Dividing the Faith

DIVIDING THE FAITH

The Rise of Segregated Churches in the Early American North

RICHARD J. BOLES

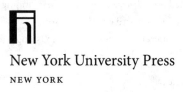

New York University Press

NEW YORK

NEW YORK UNIVERSITY PRESS
New York
www.nyupress.org

References to Internet websites (URLs) were accurate at the time of writing. Neither the author nor New York University Press is responsible for URLs that may have expired or changed since the manuscript was prepared.

Library of Congress Cataloging-in-Publication Data

Names: Boles, Richard (Richard J.), author.
Title: Dividing the faith : the rise of segregated churches in the early
   American North / Richard Boles.
Description: New York : New York University Press, [2020] | Series: Early
   American places | Includes bibliographical references and index.
Identifiers: LCCN 2020015043 (print) | LCCN 2020015044 (ebook) | ISBN
   9781479803187 (cloth) | ISBN 9781479801671 (ebook) | ISBN 9781479801657
   (ebook)
Subjects: LCSH: Race relations—Religious aspects—Christianity. |
   Segregation—Religious aspects—Christianity. | African
   Americans—Segregation—New England. | Indians of North America—New
   England—Social conditions. | African Americans—Religious life. |
   African American churches—History. | Indians of North
   America—Religious life. | New England—Race relations. | New
   England—Church history.
Classification: LCC F15.A1 B65 2020 (print) | LCC F15.A1 (ebook) | DDC
   305.800974270.089—dc23
LC record available at https://lccn.loc.gov/2020015043
LC ebook record available at https://lccn.loc.gov/2020015044

New York University Press books are printed on acid-free paper, and their binding materials are chosen for strength and durability. We strive to use environmentally responsible suppliers and materials to the greatest extent possible in publishing our books.

Manufactured in the United States of America

10 9 8 7 6 5 4 3 2 1

Also available as an ebook

For Christiane, Beatrice, and Louisa

Contents

Figures and Tables

Figures

Tables

DIVIDING THE FAITH

Introduction

Phillis Wheatley was stolen from her family in Senegambia, and, in 1761, slave traders transported her to Boston, Massachusetts, to be sold. The Wheatley family, who purchased her, treated Phillis far better than almost all slaves in the eighteenth century, and she received a thorough education, but she still longed for freedom. Wheatley began writing poetry in 1765 that frequently contained religious themes. In 1771, she was baptized and became a member of a predominantly white Congregational church in Boston. Two years later, some of her poetry was published in London, England, as a book titled *Poems on Various Subjects, Religious and Moral*. This book and the engraving of her likeness that appeared as the frontispiece are evidence that her experience of enslavement was exceptional.

Wheatley remains today the most famous black Christian from the colonial era.[1] Despite the uniqueness of her experiences and accomplishments, Phillis Wheatley's religious affiliation with a predominantly white church was quite ordinary. Thousands of African Americans and hundreds of American Indians publicly participated in and affiliated with predominantly white churches in New England and Mid-Atlantic regions in the eighteenth and early nineteenth centuries. The history of these churches and our perspective on them, however, have been whitewashed.

Most Americans today usually think of northern colonial churches as being entirely "white" institutions, but black and Indian peoples regularly affiliated with these churches. Historians have known about Phillis

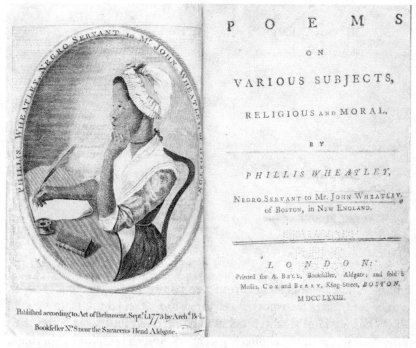

FIGURE I.1. Title page and frontispiece of Phillis Wheatley's *Poems on Various Subjects, Religious and Moral* (1773). Schomburg Center for Research in Black Culture, Manuscripts, Archives and Rare Books Division, NYPL, "Title page and frontispiece," Image ID 485600, NYPL Digital Collections, http://digitalcollections.nypl.org/.

Wheatley and some other black church members, but for a long time, they were treated as outliers in the narratives of American religious history.[2] The old Congregational churches of New England, often situated on public green spaces in quaint town centers, are iconic symbols of New England, and for many Americans, of colonial America and early American religious history as a whole. However, no broad, comparative study of black and Indian affiliation in northern churches exists that treats both changes over time and denominational differences.[3] This neglect obscures the history of interracial churches in the Mid-Atlantic and New England regions, where northerners typically worshiped in interracial but not integrated congregations from the 1730s to the 1820s.[4]

Take the First Parish Congregational Church of Hingham, Massachusetts, for instance. Although colonial Hingham had a relatively small black and Indian population in the eighteenth century, black and Indian people were active participants in this town's churches. There were eight people of African descent and three Indians baptized at the First Parish between 1730 and 1749, including "Emme George an Indian woman," "Francis a Molattoe woman," and "Jack a Negroe." Jack was also admitted to membership in the church. Black children and adults continued to be baptized there periodically into the 1770s.[5] And Hingham was hardly alone. Indeed, it was the norm. Throughout the eighteenth and early nineteenth centuries, most northern churches of various denominations baptized and admitted some blacks or Indians into their church congregations.[6]

Dividing the Faith builds on the works of a growing number of scholars who have been describing, with greater levels of sophistication, the lives of blacks and Indians in the colonial era and nineteenth century.[7] Building on this scholarship, this book furthers the conversation by demonstrating that dynamic interracial interactions in northern churches were more common and persisted longer than has generally been acknowledged. Protestant churches helped define the institution of slavery and later were on the frontline of creating the first segregated society in American history during the early nineteenth century. Much attention has been given to the remarkable story of the rise of separate black churches after the Revolution, especially the dramatic departure of Richard Allen and Absalom Jones from St. George's Methodist Church. The attention on that turning point toward racial separatism in American Christianity, however, has partially obscured the extent and depth of the long history of interracial churches that persisted even decades after Allen and Jones founded their churches.[8] During the religiously vibrant Early American Republic, both separate African American congregations and interracial churches expanded alongside one another.

The extent of interracial religious activity during the eighteenth and early nineteenth centuries in northern churches has been obscured because historians have not fully utilized the church records where congregants of color are documented and because American Christians themselves have forgotten or glossed over this history. In general, scholars of American religious history have neglected black and Indian people in northern churches, and historians studying northern black and Indian people have underutilized church records as essential sources for studying the experiences of these groups in northern society. Blacks and Indians in northern colonial churches were long understudied because of the "whitening" of New England's history that persisted until quite recently. Blacks in northern churches have also been neglected in part because many scholars of church history have tended to dismiss early conversion and church participation of enslaved Africans as nothing more than forms of oppression.[9] Only in the past decade or so have some northern congregations begun to examine the diversity of their eighteenth-century predecessors and the ways that they supported and benefited from the enslavement and displacement of African and Indian peoples.[10]

The work of later Christians who sought to integrate American churches, years after the proliferation of separate African American churches, also sometimes obscured the complicated history of racial interactions in northern churches. For example, in downtown Boston sits the Tremont Temple Baptist Church. The current edifice was completed in 1896, and above one of the church's doorways is a plaque announcing, "First Integrated Church in America—Organized 1838."[11] This congregation was founded on the principle of inclusion, as neither race nor class nor gender determined who could worship there or where people sat in the sanctuary. One of the leading founders, Timothy Gilbert, was a white abolitionist who left the Charles Street Baptist Church because African Americans were not permitted to sit in ground-floor church pews. However, this statement that Tremont Temple was the first integrated church in America can erroneously be read as implying that black, white, and Indian peoples never worshipped together in early American churches. In 1738, one hundred years before Tremont Temple was founded, nearly every church in Boston included black congregants, sometimes in large numbers. A few Boston churches of the eighteenth century also included American Indians. The sentiment behind Tremont Temple's "first" claim reflects a blind spot common in the historical memory of most Americans. Many people today assume, incorrectly, that American churches have always been firmly divided along perceived racial lines.

Tremont Temple was not the first northern church to include racially diverse members and congregants, but it was exceptional in antebellum Boston because northern churches became less interracial as the nineteenth century wore on, contrary to the narrative of racial progress sometimes associated with northern states. Americans' sense of their racial past and present is at stake in understanding the presence and influences of blacks and Indians in northern churches. The extent of interracial interactions in northern churches challenges two truisms about northern states that have fed into Americans' racial consciousness. The first is that colonial New England was fundamentally a white region with only a sprinkling of blacks in the cities and Indians along the frontier. It is no coincidence that "the North," particularly New England, has often been held up as the most "American" of regions in a country that has long associated whiteness and national identity.[12] In popular memory of the past, the North is also commonly held up as being racially progressive in contrast to the South, which is epitomized historically by plantations and Jim Crow segregation. Racism was and is a national problem, not merely a southern one. This study of people of color in northern churches, therefore, furthers the reintegration of northern colonies and states in the racial history of American church life.

How Sunday mornings became the most segregated time in American life is not a linear story of declension. Instead, it is a complex history replete with remarkable individuals who made religious choices that defied the common patterns and assumptions of American society. American Indians and African Americans (and black Americans in the colonial era) affiliated with predominantly white churches in significant numbers before slowly forming separate churches, and in the process, they influenced patterns of race relations across northern society. Many blacks and Indians affiliated with predominantly white churches even as these congregations were complicit in supporting slavery and the dispossession of Indian land.

From the early to mid-eighteenth century, most Congregational, Anglican, Lutheran, and Moravian churches in the northern British colonies were interracial congregations as blacks and Indians participated through weekly church services and the rituals of baptism and communion. These churches were dedicated to missionary outreach to these groups and made their sacramental communities relatively accessible to them. During the eras of the American Revolution and the Early Republic, northern churches became vastly more interracial as Presbyterians, Dutch Reformed Christians, Methodists, and Baptists admitted more African Americans and Afro-Indians into their churches. Separate Native American churches, especially in the 1750s, and independent African American churches after 1790, provided church alternatives for people of color. However, for a couple of decades, both interracial and segregated types of churches grew and developed side by side. In other words, churches wholly divided by the color line were not inevitable.[13] Ultimately, though, segregated churches came to dominate northern states. The ejections and withdrawals of blacks and Indians from predominantly white churches were central building blocks in the creation of widespread segregation in northern society by the 1830s.

Even if a northern town included only a small number of blacks or Indians, it is significant that many northern churches were interracial because churches were the central institutions of most colonial towns. Churches remained culturally influential organizations in the nineteenth century. Since so many churches contained people of color, these institutions helped define the place of blacks and Indians in northern society. Often this influence meant that churches reinforced colonists' widespread oppression and marginalization of blacks and Indians. Almost wherever there were people of color in New England and within every major northern city, they participated in the central institutions of these communities, and this fact alters how we think northern colonies and states operated. Although New England colonies had small shares and proportions of enslaved blacks compared to most British colonies, it would be a mistake to suggest that New England colonies were not greatly influenced by the enslavement of Africans and Indians. The activities of the enslaved blacks and Indians widely affected British colonial societies' laws, economies, and religions. In regard to religion, black and Indian agency and participation affected northern and southern churches alike.[14] New England's churches, in this sense, were not exceptional.

Interracial religious activity was common in many northern churches from 1730 to 1820. In some denominations, a majority of congregations were interracial. By interracial, I mean that people whom contemporaries judged to be of different races jointly participated in almost all the religious activities and rituals of these churches. Numerous blacks and Indians were baptized, had their children baptized, partook of communion, listened to sermons, sang psalms and hymns, and prayed along with their white fellow congregants. These churches were interracial not only because of the physical presence of blacks and Indians but also because diverse people entered through religious rituals into a defined community of a local church that believers imagined was also part of a broader and eternal spiritual community.

Interracial worship, however, does not imply that blacks and Indians received equal treatment in predominantly white churches. These churches usually did not allow blacks and Indians to vote in church affairs or to hold leadership or pastoral positions. Along with seating arranged by status and sometimes by gender, predominantly white churches required blacks and Indians to occupy segregated seats in the balconies or the back of the main floor during worship. Yet the fact remains that blacks and Indians were present in and members of a sizable number of northern churches, thereby making churches common sites of interracial relations. In turn, churches also became important sites for the contestation of racial issues from the Great Awakening to the nineteenth century's era of democratic ferment. The ways that racial issues were decided in churches influenced society more broadly because churches were one of the most common places of public gatherings and because they exercised a unique influence on society's morals.

Historians have generally overemphasized the appeal of evangelical denominations, such as Methodists and Baptists, among northern blacks in the colonial period. The fact is that significant portions of the black northerners chose to affiliate with more liturgical or subdued forms of Protestantism, particularly Anglican churches, before 1810.[15] By the antebellum era, northern African Americans overwhelmingly favored Baptist and Methodist forms of Christianity, but it is important not to assume that this later preference was common in the earlier context of the colonial era. Black and Indian people affiliated not only with evangelical and revivalist churches but also with the more hierarchical and traditional forms of Christianity. Moreover, they did so for a variety of pragmatic and principled reasons.

Black patterns of religious affiliation in New England churches differed from their participation in Mid-Atlantic churches, and both these northern regions exhibited patterns that were sometimes dissimilar and sometimes similar to black participation in southern and Caribbean churches.[16] Across the British Atlantic world, small numbers of enslaved and free black people participated in Church of England parishes and some other churches, but larger percentages of the black population participated in northern Anglican churches compared to the parishes in southern and Caribbean slave societies. As a general rule, planters in Caribbean and southern slave societies more often opposed baptizing enslaved people than the slaveholders in northern colonies, although some northern slave owners prevented their slaves from being baptized. Across the entire Atlantic world, the pursuit of education was a common reason for black and Indian people to engage with churches and missionaries, especially in Anglican and Moravian congregations.[17]

The church affiliations of Indians, Afro-Indians, and black people speak to the need in American historiography to "triangulate" racial dynamics during the colonial and early national eras.[18] By scrutinizing similar and dissimilar experiences of blacks and Indians, this book also contributes to the growing historiography on the construction of racial identities in early America and shows the need to treat churches as influential social institutions, not just religious ones. The construction of racial identities in churches affected and reflected broader social changes.

Comparing the rise of separate Indian and separate black churches reveals some of the shared experiences and also disparate conditions of these groups of people. Indians who had affiliated in predominantly white churches in southern New England withdrew and founded new churches in the 1750s, and black people, especially in the Mid-Atlantic, began establishing separate churches after 1790. These churches became segregated not only because whites did not want to extend equality and did not want to worship alongside people of color but also because Indians and blacks themselves chose to found new churches for both religious and nonreligious reasons. This comparative story also describes part of the process by which northern societies became more racially segregated as slavery collapsed and Revolutionary political principles took hold.

The chapters that follow, starting with the year 1730, progress chronologically, although their date ranges occasionally overlap. As the chronology progresses, northern churches, on the whole, became more interracial until the steep drop in interracial churches that occurred after 1820. Blacks and Indians regularly participated in Congregational, Anglican, Lutheran, and Moravian churches from 1730 to 1749, and their participation was not limited to revival-focused congregations. A wide variety of conflicts between whites, blacks, and Indians occurred in northern churches between 1740 and 1763 because of the oppression that blacks and Indians experienced in colonial society and because blacks and Indians sometimes combatted white prejudices in churches. Some of the conflicts in the 1750s influenced the rise of new, separate Indian churches in southern New England. Between 1730 and 1776, Dutch Reformed, German Reformed, and Presbyterian churches rarely baptized or admitted blacks, which stands in stark contrast to both these churches in the early United States and other denominations in the colonial period. Whites in these denominations expressed fears about the effects of interracial churches on their ability to hold men and women as chattel slaves, and they maintained church policies that made baptism less accessible to blacks and Indians.

The era of the American Revolution was a crucial turning point in race relations in northern churches. Throughout the American Revolutionary era from 1764 to 1790, a dramatic expansion of interracial worship occurred, especially in the Mid-Atlantic, despite the disruptions of the imperial crisis and Revolutionary War. Newly formed Methodist churches, an expanding number of Baptist churches, Dutch Reformed churches, and Presbyterian churches began to or increasingly included black members. Contrary to common perceptions, the development of white antislavery opinions did not commonly precede or cause this increase in black participation. Between 1791 and 1820, African Americans created separate black churches, especially in major cities, but the rise of independent black Christianity also coincided with increased black participation in predominantly white Dutch Reformed, Anglican, and Presbyterian churches. Both interracial and independent forms of black Christianity rose together in the Early Republic. Northeastern Indian churches also became interracial as blacks and Afro-Indians joined Indian communities.

Black participation in predominantly white churches swiftly declined between 1821 and 1850, and this decline affected race relations in the rest of northern society. In this period, antiblack violence peaked in northern cities, and segregation spread across northern society. In response to these developments, some Christian reformers argued that churches should be reintegrated, but more commonly, African Americans and Indians articulated radical, Christian critiques of white society and white Christians. The narrative arc of this story progresses from a surprising number of interracial churches in the mid-eighteenth century to an expansion of interracial churches during the era of the American Revolution and the Early Republic and finally to antebellum churches firmly divided along racial lines.

Church records, particularly lists of members and persons baptized, are the foundational source material for this book. These sources, written by white ministers or clerks, are the best and most reliable sources for determining levels of black and Indian participation in predominantly white churches. That said, some of the people who wrote church records did not use racial notations, so in some churches, it is more difficult to determine black or Indian participation levels. Whites, especially after 1780, increasingly described Indians or Afro-Indians as blacks, which also conceals some Indian participants in these churches. My analysis should not imply that the racial identifiers or categories used by white people necessarily matched the ways that black people and Indians identified themselves. Moreover, these sources and the records of white churches provide hardly any specific information regarding why blacks or Indians chose to affiliate with any given church. Despite the drawbacks of this information, by surveying large numbers of churches and identifying general trends, this book describes the religious choices and experiences of many northern blacks and Indians with detail and nuance. The choices and actions of thousands of blacks and Indians speak loudly about their religious experiences.[19]

Dividing the Faith does not make claims about the proportion of northern blacks or Indians who were Christians, although many of these people identified themselves as Christians. There is no reliable way to determine the portion of a city's or colony's black and Indian populations that were baptized since population data for the colonial period was so inconsistent and incomplete and since baptism was generally a once-in-a-lifetime event. Moreover, I do not assume that church attendance or participation in Christian rituals, such as baptism or communion, signifies anything concrete about the beliefs or doctrines held by the participant. Rituals can signify a wide range of meanings to the people who participate in them. Blacks and Indians practiced Christianity and adopted at least some of its theology, but they did not necessarily believe the same things as European Christians, and many of them incorporated Christianity into preexisting beliefs, rituals, and spiritual practices.[20] Without a doubt, enslaved men and women born in Africa retained and continued to practice a range of religions from West Africa, including Islam and Catholicism, but this book does not seek to examine all the religious beliefs and practices of people of African descent in northern colonies. Rather, I focus on how and when black and Indian people affiliated with churches, as institutions, and what their affiliation can and cannot tell us. I am more concerned with the range of meanings that church affiliation held to black and Indian peoples than with their internal, private religious beliefs, although these two aspects of religion were necessarily inseparable.

I generally use the term "black" to describe people who self-identified or were identified by other people as being partially or wholly of African descent. Terms such as "negro," "mulatto," "black," "African," and "colored" appear in church records, but these terms are all problematic, and "African American" is anachronistic for the colonial period. I use the term "black" not because American racial categories are self-evident or logical. It is merely the least awkward of the terms that can be used to explore race relations and changes in racial categorizations in early America. I use the term "white" to describe people of mostly or entirely European ancestry, and this category is no less constructed, contested, and problematic than "black." When possible, I identify Indians by their tribal nation or community names. Although modern Native Americans differ in their preference for the terms "Native American" or "Indian," most northeastern Indian nations today use the term "Indian" because it is treaty language. It is the word used by white officials to make all the promises they then broke, and it appears in the written historical records that connect today's Indigenous nations to their land.

The diversity evident in many eighteenth-century churches, and the changes over time in black and Indian participation in predominantly white churches, is a story that includes evidence of the tragic oppression of blacks and Indians in America. However, it also contains rarer moments in which religious beliefs challenged the prejudices of white northerners. For people more accustomed to thinking in terms of twentieth-century American churches, the rise of racially segregated northern churches may be a surprising history indeed.

1 /   "Not of Whites Alone, but of Blacks Also": Black, Indian, and European Protestants, 1730–1749

On the evening of Wednesday, October 29, 1738, church members and other congregants converged on the New London, Connecticut, meetinghouse to attend the midweek lecture service and to witness several baptisms. As many of the town's inhabitants arrived, they took their assigned seats in the high-walled box pews or benches. Church seating was a contentious issue in New London, as it was in many New England towns. A committee determined where congregants sat and assigned pews based on people's ability to pay rental fees as well as by factors including wealth, status, age, public service, family connections, gender, and race. There was such a high demand for seating that a second gallery was added above the first one. As with most services, the congregation sang psalms without instrumental accompaniment and listened to a well-prepared sermon by Reverend Eliphalet Adams.[1]

At each of the previous Wednesday gatherings in October, a child was baptized, but on this night, an adult named Phillis and four children named Ishmael, James, Ziba, and Sylvanus were to be baptized. At the appointed time, Phillis and the children proceeded toward the front of the church, likely descending narrow stairs from the galleries. They walked toward Reverend Adams, who was both the pastor of the First Church of Christ in New London and the person who held legal title to these five enslaved people of African descent. By law and custom, these slaves owed Adams their obedience and lifelong labor. Phillis stood in front of the congregation. She saw wealthier congregants nearest to her, but if she raised her eyes toward the galleries, she might have seen some of the other black people and Mohegan or Pequot Indians who attended this church. Phillis made a profession of faith and "owned the church covenant," which is to say, she affirmed her understanding of and belief in the doctrines of Christianity and submitted herself to the oversight and discipline of the church members. She was always liable to be punished by her master, but the church members could now censure Phillis or remove her from the church's fellowship for moral failings. After owning the covenant, Phillis was baptized. Next, Adams baptized Phillis's children James, Ziba, and Sylvanus, as well as a "servant child Ishmael." Ishmael was the child of another of Adams's slaves. Adams promised to educate these four children in Christianity as part of his responsibility as their metaphorical patriarch, a role typically assumed by English masters of bound laborers, when he stated, "for all whose education I also publically engaged."[2]

For Eliphalet Adams, the sacrament of baptism was a sacred duty performed regularly for the children of believing parents and adults who owned the covenant or made a profession of faith in Christ. Infants, children, and adults could all receive this sacrament, either on the testimony of a guardian's faith or by their own profession. He baptized fifty-seven people in 1738. For Phillis, the meaning and significance of her baptism are unclear as historical records provide no access to her words or thoughts. Perhaps Adams used promises or threats to pressure her into being baptized, or perhaps she made a choice herself to do so. Although a minority in the New London church, Phillis and her children were hardly the only nonwhite worshippers. In the 1730s and 1740s, at least sixteen Indians (nine adults and seven children) and fifteen blacks (eight adults and seven children) were baptized at this church. These baptisms were a small but noticeable minority among the roughly 1,080 baptisms performed there during this era, and the black people baptized at this church represented a small percentage of the enslaved population of the New London region.[3] The trend of black and Indian baptisms, though, was not limited to one location. People of color from across the region joined predominantly white churches as individuals and in small groups. Collectively, they were making those churches more representative of the diversity in British colonial societies.

In the 1730s and 1740s, long before separate black churches were formed, black Christians regularly attended and joined predominantly white churches. Although separate Indian churches dating back to the middle of the seventeenth century existed in Massachusetts, Indians also participated in predominantly white churches. In these two decades, significant numbers of blacks and Indians were baptized in Congregational churches in New England, Anglican churches from Pennsylvania to New Hampshire, and some Lutheran and Moravian churches in Mid-Atlantic colonies. Strikingly, most people in southern New England and a significant minority of people in the rest of the northern colonies experienced formal religion in interracial contexts between 1730 and 1749.

The participation of black and Indian peoples in so many of these churches is significant for several reasons. White Christians by the eighteenth century frequently believed it was their religious duty to teach blacks and Indians the doctrines of Christianity and to invite them into their churches. They thought that churches ought to contain all parts of their hierarchical society, and numerous pastors and congregants made strides in putting this ideal into practice. In some other colonies, Europeans adopted a model of Christian practice that sought to delineate boundaries of "whiteness" from "blackness" by excluding enslaved black people from churches.[4] In contrast, northern Congregational, Anglican, Lutheran, and Moravian churches generally felt that the participation of blacks and Indians in their churches helped justify their existing social order, including whites' elevated status therein. Since blacks and Indians were active in numerous churches, racial identities and slavery were created and contested in these spaces and upon religious terms. Moreover, it is crucial to examine black and Indian participation in colonial churches because it contextualizes and explains the multifaceted origins of Native American and African American forms of Christianity. In order to understand how and why churches eventually became divided along perceived racial lines, we must first understand the extent to which churches were interracial.

Even though black and Indian Christians produced few written records in this era, the patterns of their affiliation in predominantly white churches tell us much about their religious experiences. Levels of black and Indian affiliation can best be determined through baptismal and membership lists; no sources indicate how many people attended church services regularly week after week. Many churches were interracial religious communities, meaning that blacks and Indians engaged in the same religious activities as whites, including baptism, communion, public worship, singing, catechism classes, and other shared religious events. When white ministers baptized blacks and Indians or admitted them to membership, these ministers and church leaders envisioned that these people would one day be in heaven too. They imagined a spiritual community that transcended their specific time and place.

The interracial practices of churches in northern colonies contrast with the more segregated religious practices in some British slave societies. In other colonies, slave owners were more determined to prevent enslaved black people from participating in churches. In South Carolina, Barbados, and Jamaica, white people were often baptized and married in the private spaces of their homes to distinguish themselves from the small number of free and enslaved black people who were baptized and married in Anglian church buildings. White people in northern colonies did not separate their baptisms from church settings to distinguish their baptisms from those of black or Indian peoples. But, creating interracial churches was not the same as treating blacks and Indians as equals, which was not the goal of white colonists.[5]

The impressive extent of black and Indian participation in northern Protestant churches meaningfully amends our understanding of the Great Awakening's effect on the origins of African American and Native American Christianities. The participation of black and Indian people in churches was varied and not inherently connected to the Great Awakening. The Great Awakening was a disruptive period of religious controversy that dramatically changed the religious composition of New England. It was particularly connected to the traveling preaching tours of Reverend George Whitefield. Although religious awakenings occurred in earlier periods, later commentators and historians identify the revivals that occurred in the early 1740s as the Great Awakening because of the intense upsurges of religious activity that occurred in New England and also in locations across the British Atlantic world. Early forms of African American Christianity are often closely associated with evangelical revivalism, including the radical elements of the Great Awakening. However, black men and women did not solely participate in the churches that promoted or embraced awakenings. They also affiliated with Congregational, Anglican, and Lutheran churches that opposed the new revival techniques, sometimes in substantial numbers.[6]

Some scholars of religious history have overstated the role of revivalism and the Great Awakening in explaining black and Indian Christian practices in northern colonies. The emotional preaching and lay involvement in religious services of the Great Awakening played a role in black and Indian participation, but scholars have misidentified it as the primary—or even the only—source of their affiliation in Christian churches.[7] In some of the New England churches that became centers of revivalism, Indian and black participation increased from hardly any adherents to a noticeable minority of members. Some pastors who promoted revivals, such as Reverends James Davenport and Daniel Rogers, brought groups of Indians or blacks into Congregational churches.[8] The Great Awakening encouraged higher numbers of blacks and Indians to enter churches, but such participation was not necessarily tied to the pro-revival theology or styles of preaching. Blacks and Indians participated in churches before Whitefield's famous preaching tour of 1739–1740, and they joined churches whose ministers emphatically opposed Whitefield and other revivalists, so there were multiple origins of African American and Indian forms of Christianity.

I argue that the forms of Christianity practiced by eighteenth-century blacks and Indians were nearly as varied as the forms of Christianity practiced by the European colonists. The Great Awakening increased minorities' church participation in total, but "revivalism" or "the Great Awakening" are insufficient explanations for black and Indian peoples' affiliation in a wide variety of churches. They participated in Congregational, Anglican, Lutheran, and Moravian congregations. Moreover, the churches they joined ranged from passionately "New Light" (revivalist, "Whitefieldarian," or evangelical) congregations that sought to stir up revivals to staunchly traditionalist ("Old Light") ones opposed to religious excesses that disrupted communal unity. The evidence to support this argument is divided by northern regions because the New England colonies and Mid-Atlantic colonies contained different religious landscapes. After a section that addresses motivations for religious affiliation, this chapter progresses to a section about Congregational and Anglican churches in New England and ends by examining Anglicans, Lutherans, and Moravians in Mid-Atlantic colonies.

Already by 1730, blacks, Indians, and Europeans in the northern colonies had been coexisting, although rarely peaceably, for more than a century. People from these groups interacted in homes, fields, marketplaces, and churches, but the threat of violence or actual violence undergirded their interactions. During the century that followed the founding of Massachusetts Bay Colony in 1630, the number of Europeans and blacks grew considerably while war, enslavement, poverty, and diseases diminished Indian populations. Even before English and Dutch migrants created permanent settlements in what became Massachusetts and New York, the Indians who lived in the northern woodlands and coastal regions traded with Europeans and felt the devastating effects of European diseases. Epidemic diseases continued to decimate Indian communities.

Initially, Europeans were dependent on Indians for trade and even food, but as European settlements grew in strength and size, colonists increasingly sought to claim more Indian land for themselves. Some attempts were made to convert Indians to Christianity, especially between the 1640s and 1675. Puritan minister John Eliot established "Praying Towns" for Christian Indians in Massachusetts, and Thomas Mayhew Jr. and Richard Bourne established churches among the Wampanoags on Martha's Vineyard and Cape Cod. Dozens of Indians received religious training from English colonists and became missionaries and pastors to their own people. But, conflict rather than charity more often characterized English and Indian relations. Colonists waged wars against Indians, and colonists convinced some tribal nations to fight against one another by capitalizing on their long-standing differences. The Pequot War of 1636–37 and King Philip's War in 1675–76 ended with devastation for Pequot, Wampanoag, Narragansett, Podunk, and Nipmuck peoples. In addition to deaths in battle, New England colonists enslaved more than 1,300 Indians in the seventeenth century.[9]

Despite the substantial human losses from war and disease, several eighteenth-century Indian communities not only persisted but also retained control over territory and local resources. Wampanoag communities lived near Plymouth and on Cape Cod, Martha's Vineyard, and Nantucket in Massachusetts; Narragansetts had a reserve of land in Charlestown, Rhode Island, and Mohegans and Pequots held reserves in southeastern Connecticut. Montauketts and Shinnecocks maintained their homes on Long Island. More than a dozen different tribes, including Delawares and Shawnees, lived in polyglot communities on the Susquehanna River in Pennsylvania. Smaller Indian enclaves existed near Farmington, Kent, Bridgetown, and Lyme in Connecticut, near Worcester in central Massachusetts, and at Crossweeksung and Cranberry, New Jersey. The Haudenosaunee (Iroquois) Confederation remained, six nations strong, in the northern and western parts of New York. The geographic distribution of Indians meant that they were most likely to affiliate with the predominantly white congregations located relatively close to these land reserves.[10]

Colonists forcibly brought African slaves to northern colonies within the first decades of European settlement. The abundance of land and scarcity of labor, even without staple crop economies, made slaves and indentured servants economically valuable. A ship named *Desire* brought the first enslaved Africans in Boston in 1638. Colonists sold Indian prisoners of war to the West Indies in exchange for enslaved Africans. The Dutch

West India Company was especially active in bringing slaves to their New Netherland colony and to New Amsterdam (soon to be renamed New York City), where black slaves accounted for around 20 percent of the city in 1664. Enslaved blacks engaged in all types of work, from farming and fishing to skilled crafts and manual labor, and most blacks lived and worked in close proximity to whites.[11]

Enslaved blacks were numerous and economically important in the northern colonies, and the types of coercion, violence, and resistance common in American slavery were present in northern colonies. The northern population of enslaved black people exceeded 14,000 by 1720 and grew to more than 30,000 by 1750; more than one-third of these black people were in New York. Black people were mostly clustered near port cities and towns, though they could be found practically anywhere in the colonies. These societies were stratified, with Indian and black servants and slaves occupying the lowest level of the social hierarchy. Slavery was not easy or benign in northern colonies, but enslaved people in northern colonies were often allowed to learn how to read, could generally own personal property, and might access courts of law. Northerners used an array of strategies to try to control servants and slaves, including renaming them, brutal violence, and justifying their actions with religion. Christian masters hoped they could control or effectively direct the spiritual development of their slaves. Enslaved men and women, however, did not passively submit to masters and were sometimes successful in frustrating attempts to control them and in negotiating some conditions within the institution of slavery. Most black people in these colonies were enslaved, but there were also small numbers of free blacks. The northern British mainland colonies were already ethnically and religiously diverse by 1730, and they continued to become more so over the eighteenth century.[12] This diversity was reflected in many of the northern churches during the early and mid-eighteenth century.

Some black and Indian people participated in northern churches during the seventeenth century and the first decades of the eighteenth century, so this chapter's focus on the period of 1730 to 1749 should not be taken to imply that churches only began baptizing black or Indian peoples in the 1730s. Dozens of black people were baptized in the Dutch Reformed Church of New Netherland between 1639 and 1655, and a free black man named Emmanuel was baptized and admitted to membership in the Lutheran congregation in Albany, New York, in 1669. After Elias Neau began catechizing enslaved New Yorkers in 1704, the city's Anglican churches routinely baptized black adults and children. Reverend Cotton

Mather advocated for the instruction and Christianization of enslaved blacks in Boston by 1706. A thirty-year-old enslaved man named George and an unfree "Indian Boy" were baptized at Boston's Brattle Street Congregational Church in January 1709, and a dozen other black people, including three free black people, were baptized there before 1730. Four black people were baptized in 1707 at the First Congregational Church of Dorchester, Massachusetts.[13] This study begins with 1730 because it is instructive to look at baptismal rates in the years immediately preceding the Whitefield-inspired revival of 1740–42. The baptisms that occurred in the 1730s suggest that revivalism was not the only cause of black people's participation in northern churches. In the broader English Atlantic, 1729–30 was also an important turning point in Anglican proselytization to slaves because the York-Talbot legal opinion asserted that baptism did not free enslaved people, and the Virginia House of Burgesses voted to support the conversion of blacks and Indians in that colony.[14]

Understanding Black and Indian Beliefs and Motivations

Often, both material and spiritual motives were present for the blacks and Indians who participated in these churches. Church services were opportunities to see other enslaved friends and family members dispersed across a town. Some churches provided educational opportunities that blacks and Indians alike sought after. In these contexts, being a church member carried a degree of social status, and Christianity could provide a positive identity for enslaved and dispossessed peoples. The help that sympathetic ministers could provide to Indians as they dealt with legal disputes with colonists incentivized some Indians who participated in these churches.

Blacks and Indians participated in a significant number of Protestant churches in northern mainland colonies, but participation in the sacraments of baptism and communion should not simply be understood as definitive evidence of conversion or belief. Rituals can signify a range of meanings to the people who participate in them. Given the context of colonial society and the unequal power dynamics involved, blacks and Indians in these churches were not free actors. Slave owners often limited slaves' choices, and church attendance was compulsory for some slaves and servants. Black and Indian participation in these churches justified the existing social hierarchy and their low status in it. But, to the extent that enslaved people made choices within the institution of slavery or negotiated with their oppressors, some enslaved black people chose baptism and church membership for themselves or their children. Church affiliation could both support the social hierarchy and hold meaning and significance to the people who participated.[15]

Sometimes white masters applied great pressure and violence to compel slaves to adopt certain behaviors, and some masters required their slaves to attend church. Reverend James MacSparran of St. Paul's Anglican Church in Narragansett, Rhode Island, noted in his diary that he gave his slave "Maroca one or two Lashes for receiving Presents from Mingo," a male slave. MacSparran called Maroca a Christian, but he complained that she "seems not concerned about her soul nor minds her promise of chastity." In this case, MacSparran used means ranging from violence to verbal coaxing to try to get Maroca to comply with the standard of behavior that he expected of this female Christian slave. Whites compelled enslaved men and women to labor without pay, and some people compelled slaves to attend church, listen to religious instruction, or adhere to Christian morality. Some masters used a variety of inducements to encourage slaves to seek baptism, whereas others prohibited their slaves from participating in churches.[16]

Throughout the colonial era, Protestant ministers routinely owned enslaved people, participated in their commodification, and asserted their possession of people in church records with phrases such as "my servant" or "my slave." Reverend Jonathan Edwards personally traveled to Newport, Rhode Island, in 1731 to purchase his first enslaved person, who was a young woman about fourteen years of age. In the mid-1730s, the parish of the Congregational Church in York, Maine, raised 120 pounds to purchase a slave for the parish and Reverend Samuel Moody's use. A few years after this purchase, the enslaved man was not meeting Moody's expectations. The parish voted to "sell the Negro Man named Andrew belonging to the sd Parish at the best Advantage." Not only did ministers and churches use the labor of enslaved people, but they also sometimes sought a financial advantage in selling them.[17]

Although slaveholders could compel enslaved people to attend church services, Protestant churches did not mandate baptism or church membership for any adult, whether white, black, or Indian. Anglican ministers were instructed to baptize their slaves who were "willing to receive baptism."[18] The theology and practices of these churches inclined them to restrict adult baptisms to people who publicly made a profession of their beliefs. Most Protestants stressed that baptism held no value apart from genuine belief (whether it was the faith of an individual or the faith of parents standing for a child). At least in theory, baptism as a physical

act meant nothing without correct beliefs and the work of God in providing grace. Moreover, there are examples of masters who owned both
baptized and unbaptized slaves. In December 1741, at the First Church
of Abington, Massachusetts, a slave named Tony, who was owned by the
minister, "Made a Confession of his former evil & sinful life & declared
how God had met him & wrought upon him & was Baptized." Tony was
one of at least five slaves owned by Reverend Samuel Brown, but not all of
Brown's slaves were baptized, and only two became church members. As
a slave-owning minister, Brown presumably tried to convince his slaves
to profess faith and be baptized; however, church members listened to
each person's confession of sin, considered what God had "wrought
upon" him or her, and then decided whether or not to baptize or admit
each candidate.[19]

In some cases, slaves possessed wide latitude over their religious affiliation. In 1736, the Anglican minister Timothy Cutler of Christ Church
in Boston described "a negro servant to a Dissenter, and in the prime of
life, who, from great irregularities, is become a serious & somber man."
The owner of this slave was a Congregationalist (Dissenter), but this slave
affiliated with the Church of England. This unnamed slave was likely
active in the decision to practice Christianity in this Anglican church
instead of a Congregational one. Likewise, an enslaved black man named
Nero Benson, who was owned by the minister of the First Congregational Church in Framingham, Massachusetts, joined the Hopkinton
Congregational Church in 1737. Nero Benson apparently chose this
church over his master's church because of a theological dispute. These
two men, despite their status as slaves, influenced where and how they
would participate in churches.[20]

A black slave named Andreas, or Ofodobendo Wooma, expressed a
desire to join a Moravian church through baptism, and since Moravian
communities were unique among Christians in recording the spiritual
biographies of all church members, we can see in greater detail the negotiations and power dynamics involved in this enslaved man's baptism.
Andreas was both a church member and the property of the Moravian
church at Bethlehem, Pennsylvania, from 1746 to about 1771 (the church
owned most of the community's property). Andreas was born about 1729
in the Igbo nation in what is now southeastern Nigeria. After the death
of his father, he was used by an older brother to secure a loan and was
unfortunately ushered into white hands and the brutal international
slave trade. Andreas crossed the Atlantic in bondage, and a Jewish merchant in New York purchased him in 1741.[21]

After about two years in New York, there was a prospect that he would again be sold, and the fear of being sold to a bad master compelled Andreas to pray. Andreas learned the Lord's Prayer from neighbors, and he prayed: "O Lord, our neighbors said you were so good and you gave each man what he asks from you. If you will help me to a good master in this city, then I will love you for it." A Moravian merchant named Thomas Noble purchased him. In the Noble household, Andreas learned to read and was told about Christian doctrines, some of which sounded untrue to him. In a remarkable passage from his autobiographical tes- timony, Andreas stated that the Moravian Brethren "often told me that our Savior had shed his blood for me and all black men and that He had as much love for me, and everyone, as for white people, which I did not believe. On the contrary, I thought that God only loved people who were important in the world, who possessed riches, and so forth." Despite his skepticism, Andreas continued to learn about Christianity and went to school part-time. He had a New Testament and "read from it whenever [he] had the time and opportunity." Andreas was often present during morning and evening family prayers.[22]

After a moment of crisis and distress in which he contemplated sui- cide, Andreas experienced a spiritual transformation. He stated that "the Savior's love and mercy and his selfless passion and death made such an impression on my heart that I wished nothing so much as to become a genuine black offering to Jesus and a member of the congregation." He requested baptism, but Noble hesitated at first. Some Moravians were uncomfortable with baptizing blacks even though their theology pro- claimed that all people needed Christ's redemption. Noble had recently left the Presbyterian Church, which tended to not baptize black people, so his Presbyterian heritage may have made him skeptical of baptizing his slave. At the same time, perhaps Noble wished to test Andreas's faith before consenting to his baptism. Andreas met George Whitefield, the famous revival preacher, when Whitefield stayed with the Noble family in New York. Whitefield "once offered to baptize [him]," but Noble only permitted Andreas's baptism months later. He traveled from New York to the Moravian settlement of Bethlehem, Pennsylvania, met with pastor Nathanael Seidel, and was baptized on February 15, 1746, "into Jesus' death by Br. Christian Rauch and named Andreas." He took communion on the subsequent Sunday. The black woman whom Andreas eventually married, Magdalene, became a church member in 1748. Andreas spent the rest of his life with his Moravian brothers and sisters, working and worshipping along with the white church members. Other enslaved

blacks in Bethlehem did not join the church or participate in the sacraments. Moravians baptized and admitted a small number of blacks to
their church communities from the 1740s to the 1770s, especially ones
such as Andreas, whose religious experiences led him to pursue admittance to their church.[23]

The participation of blacks and Indians in many of these churches did
not necessarily mean that they adopted consistent Christian beliefs or
converted. Conversion, especially when understood as a dramatic change
in disposition or belief, is difficult to address in this context because most
people who participated in these churches (and almost all blacks and
Indians) left no written expressions to describe their experiences (Moravians were a major exception to this trend). Many of the blacks and Indians who attended or participated in these churches adopted elements
of Christianity that made sense to them, but they did not necessarily
abandon other beliefs that whites saw as inconsistent with European
Christianity. Black and Indian Christianities in the colonial era were
likely syncretic or transcultural for some. Men and women adopted and
adapted Christianity in different ways, sometimes incorporating parts of
Christianity with the beliefs and practices that they already possessed.
Some Wampanoag, Mohegan, Narragansett, and Pequot peoples identified themselves as Christian Indians, and they defined both titles on
their own terms. Blacks who were taken as slaves directly from Africa
and Indians raised in Indian communities were likely to incorporate or
syncretize Christian ideas with their already existing ones rather than
wholly convert to new beliefs. Some African slaves brought to northern
colonies were already practicing Christians. Across the Atlantic world,
including parts of the Caribbean and West Africa, black people participated in Christian churches before arriving to British colonies. West
Africans who were brought as slaves to America practiced Islam, Christianity, and a wide range of localized religious traditions, all of which
had beliefs or practices that potentially resonated with the religious practices at British colonies.[24]

Conversely, black and Indian people who were raised since childhood solely or mostly among white Christians were more likely to adopt
Christian beliefs and practices little different from those of white colonists. Clergymen wrote approvingly of the religious knowledge of some
blacks and Indians. Mr. Usher, an Anglican missionary in Bristol, Rhode
Island, noted in 1730 that "sundry negroes make application for baptism
that were able to render a very good account of the hope that was in
them, and their practices were generally agreeable to the principles of the

Christian religion." These black Christians and others like them knew Christian doctrines well enough to receive the approbation of white clergymen.[25]

For some black people, such as Flora from Ipswich, Massachusetts, their attachment to New England churches was personal and long-lasting. Flora was likely born in Ipswich in 1723 and was owned by a prominent local man named Thomas Choate. During a revival, her faith stirred, and she exhorted or preached during some of the revival meetings. The Congregational Church of Chebacco (or Fourth Church of Ipswich) was founded in 1746 by evangelicals who withdrew from Reverend Theophilus Pickering's Congregational church, and this newly formed congregation admitted four blacks among the first twenty-two members. Flora became a full church member along with another "negro" named Binah, after publicly declaring her religious experiences before the congregation in June 1746. Within a short period after joining, however, she was required to speak again in front of the congregation. Her 1748 public confession of sin was recorded, and it provides an example of the faith of an early black Christian.[26]

Flora's experience illustrates the theological views and personal commitment to a church of an enslaved New Englander. In her confession, Flora acknowledged how "spirituall Pride, Ingratitude, Unwatchfulness and Levity or Lightness" ultimately led her to fall into a worse but unnamed sin. She described the deep despair that engulfed her when she realized the extent of her rebelliousness and sin, and how she was freed from despair when "the pardoning Love of God again flowed into my Soul & caused my Heart to melt & flow with penetential streams." She asked her fellow congregants for their forgiveness, and prayed that they would "Restore me to your Charity and Fellowship and the Privileges that I have forfitted, by my Fall." Throughout the confession, Flora exhibited her knowledge of the Christian scriptures by interweaving biblical passages with her own phrases. After the confession was read twice to the congregation and several members asked her questions, the church voted to restore her to full membership status. She remained a member for the rest of her life.[27]

Despite sometimes maintaining a long-standing affiliation with a church, blacks and Indians in predominantly white churches did not participate on equal terms. Women of every race and poorer white colonists were not treated as equals to white men of higher status either, but skin color was a stark dividing line within churches. Rarely did predominantly white churches allow black men, Indian men, or any women to vote in church affairs. Prohibiting black men and Indian men from voting correlated with their exclusion from the body politic, but this exclusion may have also had the effect of gendering as female all the black men and Indian men who joined churches. Women were the largest category of church members who were usually excluded from voting, but black and Indian men could not claim the male privilege of voting either. Blacks and Indians who attended predominantly white churches usually could sit only in portions of the gallery, stairwells, or back of churches. Seating arrangements reflected the social hierarchy of the whole society, with the wealthiest people sitting in the best seats and paying the highest pew rents. At Old South Congregational Church in Boston, the church voted to have a person provide "oversight of the children & servants in the galleries" and "that in Honour to his Excellency our Governour there be a Canopy Erected over His Pew." At the Congregational Church in Suffield, Massachusetts, in December 1733, the society "Voted, that the Hind flank seat in the upper Gallery on the North side . . . and that seat and that only be for ye Negroes to sit in." Differences in status affected where people sat in church and were reinforced by the seating arrangements. In some cases, women and men also had separate seating areas, so wealth, skin color, age, marital status, and gender could all be factors in determining where people sat in church. Some Indians and blacks occasionally preached during this period, but no denomination ordained blacks or Indians between 1730 and 1749.[28]

Numerous blacks and Indians were motivated to attend churches despite substantial drawbacks and limitations that could come with their participation. Some white people, especially ministers, promoted the conversion of blacks and Indians to Christianity, but other white people were hostile to including blacks and Indians in their churches at all. Nearly all white people opposed any suggestion that blacks and Indians were their social equals. The constant use of words such as "negro" and "servant" in church records and sermons demonstrates the social distance that whites sought to maintain between themselves and black Christians. The conditions that led whites to identify black men and women as "negro" in the church records may have prevented some blacks from having access to the sacraments of communion. Some white colonists were deeply skeptical of the authenticity of black and Indian Christians, occasionally even asserting that Indianness or blackness were permanent barriers to conversion. In the 1730s and 1740s, black churchgoers did not cause white Christians to propose freeing Christian slaves. With very few exceptions, whites simply did not see slavery and Christianity as incompatible. Rather, the social hierarchy in church reflected and reinforced the social hierarchy outside of it. The acceptance of blacks and Indians in churches was often conditional or limited and certainly did not translate into acceptance into the body politic. In societies so centered around churches, the inclusion of at least some Indians and blacks implicitly validated the existing social order; however, neither segregated seating nor other reminders of low status kept blacks and Indians from participating in northern Protestant churches.[29]

Several motives influenced black and Indian participation in Protestant churches. Some blacks and Indians found comfort and emotional support in the religion of the suffering Christ, even though they worshipped with men and women who exploited them. Available written accounts suggest that Christianity could be comforting, empowering, or life-enriching to some blacks and Indians, just as it was to some whites. Church membership carried a recognized social status that could be associated with social benefits. As was the case with white Christians, a sudden illness, natural disaster, childbirth, marriage, or an unpredicted event likely prompted black people to seek formal affiliation with a church. Religious rituals and church affiliation often coincided with periods of transition and major events in people's life. Of course, some blacks and Indians considered the claims made by white Christians and wholeheartedly rejected Christianity.[30]

While there can be no simple or narrow explanation for Indian and black participation in colonial churches, they participated in so many congregations that their religious practices must be taken seriously. Black and Indian participation in Christian churches was not peripheral to northern religious life. Rather, the widespread participation of blacks and Indians in northern churches means that the quintessential churches of northern colonial societies were not simply white institutions. The presence of blacks and Indians in so many churches compelled some church leaders and religious organizations to address the conditions of these people, and the religious practices in northern colonies influenced slavery and race relations.[31]

Interracial Churches of New England

Reverend Josiah Cotton of the First Congregational Church in Providence, Rhode Island, like most of his colleagues, sought to minister to the blacks and Indians in his community and brought some of them into a formal relationship with the church. When he baptized and admitted blacks or Indians, furthermore, he articulated theological reasons for the inclusion of all people into the church. Many New England ministers felt obligated to work diligently and seek the conversion of all types of people in their community. Between 1730 and 1743, Cotton baptized two people of African descent and two Indian women. While this number is quite small, the scarcity of blacks and Indians did not necessarily undermine the importance of these events to the people involved. In January 1730, Cotton baptized "Elizabeth the Servant Child of Margaret Betty (Whose father was a Negro & Mother a White woman)." At the church service, Cotton preached from Genesis 17:13, which states that "He that is born in thy house, and he that is bought with thy money, must needs be circumcised." Cotton likely argued that baptism for Christians, like circumcision for ancient Israel, was a rite that should apply to servants in Christian households. (Did Cotton or anyone else see the irony of talking about circumcision in relation to the baptism of a girl?) Elizabeth Anthony, "an Indian Woman," was baptized and received as a church member in 1734. On December 26, 1742, in the context of widespread religious revivalism in New England, Cotton wrote that "Ann the Negro Woman Servant of Col. Jabez Bowen & Hannah Newfield a Free Indian Woman under the Cov[enant] & were both baptized, on which occasion I preached from 10 Acts 34, 35." This text is another one that supports inclusivity in churches: "Then Peter opened his mouth, and said, of a truth I perceive that God is no respecter of persons: But in every nation he that feareth him, and worketh righteousness, is accepted with him." Although little else is known about these individuals, their inclusion in this church and Cotton's sermons are noteworthy because Cotton ministered to black and Indian people long before and also during an intense period of revivalism in his congregation. Cotton supported and participated in the awakenings in 1741, but he was not a radical "New Light" minister, and he later turned against the new revival practices. A number of his congregants in 1743 accused him of being "not evangelical enough in his publick performances." They claimed that Cotton opposed "the work of God's spirit" and that he was "a preacher of damnable good works or doctrines," and these critics seceded from Cotton's church. Whether or not Cotton was "evangelical enough," he used the same biblical texts as other ministers to justify baptizing blacks and Indians, and he brought some of them into his Congregational church.[32]

Most Congregational and Anglican churches in New England were multiracial during 1730 to 1749. In churches across Connecticut, Rhode Island, Massachusetts (including parts of Maine), and southern New

Hampshire, blacks and Indians not only attended, but some were also baptized and accepted as members. In at least 121 Congregational churches, blacks and/or Indians affiliated as members or by being baptized between 1730 and 1749.[33] These Congregational churches were led by pastors who embraced the new methods of Whitefieldarian revivalism, pastors who consistently opposed Whitefield and other itinerant preachers, and pastors who first embraced the awakenings but later lessened or reversed their support for the religious changes swelling across New England in the early 1740s. Incomplete church records and inconsistent racial notations in some original and transcribed records make estimating the number of congregations that did not baptize multiple black people difficult. For Massachusetts's Congregational churches, my sample of church records included fourteen congregations whose records did not have multiple, identifiable black baptisms between 1730 and 1749.[34]

While some congregations in New England baptized only one or two blacks in a decade, other congregations baptized ten in a year. Since baptism usually occurred only once in a person's life and since blacks constituted only a small portion of the population of rural New England towns, even a few black baptisms were significant in this context. Though blacks and Indians were most prevalent in the churches of port towns or communities located near Indian land reserves, they also appeared across areas settled by Europeans. Because so many Congregational and Anglican churches in New England baptized blacks and because social conventions encouraged widespread church attendance, almost all New England churches likely included black attendees at weekly worship services.[35]

In New England, both Anglican and Congregational churches had at least pretentions toward being established churches, and as religious establishments in these colonies, they sought to entail and represent the entirety of colonial society. Anglican parishes, of course, were part of the Church of England, the legally established form of Protestantism in England, but they did not receive tax support and were not prevalent enough across New England to fully constitute an established church there. Congregational churches were dissenters from the Church of England and therefore were not officially an established church (in Scotland, the Presbyterian Kirk was officially established). However, Congregational churches across New England received tax support and functioned, at least for public worship, as all-encompassing parishes.

Congregationalists were the most numerous and influential Christians in New England. Nearly every village, town, and city in Massachusetts,

Connecticut, and New Hampshire had one or more Congregational church. Rhode Island was more heterogeneous than any other part of New England, with greater numbers of Baptists, Quakers, and Jews, but it still had Congregational churches and a few Anglican churches. Church buildings across most of New England were known as meetinghouses, and they served as the setting for local government. These churches were outgrowths of seventeenth-century Puritan churches, and they still maintained moderate to strict forms of Reformed Christianity (Calvinism). As the main public establishment in many towns, Congregational churches often sought to be relatively accessible to all nearby inhabitants. Congregationalists believed that every person in each town, regardless of social position, should attend weekly church services. Ministers' understanding of the Bible and their desire to make godly societies inclined them to include all people in their congregations, but not every person who attended church services was considered a church member. Ministers encouraged people whose "godly walk" or "conversation" was consistent with their profession to join their church as a member.[36]

Most Congregational churches had two levels of membership: full members, who could take communion and vote in church affairs, and so-called "halfway members," who could not do these two things (many of the congregations most affected by the awakenings dropped owning the covenant and "halfway" membership in the 1740s). Both types of members could be baptized and have their children and other young household members baptized. They were also both subject to church discipline. The halfway members joined by "owning the covenant," attesting to a statement of faith, which was easier than the process of becoming a full member. Full or communing members usually had to share their profession of Reformed doctrine or their relation that attested to their personal experience of God's work of salvation in their life. These professions or relations were usually shared with the pastor and existing church members, who determined whether to admit each person or not. Some congregations had relatively accessible membership rolls while other congregations sought to restrict membership, as much as possible, to the truly converted. Many regular attendees and devout parishioners in Congregational churches waited a long time—or refrained entirely— from fully joining their church because they were concerned about or feared taking communion in an unworthy manner.[37]

Despite its limitations, owning the covenant or halfway membership provided a formal place in church life and the community, and not a few blacks and Indians owned the covenant to received baptism. The original intention of the Halfway Covenant was not to provide a means for blacks or Indians to affiliate with churches, but by the 1740s, these people often affiliated with churches through this more accessible process. Servant or slave children could be baptized if their masters were members or halfway members—just as though the servant children were biological children. For example, on September 6, 1741, the First Congregational Church of Windsor, Connecticut, baptized a black person named John when he owned the covenant for himself and another named London, on account of his master's profession. In most cases, masters who had enslaved children baptized on their account were full members.[38]

Though Church of England parishes in New England were few in number compared to the Congregational churches, the wealth of some parishioners and their location in port towns made them more influential than their numbers imply. Many Church of England parishioners were slaveholders who encouraged their slaves to come to church. At the very least, blacks were baptized at Anglican churches in Portsmouth, New Hampshire; Newburyport and Marblehead, Massachusetts; Boston's three Anglican churches; and Rhode Island's four oldest Anglican churches between 1730 and 1749. Some of these congregations also included Indians.[39] At Trinity Church in Newport, Rhode Island, fifty-seven people were identified as "negro," and two people were identified as "Indian" in the baptismal records of this era. In 1746, this church was described as a "large and increasing congregation, not of whites alone, but of blacks also; no less than twelve of the latter sort having been admitted members of it, by the holy sacrament of baptism, within twelve months." Over this period, it was common in any given year for 4 or 5 percent of the people baptized to be identified as "negro" at Trinity Newport. Between 1746 and 1749, however, 10 to 25 percent of yearly baptisms were of black people. In these years, the percentages of blacks baptized at Trinity Church were close to or exceeded the percentage of Newport's population that was black, but the cause of these higher rates of baptisms is unclear.[40]

The Church of England's approach to the sacraments of baptism and communion enabled many blacks and Indians to participate in its worship. For Anglicans, baptism was also how adults became church members. Anglicans were told to teach blacks and Indians that they can "enter into the Church of Christ by Baptism." The Church of England baptized children of believing parents and used catechisms to teach them doctrines. Notorious sinners were about the only adults who were excluded from the sacrament of baptism and membership by the Anglican clergy.

For unbaptized adults, including blacks and Indians, Church of England clergy sought to educate them about the doctrines of their faith before admitting them into the church. This education often included memorizing the Lord's Prayer, the Ten Commandments, and church catechisms. Some of this material, including *Book of Common Prayer* catechisms, emphasized that all people owed obedience to superiors, including the king, parents, and masters. Once they were baptized and admitted into the church, Anglicans instructed blacks and Indians about their "Obligations . . . to love their Fellow-Christians, and frequently to join with them in the Publick Worship of God, in Prayers and Praise, and partaking of the Lord's Supper." Anglican parishes were open and available to anyone who lived nearby, and membership through baptism made these churches more accessible to blacks and some Indians.[41]

With the American colonies becoming increasingly valuable economically and militarily to Britain by the late seventeenth century, the Church of England turned its attention to bringing wayward colonists, blacks, and Indians into its fold. To that end, in 1701, leading Anglicans founded the Society for the Propagation of the Gospel in Foreign Parts (SPG). It sent ordained clergy to America and sought to enhance the prominence of the church in the colonies, especially in the colonies without a tax-supported Anglican establishment. Starting in the 1720s, the SPG gave increasing attention to catechizing and converting slaves, and they established a fund in 1729 to pay for clergy for that purpose. The SPG also owned a plantation and purchased more than four hundred enslaved people who generated profits that supported SPG missionaries. The SPG secretary wrote in 1725 that the Society does "require all their missionaries who have any negroes or other slaves of their own to instruct them in the principles of the Christian religion and to baptize them as soon as they are sufficiently instructed and are willing to receive baptism." Missionaries were to set an example for other Anglicans by educating and baptizing their slaves if the slaves were interested. Apart from sending priests to northern parishes, the SPG also encouraged the opening of schools to educate enslaved black people. In the eighteenth century, the SPG sent hundreds of missionaries to locations around the Atlantic, and most went to the mainland colonies.[42]

Congregational and Anglican churches across the European-controlled portions of New England regularly baptized blacks and Indians. Figure 1.1 shows the locations of Congregational and Anglican churches that baptized and/or admitted multiple black or Indian peoples in the 1730s and 1740s. It is clear that more blacks were baptized than

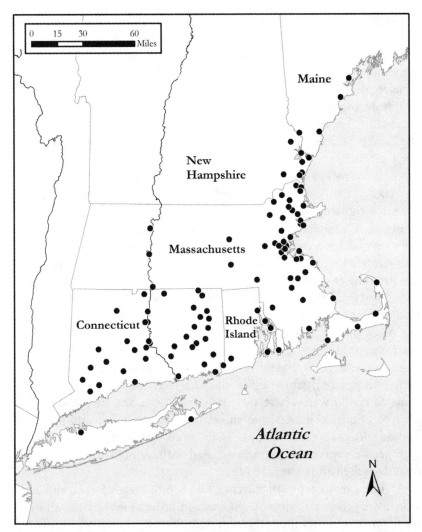

FIGURE 1.1. Map of Congregational and Anglican church locations in New England that baptized and/or admitted blacks or Indians, 1730–49. Map courtesy of William Keegan.

were admitted to full communion and membership in Congregational churches, which was often the same pattern for white church attendees. It is safe to say that the number of black people at a weekly service was higher than the number of black baptisms at each church, and, as such, black men, women, and children were present at the majority of worship services in Congregational and Anglican churches.

Boston, the largest town in colonial New England and home to Massachusetts's largest concentration of enslaved blacks, was a center for interracial religious activity. In the 1740s, Boston's population was somewhere between 7 and 15 percent black. All of Boston's oldest nine Congregational churches and three Anglican churches baptized black people during the 1730s and 1740s, as indicated in table 1.1. In some of these churches, a small number of Indians were also baptized. Most of the Congregational churches admitted some black people to full membership too. However, there were noteworthy differences in the levels of black participation in these churches.[43] The diversity of Congregational churches in this one location makes Boston a useful example for analyzing black church affiliation in New England.

Boston Congregational churches connected to the Great Awakening's revivalism baptized many black people, but some blacks were also baptized in the Congregational and Anglican churches that did not promote the revival. In other words, some of the revival-focused Congregational churches did more to recruit members than the other Congregational churches by actively seeking out black congregants, but black people still joined churches whose pastors did not do so. Black people did not always come to churches in search of emotional or enthusiastic revivalism.[44] What seems to have attracted many black people to predominantly white churches was the personal influence of pastors who were active in parish visitations and catechisms. The Congregational churches that showed the most vitality and baptized and admitted the most people were those whose minister not only embraced revival techniques associated with Whitefield but also frequently visited and catechized their congregants.[45]

Among Congregational churches, Old South, Brattle Street, and New North were the most vibrant, the most in favor of revivalism, and the most active in pastoral engagement with the laity. In the words of historian George Harper, the pastors of these three churches engaged in "systematic visitation, catechesis, religious societies, and other tools of hands-on ministry."[46] These three churches also had the highest number of baptisms of black men and women among Boston's Congregational churches. Moreover, Old South admitted five black men and four black women to full membership, and Brattle Street admitted eleven black men and nine black women to membership. In general, church affiliation appealed to both black men and black women. For enslaved black men, and women in general, being a church member was one of the only socially sanctioned positions of status that they could attain.[47] The

TABLE 1.1. Black baptisms in Boston's Congregational and Anglican churches, 1730–1749

Boston churches	Number of black baptisms	Total baptisms, 1730–49	Percentage of black baptisms
Brattle Street (Fourth) Church	46	1,134	4.06
Old South (Third) Church	35	1,158	3.02
New North (Fifth) Church	31	1,726	1.80
Second Church	22	623	3.53
First Church (Old Brick)	15	738	2.03
New Brick (Seventh) Church	9	593	1.54
West (Ninth) Church (1737–40)	8	263	3.04
New South (Sixth) Church	6	881	0.68
Hollis Street (Eighth) Church	3	313	0.96
King's Chapel Anglican	9	574	1.57
Christ Church Anglican	55	1,010	5.44
Trinity Church Anglican (1738–49)	15	432	3.47
Total	254	9,445	2.69

pastors of these churches, including Reverends Joseph Sewall, Thomas Prince, William Cooper, and Benjamin Colman, supported the revivalisms of the 1740s and actively and energetically met with parishioners and sought to bring them into the church. Benjamin Colman was so intent on welcoming slaves into the church that in a 1740 sermon, he told whites and blacks alike that "Your Ministers welcome you to the Table of CHRIST . . . [and that] the pious Master, who is CHRIST's Servant, will be glad to see his Negro above a Servant, a Brother at the LORD's Table with him."[48]

The lay devotional activities that the pastors encouraged can explain the levels of black participation in these three churches. These activities also suggest that blacks and whites experienced interracial religious activities outside of Sunday services. The pastors at these three churches were more likely than some of their colleagues to visit the homes of parishioners and encourage religious societies. In these visits, the pastors asked enslaved servants about their religious beliefs, encouraged masters to educate their slaves in Christian doctrines, and catechized white as well as black children. Joseph Sewall stated in a 1716 sermon that "Heads of Families" should teach family members "the good Knowledge of the Lord" and "Catechise their Children and Servants." Benjamin Colman went even further in a 1728 sermon, arguing that those fathers and masters who did not teach Christianity to their children, servants, and slaves risked eternal damnation. Colman warned, "His Offspring and Servants will rise up in Judgment against him, and accuse him, that he never instructed them by Word and Example in the Worship and Fear of God." For these Christians, patriarchal privilege theoretically came with the ideal of patriarchal responsibility.[49]

These pastors encouraged religious meetings among pious parishioners, in which laymen and laywomen prayed, sang, and read scripture together and where ministers occasionally preached. These activities encouraged black participation in Boston's churches. Black people, who heard the encouragements to meet privately for devotional activities, formed religious societies that complemented their attendance at regular church services (some of these societies included Indians and whites too). Reverends George Whitefield and Daniel Rogers each preached to assemblies or societies of black people in Boston. Later written accounts from enslaved and free blacks testify to the role that family devotions and conversations with white pastors had in their movement toward Christianity. Old South Church, Brattle Church, and New North Church baptized blacks before and after the Great Awakening, but they baptized and admitted a greater number of black people during the years 1740 to 1743, when revivalism was strongest in Boston. All these factors combined, including pastoral visitation, catechisms, fervent preaching, and private religious societies, led to 112 black people being baptized in these three churches compared to 63 black people being baptized in the other six Congregational churches. Evidence suggests that more black people were baptized in "New Light" Congregational churches than in "Old Light" churches, but the percentages of baptisms that were black people and black people's rates of affiliation in Anglican churches complicate this narrative.[50]

The six other Congregational churches in Boston generally contrast with the three churches above because they had fewer black baptisms, but in one of them, the percentage of black baptism was relatively high. The ministers of all these churches did not participate in the revival movement or did not as energetically encourage devotional practice outside the church walls. In total, these six churches baptized sixty-three people of African descent between 1730 and 1749, with twenty-two of these baptisms occurring at Second Church. At Second Church, 3.53 percent of all baptisms were of black people, which was a relatively high percentage among Boston churches and suggests that this church was as attractive to black people as the "New Light" congregations.[51] The absence of activist pastors and opposition to the changing religious culture of the Great Awakening in these six Congregational churches account for the fewer total baptisms and the lower numbers of black baptisms. Opposition or indifference from some people to black participation might have also existed in these churches. Boston Anglican minister Roger Price wrote in 1739 that the "baptizing of negroes is too much neglected," which suggests that some Bostonians were at least indifferent to baptizing slaves, but all of Boston's Congregational churches baptized some black people.[52]

Boston's three Anglican churches also had significant variance in the number of black baptisms. King's Chapel baptized nine black people, but Christ Church baptized fifty-five blacks between 1730 and 1749, which was 5.5 percent of the roughly one thousand total baptisms. Of these, twenty-five can be identified as female and twenty-two as male. Considering both the percentage and the absolute number of baptisms, Christ Church's minister Timothy Cutler baptized more black people than any other Boston church (even though he was a consistent opponent of Whitefield and the revivals). It seems likely that black people were often in attendance at Christ Church's services, including some who were never baptized. The claim that masters were hesitant to baptize their slaves does not seem to apply to this church. As was the case with northern Anglicans in general, an opportunity to gain an education and outreach by Reverend Cutler to enslaved blacks likely contributed to the high rate of black affiliation in this congregation.[53]

The blacks and Indians who joined the churches that opposed the new religious practices of the awakenings may not have needed enthusiastic revivalism to find meaning in Christianity, including the few who were baptized at the antirevivalist Hollis Street Church. Among the people affiliated with Hollis Street Church was Primus, an "Indian servant belonging to Hon. Anthony Stoddard," baptized in 1738, and Dinah, "negro servant to Deacon Clough," baptized in 1742.[54] Some members of the Clough family were already members of this church when Dinah was baptized, but Stoddard and his family do not appear elsewhere in these church records. Primus had no obvious connection to this church, such as a master or employer who attended. In his case and for the free black people who affiliated, we can assume they chose to attend this particular church. Some of the blacks baptized at Hollis Street were free, including John Cuffee, a "free negro" who was baptized in 1746, and a free black child named Sarah Vingus, who was baptized on October 19, 1735.

Sarah Vingus was the seven-year-old daughter of John Vingus, and their affiliation with Hollis Street Church is best understood in a wider Atlantic context. In order to have his daughter baptized, John Vingus owned the covenant on the day she was baptized. Like many white parents in New England, the desire to have his child baptized was the immediate cause of Vingus's official affiliation with this church. These church records describe John Vingus as "a free negro, baptized in his own country by a Romish priest, who also owned the covenant with us." In all likelihood, "his own country" was somewhere in Africa, perhaps the Kingdom of Kongo, whereby Kongolese royalty and others had practiced Catholicism since the end of the fifteenth century. It is also possible that "his own country" could have been a Spanish or Portuguese colony.[55] If he came from Kongo, then John Vingus was likely raised as a Roman Catholic and baptized and catechized as such. We do not know when or under what circumstances he reached Boston, but he was there and was free since at least 1725, when he married Parthenia Barteno. They were listed as "free negroes" when married by Peter Thatcher, associate minister of the New North Church. Perhaps he crossed the Atlantic as a free person, or perhaps he was brought as a slave and regained his freedom. Whatever the case, it was important to him that his daughter be baptized, and he was willing to ascribe to the doctrines of this Protestant church in order to have it done. White Christians evidently judged him worthy of being in fellowship with them. These facts suggest that Vingus was a black man who valued access to Christian sacraments in a Congregational church.[56]

The inclusion of black people in Congregational churches was so ubiquitous that even pastors who publicly opposed revivalism, such as Charles Chauncy of First Church Boston and Ebenezer Gay at First Parish Hingham, baptized and admitted some blacks to their churches (both before and after the awakenings peaked).[57] Chauncey was an ardent opponent of revivalism who famously complained that blacks and other people who "have no learning" were preaching in revival meetings. But opposition to revival practices was not the same as opposition to interracial churches, and 15 of the 738 baptisms (2.03 percent) from 1730 to 1749 at Chauncey's church were of black people. Included in these baptisms were two children of an enslaved woman named Rose, who was owned by Nathaniel Byfield. Rose was baptized and admitted as a member, and two of her other children were baptized in 1729. Byfield purchased Rose from the West Indies in 1718, when she was about thirteen years old. Byfield, in his will, wrote that Rose "proved a faithful Servent, she hath with Great Pains & Diligence learned to Read & attained to Considerable knowledge of Religion, Concerning whom I am persuaded to Believe that she truly fears God, which obliges me to set her free from the Servitude she stands obliged to Me both by Purchase & Custom." Although granting freedom to slaves was an uncommon practice in British Atlantic colonies, Byfield believed that Rose's sincere Christian faith and faithful service entitled her and her children to freedom. She was freed in 1733, upon Byfield's death. Was Rose surprised that her Christian faith led to emancipation, or had she deliberately leveraged religious devotion to gain concessions from Byfield? Had she prayed for both emancipation and salvation for her children for years before that moment? These are unanswerable questions, but it seems more likely than not that Rose valued her affiliation with this church. Her religious affiliation and experiences more resembled the experience of "godly walkers" than later Whitefieldarian converts.[58]

Even though blacks participated in most Congregational and Anglican churches in New England, there were still deterrents to their full participation, and white Christians held diverse opinions regarding black and Indian Christians. Some masters forbade the baptism of their servants and slaves on the grounds that it might suggest the equality of blacks and whites or that Christianity might be used by blacks to obtain freedom, though historians appear to have overstated this opposition. Some masters were at least ambivalent about the baptism of slaves, for Reverend Roger Price complained in 1740 that "till masters can be persuaded to have a greater value for their own souls, we have but small hopes they will be very anxious about the salvation of their negroes." On one occasion, for an ordination service in 1733, the Congregational church of Bradford, Connecticut, ordered that "no negro servant be admitted to enter ye meeting house" to leave plenty of room for white attendees.[59]

Perhaps to counter resistance among slaveholders, colonial laws tended to support the inclusion of blacks and Indians into New England churches. The Connecticut legislature in 1727 passed a law that directed masters and mistresses to attentively teach Indian servants to read English and to understand Christianity. The General Assembly in 1738 stated that infant slaves of Christian masters could be baptized on the authority of the master's faith and that it was the duty of masters to educate their enslaved children about Christianity. While these laws were not uniformly followed, the force of law promoted the religious participation of blacks and Indians.[60]

Several of Connecticut's churches, particularly those near the Mohegan, Pequot, and Western Niantic reservations had relatively high numbers of Indian participants, in addition to some black congregants. Indians were active in the Congregational churches of Groton, Stonington, New London, Lebanon, Old Lyme, Hebron, and Norwich, Connecticut. Some pastors in these towns had ministered directly to Indians since the 1720s. These pastors sought to bring Indians into their churches because they believed it was their religious duty to convert Indians and because missionary societies provided monetary incentives for doing so. Though Indians attended these churches occasionally before the awakenings, there was a considerable spike in Indian participation from 1741 to 1743, when the revivals peaked.[61] Moreover, it was not simply "radical" revivalists who were laying the foundations for Indian affiliation in Congregational churches since several moderate or even conservative pastors also worked to teach Christianity to the Indians near their churches.

The Company for the Propagation of the Gospel in New England and the Parts Adjacent in America (known as the New England Company, or NEC) provided some ministers and congregations with substantial monetary support for ministering to Indians and encouraged churches to be inclusive. Money, it seems, helped make seats accessible to Indians in English meetinghouses. For example, in 1749, the NEC pledged one hundred pounds old tenure for building a new meetinghouse in Rochester, Massachusetts, and additional money for Reverend Thomas West's salary because the church planned to make "part of the house for the use & service of the Indians." They paid Reverend Daniel Lewis of Pembroke, Massachusetts, twenty pounds in 1732 because he had "for divers years instructed a Number of Indian families in P[raying] town & having brought them to attend the publick Worship at the Meetinghouse on Lords Days in conjunction with the English." Ministers in Groton, Stonington, New London, and elsewhere were paid small sums for visiting Indian communities and because Indians attended their predominantly white congregations.[62]

The Indian and black populations in New England were clustered in different geographic locations during the eighteenth century, and these differences were a significant reason why Indians participated less uniformly in Congregational churches than did black people. Some Indians lived and worked in major cities, but the largest number of Indians resided in distinct communities and land reserves often at some distance from white population centers. Predominantly white churches with the greatest numbers of Indian participants tended to be located near Indian communities. At least forty-five Congregational churches baptized one or more Indians during the 1730s and 1740s. In many of these churches, only a small number of Indians were baptized, and they consisted mostly of Indian servants living in English households. Yet in the Congregational churches located nearest to Indian communities, dozens of Indians affiliated with these congregations. Thus, the only predominantly white churches in which Indians could find a critical mass of other Indians were those in English towns closest to distinct Indian communities. Overall, at least 289 Indians were baptized in Congregational churches between 1730 and 1749. Given the size of the Indian population and the often antagonistic relations between Indians and whites, this number of baptisms is considerable.[63]

The First Church of New London, where this chapter began, baptized Indian people who ranged from leading Mohegans to the most marginalized Indian servants. Mohegan sachem Benjamin Uncas II and seven of his family members joined this church and were baptized. Radical evangelists publicly criticized Adams as insufficiently evangelical, but Adams promoted a moderate form of revivalism that emphasized education as a means of converting people. In general, Indians did not suddenly become convinced of the truth of Christianity by revivalist preachers. In many cases, Indians learned the English language and Christian doctrine over a long period before some Indians publicly affiliated with a church. Ben Uncas II and his family strengthened their connection to Adams's church when Uncas was seeking white support against a Mohegan faction dissatisfied with his leadership.[64]

At the opposite extreme, Adams fulfilled a traditional role for a town's minister by seeking the repentance of a condemned prisoner, Katherine Garrett, who had been convicted of infanticide by a white, male jury in New London and sentenced to death. Garrett was Pequot, and in her childhood, she was sent to live as a servant with Reverend William Worthington of Old Saybrook. Indian children sometimes became live-in servants in white households to relieve their parents of the cost of raising them and in the hope of acquiring skills and English literacy, but colonial officials indentured other Indians. For some Indians and most blacks, exposure to Christianity was in the context of bonded labor to whites. After Garrett was arrested and sentenced, Adams sought to provide spiritual comfort and direction to the young Pequot woman. During the six months between her conviction and execution, Garrett regularly attended religious services. She was baptized on January 29, 1738, and admitted to communion in the First Church in New London on February 5, 1738.[65] Her status as a condemned criminal made her full participation in this church atypical, but Garrett was far from the only Indian servant who affiliated with a predominantly white church.

In a few exceptional cases, such as the Congregational church in Natick, Massachusetts, during the 1730s, Indians and whites participated in churches on relatively equal terms. Because the church at Natick was financially supported as an Indian mission, whites showed a greater willingness to have an Indian serve in the leadership role of deacon along with two white deacons. Natick was part of a long history of Indian engagement with Christianity. It was established in 1650 as the first of fourteen Indian praying towns in which the colony guaranteed Indians land in exchange for their pursuit of Christian and "civilized" reforms under the guidance of missionary John Eliot. Indians also used the town as a means of maintaining some traditional cultural practices, Indian leadership, and control of land while under colonial pressure. Both white and Indian ministers led this congregation between 1660 and 1719. Meanwhile, more and more whites acquired land in Natick, both legally and illegally. A new Congregational church was organized in Natick in 1729 by the white minister Oliver Peabody, who was employed by the NEC. Although Peabody had a condescending attitude toward the Natick Indians, some Indians were members and participants in his church. Three Indian men and five white men, including Peabody, were the original members of the new church. Joseph Ephraim Sr., an Indian, was elected to the office of deacon soon thereafter, "by a fair Majority of Written Votes." Peabody noted that "every English man in the Church Voted for him," but the Indian members "Voted for English men not unanimously." At this point, Natick's white Christians seemed to acknowledge the primacy of the Indian identity of this church and accepted some Indian leadership therein, but such cooperation did not last. Between 1729 and his death in 1752, Peabody "Baptised about 161 Indians and 413 White persons." The ratio of Indian members declined, and by 1749 only 25 Indians had been admitted to membership compared to 120 whites.[66] The Natick church was a unique case in that whites and blacks gradually displaced a Christian Indian community.

Scores of blacks and Indians were regular participants in the Congregational and Anglican churches of New England in the 1730s and 1740s. As such, the colonial religious experiences of New England were influenced by the continual and active presence of people of African and Indian descent. They attended these churches, but, more significantly, many of them were baptized and took communion. They did so in a wide range of New England churches. Historians have long been aware of black and Indian affiliation in the "New Light" congregations that were most affected by the 1740s revival, in part, because of the types of sources they have privileged. The itinerant ministers and sympathetic pastors, such as George Whitefield, Daniel Rogers, Jonathan Edwards, and Eleazar Wheelock, deliberately sought out blacks and Indians and wrote about their participation in revivals.[67] Relying heavily on the sources produced by revival participants, however, has led historians to neglect the black and Indian people who affiliated with churches before Whitefield's arrival in New England and with churches who opposed the religious innovations of the early 1740s. When the full range of New England churches is considered over two decades, a more complex view of black and Indian peoples' participation in churches and Christian sacraments emerges. Blacks and Indians participated in a broad range of church types and in most churches across New England.

Mid-Atlantic Anglicans, Lutherans, and Moravians

The Mid-Atlantic colonies of New York, New Jersey, and Pennsylvania had greater religious diversity than most of New England, but the churches of these colonies did not uniformly baptize black or Indian peoples. Anglican parishes were the most commonly interracial, followed by some Lutheran and Moravian congregations. Presbyterian and Reformed churches rarely baptized blacks before the Revolutionary era. The educational programs, pietism, and missional worldviews held by Anglicans, Lutherans, and Moravians help explain why they often sought out black congregants. The rules governing these denominations also made baptism relatively accessible to adult converts. The presence of blacks and Indians in worship services of these types of churches and their participation in the rituals of baptism, communion, and marriage were not directly tied to the revivalism of the Great Awakening.

Church of England clergy and congregations generally distrusted the awakenings as eccentric, leveling, and even devilish, though George Whitefield was an ordained Church of England clergyman. Although there were some evangelical-leaning Anglicans, they were in the minority. Some Anglican clergy campaigned passionately against revivalism.[68] Black people valued the educational opportunities that Anglican churches offered, and Church of England parishes, including New York City's Trinity Church, Staten Island's Saint Andrew's Church, Christ Church of Shrewsbury, New Jersey, Christ Church of Philadelphia, and Trinity Church of Oxford, Philadelphia, baptized numerous black people between 1730 and 1749.[69]

In addition to being baptized, some blacks and Indians took communion, were married by priests, and were buried under the auspices of the church. Their presence, as well as their selective adoption of Anglican Christianity, should not be underestimated because this affiliation was an important origin of African American Christianity, especially in New York City and Philadelphia, where separate black Anglican/Episcopal churches were formed after 1790. Black people who had been baptized and instructed in catechism classes could take communion in Anglican churches. Thomas Thompson, SPG missionary to Monmouth County, New Jersey, from 1745 to 1750, described ministering to black people: "I catechized them in the Church on certain Sundays, and sometimes at Home: and after due Instruction, those whom I had good Assurances of I received to Baptism, and such as afterwards behaved well I admitted to the Communion." In attendance at services, through the sacraments, and in catechism classes, blacks and Indians became a significant minority in the Church of England.[70]

Trinity Church in New York City was a model of the ways that Anglicans in northern colonies sought to minister to black people through education and sacraments, and hundreds of black people were baptized at this parish. Reverend Elias Neau began work in 1704 as a catechist, and he held school sessions that included enslaved blacks, free blacks, and a small number of Indians.[71] In 1726, Trinity Church sent a letter to the SPG requesting a new catechist to minister to blacks and Indians. Since "about One Thousand and four hundred Indian and Negro Slaves" were in New York, they wrote, the need for a catechist was great. "A Considerable number of those Negroes by the Society's charity have been already instructed in the principles of Christianity, have received Holy Baptism, are Communicants of our Church and frequently Approach the Altars," but many more needed instruction.[72] Reverend Richard

Charleton operated Trinity Church's school for blacks from 1733 to 1747, and from his school, fifteen to twenty black people were baptized annually. According to missionary reports, approximately 24 black adults and 195 black children were baptized at Trinity Church between 1732 and 1740.[73] Sermons and letters from members of the SPG attest to a widely held desire, especially among Anglican clergymen, to baptize blacks and Indians.

Church of England clergymen, like almost all colonial clergy, claimed that baptism did not alter the bondage of enslaved blacks. Reverend George Berkeley, while in Newport, Rhode Island, in October 1729, preached a sermon on baptism, arguing that "Our Saviour commandeth his disciples to go & baptize all nations," and he specifically stated that this included baptizing enslaved black people. He also insisted that children and slaves should be baptized under the authority of the head of Christian households, and that "Christianity maketh no alteration in civil rights," that is, in the right to own slaves. New York's legislature in 1706, at the request of Anglican missionaries, passed "An Act to Encourage the Baptizing of Negro, Indian and Mulatto Slaves." It decreed "That the Baptizing of any Negro, Indian or Mulatto Slave shall not be any Cause of reason for the setting them or any of them at Liberty." Since the 1660s, English colonists had to keep insisting that baptism did not free slaves because the "heathenism" of Africans was an early justification for their enslavement and because enslaved people kept trying to use Christianity to obtain freedom.[74]

By meeting with slaves directly and by encouraging masters to promote religion among their slaves, Anglican clergy successfully laid the foundation for interracial church life in northern colonies, but little information about individual black Anglicans has survived in archives. Although autobiographical accounts by black and Indian Anglicans are scarce, some telling demographic characteristics can be extracted from church records. Many blacks and Indians were baptized as adults, and there was a roughly equal balance between men and women. At Christ Church Philadelphia, at least seventy-eight people were clearly identified as blacks in the baptismal records between 1730 and 1749. One of these people was "Pompsey, an adult negro slave belonging to ye minister of ye parish." Additionally, at least two Indians were baptized in 1733: "John, Son of Peter & Margret Moutanne, an Indian," and "Anne daughter of Amoritta, Mr. Lawrence's Indian woman." Of the black people baptized, forty-two were male and thirty-six were female. These people appear to have been, moreover, equally divided between adults and children/infants. The high proportion of adult baptisms contrasts sharply with the typical trend among whites. English Anglicans were much more likely to have been baptized as children. Many of these black people were forcibly abducted and carried across the Atlantic as slaves, so they did not necessarily learn about Christianity from their parents. In fact, many enslaved Africans practiced Islam or other West African religions. Enslaved adults, as well as children, were targets of the Church of England's outreach.[75]

In most cases, black people who were baptized in the Church of England parishes were identified by their race, status, and master's name. Identifying black men, women, and children in this manner meant that their legal status as slaves and perceived racial identity was reinforced at the very same time white society recognized them as Christians. There were, however, some exceptions to this pattern. In a few cases, the enslaved parents were listed for a child's baptism with or without the owner's name. For example, "Salisbury, son of Richard & Dinah slaves of Griffith," was baptized in 1748 at Christ Church Philadelphia. Although black families under slavery always faced the possibility of being separated, black family relationships were, to an extent, acknowledged by churches. The white ministers implied that parents, as well as the masters, had a responsibility to raise the enslaved children in the Christian faith.[76]

In addition to the parishes located in cities and coastal areas, Anglican priests also ministered to Indians, Africans, and colonists on the outskirts of Britain's North American empire at missionary chapels. Reverend Henry Barclay recorded nearly three hundred baptisms at Queen Anne Chapel located at Fort Hunter, New York, between 1735 and 1746. Fort Hunter marked the border between English settlements west of Albany and Mohawk territory. In the setting of a military and commercial outpost, Barclay ministered to and taught Indians (he could speak some Mohawk) until he left in 1745 to become rector of Trinity Church New York. Not only was this a place of interracial trade and diplomacy, but it was also a site of interracial religious exercises, supported by the SPG.[77] Although the racial notations in these records appear haphazard and inconsistent, at least four "negroes" were baptized at Queen Anne Chapel, all slaves of John Wemp or Captain Hellen. Some of the Indians baptized there were identified as Oneida, Tuscarora, or simply as Indian. Although English and Dutch last names predominate in the records, there are dozens of Indian last names recorded.[78] These families and baptized individuals of different ethnicities likely worshipped and occasionally took communion together. Even at the edges of the empire, or perhaps especially at the edges of the empire where different cultures collided and where shared rituals facilitated trade and politics, religion often occurred in interracial contexts.

Some Lutheran and Moravian churches in the Mid-Atlantic also ministered to blacks or Indians between 1730 and 1749, but fewer blacks and Indians affiliated with these churches than with Anglican and Congregational ones. Lutheran and Moravian churches, most of which were ethnically German, were relatively young transplants from Europe, and there were fewer black people in German American communities. Nevertheless, their participation in some of these other denominations suggests that early African American and Indian forms of Christianity were not limited to one or two types of churches and were not limited to the churches that promoted the Great Awakening revivalism.[79]

During the 1730s, German Lutheran churches in Pennsylvania were struggling to become well established, but blacks occasionally participated in Lutheran churches. German and Swiss migrants were growing in numbers and were spreading out from Philadelphia in the first decades of the eighteenth century, but there were few ordained clergy among them. From 1733 until 1742, there was only one ordained German Lutheran minister, Casper Stoever, in Pennsylvania. In these nine years, Stoever baptized at least 1,418 people, some of whom were identified as English rather than as German congregants. The first German Lutheran church in Pennsylvania was organized in 1717, but dozens were planted across Pennsylvania by the 1740s.[80]

The circumstances of German colonists and their churches did not make them natural centers of interracial religious experiences. Given the early years of German congregations in Pennsylvania and the immigrant status of most Germans, their Lutheran churches baptized few blacks or Indians during the 1730s and 1740s. Most of the recently arrived German and Swiss immigrants lacked the money to purchase slaves. Some of the German migrants were themselves bound to years of service as payment for the cost of transportation to America. German farmers generally preferred indentured Germans over enslaved blacks, at least while the supply of indentured servants remained steady, so there were fewer blacks among Germans than among English or Dutch colonists. Pennsylvania Germans' pattern of eschewing slavery was similar to the practices of German colonists elsewhere. Lutherans in Ebenezer, Georgia, feared the effects of having enslaved people in their community, and they supported continuing the ban on slavery in Georgia. After 1750, when slavery was allowed into Georgia, Ebenezer Lutherans owned fewer enslaved people than was typical for southern communities. Some Germans in Pennsylvania and elsewhere owned slaves, but they owned fewer slaves on average than did English and Dutch colonists.[81] Overall, circumstances particular to German colonists hedged against black and Indian participation in their churches.

Black people were baptized in a couple of Pennsylvania Lutheran churches before 1750; there was a higher concentration of black people in Philadelphia and eastern Pennsylvania than in the Pennsylvania countryside. At St. Michael's & Zion Lutheran Church in Philadelphia, "Wilhelm Peter son of Peter & Mary (free negroes)" was baptized in 1747 (the earliest baptismal records available for this church are from 1745). At the Swedish Lutheran Church of St. Gabriel's, located about forty-five miles northwest of Philadelphia in Berks County, four black children were baptized in 1741.[82] Pennsylvania Lutherans baptized few blacks from 1730 to 1749, but the absence of blacks was mostly due to the low levels of slave ownership among German and Swedish migrants in Pennsylvania and not to a disposition to exclude blacks.

The Lutheran Church of New York, which included German, Dutch, and Scandinavian Lutherans, "was weak and struggling" until the first years of the eighteenth century, but it was accessible to blacks and Indians. Soon after his 1725 installment as the minister in New York, Reverend Wilhelm Christoph Berkenmeyer wrote to the Amsterdam Lutheran Consistory requesting their opinion about how to administer the rite of baptism. Lutherans, unlike Congregational churches, believed in the doctrine of "*de necessitate baptismi*," whereby it is necessary to baptize children as soon as possible to avoid the possibility of children dying before their baptism. In the context of New York, with its many religious groups and nationalities, Berkenmeyer wanted the opinion of theologians and church officials in Europe as to how widely this doctrine applied. He wrote to ask about whether or not the rule that "pastors must baptize all children that are not baptized when they are requested to do so" applied to children "born of savage parents."[83]

The Amsterdam Lutheran Consistory responded with statements that indicated the Lutheran stance on baptism; Lutheran churches should have, in theory, baptized some blacks and Indians. The Consistory argued that children should almost always be baptized, even if born out of wedlock, because "withholding baptism is a punishment for the child, for one deprives it meanwhile of the merits of Christ; one leaves it in a state of unbelief, since baptism is a means of planting faith in the hearts of children and thereby enabling them to accept Christ." This recommendation to baptize children extended to Christians outside the Lutheran Church, including children of Reformed parents (Reformed churches, conversely, placed more limits on who could be baptized). The requirement to baptize regardless of the parents' denomination did not, however, extend to indiscriminately baptizing Indians. The Consistory instructed that if Indian children were to "remain in the blindness of heathenism" with their parents, then they "cannot be baptized." However, "if such children at and after their baptism become Christians, to be brought up and instructed by them, they can and must be baptized, as such children, by right of cession, adoption, gift or purchase, or being acquired in any other way, can and must be regarded as personal property." In essence, Indians who professed belief were to be baptized, and Indian children raised in Christian households as slaves or servants were to be baptized under the authority of their master's faith. The letter also implied that baptism did not change the enslaved status of bondsmen and bondswomen. While the Consistory did not discuss enslaved blacks, it is reasonable to assume that Lutheran pastors would have treated them similarly because both groups were held as servants or slaves and because Europeans believed both unconverted Indians and blacks were heathens. Berkenmeyer believed that blacks and Indians in Lutheran households should be baptized, and he baptized his three enslaved people.[84]

The 1735 constitution for New York and New Jersey Lutheran congregations, written by Berkenmeyer, instructed pastors to admit enslaved people to the church as long as they seemed sincerely interested in abiding by Christian morality and promised to continue serving their masters. When baptizing black people, the constitution says that "preachers should be careful that they [enslaved people] promise not to abuse their Christianity or break the bond of submission." This concern reinforced the practice that dated from at least 1708 of requiring enslaved people to promise not to use baptism or church membership as arguments for emancipation.[85]

Black people were theoretically allowed to become communicants in Lutheran churches by the 1730s, and they certainly became communicants in later decades. At the Lutheran church in Hackensack, New Jersey, the church council, headed by Reverend Michael C. Knoll, in 1733 decided that, "If, by the grace of God, some Negroes would also be willing to come to catechetical instruction," then they would be instructed with white children and white young adults in preparation to "be admitted to the Lord's Supper."[86] The possibility of learning to read, as part of cat-echism lessons, likely appealed to black northerners.

The Lutheran churches in New York, according to Graham R. Hodges, were "sufficiently open to black membership as to be considered interra-cial communities," and they seemed to attract free blacks particularly.[87] At the Lutheran church in New York City, there were at least nineteen blacks baptized in the 1730s and 1740s. Among the individuals baptized were "Peter Jaksen, a free negro, about 20 years old"; "David, a negro slave of Niclaes Walther"; Abraham, the son of "Joseph Matthyeen and Annatje, free negreoes," and Eva, the illegitimate child of "Maria Poppelsdorf, white and an unknown negro." Some consensual sexual relations and even marriages between Germans and free black people occurred in the eighteenth century. These black individuals, some free and some enslaved, requested baptism at the Lutheran church and likely attended services there.[88]

The Moravian Church (Renewed Unity of Brethren), a mission-driven and pietistic Protestant sect from central Europe, also ministered to some blacks and Indians during the 1740s. The Moravians promoted emotional piety and focused on semi-communal living, heartfelt devo-tion to Christ, and worldwide missionary efforts. Moravians were engaged in missionary work to thousands of African slaves on the Dan-ish Caribbean Island of St. Thomas by 1740.[89] A group of Moravians from Saxony settled in Bethlehem, Pennsylvania, in 1740 to practice their reli-gion without state harassment and to minister to Pennsylvania Indians. Eventually, by the 1760s, Moravians established five communities in New York, Pennsylvania, and Connecticut for Delaware, Mohican, and other Indians interested in Christianity. Missionary work at Indian vil-lages, such as Shekomeko, New York, was a central component of the faith of these Christians. Like Anglicans, Moravians sometimes offered educational opportunities to enslaved people. Moravians also did not demand that their converts possess a high degree of religious knowledge or memorize doctrines before baptism, and Moravians sought to learn Indian languages and could be more accepting of traditional Indian practices than most English Protestants. All that was required of adults seeking baptism was a simple profession of faith, and as such, Moravians made this sacrament relatively accessible to blacks and Indians.[90]

In addition to the small number of black Moravians, including Andreas and Magdalene, Indians affiliated with Moravian Christianity in Pennsylvania, New York, and Connecticut, usually in Indian towns that were visited by missionaries. Several families of Delawares decided to be baptized by Moravians in the late 1740s and 1750s, and roughly sixty-six Delaware or Mohican women were baptized in 1749 alone. Delawares often felt pressures from growing white settlements and the more powerful Six Nations Iroquois (Haudenosaunee). Consequently, for some Delawares, Christian affiliation and missionaries were seen as means of maintaining community cohesion and local autonomy. The Moravian missionary town of Gnadenhütten, Pennsylvania, became an important site of Indian Christianity, but other Delawares were skeptical and disinterested in Moravian Christianity and white alliances.[91]

Moravian women played central roles in many of the spiritual interactions with Indians. Several eighteenth-century female Moravian missionaries in New York and Pennsylvania became close friends with Indian believers, and both Europeans and Indians found mutual support in these relationships. Moravian women such as Jeannette Mack met individually with Indian women, discussed religious beliefs with them, and encouraged their spiritual growth. When Indians were baptized in the Moravian church during the 1740s, white Moravians served as sponsors or godparents for Indian children, and correspondingly, Indians sometimes served as sponsors or godparents for white children. These relationships facilitated spiritual as well as physical support among the Indians and Europeans at the Moravian missions. The central role played by Moravian women in missionary work among Indians in the 1740s and 1750s was one of the key factors that made these missions successful examples of interracial Christianity.[92]

The Moravian missionaries who created personal friendships with Indians in Pennsylvania and elsewhere show one way in which interracial religious activities flourished in the 1740s, but such experiences were fragile and not shared by all whites and Indians in Pennsylvania and New York. New York officials persecuted the white Moravian missionaries at Shekomeko in 1744 by charging that they were in league with French Catholics and by expelling white Moravians. The migration of the white and some Indian Moravians effectively ended this Moravian interracial religious community in New York. Some religious societies that were interracial and that practiced some measure of equality occasionally existed in the early eighteenth century, but these endeavors came into conflict with the inequality and injustice that more often characterized relations between whites and Indians.[93]

In contrast to the other Mid-Atlantic churches, most Dutch Reformed, German Reformed, and Presbyterian churches did not baptize or admit to membership black or Indian peoples during most of the eighteenth century. Graham Russell Hodges, who examined baptismal records from more than fifty Reformed churches from 1680 to 1776, was able to find only "scattered black baptisms." The Dutch Reformed Church of Albany, New York, baptized at least ten black people between 1733 and 1745, but those baptisms appear to be the largest concentration of black baptism in a Reformed church before the 1780s. The Old Tennent Presbyterian Church of Manalapan (formerly Freeport), New Jersey, baptized five black adults upon their professions of faith and four black children, whose parents had been baptized previously, between 1740 and 1749. Few other Presbyterian churches followed their lead. Albany's Dutch Reformed Church and the Old Tennent Presbyterian Church were exceptions.[94]

Most Reformed and Presbyterian churches did not baptize blacks or Indians because of parishioners' direct opposition to doing so and because church policies made these sacraments relatively inaccessible, even for enslaved people in Christian homes. Writing in February 1728, James Wetmore, Anglican missionary at Rye, New York, noted that "some Presbyterians will allow their servants to be taught, but are unwilling they should be baptized."[95] Reformed and Presbyterian churches would baptize only children of members (not other household members such as servant children), and they required adults who wanted to be baptized to be admitted as communicants at the same time, which made baptism more difficult to obtain. Presbyterian and Reformed churches did not have the equivalent of the Congregationalists' Halfway Covenant, which separated adult baptisms from the requirements of full membership. More so than among English colonists, Dutch slaveholders feared that baptism would imply equality or undermine their ownership of slaves. Reformed churches also lacked missionary activities directed toward blacks and Indians, which played such a central role in the number of black baptisms in other churches.[96] After the American Revolution, however, Reformed and Presbyterian churches changed their baptismal policies, and African Americans joined these churches, sometimes in substantial numbers (see chapters 4 and 5).

In the Mid-Atlantic colonies as a whole, most Anglican and some Lutheran and Moravian churches ministered to blacks and Indians between 1730 and 1749. Their theology of baptism and missionary activities help explain why these churches included blacks and Indians, even though Germans, in general, owned fewer slaves, and German churches were often less well established than other denominations.

Throughout New England, most Congregational churches and most Church of England parishes were interracial religious communities between 1730 and 1749. Blacks and Indians regularly participated in these churches as attendees and through the rituals of baptism and communion. The presence of blacks and Indians in all these types of churches was not solely the result of Great Awakening revivals because they participated in churches before the Great Awakening began and were participants in churches whose leadership emphatically opposed the Great Awakening. Rather, blacks and Indians found various types of Protestant Christianity appealing for the spiritual and material benefits they could confer. In the middle of the eighteenth century, many of these trends continued. However, European exploitations of Indians and blacks also strained the dynamics in these churches, leading to conflicts and even the dissolution of some interracial religious communities as Indians increasingly opted for separate churches in the 1750s.

2 /   "I Claim Jesus Christ to Be My Right Master": Black-White Religious Conflicts and Indian Separatists, 1740–1763

On a November 1740 evening in Boston, an enslaved man was told to entertain the whites in attendance at his master's house by impersonating Reverend George Whitefield. The black man began with a prayer and started a sermon despite the jesting and laughter of the white dinner guests. The mood quickly turned somber, however, when the enslaved man said something akin to the following:

> I am now come to my Exhortation; and to you my Master after the Flesh: But know I have a Master even Jesus Christ my Saviour, who has said that a Man cannot serve two Masters. Therefore I claim Jesus Christ to be my right Master; and all that come to him he will receive. You know, Master, you have been given to cursing and Swearing and blaspheming God's holy Name, you have been given to be Drunken, a Whoremonger, Covetous, a Liar, a Cheat, &c. But know that God has pronounced a Woe against all such, and has said that such shall never enter the Kingdom of God. And now to conclude (saith he) except you shall repent you shall likewise perish.[1]

Although nothing else is known about this slave, his exhortation is suggestive of one type of conflict or social tension that existed between some blacks and whites in northern colonial churches.[2] Conflicts between slaves and masters were inherent to slavery, and sometimes conflicts occurred when slaves decided that they could not serve two masters— their God and the person who claimed to own them. This story is also indicative of the fact that blacks, Indians, and whites took from the same churches conflicting understandings of God's will. This slave implied that he should principally serve God, but many masters believed that God's will was for slaves to obey their earthly masters. This slave said that his true master was Jesus Christ, who receives "all that come to him." Not only did this slave insist that he answered to a higher power than his "Master after the Flesh," but he also contended that he would reach heaven instead of his master as long as this man continued to be a "hater of Religion." This enslaved black man used the message of evangelical Christianity, likely gained from attendance at interracial religious services, to critique the person and by implication the institution that kept him enslaved. A benefit of Christianity for this enslaved man was a theology that could be used to criticize his master.[3]

Social tensions and conflicts resulted from the participation of blacks and Indians in so many predominantly white Anglican and Congregational churches. The social hierarchy in British colonies, which assigned blacks and Indians to the lowest positions in society, did not always coexist easily with the egalitarian and evangelical strains of Christianity, even though social hierarchies were commonly reinforced within churches. When blacks and Indians decided to affiliate with a predominantly white church, many of them likely considered that such an association could provide them with not only benefits but also disadvantages, including the possibility of religiously oriented conflicts with whites.

Tensions, conflicts, and disruptions in relationships between blacks, whites, and Indians occurred within interracial religious communities and ranged from ordinary church discipline to church schisms and from antagonistic words to physical violence. During the middle decades of the eighteenth century, religious and personal conflicts with whites attended black and Indian participation in northern Protestant churches. In New England, especially, the 1740s through the 1750s was a period of intense religious conflicts caused by the Great Awakening.[4] Interracial conflict in churches was by no means restricted to this period, but during the late 1740s and 1750s, many Indians stopped participating in predominantly white churches and formed separate churches. Many black people, however, remained in predominantly white churches irrespective of the tensions between Christianity and their enslavement or between themselves and white Christians. Indians formed separate churches in Connecticut, Rhode Island, and Long Island roughly four decades before northern blacks formed their own churches. Although both Indians and blacks experienced conflicts with whites, only Indians had the resources and freedom necessary for maintaining separate churches in the 1750s.

Because most black northerners remained enslaved, predominantly white churches were the only formally organized places of public worship available to them.

A number of conflicting factors likely influenced the religious decisions that blacks and Indians made. The people in these groups were severely marginalized, so the decision to practice Christianity usually entailed disadvantages as well as benefits. Blacks and Indians, both individually and communally, evaluated whether the benefits derived from participating in mostly white churches were accessible only within these churches and whether these benefits outweighed the subordination that they often experienced therein. The benefits for some people included meaningful worship, spiritual fulfillment, white advocates, access to education, and the status of being a church member in colonial society. Reverend Harry Munro noted two of the benefits that attracted blacks to his church, including "the great desire the negroes have of learning" and the "care and attention to their spiritual concerns" that they received.[5] Moreover, blacks and Indians were astute observers of colonial society. They knew where power lay in their towns, and churches were accessible places with power. The disadvantages of affiliation for blacks and Indians included exclusion from the pulpit and leadership positions, implicit support for systems of exploitation, being treated as inferior or subservient, and greater white supervision over their behavior. For example, in 1767, at the First Congregational Church in Deerfield, Massachusetts, "Titus Negro Confessed the Sin of Stealing, Lying & disobedience to his Master." This church added another layer of oversight and discipline to promote obedience to slave owners. Available evidence suggests the existence of both tangible benefits and negative proscriptions for blacks and Indians in white churches, and it is difficult to imagine that they did not consider these factors when choosing whether or not to affiliate, or to continue their affiliation, with predominantly white churches.[6]

For many Indians during the 1750s, the religious and educational benefits received from affiliating with white churches could be obtained in Indian churches or from other sources without the disadvantages associated with participation in white churches. Many Indian communities, even though often poor and marginalized compared to white communities, possessed the resources necessary to maintain churches. Missionary organizations sometimes provided money for building a meetinghouse and salaries for Indian ministers and teachers. For many blacks, there were still benefits that could be derived from predominantly white churches that could not readily be found elsewhere, and the vast majority of blacks lacked even the modest autonomy and resources available to Indians. The overwhelming majority of black people were enslaved. Thus, despite conflict with whites, many blacks and a few Indians continued to participate in many predominantly white churches.

A wide variety of interracial conflicts and broken relationships existed within northern churches, and blacks and Indians faced some conflicts by merely participating in predominantly white churches. These conflicts included theological disagreements, church schisms, and resistance to slavery. Some disputes between whites and Indians correlated with the rise of separate Indian churches, but other conflicts occurred in the churches where both whites and Indians attended together. Enslaved blacks occasionally asserted their rights as church members against the wishes of owners. In growing numbers, black adults baptized their children, and sometimes blacks and Indians publicly expressed their own interpretations of Christianity, often to the surprise and disapproval of whites.

The period of 1740 to 1763 was heavily influenced, perhaps even defined, by warfare and violence. King George's War particularly affected New York, Massachusetts, and New Hampshire from 1744 to 1748. English colonists and their Indian allies fought French forces and their Indian allies along the border between the British colonies and New France. The Indians who fought alongside the English included individuals who had affiliated with colonial churches. Similar but more sustained and devastating fighting occurred between these rivals during the French and Indian War from 1754 to 1763. Whites reacted to Indian engagement in these conflicts in Pennsylvania with widespread fear and retaliatory violence not only against Indians allied with the French but also against Indians allied with English colonial authorities. Graphic written accounts of frontier warfare contributed to spreading white fear of Indian violence and shrill anti-Indian discourses. For some colonists, Indian-hating crystalized in new ways during these wars. Some white Christians transferred a growing anti-Indian animus onto Indian Christians and even attacked settlements of pacifist, Christian Indians. White distrust and animosity made Indians less inclined to remain in predominantly white churches.[7]

Even as imperial and Indian wars raged, the numbers of enslaved Africans imported to northern colonies increased dramatically, peaking in the 1750s and 1760s. The demand for slaves in Pennsylvania was partially due to a decreased availability of German indentured servants because wars made European migration more difficult and less appealing. Between 130 and 150 voyages from 1748 to 1774 brought thousands of enslaved Africans to the New York area. In 1763, Connecticut had a population of more than 14,000 whites, 4,503 blacks, and 940 Indians. In 1755, Rhode Island had 35,939 white and 4,697 black inhabitants. Recently arrived adult Africans were less likely than American-born blacks to affiliate with churches, at least during their first years of enslavement.[8]

The growing population of enslaved blacks and politicized fear of Indians were two of the broader changes that occurred in northern colonies from 1740 to 1763 that influenced white perceptions of blacks and Indians and their interactions in churches. Although these colonial wars and the slave trade are not detailed in this chapter, they form a significant part of the context of this era. In his study of the Seven Years' War, Fred Anderson argues that "this immense conflict changed everything, and by no means only for the better."[9] This change included growing white hostility and violence against all Indians and increases in the enslaved black population. Despite conflicts within and outside of churches, however, a significant portion of northerners continued to experience formal religion in interracial contexts. Because Anglican and Congregational churches continued to be more interracial than other types of northern churches, this chapter focuses on these two types of Christianity. After describing the extent of black and Indian participation in Congregational and Anglican churches from 1750 to 1763, this chapter covers the rise of separate Indian churches in southern New England and the conflicts that occurred between whites and blacks in churches across northern colonies. For black and Indian peoples, the practice of Christianity in colonial America involved some difficult choices.

Black and Indian Participation Levels, 1750–1763

Of all the Protestant denominations, Congregational churches in New England and Anglican churches throughout northern colonies had the highest levels of black and Indian participation between 1750 and 1763. However, rates of black church affiliation declined in Congregational churches and grew in Anglican parishes. Indian participation dramatically declined as they founded separate churches. Black participation remained relatively low but stable in Lutheran and Moravian churches. Many colonists continued to experience public worship in interracial settings, but at some Congregational churches, rates of black baptisms declined relative to the 1730–49 period, particularly among adults. In many locations, the number of both white and black baptisms declined in Congregational churches, but sometimes the black-to-white ratio of baptisms also fell. Fewer revival activities and conflicts within many Congregational churches likely led to a drop in adult baptisms. At Anglican churches, conversely, black participation levels tended to be higher in the 1750s and 1760s as Anglican churches offered additional religious classes in which black people learned to read and as more missionaries arrived from England. Anglicans, the official model of imperial state Christianity, expanded their reach in this era with direct support from the metropole. Anglican churches grew and expanded by recruiting enslaved and free blacks and by enticing colonists away from other churches. Some New Englanders left the Congregational churches that divided over issues of revivalism and joined Anglican parishes. Specific information about black and Indian peoples' affiliation in churches is essential for showing the extent of interracial worship. The widespread, active participation of people of color in churches led to all sorts of religious conflicts with whites. Without understanding the scope of interracial churches, we cannot accurately contextualize the conflicts therein between blacks, Indians, and whites.[10]

Black men and women continued to participate in all of Boston's Congregational churches from 1750 to 1763, but generally, they affiliated less frequently than in the two previous decades, as comparisons between table 2.1 and table 2.2 indicate. The decreased number of black baptisms at most of Boston's Congregational churches, however, stands in contrast to a relative increase in black baptisms in Boston's Anglican churches. In most of Boston's Congregational churches, the number of black baptisms decreased in both absolute and relative terms. Since black people were baptized at higher rates in Boston's three Anglican churches than in any of Boston's Congregational churches, excepting Old South Church, Anglican churches may have offered more enticements for blacks worshippers.[11]

Several factors affected the number of baptisms in these Congregational churches and led to fewer white people and fewer black people being baptized during the 1750s and early 1760s. All of Boston's Congregational churches baptized, on average, fewer people per year between 1750 and 1763 than compared to the average number of yearly baptisms in the preceding decades. Since an unusually high number of adults' baptisms occurred in the 1740s, it makes sense that fewer adults and fewer total people were baptized in the next decade. Demographic and social conditions in Boston and within some churches likely led to fewer total baptisms. Colonial populations are difficult to determine

TABLE 2.1. Black baptisms in Boston's Congregational and Anglican churches, 1730–1749

Boston churches	Number of black baptisms	Average number of black baptisms per year	Total number of baptisms	Black % of total baptisms
Brattle Street (Fourth)	46	2.30	1,134	4.06
Old South (Third)	35	1.75	1,158	3.02
New North (Fifth)	31	1.55	1,726	1.80
Second (1730–47)	22	1.10	623	3.53
New Brick (Seventh)	9	0.45	593	1.54
West (Ninth)	8	0.40	263	3.04
First (Old Brick)	15	0.75	738	2.03
New South (Sixth)	6	0.30	881	0.68
Hollis Street (Eighth)	3	0.15	313	0.96
King's Chapel Episcopal	9	0.45	574	1.57
Christ Church Episcopal	55	2.75	1,010	5.44
Trinity (1738–63)	15	1.25	432	3.47
City Totals & Averages	254	12.70	9,445	2.69

accurately, especially for black people, but it appears that Boston's white population declined somewhat from the late 1740s to 1760, while Boston's black population stayed constant or grew slightly. In some Congregational churches, however, not only did the total number of black baptisms decrease, but the percentage of black baptisms compared to all baptisms also decreased. Perhaps some churches became less welcoming to black people, or maybe other churches became more appealing. Given the trends in black baptisms, some black people may have switched from attending Congregational churches to Anglican ones. At least part of the decrease in black baptisms reflected a stabilization or normalization of black baptisms in which fewer adults were baptized and more blacks were baptized as children.[12]

TABLE 2.2. Black baptisms in Boston's Congregational and Anglican churches, 1750–1763

Boston churches	Number of black baptisms	Average number of black baptisms per year	Total number of baptisms	Black % of total baptisms
Brattle Street (Fourth)	13	0.93	441	2.95
Old South (Third)	22	1.57	522	4.21
New North (Fifth)	7	0.50	1,064	0.66
Second (1730–47)	NA	NA	NA	NA
New Brick (Seventh)	6	0.43	192	3.13
West (Ninth)	4	0.29	158	2.53
First (Old Brick)	3	0.21	224	1.34
New South (Sixth)	5	0.36	467	1.07
Hollis Street (Eighth)	1	0.07	208	0.48
King's Chapel Episcopal	32	2.29	798	4.01
Christ Church Episcopal	23	1.64	520	4.42
Trinity (1738–63)	24	1.71	531	4.52
City Totals & Averages	143	10.21	5,125	2.79

Blacks who were baptized between 1750 and 1763 at the Old South Church Boston were more likely to be children than those baptized in the previous two decades, which means that the rate of black baptisms stabilized at a level closer to the birth rate in this congregation. It became more common to see black parents listed with the baptism of black infants and children, suggesting that black adults continued their affiliation with churches by baptizing their children. At Old South, there were primarily two ways that black baptisms were recorded: (1) with the name of the baptized person followed by the status description, "negro servant of," and the master's name, or (2) the name of the baptized person followed by parents' names and the designation "negroes." The former type usually signified that the person was baptized by the authority of the white master, who publicly "engageth for his [or her] Education." In the latter group, the children were baptized by the authority of their parents, who had owned the covenant (ascribed to the doctrines of the church) and had been baptized already. From 1730 to 1749, about 30 percent of the black baptisms were done on the authority of the children's parents. Between 1750 and 1763, this group increased to roughly 55 percent. The rate of black children being baptized rose in relation to adult baptisms. There was a trend toward most people, black and white, being baptized as children. Black parents, baptized earlier, now brought their children back to be baptized upon their own authority. After the extraordinary period of the early 1740s, fewer adults were converted and baptized, which decreased the total numbers of black baptisms in many churches even though black children were regularly baptized.[13]

The records of the First Church of Watertown, Massachusetts, help explain how black participation in Congregational churches stabilized after the 1740s, whereby black people continued their affiliation with churches by having their children baptized. Three "negroes," two "mulattoes," and one Indian were baptized between 1730 and 1749. They all appear to have been adults when baptized because they publicly owned the covenant. These adult baptisms included Nymphas, a slave owned by the church's minister. In contrast, between 1750 and 1760, one "negro" adult and three "negro" children were baptized in Watertown. As an adult, "Jenny Negro woman of Saml Parry owned ye covenant & was baptized." Nymphas, Phillis, and Katy, the children of the minister's slave Nymphas, were baptized in 1753, 1755, and 1757, respectively. Since Nymphas owned the covenant and became a halfway member in 1745, it was possible in the 1750s for his three children to be baptized under his authority. The act of an enslaved man offering his children for baptism complicates traditional understandings of master-slave relations because the master was not the sole patriarchal figure in such a situation. To some degree, this church recognized the parental rights and obligation of Nymphas as he brought his enslaved children for baptism. According to census information, Watertown had seven male and five black female residents over the age of sixteen in 1755, so it seems likely that fewer than half the town's black people were baptized at this church.

Black people participated in the rite of baptism and membership in at least ninety-nine Congregational churches in New England between 1750 and 1763.[14] In comparison, 121 Congregational churches included multiple black baptisms or members between 1730 and 1749 (see chapter 1). At some of these churches, such as the First Parish Congregational

Church in Brockton, Massachusetts, the rate of black baptisms remained steady. At the Second (West) Church of Christ in Amesbury, Massachusetts, only one black child and one Indian child were baptized in the 1740s, but four black children were baptized there in the 1750s. Although these are small numbers of people, Amesbury had an estimated population of five black people over age sixteen in 1755, so a significant portion of the black people in town were connected to this church.[15]

At other churches, however, fewer blacks participated in the sacrament of baptism after 1750 due to stabilizing baptismal rates and cases when church affiliation may have become less appealing or less accessible because of local circumstances. At the First Church of Mansfield, Connecticut, only two blacks and two Indians were baptized between 1750 and 1763 compared to eight black baptisms in the two decades before 1750. The Mansfield church became bitterly divided around 1744, and in 1762, Mansfield had twenty-six black residents. The First Church of New London, Connecticut, saw a more substantial decrease. Sixteen Indians and fifteen blacks were baptized there between 1730 and 1749 compared to two blacks and one Indian between 1750 and 1763. This church also experienced a schism as a result of the awakenings and was several years without a resident pastor following the death of Reverend Adams in 1753, both of which likely effected the baptismal rate. Although the number of black baptisms fluctuated, in a significant portion of the communities in southern New England, some black people participated in Congregational church even after revivals waned.[16]

Blacks regularly and Indians occasionally affiliated with the Church of England parishes between 1750 and 1763. In fact, most northern Anglican parishes were interracial, and the rate of black baptisms increased in this era as compared to the 1730–49 period. At Trinity Church in Newport, Rhode Island, there were fifty-one black baptisms and four Indian baptisms in the latter fourteen-year period. The yearly average number of black baptisms increased from 2.85 to 3.64. Black people made up about 17 percent of Newport's population in 1748, so most black Newporters probably still had not affiliated with a church. At Christ Church Philadelphia there were 105 blacks baptized from 1750 to 1763; the yearly average number of black baptisms increased from 3.9 to 7.5 from the first period to the second. Twenty-five of the black persons baptized at Christ Church Philadelphia were identified as "free negroes." The increase in black baptisms at Christ Church was likely the result of efforts by Reverend William Sturgeon, who became "catechist to the negroes" in 1747 with the support of the Society for the Propagation of the Gospel in

Foreign Parts (SPG). Sturgeon, like many Anglican catechists, offered valuable educational opportunities for black adults and youths.[17]

One of the principal causes of the increased number of black baptisms and members in northern Anglican churches was the ministers and catechists employed by the SPG to reach out to blacks and Indians. In 1762, the SPG supported or employed seventy missionary priests, schoolmasters, and catechists in the northern colonies (compared to only ten for the southern mainland colonies). Religious developments happening in other colonies influenced Anglicans in northern colonies, but the relatively smaller size of the enslaved population in northern colonies made northern Anglicans, on average, more accepting of SPG missionaries' work among slaves. Although black people attended and affiliated with some Anglican churches in southern and Caribbean colonies, white Anglicans in these contexts expressed more opposition to baptizing enslaved blacks, and the SPG dedicated fewer resources to evangelism in southern colonies. Many of the northern SPG missionaries reported not only educating but also baptizing and admitting to communion black parishioners.[18]

Trinity Church in New York City attracted many of the city's wealthiest inhabitants and colonial officials, but numerous poor whites and enslaved blacks also attended services there. The building was enlarged in 1737 to accommodate more worshippers (see figure 2.1).

Although most of Trinity Church's records were destroyed in a 1776 fire, missionary reports suggest that black baptisms occurred at a significant level at this church. A single surviving baptismal record indicates that at least twenty-one blacks were baptized at Trinity Church New York in 1759.[19] Reverend Samuel Auchmuty was appointed as a catechist for New York City by the SPG, and he taught, catechized, and baptized scores of black people. In 1750 he wrote: "Since my last [December 1749] I have baptized about twenty-five negro infants, and eight adults, and can with truth assure you that my black catechumens daily increase, and seem to be fonder of becoming Christians than they were when I first came among them. I must acquaint you that the Masters of the slaves in this place have also become more desirous than they used to be, to have servants baptized, and instructed in the principles of our most holy religion."[20] It seemed that many blacks sought instruction and baptism at Trinity Church, and masters generally promoted the same object. For both white and black participants, baptism was a sign representing the means of eternal salvation; however, white masters hoped that Christianization would produce dutiful slaves, whereas at least some slaves sought

FIGURE 2.1. Trinity Church of New York City as it appeared from 1737 to 1776. *Trinity Church, the First Edifice, Destroyed in the Fire of 1776*, The Miriam and Ira D. Wallach Division of Art, Prints and Photographs: Picture Collection, NYPL, Image ID 801100, NYPL Digital Collections, http://digitalcollections.nypl.org/.

liberty or empowerment through Christianity. Many northern Protestants taught slaves to read the Bible at home, but Anglican churches paid instructors to teach blacks, including slaves, how to read and the doctrines of faith in weekly classes. Auchmuty reported in regular letters that he baptized 371 black infants/children and 65 black adults from 1750 to 1763 and that some were preparing to take communion. Black people participated at Trinity Church and other Anglican churches in higher numbers during the 1750s than in previous decades, perhaps in part because the number of enslaved blacks in northern colonies rose during the middle decades of the eighteenth century and because of dedicated missionary activities. As table 2.3 indicates, northern Anglican churches generally baptized black people, sometimes in substantial numbers.[21]

Writing from Westchester County, New York, Reverend Harry Munro commented on the two major benefits that blacks saw in participation in Anglican churches: "The remarkable proficiency of my young catechumens, and the great desire the negroes have of learning" and that the black people in his parish "seem to be extremely thankful for my care and attention to their spiritual concerns." Many of the Anglican churches offered both spiritual and educational benefits to blacks, which together may have been primary motivators for the black people who affiliated therein.[22]

As they had done in the 1730s and 1740s, small numbers of black people also participated in Christian sacraments in the Lutheran and Moravian churches of the Mid-Atlantic colonies during the 1750s and 1760s. The number of blacks in all these churches, however, was generally low. A couple of black people were baptized in the Lutheran churches located in Philadelphia and York, Pennsylvania, and nine black persons were baptized at the Lutheran church in New York City. In 1752, Reverend Henry Muhlenberg described one of the enslaved people at Trinity Lutheran Church in New York. He wrote that "a widow in the congregation has a Negro slave who comes diligently to our Dutch and English services and puts many nominal Christians to shame by her life." This enslaved woman evidently valued her connection to this congregation and modeled a life of faith and piety. Small numbers of black people were baptized at Moravian churches in Philadelphia and Bethlehem, Pennsylvania, and New York City. At least some Lutheran and Moravian ministers sought to minister to blacks in their Mid-Atlantic communities.[23]

Whereas hundreds of black northerners affiliated with white churches between 1750 and 1763, the trend among Indians was strikingly different. Indians participated in predominantly white churches, particularly Congregational churches, at much lower rates during the 1750s and 1760s, and this trend corresponded to the rise of new Indian churches. One or more Indians were identified in the baptismal records of only fifteen predominantly white Congregational churches, four Anglican churches, and one Reformed church from 1750 to 1763, including an Afro-Indian ("free negro" father and Indian mother) who was baptized at Scituate, Massachusetts.[24] Conversely, Indians were baptized in at least forty Congregational churches, four Anglican churches, and two

TABLE 2.3. Select list of Church of England parishes in which black people were baptized, 1750–1763

Church names	Number of black baptisms	Yearly average
Queen's Chapel Portsmouth, N.H.	2	0.14
King's Chapel Boston, Mass.	32	2.29
Christ Church Boston, Mass.	23	1.64
Trinity Church Boston, Mass.	24	1.71
St. Michael's Church, Bristol, R.I.	2	0.14
St. Paul's Church Narragansett, R.I.	7	1.00
Trinity Church Newport, R.I.	51	3.64
King's Church Providence, R.I. (1758–63 only)	9	N/A
Christ Church Middletown, Conn.	6	0.43
Christ Church Stratford, Conn.	29	2.07
St. John's Church Stamford, Conn.	21	1.50
Trinity Church New York, N.Y.[a]	436	31.14
Christ Church Shrewsbury, N.J.	30	2.14
Christ Church Philadelphia, Pa.	105	7.50
Trinity Church Oxford, Philadelphia, Pa.	3	0.21
Total	780	56.00

[a] The number 436 is based on the baptisms reported by Auchmuty in letters that are recorded in Klingberg, "The S.P.G. Program for Negroes in Colonial New York," 332–36. Marriages Parish 1746–1816 and Baptisms 1759, p. 22, Trinity Church Wall Street Archive, New York.

Reformed churches from 1730 to 1749. In addition, there were no large concentrations of Indian baptisms in this period, such as had occurred in the 1740s in places such as Westerly, Rhode Island, and Stonington, Connecticut. After the late 1740s, many Indians formed and participated in separate Indian churches, while others stopped practicing Christianity in any formal setting.[25]

Church affiliation rates are the necessary context of the religious conflicts that occurred between whites, blacks, and Indians. The rates of black church affiliation changed, declining in Congregational churches while growing in Anglican parishes, but blacks and occasionally Indians participated in the sacraments of these predominantly white churches, and they frequently attended services there. The widespread, active presence of people of color in churches led to all sorts of religious conflicts with whites.

The Rise and Limits of Separate Indian Churches

Almost as quickly and dramatically as many Indians in southern New England affiliated with Congregational churches during the 1730s and early 1740s, so too did their affiliation end. Whites treated Indians poorly before, during, and after their affiliation with predominantly white churches, but when the Indians affiliated with white churches, they did so to obtain spiritual and material benefits that were generally unavailable elsewhere. When gifted Indian ministers, such as Samson Occom (Mohegan) and Samuel Niles (Narragansett), were available to provide spiritual leadership or educational benefits, most Indians who lived in autonomous Indian communities left established churches to maintain their own congregations. Communal autonomy, Indian leadership, physical isolation, white condescension, and a theology that justified separation were influential factors that encouraged Indians to move away from mostly white churches. In a few particular locations, however, Indians and whites still worshipped together. There were limits to Indian church separatism in some communities.

During the late 1740s and early 1750s, many Pequots, Narragansetts, Montauketts, and other Indians stopped attending and affiliating with predominantly white churches and founded new churches for themselves. Unlike Indian communities in Massachusetts, Indians in Rhode Island, Connecticut, and Long Island did not have a long history of Indian churches, so those who left predominantly white churches had to start congregations from scratch. Indian churches were mostly geographically confined to Indian land reserves where resources and numbers of people were most concentrated. In a similar way, the first black churches founded after 1790 were confined to northern cities where resources and numbers of people were available and where white prejudice could be countered. The establishment of new Indian congregations was significantly affected by the extent of community resources and long histories of autonomous Indian decision making, but changing views regarding the benefits and drawbacks of church affiliation likely determined the timing of when these new churches started. Although we have few of their written words, the actions of hundreds of Indians in leaving predominantly white churches and establishing their own churches speak loudly about their religious preferences.[26]

Tensions and conflicts within religious bodies are perhaps never more evident than in cases of schisms and the formation of new churches, but the rise of independent or separate Indian churches was less about dramatic, public conflicts and more about collective decisions in favor of independence. Indians in many locations possessed the resources to maintain their own churches, even though they were economically marginalized, and many Indians decided that they could just as well practice Christianity apart from white oversight. They had articulate and sometimes literate Indians who could be ministers, many of them lived in autonomous Indian communities that owned land, and sometimes they received financial aid to pay a salary and build a meetinghouse. In Montauk on Long Island, both an English minister and Mohegan Samson Occom were employed by a missionary society. Indian churches offered the same or even greater spiritual benefits than predominantly white churches provided, and Indians could also sit in the best seats, hold leadership positions, and preach in their languages. Indian churches allowed for the freedom to experience God's spirit in less rigidly orthodox and more satisfying ways than was usually possible in the white churches that prized decorum and European traditions. Missionary societies paid for schoolteachers to live in Indian communities, so predominantly white Congregational churches, which had never put much effort into educating Indian members or their children, were certainly not needed for education. The benefits that had earlier made affiliation with white churches appealing could generally be obtained elsewhere for many New England Indians by 1750. It does not take a great stretch of the historical evidence to imagine that Indians had never intended to permanently stay in white churches and had used short-term affiliation to achieve specific goals.

As expressed by some leaders, northern Indians had several reasons that led them to favor Indian churches over predominantly white ones. Most Indians in Connecticut, Rhode Island, and Long Island preferred Indian-led religious services. Some Christian Indians were also influenced by Separate Congregational or Baptist churches, who preached that true believers should separate from the not fully purified churches. As groups of white people, increasingly after 1741, withdrew from established Congregational churches to form separate churches, they articulated biblical justifications for these schisms. Radical revivalists even argued it was Christians' duty to leave churches led by "unconverted" ministers. Some Indians easily adopted the reasons for separation that whites articulated. Indians may have also been disappointed with the little that English ministers and churches did to help them protect their lands from white theft and encroachment. Moreover, some of their fellow white congregants were the very people fleecing them. In attending English churches, Indians experienced the prejudice that was dominant in white colonial society in the forms of segregated seating and other proscriptions, and predominantly white churches did not accept Indians as pastors or leaders. The mass exodus of Indians from white churches and their decision to practice Christianity independently suggest that Indians preferred churches free from restrictions and white supervision. In most cases, Indian churches could better meet the individual and communal needs of Indians than white churches, especially after the late 1740s.[27]

The presence of Indian ministers in several communities hastened and reinforced the separation of Christian Indians from white churches. Reverends Samson Occom (Mohegan), Samuel Ashpo (Mohegan), and Samuel Niles (Narragansett) led Indian congregations in Long Island, Connecticut, and Rhode Island, respectively. Each pastor was influenced by revival preaching during the Great Awakening, affiliated with English churches, and received some education in English schools. However, they ultimately chose to practice and preach Christianity mostly away from white churches and white supervision. Their active leadership, complicated relationships with English clergymen, and relatively frequent appearances in colonial records make them important windows for understanding the rise of new Indian churches.[28]

These skilled, articulate Indian ministers were probably the greatest factor in bringing so many Indians into these new churches. Reverend Samson Occom was the most famous and influential eighteenth-century Indian minister. Occom was born in 1723 and raised in Mohegan, Connecticut. He gained some knowledge of Christianity from the Englishmen who taught and preached at Mohegan in the 1730s. Occom was influenced by revivalists in the Great Awakening, including Reverend James Davenport, and his interest in Christianity increased in the 1740s. When he was seventeen years old, as he later wrote, he found "Salvation through Jesus, and was enabld to put my trust in him alone for Life & Salvation." In 1742, Occom began serving as a counselor for Mohegan sachem Ben Uncas II, and in 1743, with the assistance of his mother, Sarah, he began studying theology and Latin with Reverend Eleazar Wheelock. Occom often traveled home and to other Indian communities while studying with Wheelock and later with Benjamin Pomeroy. He also occasionally taught at a Mohegan school. Soon after this training, his career as a teacher and minister began in earnest in Montauk, Long Island, where separate Indian Christianity thrived under his leadership.[29]

In 1749, the Montauketts on Long Island requested Occom to be their teacher, but he quickly became their minister as well, displacing an English missionary. Occom's experience at Montauk demonstrates the role that Indian leadership and separatist theology played in forming Indian churches. The English pastor, Reverend Azariah Horton, supported by the Society in Scotland for the Propagation of Christian Knowledge, preached to Indians on Long Island since 1741. However, Occom began to hold religious meetings at Montauk because, according to Occom, Horton spent "two thirds of his Time at Sheenecock, 30 Miles from Montauk." Occom led this community "together 3 times for Divine Worship every Sabbath and once on every Wednesday evening," which was more services than Horton could provide. At these services, Occom read scripture and would "expound upon Some perticular Passages in my own Toung." From Occom's account, it seems clear that the Montauketts valued his spiritual leadership, more constant residence among them, and Indian sensibilities. Horton was not always present and could preach only in English. Apart from simply teaching at the school, Occom positioned himself as this community's minister. Occom also situated himself to be a leader when he married Mary Fowler, who was from one of the Montauketts' elite families. While separatist doctrines and perhaps dissatisfactions with Horton influenced the development of Indian services at Montauk, the presence of the articulate and knowledgeable Occom made independent worship more appealing.[30]

Occom's ministry to Indian churches increased after his 1759 ordination by the Long Island Presbytery, but so did his contact with white churches. Occom promoted independent Indian churches even while his relationship to white clergy remained relatively collegial. He was first examined and approved for ordination by a group of Congregational ministers in Connecticut in 1757; however, these ministers concluded that the Presbyterians should instead ordain Occom because his ministry was centered in New York. In August 1759, Occom was examined on Latin and theology by ministers of the Long Island Presbytery, and he was ordained a minister on the next day during a public service. In subsequent years Occom preached to different Indian communities and some English churches, and he took part in Presbytery meetings with other clergymen. Some colonists were attracted to the novelty of an Indian preacher, but no English congregation would have accepted an Indian as their full-time minister. In this period, he preached to Indians at Shinnecock, Montauk, and Shelter Island Harbor, Long Island; at Mystic, Mohegan, and Farmington, Connecticut; and to the Oneidas in upstate New York. He preached at churches across Long Island where there were whites, blacks, and perhaps some Indians in the congregations. Although Occom spent the vast majority of his time ministering to Indians, he maintained relationships with white churches and ministers to secure financial resources and political allies to help maintain Indian lands and autonomy. One of the factors that made independent Indian churches possible, especially those that Occom promoted, was the limited financial support that missionary organizations provided for Occom's preaching tours and salary.[31]

Although Occom worked with white colleagues, he complained about how some white Christians treated him. White people's prejudice and Eleazar Wheelock's betrayal of his commitment to Indian education pushed Occom further toward Indian autonomy and independent churches. Occom sometimes tolerated insults and unequal treatment from whites, especially early in his career, to obtain financial resources for Indians and to promote Christianity, but conflicts with whites weighed heavily upon him. Writing in 1768 about his time of ministry and teaching on Long Island, Occom criticized the Boston Commissioners of the Society for Propagating the Gospel in New England for their prejudice, which was displayed in unequal missionary salaries. Occom received 15 pounds a year from the Boston Commissioners as he taught and preached on Long Island, but "these Same Gentlemen, gave a young Missionary, a Single man one Hundred Pounds for one year, and fifty Pounds for an Interpreter, and thirty Pounds for an Introducer." These gentlemen accused Occom of "being Extravagant" for needing more than a fifteen-pound salary for his growing family, but they willingly paid 180 pounds for a white missionary. To add insult to injury, the Boston Commissioners did not always pay him on schedule, and Occom once went two years without receiving "a peney from the Gentlemen at Boston." Occom concluded that the pitiful pay and inferior treatment were due to his indigeneity. He lamented that he did not receive just compensation and wrote that "it is because I am [a] poor Indian." Throughout his life, Occom was paid less than whites whenever he was requested by whites to do missionary or fundraising work. In 1761, Occom stated that "Ministers of all Sects and Denomination are Extremely Kind to me," and he maintained close friendships with some white clergymen for his entire life, but whites held him to different standards and treated him differently because he was an Indian.[32] The unequal treatment that Occom and other Indians experienced at the hands of their white Christian brethren contributed to their desire for autonomous churches.

Although his relationships with white ministers differed greatly from those of Samson Occom, Samuel Niles's leadership was equally important for the existence of an Indian church among the Narragansetts in western Rhode Island. Much of what we know about the religious practices of Niles and the Narragansett church comes from Reverend Joseph Fish, who preached to Pequots near his parish in Connecticut from 1757 to 1781 and to Narragansetts in neighboring Rhode Island from 1765 to 1776. Fish preached in both communities for decades, but Narragansetts and Pequots generally preferred Indian preachers. Fish wrote in a 1762 letter about how Pequots skipped his preaching to attend services led by other Indians: "The number of Indians attending, at different Lectures, is *various*. . . . [T]he principal cause, I apprehend, has been their great Fondness for the *Indian* Teachers and their Brethren, (Separates,) from the *Narragansetts*, who were *frequently*, if not *constantly*, with *Our Indians*, or in the Neighborhood, the same day of *My Lectures*." Narragansett preachers often deprived Fish of audiences at his lectures by preaching at the same time. The Narragansetts had a church of their own, led by Samuel Niles since the early 1750s, so they were generally uninterested in the monthly lectures offered by Fish (although small numbers of Indians, blacks, and whites attended Fish's lectures at Narragansett). After 1750, many Pequots and Narragansetts showed little or no interest in listening to white preachers, but Narragansetts had not always been averse to attending services led by English clergy.[33]

Many Narragansetts initially affiliated with Christianity in Reverend Joseph Park's Congregational church in Westerly, Rhode Island, following one of Reverend James Davenport's preaching tours. When Park first formed a church in Westerly in 1742, it consisted of only "fourteen Souls, eight Male and six Females, all English." Soon after hearing the preaching of Davenport and receiving encouragement from some Christian Pequots, the Narragansetts began to participate in Park's church. By 1743, since the revival started, twenty-six people joined the church, and "of those added six are Indians, and two Negroes." In the second year of its existence, at least six Narragansetts and two blacks joined this church, and there were nearly a hundred Indians who came "very constantly" to Park's services. The affiliation continued at a remarkable pace, for by February 1744, sixty-four Indians had joined the church by "a professed Subjection to the Gospel of Christ." During the 1740s, a large portion of the Narragansett tribal nation affiliated publicly with Christianity at the Congregational Church in Westerly, Rhode Island, but it did not take long for the Narragansetts to decide that they should practice Christianity apart from whites.[34]

The Narragansetts promoted religion among themselves in ways that met with Park's approval, but the devotional activities practiced in this Indian community eventually helped promote a separate church. Such independence occurred in Narragansett after 1749 because whites took actions to restrict the preaching of Samuel Niles and because the Narragansetts could maintain a church on their own. In addition to attending public worship, Park noted that his Narragansett congregants "have set up the Worship of God in their Families" and "have frequent private Meetings among themselves for Prayer and Praise." Sometimes Park met with Narragansetts in small groups "to pray with and for them, to read the Word of God, and preach, and discourse with them upon Matters of Importance." The mix of private and public religious practices was common among Congregationalists, especially those influenced by revivalism. Pastors usually hoped that private religious activities would remain orderly and would promote participation in established churches, but among the Narragansetts, it was a relatively easy transition from private devotional activities to an independent church. Since Indian communities had strong traditions of autonomous decision making and leadership, it was not hard for them to establish a church. Narragansetts transitioned from private devotional activities to a separate church, and their new church provided spiritual benefits without any white prejudice or oversight.[35]

In 1748 or 1749, many of the Narragansetts and some of the English church members in Westerly were influenced by evangelical preachers, including Stephen Babcock, and they left Park's church. The Narragansett members of Park's church were also offended that whites chastised Samuel Niles for exhorting or preaching in the church. Ezra Stiles, after a meeting with Niles, recounted that Niles "was dealt with for exhorting in the Congregation: upon which he and about a hundred Indians withdrew."[36] The withdrawal of so many Narragansetts at the same time likely reflects a communal decision-making process. Babcock and other whites organized a Separate Baptist Church, and some of the Christian Narragansetts attended this church. According to Joseph Fish, the Narragansetts left Park's church at roughly the same time as Babcock:

> They left Mr. Parks Church and Ministry, I think, about the time that one Deacon Babcock and others fell off from the Standing Churches, . . . And Were for Some time, Under the Inspection and Influence of Said Mr. *Babcock*, a Separate Baptist Teacher: till most of them took Offense at his Conduct, in Ordaining an Indian over

them, that was not Agreable to the Body of the Tribe. Upon Which Some of the Indian Brethren (as Im informed) not in any Office, took and ordained one Samuel Niles their Pastor, And he has been their Minister ever Since, for a Number of years: preaching, Administing the Supper, Baptism, and Marriage.[37]

Narragansetts took offense when the white church tried to ordain an Indian minister who did not have community support. Some of the Narragansetts proceeded to ordain another person, Samuel Niles. Niles was a baptized member of Park's church before the splits. Niles was not necessarily the driving force behind the separations from Park's and Babcock's churches since the community worked through consensus decision making, but he led the Indian church effectively for many years and was an important part of its founding. Conflicts at Park's church and then a conflict over leadership at Babcock's church were central to the rise of the Narragansett church and suggest some of the disadvantages for Indians of participating in predominantly white churches.

Joseph Fish's first impression of the Narragansett church and Samuel Niles was relatively positive, but he objected to some of the features that made this church appealing to Narragansetts, namely its autonomy and its mix of Christianity and Narragansett culture. On the whole, Fish and other white ministers seem to have doubted the legitimacy of the Narragansett church. The Narragansetts, he reported in September 1765, were "religiously Disposed; and hopefully Retain a good Measure of Serious Impressions of Truth" that was introduced by Park. Fish noted that "they give a Decent and Devout Attention to every Branch of Worship, Whether at Table, or in public Assembly." Fish had positive things to say about their minister as well. He wrote that "Niles, (Who I have known Some Years,) is a Sober Religious Man, of Good Sense and great Fluency of Speech; and know not but a very honest Man. Has a good deal of the Scriptures by heart, and professes a Regard for the Bible." However, Fish complained about their doctrines, the fact that Niles could not read, and other elements of their beliefs and practices that he found heterodox. His statements grew more critical of the Narragansett church as he spent time there and was unable to reform their beliefs. Fish wrote to a fellow pastor in July 1766 that the Narragansett Christians were "all of the Separate Stamp,—Very Ignorant:—Scarce any of them able to read a Word,—Unhappily leavind with, yea full of False Religion,—tenacious of their wild Imaginations and Visionary things."[38] He found much to criticize, but the Narragansetts responded by continuing their church and usually ignoring Fish's monthly lectures. Fish's preaching offered little to most of the Narragansetts.

Some Narragansetts, however, saw economic and political benefits from affiliating with a white church that they could not obtain from participating in Niles's church, including the Narragansett sachem Thomas Ninigret and his family. They participated in an Anglican parish to maintain the support and resources necessary for his rule and lifestyle. Many of the Narragansetts opposed Ninigret because he sold tribal land to Englishmen to pay his personal debts. He sold such a large portion of their land by 1765 that "many Narragansett feared they would lose everything." In fact, Niles and some of the Narragansett Christians may have initially welcomed Fish's monthly lectures and an English schoolteacher named Edward Deake to obtain their assistance in the dispute with sachem Ninigret and his supporters. Christianity in Narragansett divided along theological and political divides. Most Narragansetts preferred the church led by Niles and valued his leadership, but some Narragansetts affiliated with the Church of England or occasionally attended services led by white clergymen to obtain various social, political, economic, or spiritual benefits.[39]

While little evidence is available for understanding the day-to-day religious experiences of many northern Indians, the ministries of Samson Occom and Samuel Niles provide windows into the rise of Indian churches in the middle of the eighteenth century. Many Indians who earlier affiliated with Christianity in predominantly white churches now practiced Christianity in small groups and churches within Indian communities. Often Indian churches operated without the supervision or even the knowledge of whites. Dozens of Indian pastors, some of whom rarely appear in the surviving historical records, contributed to the rise of these new churches, but there were limits to the Indian separate church movement and sometimes Indians and whites worshipped together in small congregations.[40]

Conflicts between whites and Indians in churches did not always immediately lead to separate Indian congregations. In some communities, Indians lacked the resources necessary to maintain separate churches, and in Natick and Sandwich, Massachusetts, Indians and whites attended the same churches despite occasional disputes. In these towns, whites gradually joined and took over predominantly Indian churches that received financial support from missionary organizations. Indians and whites in Natick and Sandwich disagreed over the maintenance and location of the church meetinghouse. Although the location of a town's meetinghouse "was the most common occasion of dispute"

in many New England towns, the conflicts examined here were inti-
mately tied to white encroachment upon Indian settlements. Although
white encroachment threatened and undermined Indian access to these
churches, many of these Indians did not abandon Christianity or start a
new Indian-only church.[41]

The Indian Congregational Church at Natick included a substantial
number of whites by the 1740s, and the percentage of the church that
was Indian declined in the 1750s and 1760s. The conflicts that developed
between whites and Indians in the Natick church reflected broader conflicts over land, identity, and resources in this community. Some Indians
moved away, but other Natick Indians died from battles and diseases
while fighting for the English in the Seven Years' War, and the high death
rate and widespread poverty caused many of them to sell their land to
whites and left them less able to form a new, Indian-only church if they
so desired. By 1746, white residents of Natick had taken complete control
of the town government and excluded Indians from political participation, with the help of the Massachusetts General Court.[42]

For decades, whites in Natick fought over the location of the meetinghouse. However, two factors protected Indian access to the church and
meetinghouse: the continuous funding from the New England Company (NEC) and a law that required the Massachusetts General Court's
approval to move the meetinghouse. Both groups of whites, those who
sought to keep the meetinghouse in the southeastern part of town and
those who wished to move it to the center of town, sought Indian support for their side. Natick residents sent petitions in 1747, 1748, and 1749
with some Indians apparently supporting both sides, but the General
Court's committee determined that moving the meetinghouse to the
center of town was opposed by Natick Indians and the NEC commissioners, "who settled, & for more than twenty six years past have almost
wholly maintained a learned orthodox minister among said People with
very little assistance from English inhabitants." Because the church was
financed for Indians, Natick Indians maintained a measure of control
over its location, even after whites had excluded them from the town
government and after whites had become the majority in the church. The
conflict over the meetinghouse's location, however, continued. Eventually, in 1767, a new meetinghouse was built at Natick Center, and in 1798,
the Natick congregation acrimoniously split into two churches mostly,
but not entirely, along racial lines.[43]

Other conflicts were evident in this church between whites and Indians regarding the leadership and the identity of the church. Some Natick

Indians attested that they were content with Reverend Peabody, but others were dissatisfied with him and the white majority in the church, and they practiced Christianity only within their own homes. As occurred among many Indians in southern New England, some of the Indians in the Natick church withdrew from the established church. For them, but certainly not all in Natick, once the church was an English and Indian church instead of merely an Indian church, they were no longer satisfied worshipping there. Other Natick Indians may have ceased practicing Christianity entirely.[44]

The participation of whites in the Indian church at Sandwich, Massachusetts, also caused conflicts, but some Indians still attended and sought financial support from missionaries instead of moving to another church. An Indian church existed near Herring Pond in the northern part of Sandwich (present-day Bourne, Massachusetts) since the 1670s, but whites and Indians came into conflict there during the 1750s. As early as May 1756, Reverend Elisha Tupper requested that the Boston NEC commissioners fund repairs on the Indian meetinghouse, which was in poor condition. The NEC also paid Tupper a salary. In 1757, there were about seventy-five adult Indians and thirty-eight children who lived nearby the Indian meetinghouse, of which thirty-one were church members. These Indians were generally impoverished, and the difficulty of obtaining subsistence was compounded by the absences and frequent deaths of men who were "either to sea or in the army." These Indians may have justly felt angry as the heavy toll that their communities paid in fighting for the English during colonial wars. The growing number of white settlers on Cape Cod further exacerbated the difficult economic position of these Indians.[45]

The condition of the Indian meetinghouse was a problem for many years because there was no meeting place large enough for both Indian and white attendees, and these Indians held a meeting to again solicit aid in rebuilding their meetinghouse. In October 1761, "at an Indian Meeting held at the Publick Meeting House in Sandwich," they voted to petition the NEC commissioners for a new meetinghouse because their current meetinghouse had "so gone to decay that it is not fitt to meet in for the worship of God when the weather is wet cold or windy." The Indian meetinghouse must have been in a terrible condition because these Indians gathered in the Sandwich's meetinghouse where a white church met. Without a decent meetinghouse, church services were often held in private homes. The desire of some white people to attend Tupper's services forced Indians into a difficult position, but an Indian-only church was not a practical option for them.[46]

As early as 1753, whites may have been crowding out Indians at this meetinghouse because the NEC commissioners noted that "Indians at Sandwich are very much incommoded by the crouding of the English People in the Meeting House," and they instructed Mr. Tupper to make sure that "sufficient room in the House" be reserved for Indians' use.[47] Nevertheless, the issue of space was not resolved. In October 1761, as the weather was becoming colder, a petition signed by three whites and four Indians from Sandwich expressed the need for a new Indian meetinghouse and revealed the tensions caused by the interracial religious services there.

Some whites desired to attend worship with the Indians because of the presence of a white minister whom they did not have to support with tax money and because of their proximity to the meetinghouse, but their presence made some Indians feel unwelcome. The white petitioners stated that "all of us attend the Public worship in sd. Meeting house with the Indians under the ministry of Elisha Tupper which most of us have done for more than ten years past." Englishmen Thomas Swift, Zacheus Burge, and Joseph Lawren acknowledged that some reports indicating that "Indians are deprived of convenient Room by the English" at Tupper's church services, but they generally denied this charge. They stated that the Indian population near the meetinghouse included "25 men 40 women and 36 children," and the petition writers certified "that we often se the greatest part of them there [at church services] but since the meeting house is so bad there are but between twenty and thirty [Indians] that attend generally from Sabbath to Sabbath, as near as we are able to judge." Tupper separately affirmed these numbers by stating in 1761 that "generally not more than twenty or thirty assemble on the Sabbath tho there are more than an hundred who dwell within six miles."[48] The petitioners made the following arguments for why whites were not crowding the Indians out of the church:

> None of us ever saw sd. Meeting house so crowded with people (once only excepted and then the Indians had Room allowed them) but that twenty or more might have had convenient Room in it but as the meeting is held in Cold weather at a small private House where room is more scanty we must declare Truly that at such times there Minister is very carefull that every Indian should have suitable room and the English who meet there are as ready to give room so that one of

us ever saw an Indian at sd meeting but what had or might have had convenient Room to fit and had if he pleased to take it.[49]

The request for a new meetinghouse (at the New England Company's expense) and the white people's defense of their behavior suggest that the Indians felt affronted and undermined by the numbers of whites attending their services, especially when they were held in private homes. Some of the Indians felt crowded out of their church by the white presence at services. As was the case in Natick, perhaps some Indians chose to not attend church services under Tupper precisely because of competition with whites for space and the poor condition of the meetinghouse.

New England Indians used Christianity and churches to maintain their communities and traditional practices, so the increased presence of whites in these Indian churches further undermined Indians' ability to maintain a cohesive community in Natick and Sandwich. Some of the Indians left Sandwich and moved to Mashpee to be farther away from whites, but for those who wanted to participate in a church and remain in Sandwich, there were few other options available. There were disadvantages for the Natick and Sandwich Indians in the increasing white attendance at their church, but they seemingly did not have the resources, including an Indian preacher, necessary to start a new church. They could not even maintain or fix the meetinghouse without financial support from a missionary society. For the time being, in some of the older Indian churches, Indians and whites struggled within the same congregations over the maintenance of and access to a ministry even as Narragansetts, Montauketts, and others formed independent churches.[50]

Conflicts between Blacks and Whites in Churches

Given that a majority of northern Congregational and Anglican churches included black congregants and given the conditions of slavery, it is not surprising that there were religious conflicts between blacks and whites; however, these conflicts did not lead to separate black churches or a mass exodus of black people from predominantly white churches before the American Revolution. Many blacks saw benefits of affiliation that could not be gained elsewhere, and they certainly did not yet have the resources needed to establish separate churches. People of African descent affiliated with churches to gain an education, spiritual sustenance, and the status of being a church member. In rare cases, blacks used churches as venues for asserting their common humanity or opposition to slavery. Prejudice against black people, the hierarchical nature of colonial society, and the economic exploitation of black people were grounds upon which discords occurred within churches, but some of the conflicts in churches, such as disputes over theology, occurred irrespective of the skin color of the people involved. Occasionally whites and blacks both withdrew from an established Congregational church to form a separate church because of theological disputes. In 1750, "Pompey negro Servant of David Moseley" and several white church members were questioned about why they had separated from the Congregational church in Westfield, Massachusetts, and Pompey replied that he withdrew because "persons were admitted yt [that] had not Grace." Along with many of the New Englanders most affected by the Great Awakening, Pompey objected to relatively lax standards for membership in this church.[51]

Although religious conflicts regularly occurred between white masters and the black people they enslaved, relatively few sources indicate how enslaved black people felt about or experienced these conflicts. The lack of firsthand accounts written by black people was part and parcel of the systematic oppression that they faced in colonial America, but some generalization about these conflicts is possible. Most black northerners were involuntarily held as slaves, a condition that whites maintained through force and fear, but they did not submit to this condition without protest, negotiation, or resistance. The structures and means that whites used to keep black men and women enslaved were present in churches, and churches themselves could be part of the system of control and oppression. Colonial churches taught that slaves should obey masters just as children should obey parents and subjects should submit to the king. As they did in other areas of life, some black people resisted oppression in and through churches.[52]

Tensions and conflicts between black and white Christians can be seen in records of church discipline, and increased white oversight of their lives was a disadvantage of church affiliation for black people. Cases of church discipline reflect instances of discord between an individual and the rest of the church. Church members saw disciplinary cases in relational terms. A breach of morality caused discord and separation, and a sinner's repentance enabled reconciliation. These conflicts often ended with renewed uniformity in behavior and beliefs because sinners and dissenters were either expelled or reformed. Black and Indian Christians, like many white Christians, were disciplined by the churches in which they affiliated. Blacks and Indians who owned the covenant (a requirement for baptism in Congregational churches) or who became communing members, submitted themselves to the guidance and discipline of the church. Christians who sinned could be privately admonished, publicly censored, suspended from communion, or excommunicated, depending on the severity of the offense and the response of the accused person. For people in the eighteenth century, these punishments carried weighty social stigma. The goal of such discipline was to keep the church free from sin and to assist Christians in the pursuit of godly living. In many of the churches that disciplined blacks, the wayward black members were restored to full status in the church once they confessed.[53]

Black and Indian Christians usually did not receive harsher penalties in church discipline cases than anyone else, and in most churches, blacks were not more likely targets of church discipline than white congregants. However, given that many black and Indian servants lived in white households, whites exercised a greater degree of supervision over blacks and Indians than was common among white neighbors. Moreover, the First Congregational Church of Deerfield, Massachusetts, disciplined black members more often than white members. At this church, between February 1733 and August 1741, Reverend Jonathan Ashley recorded twenty-five public confessions (including ones where both a man and a woman confessed together), and nineteen of the confessions involved admitting to fornication. These twenty-five confessions included six by black people and one by an Indian woman. By 1741, only three black people were full members, and eleven black people had been baptized at this church (including Lucy Terry Prince, America's first black poet). Given these numbers, people of color confessed more often and to a greater number of sins at the Deerfield church than the white members. The rate of black people confessing to sins may have been relatively high because of white supervision of their lives or because whites prejudicially thought that black people were more inherently prone to sin. Reverend Ashley preached a sermon "to the Negroes" of Deerfield in 1750 that stressed that the first step in becoming a Christian ("Christ's freemen") was to "break off from all sin and sincerely repent of your past wickedness" and that enslaved Christians must continually "resist all temptation to sin."[54]

The First Church in Plymouth, Massachusetts, disciplined two black men, who were both slaves and church members, in 1744, but these men were eventually restored to church membership after they repented. The church voted to suspend "Nero a Negro Man belonging to Mr. John Barnes & Boston a Negro Man belonging to Mr. Thomas Foster" from communion after they were "convicted of Scandalous Offenses before the Civil Magistrate." These two men had been convicted of an unspecified crime by a public court and were likely punished by civil authorities (probably whipped), but their church also punished them. About a year later, this discipline had the desired effect on Boston, who "made Publick confession of his Offense & was Restored." Another year later, Nero also confessed and was restored. He then transferred his membership to the church in Marshfield, where he was living by 1746.[55] Once these black men repented, their status within the church was reaffirmed, and they were reconciled to the other church members.

Sira (a person of mixed ancestry) was baptized at the First Church of Brockton, Massachusetts, in March 1745, after her parents confessed to fornication, which suggests that they valued baptism for their daughter enough to undertake a public confession. The minister "baptized Sira daughter of [name crossed out] Mollato, on he and his wife owning ye Covenant and his making his acknowledgement for ye sin of fornication." Sira's father publicly acknowledged that he had "offended God, wounded religion, and wronged my own soul for which I am heartily sorry, and desire to be deeply humbled before God, and do ask forgiveness of God and his people for ye same." In this case, "mulatto" congregants were held accountable to the same standards for sexual conduct as white Christians. All Christians at this church were expected to refrain from premarital sex and to remain monogamous (although it is highly unlikely that a male slaveholder would have been punished for sex with an enslaved black woman). Since this couple likely conceived before being married, which was a relatively common occurrence among white Christians, they had to make this public confession so that Sira could be baptized. Enslaved New Englanders were permitted to marry and were sometimes held to the normative sexual morals, but marriage was not a sure safeguard against being sold away from a spouse or children.[56]

In addition to transgressions of morality, black church members were occasionally disciplined simply because they were repeatedly absent from church. Blacks who were members of Congregational churches were expected to act in a godly manner, regularly attend church services, and participate in communion. Some church members took these duties very seriously. In one instance, a black man named Primus, who was a slave to David Green and a member of the First Church of Reading (Wakefield), Massachusetts, was admonished by his church for missing services. In 1753 the church scolded him because he had "for a long Time Absented himself from ye Communion of ye Chh [church]."[57] It is unclear why this black Christian abstained himself, but his prolonged absence was noticed and found offensive to some white Christians, who admonished him to do better.

Sometimes individual blacks (like whites too) dealt with disagreements or conflicts with other congregants by separating from their church. Hewson, who was identified as a "negro servant to Sarah Christophers," became a member of the First Church of New London, Connecticut, in 1741, but Hewson "separated" from the church in 1757. In another case, a woman identified in 1750 as "Negro woman Ann" or "Sister Ann" came into conflict with the First Church of Brewster, Massachusetts, because of a difference in theology. She too separated from the church. Ann had "long absented" herself from the church community, and the church voted to send two deacons to speak to her. In November 1750, Ann testified before the members of the church regarding her long absence. She "offered her Reasons for Absenting wch were that to her understanding the Doctrine of Grace & of Assurance were not preached in that Chh [church]." She did not believe that the minister was accurately teaching foundational doctrines about salvation. Some in the church responded by trying to change her views, and "means were used to convince her of her mistake & to Show her that it was her Duty to return to our Communion." Ann, however, was not convinced, and "She declared her Purpose to continue at a Distance," perhaps leaving open the possibility of a future return to the church.[58] Like whites and Indians who were influenced by separatist doctrines, Ann asserted that her understanding of the Bible was justification enough for her withdrawal from the church. Ann voiced her theology and criticism of the church, thereby publicly disagreeing with the other members. This black woman chose not to attend the church because she did not agree with all the theology, but no other church option was immediately available to her.

While church discipline reflected common forms of disagreement within churches that any wayward believers could face, there were also conflicts in churches related more directly to the prejudice against blacks and their enslavement. Few of the conflicts that occurred between enslaved blacks and their masters, especially conflicts related to church attendance or religious matters, appear in the historical record. Some examples of these forms of conflict do exist, and it is safe to assume that they occurred more broadly because blacks did not passively accept the status that whites assigned to them in colonial society. Expectations for Christian behavior sometimes came into conflict with the enslaved status of blacks. Although enslaved black people in northern colonies legally had access to courts and although religion and public morality prescribed limits on masters' authority, in practice, northern masters maintained an immense power over their slaves. Slaves' freedom of movement, control over their bodies, and protection of family members were all severely limited. So what happened when the will of a master contradicted the slave's most cherished desires? Even in cases where both the slave and the master were members of the same church, the desire by one for productive labor or economic security and the desire by the other for protection of family or personal liberty caused conflicts or resistance. Some enslaved men and women acted dynamically and forcibly against the control of masters and mistresses, and at least a few slaves sought to use religion to check the oppression that they faced. Although power was overwhelmingly concentrated with whites, blacks negotiated and struggled for concessions. Black people leveraged church affiliation and religious beliefs in the negotiations that occurred between slaves and masters within the confines of slavery.[59]

The story of the slave who preached and claimed Jesus Christ as his right master in front of his owner's dinner guests, which opened this chapter, is an example of the tensions between black and white Christians that sometimes arose as a result of the convergence of egalitarian impulses in Christianity and race-based slavery. An opponent of the Great Awakening, Reverend Jacob Eliot, noted a worrisome case of a converted slave opposing his "unregenerate" master. While few white Christians saw any issue with holding dark-skinned Christians as slaves, many blacks saw a contradiction between their religious and social positions, and some of them publicly expressed a desire for freedom. For enslaved people across the Americas, Christianity was closely related to freedom. For example, in 1723, one or more enslaved people in Virginia sent a petition to the bishop of London that linked baptism and freedom. On March 29, 1754, an enslaved black man named Greenwich made a public statement against the type of slavery being practiced by Christians in colonial America, and he did so in the Separate Congregational Church in Canterbury, Connecticut, where both he and his owner attended. Captain Obadiah Johnson Jr., a wealthy man and church deacon, owned Greenwich and several other slaves. Greenwich's statements against slavery were undoubtedly directed toward Johnson and other congregants. Although the particular circumstances of Greenwich's speech were not recorded, a copy of this speech was saved in church records.[60]

Greenwich invoked direct authority from God, for he began his speech by saying, "As I have ben Instructed by the Lord." However, Greenwich based the rest of his appeal on an analysis of select scriptural texts, particularly from Genesis, Exodus, First Kings, Jeremiah, and Proverbs. Greenwich did not condemn all forms of slavery, for he noted some of the "just" forms of slavery described in the Bible. He did, however, critique the international slave trade and the ways that Europeans incited and benefited from conflicts in Africa. He condemned how whites "steel as many of them [Africans] and bring them over Into your Contry to make slaves of them their soul and body." He cited the biblical passage that states, "he that steel A man and seleth [sells] him or if he be found in his hands he shall surely be put to death." He also reminded the listeners that in ancient Israel, it was prescribed that enslaved Israelites must be set free after seven years of service (many Christians associated their church communities with ancient Israel because both were communities under God's covenants). Through his careful, and at times creative, reading of Old Testament scriptures, Greenwich presented a case for why he and other black Christians should be set free. In so doing, he used the same faith that he shared with white churchgoers to confront the assumptions about race and slavery that white colonists took for granted. If Greenwich had not attended this church, he would not have been able to publicly condemn his enslavement in this way.[61]

Greenwich stated that "Justise must Take Plase," but his appeal did not seem to have a major effect upon his enslaved condition. Although we do not know how his owner and other congregants reacted to his critique of slavery, Greenwich was not immediately freed. In 1765, Greenwich and his wife, Peg, became the property of Colonel Obadiah Johnson III. His critique of slavery, however, did not disqualify Greenwich from further participation in his church. The church voted in 1766 to send representatives to inquire of Greenwich about his recent absences from church and to encourage him to return to regular attendance. Soon thereafter, Greenwich became a member of the church and even voted in church business along with the other male members. After being sold to John Johnson, then to Joseph Easton, and finally to Benjamin Bacon, Greenwich and Peg were permitted in 1776 to buy their freedom for thirty pounds. Perhaps Bacon heard Greenwich speak against slavery in 1754, but he made Greenwich and his wife pay for their freedom on the eve of American independence. Greenwich remained a slave for a long time, but participation in the church had benefits for him, including a place to voice objections to slavery, the status of church membership, and perhaps, finally, a master open to the possibility of freedom.[62]

Some enslaved black people so despaired of their condition that they caused disturbances and conflicts with whites in churches, including a slave named Cato, owned by Reverend Stephen Williams of Long-meadow, Massachusetts. In January 1759, Williams wrote that "poor Cato came to me in my Study & Seems desirous to be Sold." The cause of his desire to be sold is unclear, but he remained unhappy within the Williams household for years. In 1762, his behavior was more dejected, and he disrupted a church service. On Sunday, October 31, Cato "went to the publick worship," Williams wrote, "but Spoke out Loud—at ye End of ye afternoon Sermon." In this culture, interrupting a sermon was an affront to the minister's authority. Williams prayed for Cato's salvation even as he became more "audacious" and "deprav'd" in the coming week. After throwing himself onto a white woman, Cato was whipped and sent to live with Williams's adult son. Soon after that, Cato's body was pulled up from a well. His death was likely a suicide, perhaps a last and desperate protest against his enslavement by a Congregational minister.[63]

In the spring of 1764, an enslaved man named Nim in Litchfield, Connecticut, disregarded the racial and social hierarchy within the church by repeatedly occupying a gallery pew reserved for whites, and his actions resulted in a conflict that involved threats and a physical altercation. By "Custom and Usage" only a particular gallery pew in the meetinghouse was available for "black people Servants and Slaves," but Nim had been sitting in one of the gallery pews usually occupied by whites. Several men complained to Nim's owner, Colonial Ebenezer Marsh, who ordered him to desist, and a lock was placed on the disputed pew's door. Some congregants insisted that Nim's behavior in sitting in this pew was "very insolent" and "irregular and indecent Conduct." On Sunday morning, June 8, 1764, before the service, Nim broke open the pew door and sat there anyway, and three young white men, Ashbel Catlin, Thomas Sheldon, and Alexander Alford, confronted him. Court testimonies do not agree about what happened next, but it is clear that the three men physically removed Nim from the pew. According to testimony favoring Nim, they "threw the said Negro headlong out of said Pew." The incident was adjudicated in August 1764, and the three young men were fined a nominal three shillings each plus court costs for their actions against Nim. Perhaps the court felt that violence against anyone in a church was unacceptable. In 1766, the Superior Court reversed and voided the earlier conviction. Nim may have felt some measure of satisfaction from his assault on racially segregated seating, even though he did not manage to change the practice.[64]

Of course, enslaved black people did not limit themselves to bettering their lives or fighting against oppression through religion. As black

Christians came into conflict with white Christians over the issue of slavery, some blacks chose the same severely limited forms of resistance available to slaves generally. Throughout most of the eighteenth century, northern newspapers regularly carried notices of runaway slaves. Many enslaved blacks sought to improve their lives by absconding, including some black people who participated in churches. An enslaved man named Simon from Middlesex County, New Jersey, ran away in 1740 and was described as "Pretended to be a Doctor and very religious and says he is a Churchman." In 1742, an enslaved man named Pompey York, described as a "new convert," ran away from his master. A runaway advertisement in the *Boston Weekly News-Letter* from 1760 describes "a Negro servant man, belonging to Major Robert Rogers, named Prince," who had fled his Concord, New Hampshire, master. The advertisement describes him as thirty years old and mentions that he "was in the Service the last Year," which indicates that he had perhaps fought with colonists in the French and Indian War. His white master stated that he "looks very serious and grave, and pretends to a great deal of Religion."[65] It seems likely that this unhappy owner dismissed the religious belief of this black man. This slave owner may have believed, like many white Christians, that religion made slaves more dutiful. Perhaps Prince was serious about his beliefs, and after experiencing life beyond Concord, he had no intention of continuing to serve this master. The religious beliefs of Simon, Prince, and other slaves did not prevent them from absconding and seeking better lives.

Apart from running away, enslaved black Christians engaged in other common practices that undermined or contradicted their owners' authority, such as stealing food or working slowly. Reverend James MacSparran, the rector at St. Paul's Anglican Church in Narragansett, Rhode Island, confronted disobedience and theft perpetrated by two of his baptized slaves. In August 1751, he wrote, "I have searched everywhere, and can find no Sugar, wch I suspect Maroca stole out of ye Barril last Monday, when we were all from Home. I found a Cheese wch Harry bo't of Jno. Gardner's wife on ye Hill." Apparently, the cheese (like the sugar) had not been honestly gained, because MacSparran prayed, "Gracious God, give my Servants Grace to live in a holier manner, that my Peace & Property mayn't be invaded by their evil doings . . . reform them, if it be your blessed will, from ye sins of uncleanness, stealing & lying." MacSparran had baptized Maroca and Harry at his Anglican church, but we can imagine that their prayers differed markedly from MacSparran's prayers about his "Property." Many slaves did not consider taking extra food from masters and mistresses as stealing because so much of their lives were stolen through slavery. Maroca probably did not consider Mac-Sparran a good master. MacSparran separated Maroca from two of her infant children by gifting them to white families in his parish. Enslaved blacks often participated in the same church as their owners, but sharing a church or the same faith provided no guaranteed safeguard against the worst injustices of slavery, including physical violence and separation of family members. Some Christian slaves did what they could to better their lives under slavery, including taking extra food and other acts of disobedience. Affiliating with a predominantly white church was one of the ways that some enslaved blacks sought to improve their lives under slavery, and church affiliation did not necessarily exclude the possibility of more subversive acts of resistance.[66]

Other enslaved blacks, however, chose to not affiliate with churches and resisted slavery directly. According to a 1906 town history, Reverend Theophilus Hall of Meriden, Connecticut, owned five slaves, who worked his farm, and only some of them participated in his church. At least one of the slaves was "surly and unruly," and sometime between 1730 and 1755, on "one Sunday morning the parson was obliged to whip this negro, and then went to his duties at the church." During the worship service, this slave apparently set fire to hay near the pastor's house. A congregant saw the fire from the meetinghouse. They rushed to extinguish it, and according to this account, "a short time after, this negro climbed into a chestnut tree in the southern part of the farm, and falling, broke his neck."[67]

As much as there were conflicts and tensions between blacks and whites within churches, it would be inaccurate to suggest that discord wholly characterized the story of black and white interactions there. Much of the conflict between whites and blacks was unlikely to be recorded and preserved in records, but religious conflicts between blacks and whites did not cause black people, en masse, to stop participating in Anglican and Congregational churches, especially compared to the decline in Indian affiliation. Moreover, numerous black people were active participants in Protestant churches without being in conflict or discord with whites members.

Black people's affiliation with northern Protestant churches sometimes led to conflict with earthly masters, but those who participated may have also found compelling benefits from these churches. Some black Christians used their faith to challenge or negotiate with their owners. Although blacks were not forming independent churches in this period, they were beginning to express their religious views publicly, as Greenwich and Ann did. In reality, many of the black men and women who participated in colonial churches did not fit into any simple explanatory category. Like people of faith generally, and as complex individuals, they made choices on a case-by-case basis. They sought to improve their lives and navigate relationships with both faith and pragmatism. It was not easy for many blacks to be enslaved Christians, for they experienced tensions between egalitarian promises in Christianity and the social inequalities in British America. But many kept their faith nonetheless, and, for the time being, many kept it in predominantly white churches. For some, the education and spiritual sustenance derived from participation in these churches outweighed the conflicts and prejudices that they experienced. Therefore, in a considerable portion of the Congregational churches of New England and the Church of England parishes across northern colonies, blacks affiliated publicly with Christianity between 1750 and 1763. Free and enslaved black people became members, owned the covenant, had their children baptized, were married, and were disciplined by the church authorities. As a consequence, many people in northern colonies experienced formal religion in interracial contexts.

The 1750s and 1760s was also a period when black and Indian participation in these churches changed. At many of the Anglican churches, blacks were baptized at higher rates and in greater numbers during the 1750s and 1760s as these churches provided educational, material, and spiritual benefits targeted toward blacks. In a large portion of Congregational churches, the rate of black baptisms declined. Support for revivalism waned, and so did the active outreach that brought many black people to Congregational churches in the 1730s and 1740s. In addition, black access to the sacrament of baptism stabilized, whereby fewer black adult converts were baptized and more blacks were baptized as children upon their parents' request. Indian participation in Congregational churches also declined, but more dramatically and uniformly as Indians formed new churches in Connecticut, Long Island, and Rhode Island. While both Indians and blacks were oppressed by English colonists in the eighteenth century, examining their church affiliation rates and religious conflicts is a valuable lens for highlighting the different experiences of these communities.

Narragansetts, Mohegans, Montauketts, and other Indians made a choice to leave interracial churches and start new congregations in the late 1740s and 1750s. These communities had leadership, educational, theological, and community resources to support churches, with the occasional help of missionary financial aid. Moreover, they did not face segregated seating within Indian churches. Conversely, Indians at Sandwich and Natick, Massachusetts, attended churches with white pastors and white fellow-congregants despite ongoing conflicts. As was common during colonialism, these Indians adopted and adapted parts of white society, in this case, Christianity, but most Indians decided that it was better to keep some distance between themselves and white Americans.

Blacks came into discord with whites through church discipline and theological differences, but the desires of slaves competing against the demands of masters also caused conflicts. Tensions existed as a result of the purported universality of Christianity and the inequality of British colonial society. Some individual blacks left the churches where they previously affiliated, but many more still attended and participated in church rituals irrespective of limitations placed on their involvement and the ways that churches reinforced their marginalized status. The inferior place of black and Indian peoples in colonial society was often lived out and experienced in the spaces of a church building. But, in these churches, hundreds and perhaps even thousands of blacks also received a rudimentary education and a narrative of history with a God that acted in history, which provided hope and strength. A small number of blacks used Christianity to protest against slavery, and their protests foreshadow the more prominent use of religious protests during the Revolutionary era and later generations. Religious participation, moreover, did not prevent blacks from seeking to improve their lives or subverting the authority of their owners in other ways as well. The era of the American Revolution, however, changed some of these calculations for black people and entailed a remarkable expansion of interracial worship. In the era of the American Revolution, Christianity was increasingly used as a means of protest against slavery and more northern churches baptized black people.

"Compassion upon These Outcasts": Evangelism and Expanding Interracial Worship, 1764–1776

On Thursday, August 1, 1771, the New York City Methodists held one of their quarterly "Love-feasts," which was a special religious service only for members. At these services, Methodists ate together and shared testimonies of their religious experiences to further unite and encourage their love for one another. This summer's love feast, like most eighteenth-century Methodist services, included both black and white members. Itinerant preacher and missionary Joseph Pilmore recorded that the people "spoke freely of the goodness of God, while a profound awe and divine reverence seemed to sit upon every countenance. One of the poor Negroes declared, her heart was so full of divine love that she could not express it, and many more of them were exceedingly happy in their minds." This woman and the other black members talked about how God had changed their lives, even though they were oppressed and enslaved.[1] Black men and women had spoken about their religious experiences before some racially mixed churches since the early eighteenth century, but the presence of black people and the sharing of religious testimonies in interracial contexts occurred more frequently between 1764 and 1776 than in earlier decades, especially in the Mid-Atlantic colonies.

The number of Christians who viewed evangelism to blacks and Indians as a benevolent duty seemed to reach a new peak in this era, which led to more interracial religious experiences. The expansion of Methodist churches is the clearest example of this trend. The black female Methodist in New York who professed that her heart was full of divine love was a part of something new and unprecedented in New York City and other northern cities during this era. Whether these New Yorkers realized it or not, they were part of a much broader religious transformation—an expansion of interracial religious worship across northern colonies (and later states) that began in the 1760s and continued well into the nineteenth century.

British Enlightenment ideas about how to improve society and forms of evangelical Christianity converged in the colonies in the 1760s to create the setting for an expansion of interracial churches. Enlightenment humanitarian ideals influenced Anglicans, Congregationalists, Methodists, and other Christians to put more effort into evangelizing and providing religious education for blacks and American Indians, often through missionary organizations. This culture of benevolence and companion was not the sole creation of eighteenth-century evangelical Christians. Rather, evangelicals tapped into some of the same intellectual and religious currents that influenced Anglicans and other nonevangelical Christians. As historian Catherine Brekus writes, evangelicals were "convinced that there was no greater act of benevolence than to save sinners from damnation, [so] they placed more emphasis on evangelism than virtually any other group of Christians before them." However, in the context of northern colonies, evangelical and nonevangelical Christians both agreed that promoting religious education and alleviating physical suffering were important Christian duties.[2]

Interracial love feasts did not occur before the 1760s both because Methodism was not yet established in America and because fewer denominations in the Mid-Atlantic colonies included blacks before this decade. Between the Seven Years' War and the American Revolution, however, interracial religious worship occurred in a greater variety of the northern churches than during previous eras. This expansion of interracial churches was caused by the actions of a wide variety of people, including pious laymen and laywomen, Indian church organizers, enslaved blacks, and ministers. These people had diverse motivations for their religious work, but they shared a desire to evangelize, and many white Christians viewed evangelization as a work of compassion that benefited less fortunate people. New and well-established churches alike increasingly sought out and allowed blacks to join as members, and many of the Christians involved in proselytizing expressed evangelical and humanitarian ideals as reasons for doing so. Although an ongoing imperial crisis (fights between the British government and American colonists over taxes and parliamentarian authority) filled these years, colonists' political protests did not hinder black participation in these churches. Some people, such as Sarah Osborn of Newport, Rhode Island, believed that the religion work and religious conversation were much more important than the political controversies that dominated the minds of many colonists in this era. Ministers and some dedicated laypeople sought to incorporate black people into their churches, which most of them viewed as an act of compassion and not as a challenge to the normative hierarchies of eighteenth-century colonial society. For the time being, many evangelical and nonevangelical Christians remained slaveholders.[3]

When the French and Indian War (Seven Years' War) ended in 1763 with Britain gaining ownership of most of North America east of the Mississippi River (on paper but not in reality), many colonists celebrated the expansion of their Protestant empire at the expense of Catholic France. Many Americans hoped for increased prosperity through trade and agriculture, both tied to the dispossession of Indians from their lands and the enslavement of Africans. Slave traders brought many enslaved Africans to northern colonies during the middle of the eighteenth century, and the enslaved black population reached 32,843 in the Mid-Atlantic colonies and 14,892 in the New England colonies by 1770. Many of these slaves resided in cities, but they also lived and worked almost everywhere in these regions. English colonists also hoped that the end of imperial wars would allow for the expansion of Protestant Christianity among Catholics in Canada and blacks and Indians all over the continent.[4]

Although political questions were addressed in churches and influenced by religious affiliations, for the most part, the expansion of churches, regular worship services, and the inclusion of blacks into greater numbers of churches proceeded until 1775 or 1776 without being significantly affected by tensions between England and its North American colonies. Political and social histories of this era tend to emphasize conflict and disruptions, but the history of American churches, especially in regard to their expanding outreach to blacks, suggests more stables themes until after 1775. Relations between colonists and their government in London were contentious between 1764 and 1775, and many people's attention turned toward the boycotts, protests, and economic difficulties of the imperial crisis. As Parliament sought to tax colonists directly and gain stronger control over colonial governors and legislatures, numerous colonists focused on political matters. All types of churches participated in the fasts and days of prayer, which were common responses to the political changes and social upheaval. Once the political crises reached the point of armed conflict, the normal church operations were suspended as some churches temporarily closed or

dispersed. But, until 1776 in most places, the normal rhythms of ministers preaching, baptizing, administering communion, marrying, bury-
ing, and comforting their diverse parishioners continued.[5]

The expansion of interracial churches from 1763 to 1776 is evidenced
by data from specific locations, such as Newport and New York City, and
by aggregate trends in northern denominations. Because of significant
differences in the practices, histories, and outreach methods of northern denominations, this chapter is organized into sections focused on
specific denominations. Methodist and Baptist churches had the most
significant expansion of interracial worship during this era, but more
Anglican churches included black people through baptism and communion as well. Congregational churches were the only type of church that
had declining rates of black baptisms and declining numbers of interracial churches. Most other types of churches had stable or increased levels
of black affiliation. Some Lutherans and Moravians continued outreach
to black people without a noticeable growth in black affiliation.[6] Denominational differences mattered to people in the eighteenth century, and
they still matter because comparing different types of churches helps in
identifying the causes of interracial worship.

Churches of New York, Newport, and Philadelphia exhibited the
expansion of interracial churches because more churches in these cities baptized black Americans than in previous decades, including some
Presbyterian and Reformed congregations. Congregations of six different denominations in New York City included more black people during
the 1760s and early 1770s than at any earlier point in the century. In
addition to the Anglican, Lutheran, and Moravian churches, New York
City's Reformed, Presbyterian, and Baptist churches began baptizing
black people in this era. The earliest baptisms of black people, fourteen
in number, occurred at the First Presbyterian Church, and one black
person was baptized at the Dutch Reformed Church between 1764 and
1776. The first black member of the First Baptist Church was admitted
in 1775. The inclusion of black people in these churches, especially in the
Presbyterian church, was tied to Reverend George Whitefield's revival
preaching in the winter of 1763–64. Black people joined the early Methodist society in New York City too.[7] Black people also participated in
more of Newport, Rhode Island's churches, especially in the city's Congregational and Baptist churches. In comparing the periods of 1750–63
and 1764–76, most of Newport's churches became more inclusive in
the latter years.[8] In 1770, Reverend Ezra Stiles calculated the number
of families that attended each congregation in Newport, including the

Society of Friends and the Jewish Synagogue, and he calculated that 950 families were connected to one of the Protestant congregations. As such, at least 745 families, or 78 percent of Protestant churchgoers in Newport, attended an interracial congregation in the years before the Revolution.[9]

While only extremely small numbers of Indians participated in predominantly white churches, many blacks and Afro-Indians participated in predominantly Indian churches in the second half of the eighteenth century. By examining Native American churches over the more extended period from 1764 to 1790, it is clear that black participation in Indian churches also expanded during the Revolutionary era as the number of black people in Indian communities grew. American-Indian Christianity often differed from Euro-American Christianity, but the diversity in Indian churches mirrored the growing interracial practices of other northern churches.

The advent of American Methodism and the expansion of Baptist congregations made interracial religious worship more common, especially in the Mid-Atlantic region and Rhode Island. As Baptist and especially Methodist churches began to proliferate, their ministers and laypeople were often quite deliberate in proselytizing black people. The upsurge in these interracial religious experiences resulted from an increase in deliberate outreach to blacks by ministers, preachers, and laypersons. These people viewed outreach to blacks as a duty and as an act of compassion toward disadvantaged individuals. By the 1760s, a potent mix of ideas and practices—including evangelical practices and theology from the Great Awakening, Enlightenment humanism, and British Methodism—converged in the colonies and galvanized more people to try to convert blacks and Indians to Christianity. Methodist preachers were unrelentingly driven to convert people, and they preached wherever and whenever they could find a willing audience. Other ministers used home visitations, catechism classes, and direct interactions with parishioners to inquire about the spiritual state of congregants, including servants and slaves. Some laymen and laywomen expressed a similar concern for the spiritual condition of black men and women in their homes and communities. Sometimes responding to white invitations and sometimes seeking churches on their own initiative, blacks affiliated with different churches to pursue a mix of educational, spiritual, and material benefits.[10] Several factors affected the religious choices that enslaved and free blacks made, but deliberate outreach to blacks by more religious leaders made a greater number of churches interracial.

Early Methodist Church Affiliation

The beginnings of Methodism in North America made interracial worship more common in the Mid-Atlantic colonies. Blacks were early and regular participants in Methodist meetings, societies, and churches as congregants and even as preachers. Methodists spoke to all who would listen, and their message proved especially attractive to women, the poor, and blacks because of its emphasis on spiritual equality and the importance of religious experiences over theology. More than most early evangelicals, this reform movement was influenced by Enlightenment ideas as they sought to "methodically" pursue godliness and expressed humanitarian-type compassion toward the disadvantaged. Some Methodists in the 1770s and 1780s took stances against slaveholding, which enslaved blacks found appealing. In 1774, John Wesley, a founder of Methodism, published *Thoughts upon Slavery* in London. He denounced race-based slavery as "the vilest slavery," and he called for individuals to emancipate their slaves. For the slaves, he prayed that God would have mercy and "compassion upon these outcasts of men, who are trodden down as dung upon the earth. Arise and help these that have no helper, whose blood is spilt upon the ground like water! Are not these also the work of thine own hands, the purchase of thy Son's blood?" Other early Methodists followed Wesley's lead and advocated for an end of slavery for both the sake of the enslaved and for the moral purity of British colonists.[11]

Methodism was founded in England primarily by Reverends John and Charles Wesley as a reform movement within the Church of England. The Methodist movement developed out of revival meetings, often held outdoors and led by preachers who traveled from town to town. People who were inspired by the Wesleys began organizing classes and Methodist societies, often while attending Anglican Church services, to encourage their faith and holy living. John Wesley and other itinerant preachers traveled widely and encouraged these groups on a rotating basis.[12]

The first Methodists in Britain's North American colonies were migrants from Ireland and Britain who followed Wesleyan piety. At first, these migrants practiced their piety individually and within Anglican churches. Small numbers of laymen and laywomen established Methodist meetings in the colonies in the 1760s and requested missionaries from England. Meetings in the colonies were commonly biracial. The earliest Methodist society on Long Island, founded in 1768, contained twenty-four members, about half white and half black. This ratio of black and white members was extraordinary compared to that in most northern churches. In 1773, there were approximately 180 members of the Methodist circuit in New York, 180 members of the Methodist society in Philadelphia, 200 members of the circuit in New Jersey, and four rotating Methodist preachers. Official reports did not distinguish between races, but black men and women were among these early Methodists. Although it was only in its nascent years, Methodist societies in the Mid-Atlantic regularly held interracial religious services.[13]

Early Methodists considered themselves part of the Church of England and relied on Anglican clergy for the sacraments of baptism and communion until 1785, when they formed a separate denomination. As the Methodist preachers promoted greater piety among faithful Anglicans and as most Anglican churches included black members and attendees, it is not surprising that some of the early black Methodists, like the white Methodists, affiliated with both a Methodist meeting and an Anglican parish. Methodist meetings also introduced or enhanced an evangelical style of Anglicanism in some parishes.[14]

Methodist meetings were thus a new site for interracial worship in New York City, in addition to the long-standing churches that baptized and admitted black people. Although the exact number of early black members cannot be identified, it is clear that black people participated in the earliest Methodist meetings in New York City. A "colored servant" named Betty attended meetings with the five Irish migrants who first brought Methodism to New York during the 1760s. Peter Williams Sr., an enslaved black man, and his wife, Mary Durham (aka Molly), were attendees and perhaps members of this Methodist society before the Revolutionary War. Williams converted to Methodism in 1767 or 1768 under the preaching of Philip Embury and Thomas Webb. Williams eventually helped found the first African American Methodist congregation in the city. Methodist meetings grew so rapidly in the late 1760s that they built a chapel, which opened in October 1768. When this chapel was built, according to James W. Hood's later account, "there were no Negro pews nor back seats nor gallery especially provided for the dark-skinned members. They [blacks] were welcomed in common with other members to all the privileges of God's house and worship."[15] In its early years, the spiritual equality preached by Methodists sometimes translated into relative equality in churches.

In January 1771, Joseph Pilmore described blacks at the New York City Methodist meeting, noting that "God has wrought a most glorious work on many of their souls."[16] Reverend Francis Asbury, among the earliest Methodist preachers sent by John Wesley to the colonies, also commented on the black Methodists in New York. In November 1771, Asbury attended an interracial service and noted in this journal that blacks and whites were equals before God: "I feel a regard for the people: and I think the Americans are more ready to receive the word than the English; and to see the poor negroes so affected is pleasing; to see their sable countenances in our solemn assemblies, and to hear them sing with cheerful melody their dear Redeemer's praise, affected me much, and made me ready to say, 'Of a truth I perceive God is no respecter of persons.'"[17] Asbury's willingness to preach to all people helped to make early Methodist societies interracial. For Ashbury and other Methodists, the best and most compassionate thing they could do for "poor negroes" was to introduce them to the saving gospel of Christ.

Some black people participated with and joined the early Methodist meetings in Philadelphia as well; however, sometimes masters forbade slaves from attending Methodist services because they feared that Christianity would make slaves think themselves equal to their masters. Joseph Pilmore noted black congregants in Philadelphia's Methodist meetings between 1769 and 1771, writing that "many of the poor Affricans are obedient to the faith." At a meeting in which "people spoke freely of what he [God] had done for their souls," Pilmore wrote that "even the poor Negroes came forth and bore a noble testimony for God our Saviour."[18] In noting the "poor" station of blacks, Pilmore likely believed Christianity required him to have compassion for these people. Blacks regularly attended Methodist meetings and publicly shared their faith in worship services, but on Sunday, November 10, 1771, after the morning service, Pilmore received a note from "a poor Negro Slave": "Dear Sir, These are to acquaint you, that my bondage is such I cannot possibly attend with the rest of the Class to receive my Ticket therefore beg you will send it. I wanted much to come to the Church at the Watch-night, but could not get leave; but, I bless God that night, I was greatly favoured with the spirit of prayer, and enjoyed much of his divine presence. I find the enemy of my soul continually striving to throw me off the foundation, but I have that within me which bids defiance that may be enabled to bear up under all my difficulties with patient resignation to the will of God."[19] This slave's owner restricted church attendance (perhaps thereby becoming an "enemy of my soul") but could not control the slave's desire to be a good Methodist or the slave's prayers of "defiance." This slave likely attended classes and services regularly because he or she seemed to know Pilmore and requested a ticket that granted access to members-only services.

The beginning of Methodism in America was one of the most significant aspects of the expansion of interracial worship between 1764 and 1776. Surviving written accounts demonstrate not only the presence of black worshippers but also that many black people had rich spiritual experiences in these religious meetings. Blacks affiliated with Methodism because these churches offered an attractive form of spirituality and because the preachers sought after them. The compassionate antislavery message of early Methodists was also appealing. As Methodism spread, it made interracial worship in these colonies more regular than it had been previously.

Baptist Church Affiliation

Black participation in northern Baptist churches, particularly in Rhode Island, where Baptist churches were more numerous, also increased during the period of imperial crisis. By 1776, a growing number of Baptist churches admitted at least some black members.[20] A few northern Baptist churches, such as the First Baptist Church of Swansea, Massachusetts, the Baptist Church of Upper Freehold, New Jersey, and the Second Baptist Church of Newport, Rhode Island, included small numbers of black people in earlier periods, but most Baptist churches did not. Starting in the 1760s, however, black people participated in more than a scattering of northern Baptist churches. In the 1760s and 1770s, at least seven Baptist churches in my sample admitted multiple black members, and other churches included a single black member. The relative absence of black members before 1750 and the greater inclusion of black people in late eighteenth-century Baptist churches can both be explained by examining the history and practices of these churches.[21]

The oldest Baptist churches in northern colonies were founded in the seventeenth century, but Baptist churches expanded dramatically after the middle of the eighteenth century. English Baptist churches developed out of Separatist Puritan churches in England and the Netherlands, where some English Dissenters were exiled, in the early seventeenth century. Baptist individuals and congregations developed when people decided that established churches were not pure enough and that the practice of baptizing infants was unscriptural; Anabaptist theology from German-speaking territories may have influenced some of these early Baptists. Roger Williams founded the first and oldest Baptist church in America in Providence, Rhode Island, in 1638. The First Baptist Church of Philadelphia began in 1698, and the first permanent Baptist association was created in Philadelphia in 1707. A group of Baptists began meeting in New York City in 1745 and were organized as a church in 1762. The number of Baptist churches in New England expanded rapidly between 1740 and 1790.[22]

Like seventeenth-century Puritans, early Baptists believed that churches should consist solely of converted believers. Unlike other Christians, they did not baptize infants or anyone until the person made public professions of faith for themselves and could explain God's redemptive work in their life. As a result, all the black people baptized in Baptist churches were old enough to share their personal testimony publicly. To be baptized was to be admitted as a member, as when "Ann Fox, & Candance a black woman were received by Baptisms" as members into the Upper Freehold Baptist Church in June 1766.[23]

Starting in the 1760s, and continuing into the 1780s, New England Baptist churches experienced a period of growth and stabilization, as more churches were organized, as a new association was formed, and as some Separate Congregational churches became Baptist churches. New England Baptists upheld a mixture of beliefs and practices, in part because of their different origins and competing theological perspectives. Baptist churches could lean toward Calvinist or Arminian theology, and they could worship on Sundays (most Baptists) or Saturdays (Seventh Day Baptists). Baptist churches always maintained congregational forms of governance, whereby no authority outside the members of each local church could decide policy, but some Baptists organized loosely into associations.[24]

In the 1770s, some long-established Baptist churches began to admit blacks or began to admit higher numbers of black people, including ones in Boston and Providence. First Baptist Church of Boston, Massachusetts, admitted its first black members of the eighteenth century between 1772 and 1773. The First Baptist Church of Providence, Rhode Island, began baptizing more black people in the 1770s. The rise in black participation in this church was linked to the pastorate of Reverend James Manning and a shift in the church's theology and practices. Before 1771, this church did not promote revivals, but under Manning's leadership, it became more deliberate in promoting revival and conversion of the town's white and black inhabitants. Given his actions, it seems reasonable that Manning was influenced by the idea that compassionate Christianity required him to reach out to all segments of Providence society. In 1762, Mary Ceser, an Indian, was baptized and admitted to this church, and two people on the 1770 members list were identified as "negro," having been admitted sometime previous. Seventeen black people joined this church between 1774 and 1776, during an influential period of revival. Most of them were free, but some remained enslaved. In a 1789 account, John Stanford wrote that during December 1774, "it pleased the Lord to make his power known to the hearts of Tamar Clemmons & Venus Arnold, two black women, who were soon added to the church by Baptism, and have since maintained the dignity of their profession." Elsewhere, Clemmons was identified as "molatto," and Arnold was labeled "Negro." Phillis Brown became a member in 1775, two years after Moses Brown freed her from slavery. Manning's revival activities pushed this church out toward Providence's black community, and some of them decided to join this congregation.[25]

As a result of the expansion of their membership, the First Baptist Church of Providence built a new, grand meetinghouse, which contained "126 square pews on the ground floor, a large gallery on the South, West and North; and one above on the West for the use of the Blacks." Although this church started admitting black members, they could sit only in the uppermost gallery during worship services. The admittance of black women and men into the church did not, in the minds of white Christians, alter the social hierarchies that existed in colonial society. Churches helped uphold social hierarchies along the lines of gender, class, and race, although sometimes Baptist churches in the eighteenth century had relatively more gender and racial equality than the rest of society.[26]

Some enslaved black people at Providence's First Baptist Church exercised agency in choosing how they participated in a church even within the confines of slavery. Nancy Nightingale was a slave owned by Samuel Nightingale, who was a deacon at the Beneficent Congregational Church. Nancy sought baptism and membership at First Baptist Church instead of the Congregational church, where her master held a leading position. The Baptists sent a committee to meet with Deacon Nightingale "respecting his negro girl," and they "found from her Master's recommendation of her Conduct, that there could be no reasonable exception against her joining this Church, to which her Master freely consented." As a result, Nancy was baptized and received as a member of First Baptist Church and remained a member until she transferred to a church in the Boston area in 1785. In another case, the church requested that John Jenckes inform his slave Sophia, "a black sister of the Church," that she was to attend a church meeting to answer allegations of "immoral conduct," which could have been behavior ranging from fornication to lying to stealing. Both master and slave were members of the church. She did not attend the meeting, thereby disobeying the church to which she belonged and presumably also her master. Sophia's membership was suspended in 1776, but she was restored to membership in 1785 after publicly repenting.[27] These enslaved women likely made their choices about when and how to participate in predominantly white Baptist churches, even though they faced the substantial power of slave owners and the church punished Sophia for her choices.

Black men and women in northern Baptist churches shared their religious experiences before predominantly white congregations, who accepted them as members. Rhode Island particularly experienced an increase in the number of interracial Baptist churches, but some Baptist churches in other colonies also exhibited this trend. The spread of Baptist churches after 1760 made more churches available to black and white colonists alike. But the active outreach of pastors, including Reverend Manning, and lay congregants was crucial for facilitating and welcoming blacks into these churches, and this trend also continued after the Revolution.

Congregational Churches

Black men and women participated in many of the Congregational churches of southern New England between 1764 and 1776 and found them spiritually satisfying, but the rate of their participation declined relative to earlier periods. Comparing black affiliation rates in different denominations is important here for showing how the experiences of northern slavery varied from one colony to another and for identifying the particular religious activities that made predominantly white churches appealing to black northerners. Contrary to the trend in other denominations, fewer Congregational churches included black people through membership or baptism compared to previous periods. Sixty-five Congregational churches in New England baptized or admitted multiple blacks between 1764 and 1776 (there were far more Congregational churches than Baptist or Methodist churches in New England).[28] Comparatively, between 1730 and 1749, 121 congregations included black baptisms or members, and from 1750 to 1763, 99 congregations included identifiable black baptisms or members. Part of the decline in African American church membership may have related to what historian Douglas Winiarski describes as the "fractured religious culture" of New England between 1745 and 1780. Although the number of Congregational churches with black people decreased, the archival records allow for a detailed reconstruction of the spiritual lives of several black Congregationalists from this era. Many of the Congregational churches in which blacks affiliated had ministers and laypeople who, from self-perceived compassion toward black men and women, sought to minister to their spiritual needs.[29]

While the rate and extent of black participation declined in Congregational churches overall, the decline may not have been as dramatic as it first appears because some ministers stopped using racial notations in church records during these years, for reasons that no one explained. For example, Reverend Samuel Hopkins rarely included racial notations in the records of the First Congregational Church of Newport, even though black people were baptized and admitted to this church. The ministers of Brattle Street Church in Boston also did not consistently use racial notations between 1760 and 1795; black men and women were often identified as servants but not as "negro servants." Therefore, more black men and women may have been participants in Congregational churches than the records clearly indicate. Nonetheless, there was a decline in black baptisms and membership in Congregational churches. In some cities, more black people may have picked Anglican churches over Congregational ones during the 1760s.[30]

Church affiliation was important to the enslaved and free blacks who joined Congregational churches. Take, for example, Cuffee Wright, an enslaved man owned by Reverend Sylvanus Conant. Wright joined the First Congregational Church of Middleborough, Massachusetts, and was baptized in 1773 after publicly sharing his religious experiences with the predominantly white church. A 1775 list of male church members included "Cuffey Negro" as one of the sixty-four male members of the church. In 1796, Anna Wright, "a black" and the wife of Cuffee Wright, became a full member of the church. Cuffee was manumitted in 1777 by Conant's will, and his status as a church member likely influenced Conant's decision to free Cuffee.[31]

Wright's testimony is a rare example of a surviving religious account written by an eighteenth-century black person, but he was by no means the only person of African descent who joined this church. The first black person, Margeret, joined this church in 1709. At least four black men, one black woman, and one Indian man joined this church during the revival of 1742, and several blacks and Indians were baptized there in the 1740s and 1750s. The town of Middleborough had an estimated twelve enslaved black residents over the age of sixteen in 1755, and during the 1750s and 1760s, a sizable portion of these blacks attended the First Church or other churches in town. Middleborough was also home to a small Wampanoag community, and some Wampanoags lived in white households as servants. The Separate Congregational Church in North Middleborough baptized five black people between 1760 and 1766.[32]

Though whites widely believed in innate black inferiority, Reverend Conant argued that God did not judge people's appearances and that all people were equal before God. In a sermon given on the occasion of the execution of a black man named Bristol for murder, Conant argued that blacks and whites were made "of the same Kind of Flesh and Blood" because God "made of one Blood, all Nations of Men." Even though Conant profited from the enslavement of black people and did not seem to promote abolition, he felt a strong religious duty to open the way of salvation for the black men and women in his household and congregation. In theory, slavery itself was not sinful, but masters had a duty to be compassionate and just toward their slaves, especially in leading them to salvation. As was common with many slave-owning clergymen, Conant likely taught Cuffee to read and perhaps how to write. Conant regularly led his whole household in prayer, singing, and other devotional activities, and such practices formed the basis for Cuffee Wright's religious knowledge.[33]

Wright's testimony reflected many of the dominant themes and conventions of Congregational confessions during the eighteenth century, but it also subtly revealed his experience as an enslaved black man in New England and why church affiliation was meaningful to him. The dominant theme in the document was his change from a life of sin to submission to God. This Christian theme is established in the first lines with the imagery of being brought by God's mercy "out of Land of Darkness unto the Land of gloryous gospel Light." This phrase contrasts life before and after salvation, but it also reflects a Protestant geography of the Atlantic world that viewed Africa as a land without "true" religion and New England as a land of "gloryous gospel Light." The phrase is reminiscent of Phillis Wheatley's poem "On being brought from Africa to America," which was published in 1773. Wheatley stated that "'Twas mercy brought me from my pagan land." Wright also referenced the hardships of slavery and the comfort that Christianity afforded him with a biblical passage: Psalm 119:71, "it is good for me that I have been afflicted That I might Learn thy Statutes." Although many whites still used Christianization as a justification for slavery, Wright was speaking about his personal experience of being "Comforted with things of nather [nether] world." Wright believed that he was "unwordy the lest of all gods marcys" [unworthy of the least of all God's mercies], but he believed that God had made payment for his sins and redeemed him. Highlighting his transformation, Wright indicated that now "Sin is greff [grief] to me— Christ is presus [precious] to my Soule." Wright expressed his religious experiences in terms that resonated with the predominantly white audience but also in terms specific to his own experiences.[34] For at least some blacks, such as Wright, Protestant churches were appealing because they provided comfort and spiritual fulfillment.

Although some of the late eighteenth-century records did not uniformly include racial notations, black people participated in Boston's Congregational churches at lower rates and smaller numbers than in previous decades. In Boston and perhaps other communities, it appears that ministers and laypeople were less active in proselytizing, catechizing, and encouraging black parishioners than in previous decades. Boston, more than most places, was preoccupied with political events in the 1760s. In most of Boston's Congregational churches, only between one and three blacks were baptized from 1764 to 1776. As had been the case in earlier periods, the two Congregational churches with the highest numbers of black participants were Brattle Street and Old South. Included among the black people baptized at Brattle Street were slaves owned by John and Dorothy Hancock. "Cato (adult) servant to Mrs. Hancock" and "Frank (servant to Mrs. Hancock)" were baptized in 1768, and Cato's children were baptized in 1769, 1770, and 1773. Even as John Hancock was busy organizing protests against British taxes, his household engaged in ordinary religious practices. At least thirteen black people (seven males and six females) were baptized at Old South, the site of the now-famous protest meetings that preceded the Boston Tea Party. Newton Prince, a free black man who testified as a defense witness for the British soldiers involved in the Boston Massacre, was a member of Old South during the 1770s, but the date of his admission is unclear. At least four black men and one black woman were admitted as new members of Old South between 1764 and 1776. This one woman was black poet Phillis Wheatley, and her life, though exceptional, allows us to examine the roles of Christianity and church affiliation for a black woman before the Revolution.[35]

In 1761, slave traders transported a young Senegambian to the Americas as a slave. John Wheatley of Boston purchased her as a servant for his wife, Susanna Wheatley. They named her Phillis Wheatley and estimated that she was about seven years old at the time. Although it was relatively common for Congregationalists to teach slaves to read, Phillis received an unparalleled education for women and especially for a black woman, which included studying Latin. Phillis was treated better than most slaves in this household or most colonial households. In one letter to black Newporter Obour Tanner, Phillis even stated that she "was treated by her [Susanna Wheatley] more like her child than her servant." Nevertheless, Phillis was a slave and expressed a desire for freedom. Wheatley expressed evangelical Christian beliefs and political ideals that favored universal liberation.[36]

Phillis Wheatley's writings suggest that church attendance, religious practices, and faith were essential to her. "Phillis Servant to Mr. Wheatly" was baptized and admitted to membership at Old South Congregational Church on August 18, 1771. In July 1772, Phillis wrote that she had been ill and was staying in the country to recover, but she "came to town this morning to spend the Sabbath with my master and mistress." Phillis began writing poetry around 1765, and she favored religious themes. In 1773, some of her poetry was published in London as a book titled *Poems on Various Subjects, Religious and Moral.*[37]

Phillis Wheatley expressed her faith not only in published poetry but also in her private correspondence. From 1772 to 1779, Phillis Wheatley corresponded with Obour Tanner, who was an enslaved woman in Newport, Rhode Island, and they often encouraged each other's faith. Wheatley asked Tanner for prayer, and Tanner requested books from Boston. Responding to one of Tanner's letters, Wheatley stated, "Your Reflections on the Suffering of the Son of God, & the inestimable price of our immortal souls Plainly demonstrate the sensation of a Soul united to Jesus." As Wheatley struggled with poor health, she was encouraged by "him who declar'd from heaven that his strength was made perfect in weakness!" For her, religion brought comfort and meaning, and perhaps also empowerment.[38] In a 1773 letter to Englishman John Thornton, she commented that God was no respecter of persons, being the maker of all. God, she wrote, "therefor disdains not to be called the Father of Humble Africans and Indians; though despisd on earth on account of our colour, we have this Consolation." In a 1774 letter to Reverend Samson Occom (Mohegan), Wheatley discussed the enslavement of blacks and argued that in every person "God has implanted a Principle, which we call Love of Freedom; it is impatient of Oppression, and pants for Deliverance."[39] While most of Phillis Wheatley's life experiences were extraordinary and exceptional, she was far from alone in her embrace of evangelical Christianity or her affiliation with a predominantly white church.

Contrary to the trend among many Congregational churches, black affiliation increased during the 1760s at Newport's two Congregational churches. In these cases, both laypeople and ministers encouraged black people to join. The ministry of Sarah Osborn caused more black people to affiliate with these churches than had ever done so previously. Despite the objections of several Newporters and area ministers, including Reverend Joseph Fish of North Stonington, Connecticut, Osborn facilitated a spiritual revival through house-meetings among women, young people, and black people. Sarah was born in London, England, in 1714, migrated as a child to Boston, and moved to Newport in 1729. She married Samuel Wheaten, who died at sea two years later. Sarah began providing for herself and baby son by operating a school. She joined the First Congregational Church in 1737 and began holding weekly religious meetings for women in her home in the early 1740s. She married Henry Osborn, who was a widower with three sons, in 1741 and continued to operate a school despite chronic illness and decreasing mobility. In the late 1760s, her home became the center of a city-wide religious revival that included many black Newporters.[40]

Osborn felt that being compassionate toward people in need of spiritual encouragement was more important than her convenience. She worked tirelessly to evangelize, which she considered the most important way to help those in need. She gave generously with her limited resources, but she believed that helping people to put their faith in Jesus was more compassionate and important than simply relieving physical suffering. Until at least the 1770s, she did not oppose slavery, and she owned an enslaved boy named Bobey since his infancy (friends gave him as a gift). Phillis, Bobey's mother, was owned by Timothy Allen. Phillis joined the same church as Sarah Osborn in 1757 and also attended Osborn's women's prayer group. Osborn believed that black people should join churches and were equal before God, but she did not treat them as equals on earth. She was condescending toward the black people around her. White people, including Osborn and ministers such as Pilmore and Asbury, often believed that they knew what black people needed better than they knew their own needs. Osborn nearly sold Bobey away from Newport despite Phillis's vocal opposition. For most of her life, Osborn believed Christianity would make slaves more obedient to their masters.[41]

The Newport revival began in 1764 or 1765, when black men and women and young white people started meeting in the Osborn home. She wrote to Reverend Joseph Fish that "there is several Ethiopians thotful who Having their Liberty to go where they like on Lords day Evening have ask'd Liberty to repair to our House for the benefit of family prayer reading etc. and I Have thot it a duty to Encourage them." This group met for prayer, singing, and religious exhortations, and it continued to grow in size for more than a year. In 1766, another group of blacks, who may have been free persons, began meeting at Osborn's house on Tuesday nights. Other groups of mostly white people organized meetings for different weeknights. By July 1766, as many as 300 people were meeting weekly at her home, and the attendance rose to approximately 525 people by January 1767, including at least 70 black people. Although most people stopped attending by April 1768, there were still around 60 blacks who met there. Osborn knew that many people disapproved of her meetings and ministry to black people, but she was determined to continue the work that she believed God had initiated, even if some people considered this work to be outside women's proper sphere of activities. She mostly had the support of Deacon Nathan Coggeshall from her church, and the strict rules for enslaved attendees may have alleviated the fears of some slave owners.[42]

Sarah Osborn's revival was a major factor in increasing the number of black people who affiliated with churches in Newport, but the ministers of First and Second Congregational churches were also active in seeking black adherence and participation. Osborn promoted religion in her home, but access to Christian sacraments in the church was under the control of men. For example, Quaum (later called John Quamine) attended Osborn's house meetings, and then in July 1765, he was baptized and admitted as a member of the First Congregational Church. Reverend William Vinal was pastor of First Church from 1746 to 1768, and Reverend Samuel Hopkins was pastor of First Church from 1770 to 1803. Reverend Ezra Stiles was pastor of Second Congregational Church from 1755 to 1778. All three men baptized black people at their churches and admitted some black people to full membership. Starting in 1770, Hopkins and Stiles held evening meetings at their homes for blacks and other people.[43]

The First Congregational Church baptized at least twelve black people between 1764 and 1776 (racial notation were inconsistent in the records). William Vinal baptized and admitted to communion at least three blacks, including Obour Tanner in July 1768. Obour Tanner corresponded with Phillis Wheatley for years and was married to a man named Barra Collins by Samuel Hopkins in 1790. She likely attended the meeting at Osborn's house. Hopkins became pastor of First Church, in large part because of the lobbying of Sarah Osborn and members of her female religious society. By 1776, Hopkins baptized at least nine blacks, including "Jenny Folgier, a free negro" and "Cato Coggeshall, servant of Deacon Nathan Coggeshall." Five black adults were admitted to full membership. Adults were baptized at First Church only if they became full church members, and Hopkins baptized only infant children of full church members, which made baptisms less accessible to black congregants in this church than at the Anglican Church.[44] Nonetheless, some black people publicly affiliated with First Congregational Church, and others attended services there.

Some of the black people who affiliated with this church found it spiritually fulfilling, but the antislavery message that Samuel Hopkins began to preach by 1775 was also encouraging. Hopkins was one of the earliest and most vocal Congregational ministers who opposed slavery, but his reforming spirit was at odds with Newport, a center for the slave trade and related products, including about thirty distillers. It was precisely his exposure to the workings of the slave trade that began to turn Hopkins toward abolitionism. Once he decided that slavery was injurious to Africans, Americans, and the spread of the gospel, Hopkins determined to speak against it. He may have preached against the slave trade to his congregation as early as 1771 and against slaveholding by 1773. Although his congregation did not include the city's wealthiest slave traders, some of his congregants owned one or more slaves. Hopkins spread his antislavery message beyond his congregation by publishing *A Dialogue Concerning the Slavery of the Africans* in 1776, which thoroughly denounced slavery.[45]

At the Second Congregational Church, Ezra Stiles catechized, baptized, married, and admitted to membership black people between 1764 and 1776, but he was not a dedicated abolitionist like Hopkins. Stiles seems to have reached black congregants through personal interactions. This church had seven black members in 1772, including "Phyllis Negro Servant of Gov. Lyndon & wife of Brother Zingo [who] was baptized & admitted into full communion in the public congregation." Stiles held weekly catechism classes between 1768 and 1775, and blacks almost always attended his classes with whites. There were twenty white boys, thirty white girls, and four black people in his class on April 26, 1770, and on May 8, 1775, there were thirteen white boys, thirty-three white girls, and nine black people.[46]

In 1770, Stiles calculated the size of his congregation and found "six hundred & eight souls, Men Woman & Children Whites inclusive of infants; besides about seventy souls Negroes." He also noted that the

FIGURE 3.1. Ezra Stiles, minister of Second Congregational Church, Newport, Rhode Island, routinely ministered to black congregants. *Rev. Ezra Stiles, D.D., L.L.D., president of Yale College, 1777–1795*, The Miriam and Ira D. Wallach Division of Art, Prints and Photographs: Print Collection, NYPL, Image ID 421782, NYPL Digital Collections, http://digitalcollections.nypl.org/.

"congregation consists of 608 souls whites & upward of which 364 whites are baptized, & about a dozen negroes baptized." Of the 678 people (blacks and whites) whom Stiles counted, only about seventy were members in full communion, six of whom were blacks (8.57 percent of the members). The roughly seventy blacks who attended Second Church sat in a designated portion of the gallery. Wealthy slave owner Caleb Gardner rented a pew on the ground floor of the church and also one in the gallery. The gallery pew was perhaps reserved for his slaves. In his records, Stiles recorded how often members received communion, which occurred at most six times a year. The black church members were regular partakers of communion, including "Brother Caesar Negro" and "Sister Betty Negro," who were present at every communion service from 1773 to 1775. Blacks publicly affiliated with this church because the pastor sincerely welcomed them into the church and because of the benefits of affiliation, including educational opportunities and access to the rituals of baptism and communion.[47]

Black men and women continued to be baptized, married, and admitted as members in Congregational churches in New England, but Congregational churches as a whole were not part of the expansion of worship evident in other northern churches. For some enslaved black New Englanders, including Cuffee Wright and Phillis Wheatley, the Congregational tradition provided spiritual comfort. Wheatley's and Wright's words suggest the adoption of a Christian identity attuned to their personal experiences of oppression. The active work of ministers and lay members, such as Sarah Osborn, was important for welcoming blacks into these churches. Individual relationships between enslaved blacks and concerned whites paved the way for the inclusion of black people in many types of predominantly white churches.

Anglican Church Affiliation

After the Baptists and Methodists, the Church of England experienced the next most substantial increase in the number of interracial congregations. Black people continued to participate in most of the Anglican churches between 1764 and 1776 in which they had previously affiliated, but additional parishes also baptized black people. Church of England priests routinely baptized and catechized more free and enslaved blacks than any other denomination in northern cities. Between 1750 and 1763, at least fifteen predominantly white Anglican churches baptized black people. Between 1764 and 1776, that number jumped to nineteen congregations, whose locations are displayed in figure 3.2.[48] Almost all of the Anglican churches that included black people were located in places that had ocean or river ports with direct commerce with England and other colonies. Several of them were located in colonial capitals. Merchants and government officials tended to have a preference for Anglican churches, and these people, among the wealthiest northerners, were commonly slaveholders. The Church of England was among the most popular of denominations for urban black people because they offered free education and relatively easy access to sacraments.

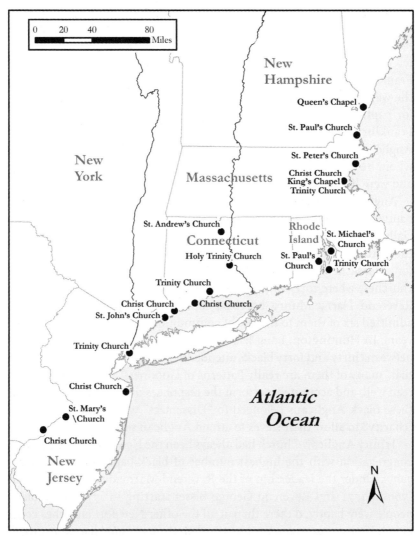

FIGURE 3.2. Map of northern Anglican churches that baptized multiple black people, 1764–76. Map courtesy of William Keegan.

Between 1764 and the Declaration of Independence in 1776, Anglican clergy and churches continued ministering to their congregations and seeking to expand their reach in colonial society. Anglicans were aware of brewing hostilities, but the imperial crisis did not much affect catechizing, baptizing, marrying, and worshipping until 1776. Catechism classes continued in many cities, especially for enslaved and free blacks, often funded by the Society for the Propagation of the Gospel (SPG) or the Bray Associates in London. Black men, women, and children were baptized in significant numbers, and some black people were admitted to communion. For example, in 1774, the Royal Governor William Franklin (the son of Benjamin Franklin and a staunch Loyalist during the war) presented Anthony Harley, "child of Knowlton a negro man," for baptism at St. Mary's Church, Burlington, New Jersey. Governor Franklin owned both people. When Godfrey Malbone established an Anglican church in Brooklyn, Connecticut, the enslaved black people whom he owned did much of the construction work on the 1771 edifice and were likely among the attendees of this church.[49]

Anglicans in each colony between Pennsylvania and New Hampshire baptized black men, women, and children between 1764 and 1776, especially in the parishes with an assistant minister or catechist who directed their attention toward slaves. Almost half of all black baptisms in Boston, Massachusetts, during this period occurred at the three Anglican churches, where forty-one blacks were baptized. In Albany, New York, Reverend Harry Munro baptized more than fifty black people and admitted six of them to the rite of communion in the pre-Revolutionary years. In Huntington, Long Island, Reverend James Greaton noted that between thirty and forty blacks attended services at his church. He wrote that "many of them are really Patterns of Goodness" and "some of them read well, and accurately perform the responses of the Church." Some of these black Anglicans belonged to "Dissenters" who possessed enough "charity" to allow their slaves to attend Anglican services.[50]

Trinity Anglican Church had always been the Newport, Rhode Island, congregation with the highest number of black baptisms and congregants. Under the leadership of the Reverend Marmaduke Browne from 1760 to 1771 and Reverend George Bisset starting in 1771, more black people were baptized there than at all the other Newport churches combined. Fifty-one people were identified on the baptismal list as "negroes" during this period, and at least twenty-one of them were adults. Most of these baptisms occurred in the early 1770s: fifteen in 1772, thirteen in 1773, and nine black baptisms in 1774. Baptisms of white persons in these years were also higher than usual, so the cause of this spike in baptisms likely affected everyone in the congregation. The newly arrived Reverend Bisset likely encouraged more of the congregation to be baptized.[51]

Both Browne and Bisset expressed compassion (aligned with Enlightenment humanism) for blacks in Newport and sought to include them within the church as a means of ameliorating their condition. Browne recognized that some of his Anglican parishioners regarded blacks as inferior beings and neglected their spiritual (not to mention their material) well-being. He speculated that "Could people be brought to consider their slaves as of the same species with themselves they would pay more regard to their temporal & eternal welfare than the planters in America general do." Browne, remarkably for the time, even expressed the opinion that blacks would be better left free in Africa than enslaved and without religion in North America. He wrote in 1768, "I shudder when I reflect on the load of guilt. . . . I would wish they would either leave them in a state of liberty or at least make them some sort of amends for the loss of it by teaching them with humility & instructing them in the truth of Christianity."[52] Influenced by the humanitarian rhetoric of the Enlightenment, Browne felt a duty to minister to the enslaved blacks in Newport, a view shared among most Anglican priests.

The educational opportunities that Trinity Church and other Anglican parishes offered appealed to black people. A charity school for educating blacks, funded by the Bray Associates in London, opened in the early 1760s, and the church had a lending library of books available to the whole Newport community. Mrs. Brett operated the school, while the rectors occasionally visited, and Reverend Browne worked to increase enrollment. By 1771, enrollment was at "thirty pupils, negro children, who were to be taught reading, writing, sewing, etc." In the spring of 1774, there were thirty-eight black students. The last names of masters who sent slaves to the school match many of the last names of the black people baptized at Trinity Church, so there was a strong correlation between being educated at this school and affiliation with the church.[53]

It is plausible that some blacks were attracted to Newport's Trinity Church because they saw church affiliation as a means of obtaining practical benefits as well as religious ones. In one remarkable instance, a slave received his freedom because of the church. In 1765, the vestry voted to have "the Church Wardens hire a room for Markadore, formerly a slave of Nathaniel Kay, Esq., deceased, set him free and pay his rent for one year." The church received this enslaved man as an estate bequest, but instead of selling him or using his services, it freed him and gave him a place to live. Such generosity was uncommon, but black people knew that church affiliation could bring tangible benefits such as education, access to white patronage, and a place to socialize.[54]

As much as Trinity Church Newport was a center of black religious affiliation, hindrances prevented the participation of some enslaved blacks. Whites did not treat black Anglicans as equals. Many blacks attended this church and affiliated with it, even though they experienced the exclusionary practices common in most churches, such as segregated seating. Seating was held at a high premium at Trinity Church, and some of the city's wealthiest citizens paid large sums of money to secure ground-floor seating. Black people were required to sit in a designated part of the gallery, while whites purchased pews in other parts of the gallery. In 1772, the church voted to move the black seating area and exchange it for another section, thereby "removing the negroes to the west end of the Church, provided it be agreeable to the proprietors of the pews behind the organ to exchange their pews for those to be built at the south side of the gallery, where the negroes now sit." Church leaders believed that "the negroes can be as well accommodated" since whites had sat where the blacks would henceforth sit.[55]

Philadelphia's united Church of England congregations, Christ Church and St. Peter's Church, also baptized far more blacks between 1764 and 1776 than did any other church in the city. What is even more telling about these baptisms is the number of free blacks who affiliated. At least 128 blacks were baptized during these years. John Penn and James Hamilton, both of whom served as governor, each had at least one slave baptized at Christ Church in 1766. Of all the baptisms, twenty-five (representing almost 20 percent of all the black baptisms) were identified as free persons. Many of the free blacks in Philadelphia, as well as many enslaved blacks, chose to affiliate publicly with and attend Christ Church or St. Peter's. This pattern was similar to trends elsewhere in the English Atlantic. A large portion of the free black population on the island of Barbados affiliated with the Anglican Church. Philadelphia's congregations included not only some of the wealthiest members of Philadelphia society but also dozens of free blacks and hundreds of enslaved Philadelphians. Some of the members of this congregation were evangelical Anglicans, who embraced the Methodist calls for piety and heartfelt devotion.[56]

In Philadelphia, the Anglican Church included both Patriots and Tories, but it managed to stay generally united until 1773 or 1774. Several prominent members of Christ Church played roles in protesting and organizing opposition to the new taxes installed during the imperial crisis. In September 1774, the Continental Congress made Anglican minister Jacob Duché its chaplain, and the Continental Congress worshipped at this church on a July 20, 1775, fast day. The Anglican clergy, like many Philadelphians, believed that the rights of colonists were being infringed upon, and they supported moderate measures of seeking redress. However, independence was a question that split the pastors and congregation, including its black members. As Anglican clergy had sworn allegiance to the king and were required to pray for him at each service, the Declaration of Independence made neutrality or even conservative protest impossible. Some northern Anglican churches ceased holding services in 1776 instead of omitting prayer for the king.[57]

After 1776, the war further disrupted Anglican congregations. Nevertheless, more Anglican churches included black people during the era of the imperial crisis than in preceding decades, and the church's successor in the United States continued this tradition of inclusion into the nineteenth century. Like the Baptist and Methodist churches, a greater number of Church of England parishes included black people than during previous decades, and they often baptized more black people than other denominations. The expansion of black Anglican baptisms and members was tied to the education-focused outreach to black people started earlier in the century. Anglican ministers felt duty-bound to show compassion, through religion, to the enslaved blacks in their parishes.

Indian Church Affiliation, 1764 to 1790

As had been the case since the 1750s, only small numbers of Indians affiliated with predominantly white churches from 1764 to 1790. The French and Indian War, completed in 1763, intensified Indians' distrust of colonists and colonists' hatred of Indians. However, black people participated in more Indian churches in the 1760s and after the Revolutionary War as increasing numbers of free black people resided near and within Indian communities. When white people moved close to or visited Indian communities, they also sometimes attended Native churches. Indian Congregational, Baptist, and Presbyterian churches differed from predominantly white churches. They were fewer in numbers and often isolated from white congregations of the same denominations. These churches often supported tribal-community self-governance and autonomy. However, despite the differences between white and Indian churches, the latter also experienced a growth in racial diversity starting in the 1760s.

White missionaries visited Indian communities throughout northern colonies, and some ministers of English congregations baptized Indians when visiting their communities. Philadelphia's Anglican minister Richard Peters baptized twenty-four Indians in 1768, and these baptisms demonstrate Anglicans' willingness to include diverse peoples within the Church of England. Pennsylvania's governor requested that Peters, who had "long experience in Indian affairs," attend a treaty conference at Fort Stanwix in 1768. At this conference, colonists hoped to gain land and delineate the boundaries of Indian and British territory in New York and western Pennsylvania. In addition to the political work that Peters conducted, he baptized many Haudenosaunee (Iroquois) and other Indians who desired baptism, which these Indians may have interpreted as a sign of friendship with the British. The Indians hoped that by forming strong ties with the British officials, and by ceding vast territory, the British would prevent further white settlement on Indian land. The Indians baptized at Fort Stanwix included adults and children who were Tuscarora, Oneida, Delaware, Mohawk, Onondaga, and Shawnee.[58]

Some Indians residing or working in towns distant from Indian communities attended and sought baptism for themselves or their children in predominantly white churches. Likewise, some individuals who moved back and forth between Indian communities and northern cities participated in both white and Indian churches. The First Moravian Church of Philadelphia baptized Jacob, son of "Renalius & Cash, Christian Indians" in 1764 in addition to five blacks between 1764 and 1776. These Indians were likely taking refuge in Philadelphia away from the Paxton Boys, who had recently murdered Christian Indians in Pennsylvania. They had likely practiced Christianity with a great deal of autonomy in their community before going to Philadelphia.[59] Table 3.1 includes predominantly white churches in which one or more Indians were identified in the baptismal or membership records.

Predominantly white churches baptized only a small number of Indians, but some Afro-Indians who identified themselves as Indian were likely labeled in church records as "negro." Whites had difficulty categorizing and describing people of mixed ancestry. For example, at Trinity Church in Newport, a daughter of Jane Thurstin, baptized in 1787, was identified as "Mulat [mulatto] or Indian." Additionally, one person who was part European and part Indian was baptized in Pennsylvania. At the Corner Church in Berks County, Pennsylvania, "Maria Sarah Buss, born in wild heathenism by her mother Maria Sarah and an Indian father on __15, 1762," was baptized in October 1767.[60] The child's mother may have been a captive during the French and Indian War. Being a member of an Indian community involved more than Indian ancestry, and these German Christians likely sought to incorporate Maria as a non-Indian, but she was the daughter of an Indian man and is included within this tabulation to suggest that attempts to categorize and label people by "race" are often problematic.

TABLE 3.1. Select list of churches in which one or more Indians were baptized or admitted and approximate numbers, 1764–1790

Church name	Number of Indians	Years	Notes
CONGREGATIONAL CHURCHES			
First Church Yarmouth, Mass.	3	1765–76	Children of Samuel & Mehetable Whitney (Indians)
Second Church in Rochester (First Mattapoisett), Mass.	1	1779	Indian woman baptized & admitted to membership
Barnstable, Mass., East Parish Church	1	1769	Indian woman baptized & admitted to membership
Old Saybrook, Conn. Congregational Church	2	1768	Indian woman Olive owned covenant & child baptized
First Church New Haven, Conn.	1	1769	Carelot "a squaw" baptized
Westchester Congregational Church, Colchester, Conn.	1	1773	Baptized "Pomp Indian Negro Boy"
EPISCOPAL CHURCHES			
St. Michael's Episcopal Bristol, R.I.	2	1764–80	An Indian child and an Indian adult baptized (no relation)
St. Paul's Church Narragansett, R.I.	2	1787	Patience and Oliver, of Sara Indian, baptized
Trinity Church Newport, R.I.	1	1787	"Mulat or Indian" daughter of Jane Thurstin baptized

TABLE 3.1 (*continued*). Select list of churches in which one or more Indians were baptized or admitted and approximate numbers, 1764–1790

Church name	Number of Indians	Years	Notes
Christ Episcopal Church Philadelphia records	24	1768	Indians baptized by Christ Church Rector at Fort Stanwix, N.Y.
Trinity Church of New Haven, Conn.	1	1772	Moses Paul an adult Indian of the Mohegan tribe in the jail house
BAPTIST CHURCHES			
Tiverton, R.I., Baptist Church	1	1788	Phear Slocum (Indian) baptized
First Sabbatarian Church, Hopkinton, R.I.	1	1786	James Warmsley (Indian)
Third Baptist Church Middleborough, Mass.	1	1774	"Indian woman from between Sandwich & Plymouth"
First Baptist Church Groton, Conn.	1	1764	John "Indian boy of Mrs. Palmmers"
Second Baptist Church Newport, R.I.	1	1774	"Susanna Pain Indian"
REFORMED, LUTHERAN, AND MORAVIAN CHURCHES			
New Bethel or Corner Church, Albany, Pa.	1	1767	Indian father and white mother
Schenectady, N.Y., Dutch Church	1	1785	"John, sen Indiaan van de Cayugas"
Reformed Church Schoharie, N.Y.	23	1767–78	Mostly Indian children
Reformed Dutch Church, German Flats, N.Y.	4	1786–90	Children of 2 different Indian couples
First Moravian Church Philadelphia, Pa.	1	1764	Jacob son of Renalius & Cash, "Christian Indians"

It was more common for blacks and Afro-Indians to attend Indian churches than for Indians to participate in white churches. During the Revolutionary era, an increasing number of blacks and Afro-Indians participated in predominantly Indian churches, thereby transforming Indian churches into sites of interracial religious worship. This period also saw an increase in Indians preaching to white and mixed audiences in northern churches following the trend established by Mohegan minister Samson Occom in the 1750s. Moreover, some whites attended predominantly Indian churches, such as those at Natick, Sandwich, and Stockbridge, Massachusetts.

More free black people participated in Indian churches in large part because the presence of blacks in Indian communities grew substantially. Indian-black intermarriage became common, especially in New England. The autonomous Indian communities in New England were attractive to free blacks, especially free black men. Indian women usually outnumbered Indian men because of the high death rates for Indian men serving in the military and seafaring. Free black men were often attracted to the relative distance from whites and the availability of land on Indian reserves.[61]

Reverend Gideon Hawley, a missionary to the Wampanoags at their reserve in Mashpee, Massachusetts, revealed how racially diverse that community and his church became in this period. Hawley stated that the Mashpee Wampanoags were "Christianized and in a measure civilized and perhaps this tribe more than any other." During the Revolutionary era, he began to note more frequently the number of non-Indians residing at Mashpee and attending church with the Wampanoags. The relative availability of land at Mashpee, and its isolation from the Revolutionary War's battles, appealed to Indians, blacks, and whites.[62] By 1782, the Wampanoags noted, "the Indian & melatoe [mulatto] Inhabitants of Mashpee have increased and are now more numerous."[63] In 1787, Reverend Hawley provided a detailed description of how diverse the Wampanoag community had become:

> In the late & present distressing day this Mashpee has been an Asylum for the poor Natives & their connections, which are becoming exceedingly various & mixed; for we have had an East Indian, a native of Bombay married to one of our females and another from Mexico, besides several Dutchmen from Gen. Bourgoyne's Army, who have formed connections with our women and comform'd to

the Indian manners. From Mohegan and other places in Connecticut, from Narragansett & other places in Rhode Island, as well as from various towns in the Massachusetts where Indians have been of that precious plant which they have planted manured & watered in this church & congregation for so long a term.[64]

Hawley described Mashpee, including his church, as a refuge for many people, including Europeans, blacks, and Indians from other New England tribes. In 1791, Hawley noted that the female Wampanoags at Mashpee had "mixed with negroes, English, Germans {Burgoyne's men} &c &c."[65] These new inhabitants concerned some Wampanoags and, at times, Hawley too. Together, they petitioned to have white and black squatters removed from Mashpee, arguing "the coming of Negroes & English who have unhappily planted themselves here has wronged us and it is to be feard that they & their children unless they are removed will get away our Land & all our Privileges in a Short time."[66] Hawley wrote, "in the year 1788 we had on the Mashpee Lands 25 families of poor Whites, who had located themselves without any legal title to the land." By 1795, seven of these families had left, and others were paying rent.[67]

Indians, Afro-Indians, blacks, and whites attended services at Hawley's church and probably attended services led by Indian ministers who visited Mashpee. The church at Mashpee, like the community more broadly, became more racially diverse. In December 1805, Hawley wrote that "The Indians occupy the pews & fore seats in my meeting, and the whites set back—At my meeting the Indians or Blacks are the principals or chiefs; as they ought to be—mixing whites & Indians is bad for the latter."[68] In a striking reversal of the standard church hierarchical seating arrangement, whites at this Wampanoag church sat in the back seats during services. Indians, Afro-Indians, and blacks sat in the church's better seats. It is not clear whether Wampanoags or Hawley suggested this seating arrangement, but anyone in that congregation would have noticed the uniqueness of this arrangement and would have understood that, in this space, Wampanoags were preeminent.

Elsewhere, too, blacks increased their presence in Indian communities and churches. Hawley wrote about an April 1770 Sunday service with the Indian church near Sandwich, Massachusetts, where "thirty & forty black hearers . . . attended with grt [great] seriousness."[69] In the 1760s and 1770s, Congregational minister Joseph Fish went monthly to western Rhode Island to preach to the Narragansetts, among whom he noted the presence of blacks, Afro-Indians, and whites. In February 1769, he preached "to Sixty Indians, Including Negros." While most of the Narragansett Christians stopped listening to Fish's lectures, there was still a small and diverse group who occasionally attended. Fish preached in July 1771 to "16 Indians and Mustees; and about a Dozn. Whites" and in August to "about 9 or 10 Indians and negroes."[70]

Between 1787 and October 1791, Presbyterian missionary Samuel Kirkland labored among the Oneida in upstate New York, and occasionally his congregation was interracial when white people visited the area. Kirkland preached in both English and Indian languages and traveled between several towns.[71] Kirkland recalled an interracial worship service that took place at a 1790 treaty signing between New York State and the Onondaga and Cayuga Nations: "There were Indians from near ten different nations & of different languages . . . with some white people, all visibly worshiping the same God together." Other white travelers in Oneida territory were, according to Kirkland, touched by "much seriousness & decorum, and the harmony of their music."[72]

At the same time that blacks and some whites comprised a growing proportion of Indian churches at Mashpee, Sandwich, and elsewhere, other Indian communities made the conscious decision to exclude blacks, whites, and mixed-raced people. In 1772, a group of Mohegans in Connecticut, including Reverend Samson Occom, resolved that women who married "strangers" had to leave the tribe and that the children born of Indian and black relationships would have no customary rights in the nation, such as access to communal lands. These Mohegans at least partially adopted racial biases that were similar to those of white colonists. The Mohegans were engaged in legal efforts to secure their remaining ancestral lands, and their land rights would have been further eroded if whites saw "blacks" or "people of color" instead of "Indians" seeking to maintain claims to Mohegan lands. Likewise, the Oneidas of upstate New York told Samuel Kirkland that they "firmly resolved never to admit any white People to settle amongst us or near us except a Minister & schoolmaster who are as one of us." The Oneidas said that they have "seen the fate of Stockbridge," a Christian Indian community in Massachusetts that whites displaced, and they did not want the same fate. When Christian Indians from New England and Long Island, including Reverend Occom, migrated to Oneida country to create a multitribal Christian-Indian community, they sought to remain free from white and black settlers. Driven by attempts to maintain their resources and identity against the pressures of colonization, some Indians enacted exclusionary policies that sought to prevent the incorporation of blacks and whites into their communities.[73]

With some exceptions, the overall trend among New England Indians between 1764 and 1790 was a movement toward greater diversity and racially mixed families, communities, and churches. Indian adoptions of outsiders was not a new phenomenon, and these people continued to be Wampanoag, Narragansett, etc., but Indians and white Americans both noticed the changed composition of some tribes. Numerous free blacks moved into Indian communities and married Indians, thereby changing the racial and perhaps political contours of these Indian communities, many of which had had their own churches since the 1750s or earlier. The story of Indian Christianity, although mostly distinct from white denominations and churches between 1764 and 1790, exhibited an expansion of interracial religious worship.

In large portions of northern colonies between 1764 and 1776, it became more common for black people to affiliate with predominantly white Protestant churches. Growing numbers of Baptist, Methodist, and Anglican churches included black people in these years. As these denominations formed new congregations or expanded missionary activities, they usually gained black attendees and members. One reason why many blacks were attracted to Methodism was their antislavery stance and the denomination's relatively compassionate attitude to the suffering of slaves. Antislavery opinion (or the lack thereof in other denominations) was only one of several factors that blacks considered when making religious choices (as chapter 4 elaborates). Many black people affiliated with the churches that offered education and that made sacraments accessible to them and their children.

In churches that included black members and attendees, ministers such as Marmaduke Browne and laypeople such as Sarah Osborn described a duty to be compassionate to "poor," enslaved black people by encouraging their conversions and access to the church sacraments. Methodists, Anglicans, Congregationalists, and others participated in Enlightenment-inspired work to address the needs of those who suffered in colonial America. Although sometimes they attended to the physical needs of poor people, many Christians believed that people's spiritual condition was most critical. They evangelized and sought to bring unchurched people into their congregations.

Despite the disruptions of war after 1775, the trend toward greater diversity in churches continued not only between 1777 and 1790 but also into the 1820s in some denominations. Even the Presbyterian and Dutch

Reformed churches, so resistant to accepting black members before 1776, sometimes embraced substantial numbers of African Americans in subsequent decades. What began in the 1760s as a slow expansion of interracial churches remade northern religious worship by the 1810s. Looking ahead, as churches became more interracial, they played an influential role not only in promoting a gradual end to slavery but also in setting standards for race relations in northern society. The long expansion of interracial northern churches, from the 1760s through the 1810s, is particularly noteworthy because of what happened afterward. The spreading of interracial churches slowed in the 1820s and then reversed in the 1830s. Neither the expansion nor the contraction was inevitable, but these developments had profound effects on northern society and for race relations in the entire nation.

4 / "Slavery Is a Bitter Pill": Interracial Churches, War, and Abolitionism, 1776–1790

On August 8, 1776, a group of Continental soldiers in the First Battalion of Pennsylvania's militia "Heard a sermon from an Indian." These Pennsylvania soldiers were likely stationed in Elizabeth, New Jersey, at the time, just weeks before the British army's assault on New York. As John Pitman noted in his journal, this unnamed Indian preached from Hebrews 2:3—"how shall we escape if [we] neglect so great [a] salvation." Pitman commented that it was an "Arminion Sermon," meaning the preacher implied that all people, and not simply the predestined, could accept God's offer of salvation. Without additional comment, Pitman switched topics and noted that "About 20 of Parmer & Leils Company deserted."[1]

On Sunday, August 5, 1785, an entirely or mostly white congregation in Rutland, Vermont, heard the black Congregational minister and Revolutionary War veteran Lemuel Haynes preach from Second Peter 1:10 and Numbers 23:10. Haynes noted that "the people gave remarkable attention." The next day Haynes moved onto Pawlet, near the border with New York, where he continued his Vermont preaching tour to predominantly white churches.[2]

In early September 1786, a black man, probably Harry Hosier, preached at the John Street Methodist Church in New York City to an audience that included white and black people. Benjamin Rush, Thomas Coke, and others praised Hosier for his preaching ability during his ministerial career.[3] The *New York Packet* on September 11, 1786, reported the following about the service:

Lately came to this city, a very singular black man, who, it is said is quite ignorant of letters, yet he has preached in the Methodist church several times, to the acceptance of several well disposed judicious people,—He delivers his discourse with great zeal and pathos, and his language and connection is by no means contemptible.—It is the wish of several of our correspondents, that this same black man may be so far successful, as to rouse the dormant zeal of numbers of our slothful white people, who seem very little affected about the concerns of another world.[4]

Apparently, the people who heard him well-received this black man's preaching, and some of them believed that he could arouse a religious conversion among whites who were indifferent to Christianity.

As these three examples suggest, between 1776 and 1790, white northerners occasionally heard black and Indian preachers, and interracial religious worship occurred in a greater variety of settings. In these and other cases, blacks and Indians were remarkably bold in preaching the gospel, and at least some whites were receptive to their messages. In particular, the 1776 Indian preacher must have had great confidence in himself since he preached a relatively controversial theology to a group of armed white men. Blacks, Indians, and Afro-Indians asserted their independent Christian judgment during the Revolutionary era and used Christianity to argue in favor of their liberation, and they often did so in interracial contexts. Through the year 1790, most black Christians in northern states still associated with predominantly white congregations because separate black churches had not yet formed. Conversely, very few Indians affiliated with any type of white church.

Northern religious life transformed substantially during the era of the American Revolution; from 1776 to 1790, the expansion of interracial churches that began in the 1760s continued. The war changed the religious landscape and, at times, made public worship impossible, but the Revolutionary era also witnessed the opening of new venues for interracial religious meetings. Black people continued to affiliate with some Congregational and Lutheran churches, and they participated in many urban Anglican and Episcopal churches. Reformed and Presbyterian churches attracted more black congregants and members than in earlier decades, and Methodist and Baptist congregations also made interracial religious worship more common. The ordinations of the earliest black preachers and ministers meant that there was also an increased chance of whites listening to black men preach. The Revolutionary War and

establishment of the United States did not generally hinder black participation in northern churches. Rather, this turbulent period of political,
social, and economic change was marked by a slight expansion of interracial worship.

The upsurge in interracial religious experiences resulted from practical changes that made baptism more accessible to black people in
some denominations and, most importantly, from deliberate outreach
to blacks by numerous preachers. In theory, the growth in white people's antislavery views and whites' deliberate outreach to blacks would
seem to have been mutually reinforcing. In fact, there is little evidence,
except for the Methodists, that increasing levels of black participation in
churches directly followed growth in antislavery activism among northern denominations. Historians have suggested that increasing numbers
of black churchgoers in the last quarter of the eighteenth century was the
result of a rise in antislavery advocacy in churches. Speaking specifically
about Baptists and Methodists, Nathan Hatch writes that "what made
this witness to slaves credible was the number of white preachers willing
to preach against slavery in the face of entrenched opposition."[5] However, the expansion of interracial religion and the increasing number of
churches in which blacks affiliated cannot easily or always be linked to
antislavery Christianity, at least in northern states. Blacks affiliated with
different theological traditions and pursued the educational, spiritual, and
material benefits that even proslavery denominations offered. While it is
true that black people's affiliation with the Methodist churches expanded
in part because of the attractiveness of that denomination's antislavery
statements, black affiliation levels among Baptist and Reformed churches
also increased before these denominations articulated objections to slavery. Moreover, black participation in Congregational churches declined
even as more Congregationalists opposed slavery. Blacks attended the
churches and denominations that preached antislavery messages, and
the presence of blacks in churches likely helped push some white Christians toward antislavery views, but black men and women also attended
churches that did not explicitly promote emancipation. There was not a
simple relationship between a church's stance on slavery and the number
of its black attendees or members.

A constellation of factors, not just antislavery theology, affected
the religious choices that enslaved and free blacks made. Slaveholders
sometimes restricted the religious options of enslaved black people, and
not all ministers were equally accessible or interested in caring for the
spiritual concerns of black people. During these fraught times of war

and instability, many people from all parts of society sought reassurance and consolation from the religious institutions and clergy in their communities. As some African Americans gained freedom, they may have expressed that new liberty not only through moving and finding employment but also from joining a church of their choosing. Emancipation led some black men to begin careers as preachers.

The Revolutionary War caused substantial challenges for northern churches, including the destruction of buildings and the dislocation of congregants. Church buildings were destroyed or severely damaged in Boston, Newport, and New York City, among other locations. Fire destroyed several church buildings in New York City in 1776, and the military converted others into barracks and hospitals. There were nineteen church buildings in New York City in 1775, but "only nine were fit for use when the British left" in November 1783. In addition to property loses, congregations lost members from death and the loyalist migration out of the United States. In many cases, the loss of property, people, and clergy was staggering.[6]

Of all the northern denomination, the war had the greatest direct consequences on the Church of England. After the Declaration of Independence, several northern states forbade prayers for the king or preaching that acknowledged him as sovereign. Even apolitical Anglican ministers had to suspend services or not pray for the king as their liturgy and ordination required. Many northern Anglican churchmen were outspoken Loyalists, which made their churches targets for Patriots during the war and suspect in the minds of many Americans. By 1783, only nine of the prewar Anglican ministers remained in the northern states. However, Anglican churches made quick progress in forming a denomination with a representative national assembly, the General Convention of the Protestant Episcopal Church in the United States. By 1790 the Protestant Episcopal Church of the United States, the new Anglican denomination in America, had regained much of what it lost during the war.[7]

The era of the American Revolution witnessed a remarkable development of antislavery attitudes among northerners that slowly promoted the end of legal slavery, and many of the people who promoted emancipation did so for religious reasons. The Society of Friends, or Quakers, were the earliest and most vocal opponents of slavery, but some other Christians followed their lead in the 1770s and 1780s. The antislavery stances articulated by Methodists, some Congregationalists, and various other individual Christians reshaped public opinion about slavery, even if antislavery advocates remained in the minority. Quakers and

Methodists were the most prominent antislavery Christians, but some individual Anglicans, Presbyterians, and Lutherans also opposed the slave trade and supported gradual emancipation. Gradual emancipation legislation was more politically palatable because these laws did not deprive slave owners of their human property and allowed them to profit from indentured black children for decades.[8]

Antislavery activities by black men and women, in the form of petitions, lawsuits, and running away, significantly influenced the gradual end of slavery in northern states, and blacks explicitly used Christianity to justify emancipation in their petitions. Most of the antislavery documents written by black people from this period used Christianity alongside republican ideals in advocating their case. A group of black people petitioned the Massachusetts Legislature in 1773 seeking emancipation. They testified to the injustice of slavery and referenced their religious beliefs: "We have no property! We have no wives! No children! We have no city! No country!" The slaves' petition cried, "But we have a Father in Heaven, and we are determined, as far as his Grace shall enable us, and as far as our degraded contemptuous life will admit, to keep all his Commandments." In 1780 a group of enslaved blacks in Hartford petitioned for the freedom of Connecticut's slaves, and they directly quoted nine biblical passages and referenced several others. These slaves possessed a detailed knowledge of scriptural texts, and they skillfully interpreted them to show the justice and necessity of emancipation. These petitions flowed from lifelong experiences of oppressive bondage and frequent participation in religious exercises. These black people told the legislators that they "pray to god that he would send forth his good Spirit unto your harts and Remind you of your Duty and make you the insterments of Binding up the Brokenharted and of Proclaiming Liberty to the Captives." While many whites did not believe that Christianity required an end to slavery, black believers made direct connections between Christianity and emancipation.[9]

Antislavery opinion began to grow among white northerners during the early 1770s as black Christians promoted emancipation and some whites confronted the hypocrisy of holding slaves while trumpeting their natural right to liberty, but many northerners remained fully committed to slavery. In 1764, James Otis of Boston argued that all men, including blacks, were by right born free. During the imperial crisis and Revolutionary War, such views built into an audible chorus critical of slavery. Blacks quickly applied Revolutionary rhetoric, like Christianity, to their own lives and used the same language as white Patriots to petition for an end to slavery. When whites refused to respond, blacks took action to liberate themselves, particularly after the British offered freedom in exchange for military service. Eventually, the Continental army addressed its manpower shortage by also granting freedom to black men who enlisted. After the war, self-emancipation continued as self-liberated black people joined the nascent African American communities developing in northern cities.[10]

From the perspectives of black northerners, emancipation moved at an incredibly slow and tenuous pace, especially in New York and New Jersey, but a shift away from slavery began by the 1780s. Several states prohibited the importation of new slaves in 1774, and between 1780 and 1804, northern states enacted gradual emancipation measures that put legal slavery on a gradual road to extinction without immediately freeing anyone. Gradual emancipation slowly changed the legal condition of northern blacks born after the laws were enacted; however, black freedom did not usually mean black equality or economic advancement. Often, whites still felt entitled to labor and deference from blacks, and "the state of being free continued to draw its meaning from the state of enslavement that had preceded it." By the time of the 1790 Federal Census, 27,054 northern African Americans were free, but 40,420 remained enslaved. The vast majority of these slaves resided in New York and New Jersey.[11]

Northern society dramatically changed during the era of the American Revolution, including freedom for a sizeable number of blacks. The free black communities in northern cities formed benevolent associations in the 1780s and after 1790 organized independent black churches. But, between 1777 and 1790, a greater variety of white churches included black men and women than ever before. The rising levels of black participation in Baptist, Methodist, and other churches exhibited the growing options available to blacks and an increased variety of interracial churches. The presence of antislavery sentiment was sometimes a reason for why blacks joined a church. However, on the whole, churches' stance on slavery was not the determinant factor in the expansion of interracial worship in either New England or Mid-Atlantic states. As they had done for decades, black northerners sought spiritual comfort and practical educational and social benefits from a variety of churches.

New England Churches

Antislavery opinions spread among many whites in New England during the Revolutionary era, and some churches and ministers spoke out against the slave trade and slavery, but black New Englanders' religious affiliation was not often directly linked to churches' stance on slavery. All denominations had some proslavery and some antislavery members, although those in favor of emancipation grew more prominent over time. Despite the growing numbers of Congregational pastors who spoke out against slavery, black affiliation levels in Congregational churches declined overall. Most Anglican churches in New England were not expressly opposed to slavery, but black people sometimes affiliated with them in substantial numbers. Black affiliation rates in New England Baptist churches also rose before most of these congregations and before Baptist associations spoke publicly against slavery.

White New Englanders, on the whole, developed broader and earlier antislavery feelings than people in the Mid-Atlantic, but slaveholders were not always inclined to voluntarily grant freedom to black people. Vermont and Massachusetts were among the first states to take steps to end slavery. Blacks vigorously pursued their freedom in these states, and increasing numbers of whites opposed the institution or were ambivalent about its continuation. In 1777, the new Vermont constitution freed all enslaved blacks who were "of age." However, the "of age" clause enabled masters to keep some blacks as slaves for years. Blacks petitioned the Massachusetts legislature in 1773 and 1774, but they did not convince the legislators to pass an emancipation bill. As more churches and ministers spoke against slavery, the willingness of the Massachusetts public to support the institution diminished. As enslaved black people in Massachusetts vigorously pursued freedom in the 1770s, many white people stopped claiming the legal right to control people as slaves. Successful freedom suits and changing attitudes about slavery destabilized the social structures necessary for maintaining slavery. The actions of blacks and their white allies gradually undermined the ability and willingness of people to hold slaves in Massachusetts as public support for policing slavery diminished. A series of judicial cases in Massachusetts, including the 1783 Quok Walker case, helped to bring about the end of legal slavery in the Commonwealth. Chief Justice John D. Cushing of Massachusetts gave the opinion that slavery was incompatible with the new state constitution, but his opinion was not widely published.[12]

Rhode Island and Connecticut enacted gradual emancipation laws that took generations to end slavery and that did not have an adverse financial effect on slave owners. Rhode Island passed a gradual emancipation law that made black children born after March 1, 1784, "apprentices" who would be free at age eighteen for women and age twenty-one for men. Although the Connecticut legislature voted against emancipation bills in 1777, 1779, and 1780, it passed an emancipation law in 1784 that freed black and mulatto children born after March 1, 1784, when they reached age twenty-five. The Connecticut law did not unconditionally free anyone until 1809, but more and more blacks gained their freedom in New England through military service, private manumission agreements, and absconding.[13]

Though black men and women continued to participate in some of the Congregational churches of New England between 1777 and 1790, their overall rate of participation in these churches declined, even though some prominent Congregational pastors supported emancipation. Twenty-nine Congregational churches included multiple black people through baptism or membership between 1777 and 1790, down from sixty-five Congregational churches that did so between 1764 and 1776.[14] For the individual black men and women who were baptized or admitted as members, their affiliation was likely still significant or meaningful because of the spiritual and material benefits the churches conferred.

Some of this decline may have been the result of a static birth rate and the absence of numerous black men from New England between 1776 and 1781. Many black men from New England enlisted in the Continental army, and a small number of other black New Englanders sought liberty and sanctuary with the British army. Blacks serving in arms reduced the black population in some communities and perhaps temporarily reduced the birth rate among black New Englanders, thereby reducing the number of potential black baptisms at least until 1781. The black population of New England seems to have been static between 1777 and 1790, whereas the white population in New England grew by roughly 50 percent. The black population of New England also began shifting toward larger cities. Some New England towns had fewer black residents and consequently fewer black church attendees.[15] Due to the war, demographic shifts, and possibly because of changing attitudes among whites, blacks participated in fewer Congregational churches between 1777 and 1790 than they had in previous decades.

Paradoxically, this decline of black participation in Congregational churches took place during the same period when numbers of

Congregationalists spoke publicly against slavery. Some Congregational church members and ministers owned slaves in this period and into the Early Republic, but other Congregationalists spoke out against the practice. The mixed, contested attitudes about slavery are well exemplified by the case of Benjamin Colman and Reverend Moses Parsons of Byfield parish in Newbury, Massachusetts. Around 1774, Colman, a deacon in the church, began to denounce slavery forcefully. Colman's antislavery activity turned into a conflict with the church's minister by 1780 because Parson continued to own at least one slave. Parson was the minister in this parish from 1744 to 1783 and owned two male slaves and one female slave. Parson apparently offered freedom to all three slaves, but Violet refused to be set free.[16] A descendant of Parson wrote:

> When it was generally believed that slavery was unlawful in Massachusetts, he [Reverend Parson] summoned his slaves into his sitting-room, and there, in the presence of his children, declared to them that they were free. The men accepted . . . Not so for Violet. "No, no, master," she said, "if you please, this must not be. You have had the best of me, and you and yours must have the worst. Where am I to go in sickness or old age? No, master; your slave I am, and always will be, and I will belong to your children when you are gone; and by you and them I mean to be cared for."[17]

Violet felt that freedom would be a greater burden to her than slavery, given the difficulty that she would have in providing for herself as an elderly woman (Violet was baptized in March 1764 after owning the covenant). Deacon Colman, however, continued to promote abolition and insulted Parsons by questioning his attempt to free his slaves. In December 1780, Parsons and Colman brought charges against each other in front of the church members. Parsons said that Colman had slandered him by accusing Parsons of "the wicked Practice of man stealing" and for offering to "sell his Slave (as he call'd her) for a large sum of money." The church members found the charges against Parsons to be false, and in March 1781, they voted to suspend Deacon Colman from membership and communion until he repented for offending the pastor. He was also removed from the office of deacon. It was not until 1785, nearly two years after Parsons's death, that Colman apologized for the "excessive vehemence & asperity" in his treatment of Parsons and asked "forgiveness of this Church." Some Congregationalists opposed slavery with all their might, but others willingly kept slaves or only gradually moved away from slaveholding as the institution slowly ended. Some

Congregationalists, unlike both Colman and Parson, continued to feel entitled to own enslaved people.[18]

The influence of a few vocal Congregational pastors did convince some New Englander to free their slaves and pushed New England states to adopt gradual emancipation laws. Reverends Samuel Hopkins of Newport, Rhode Island, Nathaniel Niles of Newburyport, Massachusetts, and Levi Hart, Ebenezer Baldwin, and Jonathan Edwards Jr. of Connecticut were all vocal promotors of abolitionism.[19] Their sermons against slavery helped promote antislavery opinions and legislation in New England. Doubtless, their promotion of universal liberty was a factor that attracted blacks to some Congregational churches. Other pastors supported emancipation by freeing their slaves. Reverend Josiah Stearns of the Congregational Church of Epping, New Hampshire, "was the owner of a negro, whom he had purchased when quite young." The church records continue, "but when the struggle for freedom commenced, feeling how utterly inconsistent it was for him to be exciting himself for his own liberty, whilst he held one of his fellow-creatures in bondage, he called his servant to him, &, after explaining fully his reasons for the course he intended to pursue, pronounced him henceforth free." This slave's name was Peter, and he owned the covenant and was baptized at this church in 1778. Peter "shouldered his musket & did good service in the common cause as a free man," but Peter died in July 1788.[20]

Congregational churches in both Boston and Newport had a smaller number of black participants, and some Anglican/Episcopal churches in these cities baptized more black people than the Congregational churches. Four of the nine oldest Congregational churches in Boston recorded no black baptisms between 1777 and 1790, and the other Congregational churches in this city baptized only one to three black people each. Some of Boston's ministers spoke against slavery, including Reverend Charles Chauncy of First Church. Chauncy's stance against slavery did not draw many blacks to affiliate with his church. The sharp decline in black affiliations in these urban Congregational churches paralleled the decline in black affiliation with Congregational churches throughout New England, but British occupations severely weakened Boston's and Newport's churches. From 1783 until 1790, there were only nineteen baptisms recorded at the Old South Church of Boston, including the baptism of one black person. Only one black woman was admitted to membership in Old South between 1777 and 1790.[21]

Despite Samuel Hopkins's antislavery activism, the First Congregational Church of Newport did not have a monopoly on black affiliation, and Newport's two Congregational churches had fewer black baptisms and members than compared to the period when Sarah Osborn's revival swept the city (see chapter 3). British occupation was terribly disruptive to these churches and caused fewer white and fewer black baptisms.[22] At least eight black people, and in all likelihood more, were baptized at First Congregational Church between 1781 and 1790. Samuel Hopkins did not write racial notations in church records from this period, and blacks were listed with last names, so it is difficult to determine the exact number of black people who affiliated with First Church. The eight baptisms that were definitely of black people were all children of Newport and Limas Gardner. On August 26, 1781, the church "received Newport Gardner" as a member. On the same day, Hopkins baptized two of their children: Prince and Dinah. Between 1782 and 1789, Solomon, Silva, Elizabeth, Jacob, Ahema, and Amy Gardner were all baptized. Five more Gardner children were baptized between 1792 and 1800 after Newport Gardner had gained freedom for himself and most of his family.[23]

Newport Gardner's given name was Occramer Marycoo, and a slave ship brought him from Africa to Newport at about age fourteen. Caleb Gardner purchased him and gave him the name Newport. He was educated and became so proficient in music that his master permitted him, while still a slave, to operate a music school. In the nineteenth century, William Piersen wrote that "Gardner became known for his abilities as a composer and as a director of a popular singing school in Newport; he could also cipher, write passable poetry, and speak French, and was highly regarded for his devotion to the Christian faith." He may have attended Second Congregational Church before the Revolution, where Caleb Gardner attended, but he became friends with Samuel Hopkins in the 1780s. Even while still enslaved, Newport Gardner associated with the first black organization in Newport, the Free African Union Society, founded around 1780. In August 1789, the Free African Union voted that "Mr. Ocrmar Mirycoo, or Newport Gardner be, and he is hereby admitted with the Privileges of having a Voice in the said Union Society . . . and that whenever he shall be free, he shall be admitted and received into the said Union Society." In the nineteenth century, Newport Gardner was one of the founders of the first black church in Newport, but during the 1780s, he affiliated with the predominantly white First Congregational Church.[24]

Black people, including the Gardners, may have chosen to affiliate with Newport's First Congregational Church for various reasons, but the antislavery message that Samuel Hopkins began to preach in the early

1770s certainly did not discourage black affiliation. Samuel Hopkins was one of the earliest and most vocal critics of slavery in New England, and he published *A Dialogue Concerning the Slavery of the Africans* in 1776. Eventually following their pastor's lead, the First Congregational Church voted in March 1784 "that the slave trade and the slavery of Africans, as it has taken place among us, is a gross violation of the righteousness and benevolence which are so much inculcated in the gospel; and therefore we will not tolerate it in this church." Hopkins continued the antislavery crusade in Rhode Island, even after the first gradual emancipation law passed because Rhode Island citizens still engaged in the African slave trade between 1780 and 1807.[25] It seems apparent that Newport Gardner and other enslaved blacks appreciated Hopkins's antislavery advocacy, but the church's position on this issue did not grant First Church a monopoly of black congregants since many black people also attended the Episcopal and Baptist churches of this city.

In an ironic coincidence, Lemuel Haynes became the first black man ordained as a Congregational minister during the same period that black participation in Congregational churches declined. Haynes was born in West Hartford, Connecticut, in 1753. A fellow minister wrote an 1837 biography and stated that Haynes was a "coloured man, his father being of unmingled African extraction, and his mother a white woman of respectable ancestry in New-England." At five months old, one or both of his parents took him to Granville, Massachusetts. As was common for black children in New England, white authorities bound Haynes as a servant until age twenty-one and placed him in the house of David Rose, a deacon at the local Congregational church. Like many black people in white colonial households, Haynes participated in family religious devotions and attended church. Farmwork and household labors occupied much of his early life. As a servant, he was "obliged to labour hard through the day." As a young adult, perhaps after the death of Mrs. Rose, Haynes experienced a sense of conviction for his sins and a hope for salvation. Soon thereafter, Reverend Jonathan Huntington baptized him, and Haynes joined the East (First) Granville Congregational Church.[26]

The Revolutionary period was characterized by Haynes's active pursuit of freedom and his development as a Congregational minister, including preaching to whites. At the close of his indenture, in 1774, Haynes enlisted as a minuteman, and after fighting broke out in 1775, he joined the army in Roxbury for the siege of Boston. He traveled with General Henry Knox's expedition to Ticonderoga to bring the artillery pieces that eventually drove the British from Boston. After this military service, Haynes returned to Granville, farmed, and began to consider a religious vocation. Based on his personal study of theology, he gave a sermon to the Rose family, and their reception of his sermon encouraged his pursuit of the ministry. Haynes also wrote an essay in the mid-1770s titled "Liberty Further Extended: Or free thoughts on the illegality of Slave-keeping." This essay criticized slavery on both religious and political grounds, in a similar fashion to the antislavery critiques written by contemporaries such as Samuel Hopkins. According to his early biographer, "It became known that he possessed uncommon gifts in prayer and exhortation; and, the parish being destitute of a minister, he was frequently called upon to read approved sermons, and to lead in the devotional exercises of the house of God." Even before his formal training, Haynes was taking a public role in his predominantly white church.[27]

In 1779, Haynes began his professional education and his long career ministering to predominantly white congregations by studying Latin and theology with Reverend Daniel Farrand in Canaan, Connecticut. After mastering Latin with Farrand, all along paying his way with farm labor, he studied Greek with Reverend William Bradford in Wintonbury, Connecticut, while working as a school teacher. On "Nov. 29th, 1780, several ministers of high respectability 'having examined him in the languages and sciences, and with respect to his knowledge of the doctrines of the gospel, and practical and experiential religion, recommended him as qualified to preach the gospel.'" In the following year, a new church was organized in Granville (Middle Granville), Massachusetts, and Haynes was invited to supply their pulpit. According to Cooley, "all classes and ages were carried away with the sweet, animated eloquence" of Haynes's preaching. He continued as their preacher for five years and within that period married Elizabeth Babbit. Haynes was formally ordained as a minister on November 9, 1785, with the support of the Granville congregation. He then served as a minister—preaching and administering the sacraments—in Torrington, Connecticut, for about two years, and he went on preaching tours of Vermont. In 1788, Haynes accepted the invitation to become pastor of the West Church in Rutland, Vermont. He served this "white" congregation for three decades.[28] The frontispiece from his 1837 biography (figure 4.1) depicts Haynes as a respectable and resilient New England minister. Although many Congregational churches included black congregants since the 1730s and whites occasionally heard black men and women exhort in Congregational churches during the 1740s and 1750s, it was only after

FIGURE 4.1. Reverend Lemuel Haynes. Frontispiece from
Timothy Mather Cooley, *Sketches of the Life and Character of the Rev. Lemuel Haynes, for Many Years Pastor
of a Church in Rutland, VT, and Late in Granville, NY*
(New-York: Harper & Brothers, 1837).

the Revolutionary War that some whites listened to the preaching of a
black Congregational minister.

Blacks participated in most of New England's Anglican/Episcopal
churches between 1777 and 1790. As they had done before the war, some
Anglican priests baptized and catechized more free and enslaved blacks
than any other Protestant denomination in northern cities. At least thirteen Anglican parishes in New England baptized multiple black people
between 1777 and 1790, whereas fifteen had done so between 1764 and
1776. These churches included black people despite the war's disruptions
and the church's lack of a denomination-wide antislavery stance. Some

black people valued their connections to these churches because of satisfying spiritual worship and for the educational opportunities that they made available.[29] In one Episcopal parish, the ability to network with other black people seems to have made the church especially appealing.

Some individual Anglicans and a few Anglican ministers opposed slavery or the slave trade, but neither individual churches nor the denomination explicitly opposed slavery. The main Anglican missionary organization, the SPG, had helped propagate a proslavery Christianity across the British Empire by the 1760s and owned a plantation and hundreds of slaves on Barbados. Some Episcopalians, like other Christians, slowly moved away from slaveholding by individually freeing their slaves, and many Episcopalian priests retained their long-standing desire to include blacks within their churches, but these two trends were not necessarily connected. The Anglican minister Samuel Andrews in Wallingford, Connecticut, in a July 1775 sermon questioned whether holding slaves was consistent with the pursuit of political liberty, but he was a Tory during the Revolution, and few other clerics openly condemned slavery.[30]

Many black Bostonians decided to affiliate with Trinity Episcopal Church over other churches after 1776. While Christ Church and King's Chapel were closed temporarily after the British evacuation, Trinity remained open because Reverend Samuel Parker did not leave with the British and was willing to omit prayers for the king. Trinity had by far the greatest number of black baptisms of any Boston church both before and after the British occupation of the city, but its share of the city's black baptisms grew substantially after the occupation. Of fourteen Boston churches, nearly 68 percent of all black baptisms between 1777 and 1790 occurred at Trinity Church. Although the records do not always or consistently include racial notations, it is clear that at least twenty-one blacks (ten male and eleven female) were baptized there between 1764 and 1776 and at least forty-six (twenty-one females and twenty-five males) were baptized there between 1777 and 1790. Trinity Church in this period included economic, occupational, and racial diversity. Among the participants at Trinity Church were leaders of Boston's early black community, including Prince Watts, who owned a soap-making business, and George Middleton.[31]

George Middleton and his family affiliated with Trinity Episcopal Church between 1777 and 1790, and according to oral tradition, he was a commander of a unit of black soldiers known as the Bucks of America that functioned as a home guard during the Revolution. John Hancock presented this group with a flag sometime during his governorship

(1780–85). Middleton was also a black Mason, and he was the third Grand Master of Boston's African Lodge. Middleton, along with Lodge founder Prince Hall, petitioned for a school to be opened for black children in Boston at the turn of the century and advocated for equal rights for blacks.[32] George Middleton married Elsey Marsh on March 11, 1781, at Trinity Church. He was baptized there in 1781 and his wife, Elsey (aka Alice), was baptized in 1782. Their three children were baptized between 1783 and 1786. Prince Hall may have attended Trinity Church in the 1780s because his name appeared as the sponsor or godparent at four baptisms of black people. The role of godparent was consistent with the other ways that Hall was a leader in this community. Part of the appeal of Trinity Church for black Bostonians may have been its concentration of community leaders and other black people. It was a church where blacks could network together and with a wider cross-section of Boston society.[33]

Trinity Church in Newport, Rhode Island, exemplified the experiences of Anglican churches in New England during the war and how black people continued to affiliate with them. The British armed forces took Newport without meeting much resistance in December 1776. During the occupation, services continued at Trinity Church, but some of its members fled the city. In 1777, twenty people were baptized at Trinity, including one black man. The British army withdrew from Newport in October 1779, and Reverend George Bisset left with them. After being reorganized, Trinity Episcopal Church baptized more black people, but it took years for the church to rebound. Between 1780 and 1785, there were relatively few baptisms at Trinity Church as the congregation slowly regained members. There were only three black baptisms between 1780 and 1785, but the church lacked a settled pastor until 1786, when Reverend James Sayre was installed. Between 1786 and 1790, twenty-two blacks were baptized at Trinity. Also, Phoebe, a "Mulat or Indian, Daughter of Jane Thurstin," was baptized. With a settled minister again, black affiliation with Trinity Church increased, thereby continuing the long-standing allegiance that black people felt toward the Anglican/Episcopal church in that city.[34]

During the Revolutionary era, black participation in the Baptist churches of New England increased more substantially than during any previous era, and churches' outreach to black people better accounts for this increase than Baptist antislavery politics. In the sample of churches from 1777 to 1790, nine predominantly white Baptist churches in New England included multiple black members (up from four between 1764 and 1776).[35] The increase in black participation in Baptist churches during the Revolutionary era was not limited to northern Baptist churches. For example, the Baptist church of Welsh Neck, South Carolina, was founded in 1738, but it did not include any African American members until 1779. Baptist churches across America evangelized black people more frequently after the 1760s. Black members were often small minorities in northern Baptist churches, but the trend toward greater inclusion is clear. The Seventh Day Baptist Church of Newport, Rhode Island, for example, included only five black members by 1784, but these five people accounted for a little more than 10 percent of the total membership.[36]

By 1790 New England Baptists had begun to take antislavery positions, but it does not appear that the rise in black participation in Baptist churches during the 1770s and 1780s can usually be tied to white pronouncements against slavery. The Baptist preacher Ebenezer Smith from Ashfield, Massachusetts, made strong statements against slavery by 1773 and lay Baptist exhorter James Allen urged abolition, but few other New England Baptists spoke out against slavery until the late 1780s. The prominent Baptist leader Isaac Backus did not speak out against slavery until nearly the end of his life. Like other Christians, the early antislavery Baptists linked opposition to slavery to the Revolutionary calls for freedom from British oppression, but it took longer for most Baptists to directly oppose slavery and the slave trade.[37]

Near the end of the 1780s, after prominent Baptist churches included more black members, Baptist Associations and more individual Baptists spoke out against slavery. In 1787 the Warren Association, which was the general organization among New England Baptists, took a stand against the slave trade. The Association, however, did not take a stand against slavery itself in this period. The Association in 1787 approved the following statement:

> Notwithstanding the great expense of blood and treasure during the late war, to ward off slavery from ourselves, we are informed, that in various parts of this country many have recurred to the horrid practice of sending our shipping to Africa, to bring from thence the natives and to sell them as slaves in the West-Indies: And as man stealing is a capital crime by the law of God–see Deut. Xxiv.7—I Tim. i.10–we, therefore, earnestly desire all our brethren to guard against giving the least countenance to that heaven-daring wickedness.[38]

The Warren Association recognized the inconsistency of slave trading with the principles of the American Revolution, and they called slave trading a sin based on passages from Deuteronomy and First Timothy. The Association did not demand emancipation for slaves currently held in bondage in New England.

While the war disrupted some Baptist churches, it also provided a unique opportunity for a few black Baptists. The Second Baptist Church of Richmond, Rhode Island, was founded in November 1774, and nearly two years later, "Frank, a negro," was received as a member. Frank, like other black people during the Revolution, saw an opportunity to obtain freedom after the commencement of hostilities. He ran away from slavery in 1778, and the church "suspended [him] for leaving his master and joining the British troops in Newport, our enemy, July 11, 1778." The majority of white Baptists in New England supported the Revolution, but this black Baptist saw greater hope for liberty with the British army. His actions mirror the thousands of former slaves in the South and in New York who sought freedom by fighting for Britain.[39]

Numerous Baptist churches were founded in the latter decades of the eighteenth century, and some of these new Baptist churches included black members. The First Baptist Church of North Kingstown, Rhode Island, was organized in November 1782, and at least a couple of black men were included among the founding members. The list of twelve men and twenty women, who were original members of this North Kingstown church, does not include racial notations, but the names of two members, Cuffee Congdon and Cudjo Selvis, suggest African ancestry. As the Baptist denomination grew in New England, it also tended to become more interracial.[40]

Churches that began admitting blacks during the 1760s or 1770s often continued to do so during the war and into the 1780s. Seventeen black people joined the First Baptist Church of Providence, Rhode Island, between 1770 and 1776, and three more people identified as black joined between 1789 and 1790, including William Ceaser, who was an Afro-Narragansett. "Yochy Fenner, & Sambo" were members of a Baptist church in Smithfield until they transferred their membership by letter to First Baptist Providence. They were both born in Africa and were formerly slaves of John Fenner of Smithfield, Rhode Island. The white leaders and members of First Baptist Providence took their responsibility for shepherding black members seriously, and they used the church discipline process to try to encourage godly living and unity within the church. The congregation may have helped mediate relationships between slaves or servants and their masters or employers. In 1785, the church reported, without more detailed, "that the difficulty that had Subsisted between our Black Sister Philis Bowen & Her mistress appeared to have been fully settled." Disputes between black and white people fell within the purview of the church's concern.[41]

Baptists' views on slavery seemed to be congruent with the general antislavery opinions that developed in New England during the Revolutionary era and, in most cases, antislavery views were not a determinant factor in causing the rise in black affiliation with Baptist churches. Black people within Baptist churches, however, may have helped push Baptists toward antislavery views. The increase in black participation in the First Baptist Church of Providence, which began in the early 1770s, likely influenced Reverend James Manning's adoption of antislavery principles. The First Baptist Church's meeting minutes record no statements about slavery before the 1850s. Of pew owners, 40 out of 131 were slaveholders in 1775, and Manning owned three slaves. Ownership of slaves fell sharply after the Revolution, and in 1790, only one or two pew owners at this church still owned slaves. In 1784, Manning freed his last slave and joined the Providence Society for Promoting the Abolition of Slavery, founded in part by Moses Brown, who had been a Baptist but joined the Society of Friends in 1774. Black participation started and grew at First Baptist Providence before Manning or this church spoke or acted against slavery, so the early black members may have helped influence Manning's adoption of antislavery principles in the 1780s.[42]

Blacks also participated in both the First and Second Baptist churches of Boston, Massachusetts, for the first time, thereby increasing the variety of interracial churches in Boston. First Baptist Church had admitted two black people between 1772 and 1773, and it admitted another three by 1790. Second Baptist Church did not admit any black people between 1764 and 1776, but three were admitted to the membership there by 1790, including a black woman named Chloe Spear.[43]

Chloe Spear was born in Africa and, like Phillis Wheatley, was kidnapped and made a slave while still a child. Spear was brought to Boston via Philadelphia, and likely became the slave of Captain John Bradford (her memoir only calls him Mr. B.). As related years later by a fellow member of the Second Baptist Church, Chloe's master took her to the Congregational church on Sundays, but Chloe "did not understand the preaching," and she engaged in "playing, eating nuts, &c." with other black people in the gallery during the service. Unlike Phillis Wheatley, Chloe Spear did not have an owner who sincerely endeavored to educate her, but she slowly learned to read. At this point, church attendance was an opportunity to socialize with other black people. During the

Revolution, Chloe's master moved his whole household out of Boston to the town of Andover, where she received some religious instruction from a Mr. Adams. When the family returned to Boston, Chloe joined the New North (Fifth) Congregational Church: "Chloe negro servant to Capt. John Bradford" became a member on February 2, 1777. Sometime after 1780, Chloe was considered free, but she continued as a servant in the Bradford household and married a man named Caesar Spear. She attended the New North Church, but some nights she also went to the evening services at Second Baptist Church. Chloe eventually became convinced of "the doctrine of believers' baptism by immersion," and Reverend Gair baptized and admitted her to the Second Baptist Church in 1788. She remained a member there until her death in 1815, and along with other black people.[44]

Although New England states committed themselves to an eventual end to slavery by 1785, the relationships between religiously motivated antislavery politics and black people's church affiliation should not be understood as a simplistic cause and effect. Black New Englanders routinely advocated for emancipation, and given their use of religious and political justification, they likely argued for abolition in churches as well as in other places of public discourse. But black New Englanders had other spiritual and temporal goals—not to mention long-standing habits and still circumvented freedom—that influenced their religious choices sometimes more than antislavery politics.

Mid-Atlantic Churches

Excepting the Methodists, most Mid-Atlantic churches did not take public stands against slavery before they experienced a growth in black members. Throughout the Revolutionary War and into the 1780s, in many locations, pastors and laypeople sought out (or at least allowed) black people to affiliate with their churches. Black people in Mid-Atlantic cities had multiple church options available to them, and they chose to attend or affiliate with several denominations, including ones that countenanced slavery. As a result, black attendees and members were found in Reformed, Presbyterian, Lutheran, Anglican/Episcopal, Baptist, and Methodist churches between 1777 and 1790. There remained barriers to black affiliation in some congregations, including stringent requirements for baptism and the opposition of some masters, but an increase in black affiliation with Mid-Atlantic churches occurred during the Revolutionary era and accelerated after 1790.

Mid-Atlantic states had substantially more slaves than did New England ones, and New York and New Jersey were much slower to enact gradual emancipation laws than were other northern states. To most enslaved black people, the way that slavery ended in Mid-Atlantic states was a disappointing betrayal of America's Revolutionary principals. Pennsylvania, in 1780, became the first northern state to enact a gradual emancipation bill. Pennsylvania's law stipulated that the male and female children of enslaved women born after the law's passage were indentured until age twenty-eight (this act fully freed no one until 1808). This period of indenture differed little from slavery because whites continued to control the most productive years of black people's lives, and some masters sold black people into perpetual slavery elsewhere. But, the free black population of the Mid-Atlantic grew after the 1770s, especially as some slaveholders voluntarily emancipated their slaves. The New York legislature voted in 1781 to free blacks who had served in the American army, but New York did not institute a gradual emancipation bill until 1799. New Jersey did not pass a gradual emancipation bill until 1804; all earlier legislative attempts failed, and slaves could still be imported into New Jersey until 1786.[45]

When gradual emancipation laws were enacted, legislators from all types of Christian denominations joined together to provide the necessary votes. A coalition of people from different denominations secured the passage of Pennsylvania's 1780 gradual emancipation bill: nineteen Presbyterian legislators supported emancipation while eleven opposed the bill; one German Lutheran supported it while four opposed it; one German Reformed legislator supported emancipation while three opposed it; three Episcopalians supported gradual emancipation while two opposed it; and, finally, two Baptists and a French Huguenot supported the emancipation bill.[46]

Mid-Atlantic denominations commonly had both proslavery and antislavery members, so most denominations remained silent on the issue of slavery even as slaveholding diminished over time. Most churches and denominations allowed members to own slaves well into the nineteenth century, but the number of slave-owning members often decreased between 1775 and 1790. Philadelphia's Presbyterians dropped from 55 slave owners to 21 by 1790, and Philadelphia's Episcopalians dropped from 118 slave owners to 75 by 1790. For these Presbyterians and Episcopalians, freeing slaves was an individual's decision. These churches did not publicly encourage emancipation. Nevertheless, more free and enslaved blacks were baptized at Anglican/Episcopal churches than at any other type of church in Philadelphia and elsewhere. No denomination in Pennsylvania with black members, except for the Methodists, had a strong antislavery message, so the black people who affiliated with the Episcopal, Presbyterian, Baptist, and Lutheran churches did so irrespective of the churches' official stance on slavery. Some individual black people leveraged church affiliation in their pursuit of liberty, but the connection between abolitionist politics and church affiliation in these churches was tenuous.[47]

Black people participated in a greater number of the Dutch Reformed churches between 1777 and 1790 than in previous decades, and they continued their participation in some of the Presbyterian churches that began admitting blacks in the 1760s. The number of black baptisms in Presbyterian and Dutch Reformed churches remained very small compared to the black population of the Mid-Atlantic and compared to the number of churches that did not baptize blacks, but some black people affiliated in these churches in search spiritual fulfillment, education, and social connections. From the sample of churches in this study, five Presbyterian churches baptized two or more blacks between 1777 and 1790; in contrast, six Presbyterian churches did so between 1764 and 1776, and only one Presbyterian church did so between 1750 and 1763.[48] At least eight Dutch Reformed churches baptized multiple black people in these years, whereas just two German Reformed and two Dutch Reformed churches did so between 1763 and 1776. Overall, a small but evident expansion of interracial religious experiences occurred in Reformed churches of the Mid-Atlantic, which was the inverse of the pattern that existed among New England's Congregational churches.[49]

The slight rise in black participation in Dutch Reformed churches was not tied to any changes in white people's attitudes toward slavery, which did not noticeably change in the eighteenth century. Neither denominational nor congregational organs spoke out against slavery or the slave trade. Lay leaders and ministers continued to own enslaved blacks, including Reverends Simeon Van Arsdale and Peter Studdiford. Dutch Reformed Christians were certainly not on the vanguard of the budding northern antislavery movement.[50]

Nevertheless, some Dutch Reformed churches became more open to black congregants. While Dutch Reformed churches did not much alter their support of slavery, there was a slight change in these Christians' attitudes toward black people after 1776. One cause of this change likely came from abroad. In 1779, the Classis of Amsterdam, the Reformed church governing body directly responsible for the congregations in

America, wrote to overseas congregations to encourage Christians to instruct enslaved people in their households about Christianity and when appropriate to baptize them. As with similar statements from other denominations, the Classis noted that baptism and conversion do not release slaves from service to their master or mistress.[51] These instructions likely influenced some Reformed Christians in America, and in the subsequent years, Reformed pastors in America took additional steps to make their churches more accessible to black people. In 1783, church leaders in America addressed a question regarding the admission of slaves to church membership. At the denominational meeting, they asked "whether the consent of masters and mistresses is necessary to slave's uniting with the church." The ministers indicated that consent was not biblically required, as "the Scriptures make no such condition," but they believed it would be prudent and "proper to consult masters as to the character of the slave, and seek to preserve the peace of the household." The ministers also agreed that marriages recognized by enslaved men and women (but not officially conducted by clergy) should not be a barrier to church admittance.[52] These decisions indicate that Dutch churches had begun addressing *how* enslaved men and women should be included in their churches, not *whether* they should be included.

The Reformed Dutch Church of New York City was one of the Mid-Atlantic churches that became more diverse after the British evacuated the city in 1783. This congregation, later known as the Collegiate Church, consisted of three church buildings after 1769. No baptism records exist for this church between October 1776 and July 1780. Between five and seven black persons were baptized by this Reformed church between 1783 and 1790. In September 1783, Catharina, daughter of "Abraham & Nell, Servant," was baptized. It seems highly probable that they were black people. Additionally, five black adults were baptized and presumably admitted to this church, including Ponetta, "an adult negro woman" who was baptized "upon the confession of her faith."[53] The Dutch Reformed Church of New York City, like some of the other Reformed churches, began to include black members during the Revolutionary era.

In 1786, Mid-Atlantic Presbyterians also moved toward making access to baptism and church admittance more routine and possible for enslaved black children. Before the church's governing body, church elders debated "whether Christian masters, or mistresses, ought in duty, to have such children baptized as are under their care, though born of parents not in the communion of any Christian church?" This question was directed to the conditions of enslaved black children. The Synod concluded that "Christian masters and mistresses, whose religious professions and conduct are such as to give them a right to the ordinance of baptism for their own children, may and ought to dedicate the children of their household to God, in that ordinance, when they have no scruple of conscience to the contrary."[54] This decision made baptism of black children easier because enslaved and indentured children could now be baptized on the authority of masters, even if the child's parents were not church members. Congregational, Anglican, and Lutheran churches had come to this same conclusion decades earlier. Presbyterians in the 1780s made changes to how baptisms were administered and thereby made this rite more accessible to black children.

Most Presbyterians, much like the Dutch Reformed churches, did not promote antislavery activism. A few Presbyterian ministers adopted antislavery positions in the 1770s, including New Jersey Presbyterian minister Jacob Green, who denounced slavery in 1776 on both religious and political grounds. By 1782, Green's congregation prohibited members from owning slaves, but it remained the only Presbyterian congregation to enact such a rule in this era. Physician Benjamin Rush, a lay leader at Philadelphia's Second Presbyterian Church until 1788, when he became Episcopalian, also published early statements against slavery. However, it seems that most Presbyterians did not speak out against slavery, and the denomination was slow and conservative in taking a stand against this injustice.[55]

In 1787, the Synod of New York and Philadelphia resolved that they did "highly approve of the general principles in favour of universal liberty that prevail in America and the interest which many of the states have taken in promoting the abolition of slavery." However, they also worried that moving people "from a servile state to a participation of all the privileges of civil society without education and without previous habits of industry may be in many respects dangerous to the community." They therefore suggested that masters "give those persons who are at present held in servitude such good education as to prepare them for the better enjoyment of freedom" and to allow some slaves to earn money for procuring "their own liberty at a moderate rate that thereby they may be brought into society with those habits of industry that may render them useful citizens." In essence, they believed that blacks were not prepared for liberty and were not accustomed to "industry." These Presbyterians suggested measures that were, in some ways, more conservative than the gradual emancipation laws enacted seven years earlier in Pennsylvania. As a denomination, Presbyterians were not advocates for immediate emancipation, but they began to make access to the sacraments easier for black people. The knowledge that black people would eventually gain freedom may have encouraged some Presbyterians to invite black people to participate in their churches as a way to "prepare them for the better enjoyment of freedom."[56]

In the late 1770s and 1780s, the number of black baptisms in Philadelphia's and New York City's Presbyterians churches increased. In Philadelphia, First Presbyterian, Second Presbyterian, and Scots Presbyterian churches baptized small numbers of black people during these years. First Presbyterian Church, which apparently did not baptize any blacks in the colonial period, baptized two black people in 1780 and 1781: "Neptune Turell a mulatto man about 23 years old" and "George, a negro child, son of Robert and Phillis Boardley." Neptune Turell was probably admitted as a church member when baptized, and at least one of George's parents was likely a church member at the time of his baptism. Second Presbyterian baptized five black people.[57] At the Scots Presbyterian Church, founded in 1766, one black child was baptized. The pastor wrote: "Isaaec Worley Till son to Hannah a fre Nigroe woman in full Communion with the Church was born in Gen: Washington's Camp Valey Forge nineteen months ago & baptized on this 4th Sabbath of Augt 1779." Hannah, a free black woman and a member of the Scots Presbyterian Church, likely fled Philadelphia during the British occupation and sought employment with the Continental troops at Valley Forge, where her son was born. They returned to Philadelphia after the British left, and her child was baptized in the reopened church. Likewise, on November 26, 1783, the First Presbyterian Church of New York City "was collected, by return of the Rev. Dr. Rodgers and the exiled people, after a dispersion of seven years two months and twelve days." Between 1785 and 1790, two black men and three black women were baptized by the First Presbyterian Church in New York City.[58] As Presbyterian churches moved toward making access to baptism and church membership more accessible, small numbers of free and enslaved blacks affiliated with these churches.

Lutheran churches had been theologically and practically open to baptizing blacks for a long time (see chapter 1), and some Lutheran churches baptized black people during and after the war. Within my sample of churches, between 1764 and 1776, six Lutheran churches baptized multiple blacks. Between 1777 and 1790, seven Lutheran congregations did so, including ones in New York City, Albany, Brunswick, Claverack, and Athens, New York, and churches in Gloucester County, New Jersey, and Stouchsburg, Pennsylvania.[59] Other Lutheran churches baptized only a single black person in this period. Along with the other churches, Lutheran congregations were places of interracial worship in the Mid-Atlantic.[60]

New York City's Lutheran churches baptized some black people both during and after the British occupation. Trinity Lutheran Church, which had Dutch roots and was predominantly Loyalist, baptized three black men and three black women during the occupation even though the church's building was destroyed in 1776. The black people who participated in this congregation were likely Loyalists, but they reflected a diversity of background: Jack Genette, who was "a negro man working in Col. Grouts artillery," had a son baptized in 1778. Richard Bratison, who was "guinea born," and Jenny, his wife, were the sponsors for the baptism of Charlotte, the daughter of "John Midler and Diana, his wife, Mulatto." The daughter of John Mosson and Sarah, his wife, who were "Mulattos from Virginia," was baptized in 1783. John Mosson may have been one of the three hundred blacks, members of the Ethiopian Regiment, sent to New York from Virginia by Lord Dunmore. Many New York City Lutherans left when the British evacuated (three thousand black Loyalists left New York City with the British too). The remaining Lutherans from both Trinity Dutch Lutheran and Christ German Lutheran churches united in 1784 under the pastorate of Johann Christophe Kunze. In this reorganized Lutheran church, at least one black person was baptized between 1784 and 1790.[61]

As they had done for many decades previous, black people participated in the urban Anglican/Episcopal churches of the Mid-Atlantic between 1777 and 1790, even though these churches did not directly advocate for emancipation. In New York City and Philadelphia, Anglican/Episcopal priests routinely baptized and catechized free and enslaved blacks. Episcopal churches at Hempstead, Long Island; Swedesboro and Trenton, New Jersey; and Lancaster, Pennsylvania, also baptized multiple blacks. New parishes and old ones alike included blacks, thereby making the Church of England and Protestant Episcopal Church among the most interracial of denominations in Mid-Atlantic states.[62]

When British troops withdrew from a given location, Anglican churches often reopened with new independence-leaning leaders, and they ministered to black and white congregants. After the British army abandoned Philadelphia, Patriot-leaning members reorganized Christ Church Philadelphia, and they made William White, the only Anglican minister left in the city, the rector. Christ Church's building was largely intact after the war, and Reverend White ministered to numerous black

Philadelphians. Seventy black people, forty-three females and twenty-seven males, were baptized at the Episcopal churches of Philadelphia between 1777 and 1790. The Episcopal Church, as had been the case in all previous periods, baptized more blacks than any other denomination in Philadelphia.[63]

Trinity Anglican/Episcopal Church ministered to black people not only while New York City was under British rule but also after Americans regained control in 1783. Fire destroyed New York's Trinity Church buildings in 1776, but services were held elsewhere. Although the baptismal records do not uniformly include racial notations, at least fourteen (but perhaps more) blacks were baptized at Trinity Anglican Church between 1776 and the British evacuation in November 1783. Some of the black people who sought freedom for themselves and their families among the British troops attended Trinity Church. Despite the war, this church's longtime focus on educating, proselytizing, and baptizing black people continued. After the British evacuation, Reverend Samuel Provoost became rector. Under his leadership, at least twenty-six black people were baptized at Trinity Church or its chapels by 1790, and the school for blacks was restarted in 1787. Some laypeople at this church were important public advocates for ending slavery, including James Duane, John Jay, Robert Troup, Matthew Clarkson, Alexander Hamilton, and others members of the New York Manumission Society (some of these men continued to own slaves but publicly called for legislative and private actions to end slavery). But, the actions of individual Anglicans/Episcopalians in support of emancipation followed behind the long-term affiliation of black people at this church and not vice versa.[64]

As the Episcopal Church expanded after the war, so did black participation. In 1789, Robert Ayres, who had been a Methodist itinerant, was ordained by Episcopal Bishop William White. After his ordination, Ayres traveled to western Pennsylvania, where he served the scattered Episcopalian settlers near Pittsburgh. In August and September 1789, Ayres baptized seventeen black people in and around Brownsville, Pennsylvania. As Episcopal churches spread into the backcountry and out of large cities, they also sought to incorporate black people into their religious communities.[65]

Some Mid-Atlantic Baptists opposed the slave trade or slavery starting in the 1770s, but not all did so. As was the case with New England Baptists, the connection between black affiliation and churches' stances on slavery was not always evident. In the sample of congregations, between 1777 and 1790, four Baptist churches admitted multiple black people to membership, whereas three did so between 1764 and 1776.[66] Baptist opposition to the slave trade was more widespread than commitments to universal emancipation. Reverend William Rogers of Philadelphia served as a vice president of the Pennsylvania Society for Promoting the Gradual Emancipation of Slavery, and some other Baptists voiced their distaste for slavery. The Philadelphia Baptist Association in 1789 approved a resolution in favor of gradual abolition, which indicated "their high approbation of the several societies formed in the United States and Europe, for the gradual abolition of the slavery of the Africans, and for guarding against their being detained or sent off as slaves, after having obtained liberty; and do hereby recommend to the churches we represent to form similar societies, to become members thereof, and exert themselves to obtain this important object."[67] This statement against slavery dates from roughly nine years after Pennsylvania legislators passed their gradual emancipation bill. Given the relative mildness of this statement ("gradual abolition") and its date of approval, it does not seem that an antislavery stance was the direct cause of black participation in Baptist churches during the 1770s and 1780s.[68]

The number of free and enslaved black members increased at the First Baptist Church of New York City between 1784 and 1790, despite the fact that the church did not oppose slavery, and some congregants continued to own slaves. This church, organized in 1762, admitted its first black member in 1775, but the church was dispersed for nearly eight years. Between 1783 and 1790, eight black people were admitted as members of this church. Four appear to have been free, including "Fanny a black woman [who] was received in the Church on profession of her faith the 5th September 1784 having been baptized in London by Mr. Martin." The black men and women who joined this church underwent the same requirements for membership as whites, including "the imposition of hands." For example, when "Charity, a black woman," was received in 1787, she was baptized along with six white people. Afterward, some members of the church accepted them into the church by praying for them with hands placed on the new members. This church did not take any stand against slavery until 1808, and at least a couple of people remained slaveholding members of this church until 1819. The addition of black members, which accelerated after 1790, was not likely caused by antislavery statements.[69]

Finally, it is important to consider the Methodists, who did adopt a denomination-wide antislavery position. In Methodist societies and classes, blacks were regular participants as congregants, members, and even as preachers. Organized Methodism arrived in the northern colonies in the 1760s, and its British character put it at a cultural disadvantage during the war. However, the relentless energy of its itinerant ministers enabled Methodists to regain losses and expand dramatically after 1783. Methodist meetings were often interracial because Methodists disavowed slavery and deliberately sought to include blacks in their meetings. With the growth of Methodism came a substantial growth in interracial churches in Mid-Atlantic states.

Methodists were second only to Quakers in their vocal and official stances against slavery, and their stand against slavery was one prominent factor that made Methodism appealing to some black people. Unlike most Quakers, however, Methodists regularly sought after and accepted blacks into their religious meetings and societies. John Wesley condemned slavery in the 1770s, and in April 1780, the conference of Methodist preachers in America acknowledged "that slavery is contrary to the laws of God, man, and nature, and hurtful to society, contrary to the dictates of conscience and pure religion, and doing that which we would not others should do to us and ours." They also advised that all their "friends who keep slaves" should free them, and they required all traveling preachers who owned slaves to make promises to free them. In 1784, the annual conference took further steps to end slaveholding among its members and ministers by suspending ministers who would not emancipate their slaves (in states where emancipation was allowed by law) and by allowing for the possibility that Methodist members who purchased slaves could be expelled. Statements at the denomination level did not mean that Methodists were uniformly opposed to slavery. Some northern Methodists continued to own slaves, and Methodists eventually dropped their official opposition to slaveholding. Nevertheless, these policies put the Methodists on the vanguard of religious opposition to slavery during the Revolutionary era.[70]

When Methodist membership levels began to pick up rapidly after 1780, many blacks made Methodist worship services into interracial events. Numerous new Methodist societies and classes were organized during the 1780s, and both blacks and whites affiliated in growing numbers. The Methodist Episcopal Church became a distinct denomination in 1785 with Reverend Francis Asbury as the bishop. In 1786, for the first time, the annual convention publication listed numbers of black and white Methodists separately. New York listed 178 white and 25 black Methodists. Long Island listed 146 white and eight black Methodists.[71] In 1787, the Methodist conference articulated what had been its long-standing practice regarding the inclusion of black people. Regarding the "spiritual welfare of the coloured people," the conference required "all our Ministers and Preachers . . . to leave nothing undone for the spiritual benefit and salvation of them, within their respective circuits, or district; and for this purpose to embrace every opportunity of inquiring into the state of their souls, and to unite in society those who appear to have a real desire of fleeing from the wrath to come, to meet such in class, and to exercise the whole Methodist discipline among them."[72] Numerous preachers followed this admonition, and by 1790, most Mid-Atlantic Methodist societies included black members (see table 4.1). Formal church membership, of course, did not account for the full extent of black participation within the Methodist movement. Many more black people heard Methodist preachers and attended Methodist meetings without officially joining. Since Methodist itinerants preached not only in cities and churches but also on rural farms and in private households, black people across the Mid-Atlantic had abundant opportunities to hear the Methodist gospel. While not accounting for all levels of participation in churches, the official members' lists show that Methodism was an interracial religious movement that greatly expanded the number of mixed-race religious settings.[73]

In New York City, both during the war and after, the John Street Methodist Church included black people, and it had significantly high numbers of black members by 1790. Weekly class meetings were usually segregated, especially after 1786, but black and white Methodists attended Sunday services together. Peter Williams Sr. continued his affiliation with the John Street Church and became their sexton (see figure 4.2). The man who owned him, Mr. Aymar, was a Loyalist who left New York with the British. As a result of Williams's initiation, the trustees of John Street Methodist Church purchased Williams in June 1783 for forty pounds, and they immediately employed him as church sexton. Williams began making payments to the trustees to gain his freedom, which he obtained in November 1785. Williams also worked as a tobacconist, and his wife, Mary, worked as a cook in the church parsonage. His path to freedom was unusual, but Peter and Mary were hardly the only black members of this Methodist church, and they were not the only black people to leverage church affiliation for practical benefits.[74]

The Methodist Church in New York offered a spiritual environment that was especially appealing to black women, who swelled the black membership levels to a substantial proportion. In 1786, the church's preacher reported that the New York City Methodist Church included

TABLE 4.1. Examples of Methodist societies and number of white and black members, 1790

Methodist society circuit locations	Number of white members	Number of black members	Percentage of black members
Philadelphia, Pa.	214	24	10.1
Chester, Pa.	317	9	2.7
Bristol, Pa.	53	7	11.7
Huntingdon, Pa.	190	4	2.1
Pittsburgh, Pa.	97	0	0.0
Burlington, N.J.	353	12	3.3
Trenton, N.J.	429	33	7.1
Salem, N.J.	933	21	2.2
Elizabeth, N.J.	237	16	6.3
Flanders, N.J.	322	7	2.1
Long Island, N.Y.	268	9	3.2
New York, N.Y.	522	102	16.3
Newburgh, N.Y	324	8	2.4
Dutchess, N.Y.	405	5	1.2
Columbia, N.Y.	379	3	0.8
Albany, N.Y.	264	3	1.1
Litchfield, Conn.	66	1	1.5
New Haven, Conn.	9	0	0.0
Totals	5,382	264	4.7

Source: Minutes of the Methodist Conferences, vol. 1 (1813), 94–95.

178 whites and 25 blacks, but the number of black people proliferated in subsequent years. By 1790, New York's Methodists included 522 white members and 102 black members, most of whom were women. Black members comprised over 16 percent of the entire church membership. The black Methodist members in New York were roughly 70 percent female in 1786 and around 78 percent female by 1791. In 1790, the Methodist Church of New York City contained the highest percentage of black members by far of any predominantly white church

FIGURE 4.2. Peter Williams Sr. was an early African
American member of the John Street Methodist Church.
He bought his freedom by working as the church sexton.
The Miriam and Ira D. Wallach Division of Art, Prints and
Photographs: Print Collection, NYPL, *Peter Williams, the
Old Colored Sexton of the John St. Methodist Church*, Image
ID 431089, NYPL Digital Collections, http://digitalcollec-
tions.nypl.org/.

in the city and one of the highest percentages of black members of any
northern church.[75]

White Methodists often preached to black people, sometimes opposed
slavery, and occasionally listened to black preachers, but racial prejudice
still affected relations between white and black Methodists. Reverend
Francis Asbury and other white preachers traveled with Harry Hosier,

who was often known as "black Harry" and who served as a coachman for Asbury. Hosier's preaching extended from upstate New York down through southern states. He drew large crowds of listeners, but he was ordained only to the level of deacon. Asbury and Hosier first preached together in the South, and they traveled together to Philadelphia in September 1781. But as Asbury began to head back south, Hosier expressed an unwillingness to return to Virginia. Asbury wrote that "Harry seems to be unwilling to go with me: I fear his speaking so much to white people in the city has been, or will be, injurious; he has been flattered, and may be ruined." Methodists expressed the sort of paternalistic racism common among antislavery advocates and other "friends" of black men and women. In the same year that the Methodists took a stand against slavery, they also suggested that "proper white persons" ought to oversee "coloured" Methodists and that blacks should not "stay late and meet by themselves."[76] Even relatively egalitarian and progressive whites still expected deference from blacks within their churches.

Included among the Mid-Atlantic Methodists during the Revolutionary era was Reverend Richard Allen, who initially preached to interracial religious meetings and later founded the African Methodist Episcopal Church in Philadelphia. Born enslaved in 1760, he experienced many of the privations of slavery, including unrequited labor and separation from family members. He wrote little of his early life but said, "Slavery is a bitter pill." At age seventeen, in 1777, Allen heard a Methodist preacher, and he quickly converted. Allen wrote many years later that he "was awakened and brought to see myself, poor, wretched and undone, and without the mercy of God must be lost." After wavering between bouts of joy and despair, fluctuating from hope of salvation to a dread of condemnation, he experienced a spiritual rebirth: "Now my confidence was strengthened that the Lord, for Christ's sake, had heard my prayers and pardoned all my sins." He joined the Methodist class and went "from house to house, exhorting my old companions, and telling all around what a dear dear Saviour I had found."[77]

Allen and his brother began to participate in Methodist meetings and classes. They also utilized Methodism to convince their owner, Stokeley Sturgis, to allow them to purchase their freedom. They gradually persuaded Sturgis of the benefits of religion, the need for his own salvation, and the immorality of slavery. During the summer of 1779, Allen convinced Sturgis to allow Methodist meetings in his home, and preachers, including Asbury, delivered the gospel message there. By January 1780, Allen and his brother had an agreement that allowed them to work independently to buy their freedom. Allen had five years to pay two thousand dollars or sixty pounds, but he paid the price within three and a half years by hauling bricks, chopping wood, and other labors. After securing his freedom and a letter of introduction from Sturgis, Allen set out to preach the gospel.[78]

On September 3, 1783, Allen left Wilmington, Delaware, and headed into the New Jersey countryside to preach. Over the next three years, he worked to support himself and spent available time preaching to all who would listen as he traveled widely from New York down to South Carolina. He was well received by whites and blacks alike and even preached to Indians for two months. Allen followed a preaching trajectory similar to that of other Methodist itinerants, for he traveled widely to address large and small groups. In many of these locations, he joined white Methodist preachers, such as Benjamin Abbott and Joseph Budd. Regarding his time in Radnor, Pennsylvania, in 1784, Allen wrote that he preached "to a large congregation of different persuasions" and that "there were many souls cut to the heart." Near Lancaster, Pennsylvania, Allen also "had comfortable meetings with the Germans." Allen and other black Methodist preachers increased interracial religious worship throughout the Mid-Atlantic by preaching to all who would listen.[79]

In 1786, after being a circuit preacher for more than two years, Allen received an invitation from a Methodist elder in Philadelphia to come and to preach to the black people attending St. George's Methodist Church. Allen began holding a 5:00 a.m. service every day, and he often preached in the afternoon and evening. Soon, the number of black Methodists in Philadelphia grew, and Allen's work shifted away from promoting Methodism generally and toward promoting black Methodism. Sometimes Methodist classes, which functioned as the most intimate level of religious affiliation, were organized by demographic groupings, such as single women or single men. Methodists recognized that people could be effectively encouraged by people similar to themselves, and Allen began organizing classes and prayer meetings solely for black attendees at St. George's Church. By 1787, Allen proposed that he could encourage more black conversion to Methodism by creating a black Methodist church. However, other "blacks resisted Allen's overtures about a separate church," and white leaders at St. George's Church emphatically disapproved of Allen's idea. In the meantime, instead of a black church, Allen, Absalom Jones, and six other men formed the Free African Society, which was "a quasi-religious but nondenominational organization" that promoted the financial and educational development of black Philadelphians. Separate black churches were still a few years away. In the meantime, the expansion of interracial worship continued among Philadelphia's Methodists. In 1790, Philadelphia reported to the Annual Conference that their church included 215 whites and 24 blacks, so blacks accounted for a little more than 8 percent of the membership. According to Allen's account, a class or society of blacks at St. George's included forty-two members in 1786, and in these years, "many souls were awakened."[80]

Through hardships and conflict, the period of 1776 to 1790 ushered in tremendous changes to American society and government, including freedom for thousands of formerly enslaved African Americans. Despite the disruption caused by war and the establishment of a new nation, it became more prevalent than ever before for black people to affiliate with predominantly white Protestant churches. The expansion of Methodist congregations in the Mid-Atlantic was the most significant aspect of the expansion of interracial worship in this period, but other types of churches also sought out and baptized hundreds of black people who found appealing spiritual and temporal benefits from church affiliation. Whites also more often listened to black and Indian preachers, including Congregational minister Lemuel Haynes, Methodist preachers Richard Allen and Harry Hosier, and others. Viewed from the perspective of 1750, this expansion of interracial churches is quite remarkable, since only the Congregationalists and Anglicans uniformly included blacks during the 1740s and 1750s. Never before had so many types of churches, especially in Mid-Atlantic states, baptized and included black people as members. Precisely because the number of interracial churches rose between the 1760s and 1780s, the rise of separate black churches after 1790 was also a multifaceted process that included several denominations and different forms of Christianity. The variety of interracial churches during the Revolutionary era was a necessary precursor to the development of separate African American Episcopal, Methodist, Baptist, and Presbyterian churches during the Early Republic.

Black affiliation with predominantly white churches had a complicated relationship to the growth of antislavery sentiment and the slow decline of northern slavery. A remarkable number of white Christians, who had never before expressed qualms about slavery, began to call for the abolition of the slave trade and emancipation. While most churches and denominations had some members who held antislavery opinions, including Anglican and Presbyterian churches, the loudest calls for abolition among white people came from Quakers and Methodists and a vocal minority of Congregationalists and Baptists. One reason why many blacks were attracted to Methodism was its antislavery policies, but an antislavery position (or the lack thereof) was only one of several factors that blacks considered when making religious choices. Black people's affiliation with Baptist, Anglican, Lutheran, Reformed, and Presbyterian churches was usually not caused by a denominational antislavery stance. In most cases, the individuals in these groups who articulated antislavery beliefs did so in the late 1780s and after black participation levels had already risen.

Other factors besides antislavery politics proved critical for increasing black participation in these predominantly white churches. Reformed and Presbyterian churches amended their practices so baptism could be slightly more accessible to black people. Reformed churches made changes in response to the Classis of Amsterdam's instructions and their context of the Revolutionary era's calls for freedom and equality. Presbyterians began to baptize unfree children in households of white Christians, such as was commonly done by Anglicans, Congregationalists, and Lutherans. These denominations contained ministers who were attentive to the spiritual needs of black people in their communities, even if they did not advocate for their freedom. As had been the case in earlier eras, many blacks affiliated with the churches that offered them an education. As African Americans slowly gained freedom from slavery, they were also freer to make choices about religious affiliation.

What is at stake in this discussion of church affiliation and political abolitionism is the agency of black people and the authenticity of their religious beliefs. The black men and women affiliated with northern churches during the Revolutionary era were not two-dimensional historical actors whose decision-making process was deterministically driven by a pursuit of emancipation. Without a doubt, northern black people wanted freedom and fought for abolitionism. Moreover, they were disappointed that gradual emancipation bills did not spread freedom rapidly. Nevertheless, other constraints and goals also influenced their religious affiliation. Where did other black people worship? Which ministers offered to baptize their children and welcomed them to the communion table? Where could they attend classes or learn to read? What theology and liturgy felt the most satisfying or comforting? Which denomination had their master's or mistress's approval, or what church could help them find an employer? What church was still open after the destruction of the war?

These questions and other ones related to individual circumstances sometimes made decisions about church affiliation less predictable. Although the specific motives of many black northerners are often unrecoverable from the extant historical record, their actions speak and indicate that black people affiliated with many types of churches and not exclusively antislavery denominations.

5 / "To Restore Our Long Lost Race": The Rise of Separate Black Churches, 1791–1820

On July 17, 1794, a group of white ministers dedicated the "African Church of the City of Philadelphia," also known as the African Episcopal Church of St. Thomas. Reverend Samuel Magaw, rector of St. Paul's Episcopal Church, and Reverend James Abercrombie, of Christ Church and St. Peter's Church, officiated. In proud attendance were many black Philadelphians, including the trustees who founded the church and built its edifice: Absalom Jones, William White, William Gray, William Gardner, William Welcher, and Henry Stewart. Also present were "venerable clergy of almost every denomination, and a number of other very respectable citizens." Perhaps the crowd nodded in approval when Magaw stated that "slavery is a hard allotment" and that this church had a duty to show "compassionate love to your brethren, who are yet in darkness, or bondage, in other parts of the world."[1] Black men and women founded this church and dozens of other separate black churches in northern states after 1790, often, but not always, with the assistance of white people. Conversely, during the same period that this predominantly black Episcopal church ministered to Philadelphia's African American community, other black men, women, and children were baptized in the predominantly white Episcopal churches in town. Even while many black northerners left predominantly white churches and founded churches of their own, some predominantly white churches became more racially diverse. The formation of separate black churches after 1790 is often described as the end of interracial worship in northern

FIGURE 5.1. Black Philadelphians gathering for worship at their Episcopal church. *A Sunday Morning View of the African Episcopal Church of St. Thomas in Philadelphia. Taken in June 1829, Drawn on Stone by W. L. Breton* (Philadelphia: Kennedy & Lucas' lithography, 1829), Historical Society of Pennsylvania, Library Company of Philadelphia digital repository, www. librarycompany.org/.

states, but, in fact, African American religious activity also increased in predominantly white churches between 1791 and 1820.

The formation of separate black churches was hardly the end of inter-racial churches. Whereas Indian participation in predominantly white churches dropped to minuscule levels after they founded a wave of separate Indian churches in the 1750s (see chapter 2), black participation in some white churches and denominations rose in the same period that dozens of black churches were founded. There was, for example, a remarkable rise in the number of Dutch Reformed and Presbyterian churches that baptized and admitted blacks from 1791 to 1820. Additionally, numerous Methodist, Baptist, Episcopal, Congregational, and some Lutheran churches baptized or admitted African Americans to membership. The continued participation of black people in predominantly white churches occurred because many northern blacks, especially those who lived away from major cities, still lacked the resources necessary to support independent churches. In numerous communities, predominantly white churches remained the only option for black people. Moreover, some black men and women, even in major cities, affiliated with predominantly white churches because of long-standing attachments to those congregations, preferences for certain theological traditions, and educational opportunities. Black people affiliated with these churches despite usually being excluded from leadership positions and the best pews.

The first independent black churches were founded in northern cities after 1790 as black communities acquired the resources necessary to maintain churches, as more black people gained freedom, and as whites exhibited prejudice against black people in churches. As leading white Presbyterians in Philadelphia stated, blacks sought their own churches because it had become "inconvenient and unpleasant" for them to remain in white churches where segregated seating, white paternalism, and proscriptions against black voting and leadership existed. The priorities for white and black Christians were not always aligned. In an exceptional case, Reverend John Pitman of the Baptist church in Pawtuxet, Rhode Island, noted in his 1793 journal that "a black woman came to service her name is Margaret. She ran away from Thomas Weeks of Warwick [and] I wrote to him."[2] A black church or an African American pastor would not have reported the whereabouts of a runaway, as this white pastor seems to have done. However, white prejudices were not the only reason that blacks decided to form independent churches. Black churches appealed to many people because they became centers for the development of community leaders, antislavery activism, cultural activities, and other pursuits. One of the greatest advantages of these independent churches, like the advantage of separate churches for Indians, was that they became platforms where black leaders could freely articulate Christian critiques of the racism and exploitation that they experienced. These churches provided satisfying spiritual communities and essential support structures that met the education, political, and occasionally economic needs of blacks and Afro-Indians in northern cities.

The development of black churches and increased black participation in some predominantly white churches were part of a remarkable movement of church planting, denominational strengthening, and religious revivalism that Nathan Hatch has termed the "democratization of

American Christianity." Itinerant and revivalist preachers, new religious groups, missionary societies, proliferating religious publications, ecclesiastical controversies, and widespread, popular engagement with diverse religious traditions all dominated the religious movements of this era. One of the common elements of the religious culture from the 1780s to the 1830s, according to Hatch, was that many of the new religious movements "challenged common people to take religious destiny into their own hands, to think for themselves, to oppose centralized authority and the elevation of the clergy as a separate order of men." In this period, black people also started to transform the core characteristics of black Christianity. During earlier eras, most black and white Christians in the Northeast were Anglican or Congregational. By the middle of the nineteenth century, African American Christians were predominantly affiliated with Baptist and Methodist churches, so much so that these denominations became nearly synonymous with African American forms of Christianity. All northerners, including blacks, increasingly had options in choosing where to worship, and this freedom of choice was a valued privilege for enslaved and formerly enslaved people.[3]

The period of the Early American Republic was an era bursting with optimism, population movement, new technologies and ideas, and reform movements. Northerners, both black and white, created benevolent societies, schools, and cultural institutions. White Bostonians expanded the public school system and founded institutions, including the Boston Athenæum, the Massachusetts General Hospital, many new churches, and the Handel and Haydn Society. Black Bostonians built a meetinghouse for their Baptist church, founded a school, expanded their Masonic Lodge, and started a mutual aid organization called the African Society. Similar patterns of institution building occurred in all northern cities and some towns. Americans migrated from rural to urban centers and from eastern towns to western or northern frontiers. Denominations that were organized with new constitutions following the Revolution now strengthened their institutions, gained new members, and sent missionaries to the frontiers.[4]

The creation of separate black churches and the continued participation of black people in numerous predominantly white northern churches, in some substantial ways, mirrored the religious developments in southern states. The earliest black congregations in North America were formed in southern locations, but many evangelical and nonevangelical southern churches were also biracial until after the Civil War. Religious developments in Maryland and Virginia, especially the spread of African American Methodist and Baptist churches, influenced similar congregations in nearby Pennsylvania and other northern locations. Black Methodists, including Richard Allen and Harry Hosier, preached in both northern and southern states. Between the Revolution and Nat Turner's Rebellion in 1831, white Christians in Virginia and elsewhere allowed black southerners relatively more religious autonomy. In this context, much like in northern states during the same era, both interracial and separate black churches expanded. After 1831, as historian Charles Irons argues, white southerners more actively sought to control and supervise black Christians. As members of slave societies, antebellum southerners had more of an ability and desire to control visible African American religious institutions than did their northern counterparts.[5]

Although many excellent studies describe the separate black churches founded during this era, scholars have generally missed the fact that black participation also increased in numerous predominantly white churches at the same time.[6] In other words, black Christianity, in all of its forms, was on the rise between 1791 and 1820. As much as the development of separate black churches and denominations was a central part of the religious history of this period, interracial religious worship was still common in many northern locations.

The Rise of Separate Black Churches

Between 1791 and 1820, black northerners established a significant number of separate churches that provided social, political, and leadership assistance that very few, if any, predominantly white churches provided. The schools, mutual aid societies, and abolitionist organizations founded by African Americans and black churches often supported each other. There is little evidence that black northerners left predominantly white churches over theological disputes, although distinct black theological traditions developed over time. It seems that many blacks withdrew from white churches because independent black churches fostered the development of black leaders, the support of other cultural institutions, and the regular worship of God without segregated seating. African American leaders also believed that more black men and women would be converted in separate churches than could be reached in interracial churches because therein they could hear the gospel from ministers whose experiences resembled their own.[7]

Black people in Mid-Atlantic cities founded a greater number and variety of churches than blacks in New England because of their superior numbers and resources. New York City and Philadelphia had five and seven black churches, respectively, by 1820. These two cities attracted free blacks after the Revolution, including some black southerners who recently gained their freedom. New York City's free black population increased by 600 percent between 1790 and 1810, but slaveholdings also expanded in the 1790s as eventually one-third of white men in the city were slave owners. By 1800, New York and Philadelphia were over 10 percent African American. New York City, unlike Boston or Philadelphia, however, still contained more than 2,800 slaves in 1800. Philadelphia had the largest free black community in the North. Although most blacks occupied the lowest positions in the economy, Philadelphia's African American community also included some wealthy artisans and a few professionals. Because of its size and relative affluence, this community had the resources necessary to form and maintain several separate churches. In contrast, black residents in Boston in 1800 made up 4.71 percent of the city's population. The small size of Boston's and other northern black communities delayed the development of multiple black churches.[8]

Methodist (including African Methodist) churches were overwhelmingly the most common form of independent black churches in northern states, but by 1820 there were also at least two black Baptist churches, two black Episcopal churches, and one black Presbyterian church in New York City and Philadelphia. Between 1795 and 1819, black New Englanders established a total of three Baptist and three Methodist churches. People in New York City and Brooklyn established seven black churches between 1796 and 1819, while Flushing and Geneva, New York, each had one black church. At least six African American Methodist churches were founded in New Jersey between 1800 and 1818. African Americans founded one Episcopal, one Baptist, one Presbyterian, and at least fourteen Methodist churches in Pennsylvania before 1820. York, Lancaster, Harrisburg, Carlisle, Allentown, Pittsburgh, and a few other Pennsylvania towns each had one black church by 1820.[9]

Not all black northerners shared the same denominational preferences, but black Baptists, Methodists, Episcopalians, and Presbyterians each followed a common pattern in forming separate churches.[10] Black northerners began organizing informal religious services before separate churches were formed. Black leaders often confronted segregation and restrictions on their leadership within white churches. They justified separate and independent churches by arguing that they could more effectively evangelize unchristian blacks. African American churches received support from white church leaders, but paternalism and attempts to control black churches convinced some African American Christians, particularly Methodists, that separate denominations were a necessary safeguard to their independence.[11]

As had been the case with the founding of new Indian churches in the 1750s, talented leadership was necessary for the establishment of separate black churches. Men such as Richard Allen and Absalom Jones of Philadelphia, Peter Williams Jr. of New York, and Thomas Paul of Boston were crucial in the formation of black churches even though women often outnumbered men on church membership rolls. These pastors were renowned for their preaching and their dedication to parishioners. The limited avenues available for African Americans to develop as leaders in predominantly white churches made those congregations less appealing to black men. While some people, such as Lemuel Haynes of Rutland, Vermont, and Charles Bowles of New Hampshire and Vermont, ministered to predominantly white churches in places that lacked clergy, the vast majority of northern Protestant churches would not have accepted a black man as a minister or even as a deacon or vestryman.

Independent black churches often grew out of informal religious meetings held in homes and public spaces. The Free African Society of Philadelphia, founded in 1787 as a mutual aid association, began holding occasional interdenominational religious services in a rented room in 1791 before the members of this organization formed a separate congregation. Eventually, the majority of the Free African Society members formed the St. Thomas African Episcopal Church, and a minority of the members formed Bethel African Methodist Episcopal Church. The first religious services held by black Bostonians, perhaps as early as 1789, were also interdenominational meetings in rented halls. Thomas Paul, a black Baptist from New Hampshire, began leading these meetings before organizing a separate black Baptist church in 1806. Many of the attendees remained members of predominantly white churches, including approximately three dozen black Baptists.[12]

The first black Episcopal congregation in New York City began as an outgrowth of an educational organization. Around 1807 some black people at Trinity Episcopal Church organized the African Episcopal Catechetical Institution, and Trinity Church provided twenty-five dollars to hire an instructor. This organization took over the work of teaching blacks about Christianity and basic literacy, which had been supported by the church since the first decade of the eighteenth century. This group eventually developed into an African Episcopal congregation. Around

1809 or 1810, the African Episcopal Catechetical Institution began using a rented room at the African Free School to hold classes and perhaps religious services, but no sacraments were administered because ordained clergy did not regularly participate. This group soon began to seek the ordination of a black man so they could function as a distinct Episcopal congregation. Peter Williams Jr. was licensed as a lay reader between 1810 and 1812, and he was later ordained as a deacon and then as a priest. He led the St. Philip's Episcopal Church from its founding to his death in 1840.[13]

The creation of many separate churches resulted from confrontations over segregated seating in predominantly white churches and restrictions on black leadership roles. The desire to serve as pastors and in leadership capacities motivated the formation of black churches. Philadelphia's St. Thomas African Episcopal Church and Bethel African Methodist Episcopal Church, led respectively by Reverends Absalom Jones and Richard Allen, developed at least partially as a result of white proscriptions against black leadership at the predominantly white St. George's Methodist Church. "We established prayer meetings and meetings of exhortation [at St. George's], and the Lord blessed our endeavors," Allen observed in his autobiography, "but the elder soon forbid us holding any such meetings . . . and when the colored people began to get numerous in attending the church [St. George's], they moved us from seats we usually sat on, and placed us around the wall." At roughly the same time as the Free African Society began holding some separate services, conflicts between white and black Methodists increased the incentives for creating a separate church.[14]

After work on a separate church had begun, tensions between whites and blacks at St. George's disrupted a public worship service and hastened the departure of many black people from this congregation. One Sunday morning in 1792 or 1793, as black worshippers arrived for the service, the sexton instructed them to sit in the newly constructed gallery. Previously, they occupied benches on the main floor. As Allen recalled it, the black Methodists, including himself and Jones, found seats near the front of the gallery, "over the ones we formerly occupied below." As the congregation knelt to pray, however, one of the trustees interrupted Jones's silent prayers and demanded that he move to the back of the gallery. Jones asked to wait until the prayer was over, but the trustee pulled Jones "up off of his knees" and demanded that he move. As Allen explained years later, "By this time prayer was over, and we all went out of the church in a body, and they were no more plagued with us in the church."[15] Allen cited this incident as a turning point in the development of independent Methodist churches. In other congregations as well, the tensions between white and black worshippers helped to motivate the development of separate churches. AME Zion Bishop John Moore in 1885 wrote that "race prejudice, and proscription" caused New York City's black Methodists to worship separately starting in 1796. Specifically, white Methodists "licensed a number of colored men to preach, but prohibited them from preaching even to their own brethren, except occasionally, and never among the whites." These black preachers asserted that they should be allowed to preach the gospel as freely as white ministers.[16]

The first black Presbyterian church of Philadelphia was also created in part because blacks no longer willingly endured the limitations they faced in predominantly white congregations. Reverend William Catto wrote in 1857 that, "about the beginning of the present century, it became a subject of considerable conversation among the few colored people in Philadelphia whose preferences were Presbyterian, of raising a Presbyterian Church. The idea seemed to be general among them." Black Presbyterians supported the plan for a separate church, and Catto stated that they wanted "an organization of colored people where church government could be committed to, and governed by them, . . . without separating from Presbyterian bodies, or alienating themselves from their fellow Christians."[17] They desired to remain Presbyterian, but they also wanted to participate fully in the church, which was something that whites prevented in interracial churches. Statements from white Presbyterians reinforce this conclusion. The Evangelical Society of Philadelphia, founded by white Presbyterians in 1806, assisted black Presbyterians in forming a separate congregation. This white society published a plea for funds, arguing that "There are many, who from education or principle, are attached to the Presbyterian church. These find it to be inconvenient and unpleasant, for reasons which need not now be stated, to attend the houses of worship frequented by the white people. They are anxious to form a Presbyterian congregation among themselves; and they ought to be assisted and encouraged." While these people, including all the pastors of Philadelphia's Presbyterian churches, avoided acknowledging that it was blacks' second-class status that made churches "inconvenient and unpleasant" to black Presbyterians, these white Presbyterians sought to encourage the formation of a separate black church.[18]

A religious conviction was another powerful motivation for the creation of separate black churches. African American leaders believed that more black northerners would be reached by the gospel message and would be converted within black churches than through interracial ones. The leaders of Philadelphia's St. Thomas Episcopal Church stated in 1810 that the primary "causes and motives" behind the establishment of their church was "for the purpose of advancing our friends in a true knowledge of God, of true religion, and of the ways and means to restore our long lost race, to the dignity of men and of Christians." A separate black church, they believed, would facilitate both the Christianization of other blacks and their elevation in American society. Richard Allen's reason for organizing an African Methodist Church followed a similar logic. He chose to remain Methodist and form a black Methodist congregation because he believed that such a church was better suited to ministering to Philadelphia's blacks than the Episcopal Church. The primary purpose of both St. Thomas Episcopal Church and Bethel AME Church was the conversion and elevation of black Philadelphians.[19]

In 1817, the founders of St. Philip's Church told the vestry of Trinity Church in New York that a separate black Episcopal church was necessary to maintain and grow the number of black Episcopalians in the city. These black leaders wrote about the "disposition" that many black New Yorkers "manifested to conform in all things to the rites & ceremonies of the church." A separate black parish could enable "the attachment of a large number of coloured persons" who appreciated the Episcopal liturgy. Conversely, these black Episcopalism warned, "it is most evident that if some such arrangement is not soon made there will be a great falling off in that class of Episcopalians." They furthermore stated that "some hundreds have already left the church, whom they have reason to believe, would not have done so had some such provision been made for their accommodation." Finally, the petitioners felt "anxious" that unless funds could be raised and a separate black Episcopal church formed, then more people would "be led to Depart from that form of worship, and those doctrines, which they believe to be most scriptural and most conducive to the interests of true religion." A significant number of blacks were attracted, in the words of Reverend Peter Williams Jr., to "the doctrines and worship of our holy and apostolic church," so they sought to maintain Episcopal worship in a black parish where they could avoid the hindrances of worshipping with whites but still enjoy the spiritual tradition they desired.[20]

The formation of separate black churches usually proceeded with the support of influential white clergymen and laypersons. Methodist Bishop Asbury met with the black Methodist classes in New York City in 1795 and discussed the possibility of forming a separate black church. In response to their request, he granted permission for them to form a separate Methodist church. Initially, this black Methodist church was supported by some white ministers who officiated at services in conjunction with the four black men who were exhorters. Bishop Asbury continued to visit and provide support to this African Methodist Episcopal Church, known as Zion Church. In 1815, the year before his death, Asbury wrote, "I spoke a few words at the African chapel, both colours being present." Other white clergy routinely preached and administered sacraments during the early years of this church because no black leaders had yet been ordained.[21]

Support for separate churches often came in the form of ordinations of black ministers, although whites were sometimes slow and reluctant to ordain black men. In October 1794, the Church of St. Thomas in Philadelphia officially proposed Absalom Jones to Bishop William White as a candidate for ordination. Jones was ordained a deacon in 1795 and a priest in 1804, thereby making him the first black Episcopal priest in the United States. White Methodists and Baptists also ordained black deacons, exhorters, and pastors.[22]

Whites assisted in the creation of black church buildings by contributing financially and sometimes by consecrating the churches, and state laws governing incorporation also helped these young congregations. The legal incorporation of their churches gave black people a corporate legal standing that protected their institutions and rights better than the law protected individual people of color. White Methodists Francis Asbury and John Dickins helped dedicate Bethel African Methodist Church in 1794. In 1805, the predominantly white Baptist churches of Boston received letters from Scipio Dalton and Cato Gardner requesting help in establishing a black Baptist church. Eventually, white Baptist ministers led the dedication service for the African Meetinghouse (shown in figure 5.2), and this black church joined the same association as Boston's other Baptist churches and remained on reasonably good terms with white churches.[23]

Financial support from Trinity Episcopal Church was essential to the formation of St. Philip's Episcopal Church, even though black New Yorkers sacrificially worked to support their church too. In November 1817, eight men, the managers of the African Episcopal Catechetical Institution, petitioned the vestry of Trinity Church for financial aid, and the vestry voted to provide three thousand dollars for a "school House & place of worship" for black Episcopalians. Upon the request of Peter

FIGURE 5.2. The African Meetinghouse of Boston, Massachusetts, built by the First African Baptist Church in 1806. S. N. Dickinson, *The Boston Almanac for the Year 1843* (Boston: Thomas Groom & Co. 1843), 88.

Williams Jr., the vestry also agreed in 1819 that Trinity Church would pay the rent for the new church's property for seven years and provide the loan guarantee that was needed to finance the construction of the church building.[24]

The First African Presbyterian Church of Philadelphia was established cooperatively by white and black leaders. The Evangelical Society found a temporary meeting place for the black congregation and paid Reverend Gloucester's salary for at least three months while the congregation began. In 1809, the Evangelical Society aided Gloucester's congregation in obtaining a permanent church building. The white committee sought a suitable piece of land at the corner of Seventh and Shippen (now Bainbridge) Streets, "after consulting with the people of colour." With the money raised, the African Presbyterian Congregation built "a substantial brick church" and took the deed into their possession.[25]

White financial support and ordinations were important for the creation of the first black churches, but some black congregations soon found white support overbearing or even obstructionist. For years, Bethel Church in Philadelphia and Zion Church in New York remained black churches within the predominantly white Methodist denomination. However, these congregations and others eventually formed African American Methodist denominations and separated from white churches because white leaders were controlling and hostile. When articles of corporation were written for Bethel Church Philadelphia, white leaders assigned themselves certain powers, including the right to preach twice a week at the black church. A legal dispute occurred in 1807 when a white Methodist minister tried to use those powers to gain control of Bethel Church, but church members amended the articles of incorporation to grant the trustees more control over their church. White Methodists did not relent in their attempts to control Bethel, and they even confiscated the church's building and put it up for auction. Allen and the congregation were forced to purchase their building a second time for a staggering price. White Methodists filed lawsuits against Bethel, but the church's leaders persevered and maintained control of their church. Afterward, Philadelphia's black Methodists realized that complete independence from white Methodists was the only way to guarantee the control of their church. At a meeting in 1816, African Methodists from Pennsylvania, Maryland, and New Jersey formed the African Methodist Episcopal (AME) denomination and made Richard Allen the first bishop. White peoples' attempts to undermine this church helped convince Allen and others of the need for a separate black denomination.[26]

By 1820, members of Zion Church in New York City also contemplated separation from the predominantly white Methodist denomination. As some white Methodists sought to change the powers that ministers had over church property, the Zion Church leaders feared that their property could be taken from their control. In 1820, the African Methodist Episcopal Zion Church incorporated as a separate denomination. Leaders sent a message to the white Methodist conference to explain "that when the Methodist Society in America was small, the Africans enjoyed comfortable privileges among their white brethren, but as the white element increased, the Africans were pressed back; therefore, it was thought necessary for them to have separate places of worship, giving the Africans a better opportunity of full religious enjoyment and privileges." They explained that within the white Methodist denomination, "they have been too limited in their ministerial privileges" because the denomination put restrictions on black preachers. Thus, the separate denomination was necessary, like the separate congregation, "to promote the spiritual interest of our people generally." Most black Presbyterian, Baptist, and Episcopal congregations, conversely, remained in denominations or associations with white churches despite race-based limitations.[27]

Between 1791 and 1820, numerous black northerners participated in founding separate churches, many of which became flourishing congregations. The First African Baptist Church of Boston was constituted in 1805 with nine men and fifteen women members. By 1819, this church included more than one hundred members.[28] Black people in Philadelphia and New York City, in particular, could choose between several independent and thriving congregations. There were 1,426 members of the two black Methodist churches in Philadelphia, 560 members of St. Thomas's Episcopal Church, 300 members of the African Presbyterian Church, and 89 members of the black Baptist church by 1813. Almost half of the black adults in Philadelphia were members of these five churches. These churches were centers of black activism on issues ranging from abolitionism to African colonization movements.[29] By 1820, thousands of African Americans worshipped in independent or quasi-independent churches.[30] Although they found different theological traditions appealing, many black Methodists, Baptists, Episcopalians, and Presbyterians agreed that separate black churches benefited their communities. The distancing of whites and blacks in northern churches, however, eventually contributed to changes in racial categorizations and the beginnings of more deliberately imposed segregation across northern society.

Blacks and Indians within Predominantly White Churches

Between 1791 and 1820, during the same period when black churches were formed in northern cities, hundreds of black people participated in a significant number of northern predominantly white churches. Reformed and Presbyterian churches in the Mid-Atlantic states, in particular, reversed their long-standing reluctance to include blacks as members in their congregations. In varying degrees, black people also affiliated with predominantly white Congregational, Episcopal, Baptist, Methodist, and Lutheran churches. Although very few Indians affiliated with predominantly white churches during this era, Indian churches in New England were often racially inclusive as dozens, if not hundreds, of African Americans moved into Indian communities.

Some enslaved and free blacks affiliated with white churches because separate black churches were slower to form in small towns and because slavery still circumvented the freedom of numerous African Americans. Others affiliated with predominantly white churches and denominations in which their families had long-standing connections. Between 1791 and 1820, Methodist and Baptist churches expanded significantly, developing from marginal religious communities before the Revolution to influential and widespread denominations.[31] As these churches founded new congregations, they included black members. Many of the separate black churches founded after 1790 were Methodist or Baptist, but other Methodist and Baptist churches still included enslaved and free blacks for the time being, especially in locations where there were too few blacks to establish separate churches.

The remarkable increase in the number of Reformed and Presbyterian churches that baptized blacks was a continuation of the expansion of interracial churches that began in the Revolutionary era. Blacks participated in more of these churches because these denominations enacted rules that made baptism and membership more accessible to African Americans, and they were welcoming enough to convince some blacks to join. White leaders and pastors put the new policies into practice by reaching out to black people, asking them about their spiritual state, and encouraging their participation in sacraments and devotional activities.

More Reformed churches baptized and admitted blacks to membership between 1791 and 1820 than during any previous period. Black people affiliated with at least thirty-two Reformed churches in New York and New Jersey during these years.[32] This was a substantial increase from the nine Reformed churches in which black people affiliated from 1764 to 1790 (only three Reformed churches from 1764 to 1776 and eight from 1777 to 1790). Several of these churches were founded in the seventeenth century, but few of them had baptized blacks during the hundred years preceding 1791. In towns along the Hudson River Valley, from New York City harbor to Albany, in towns west of Albany, and scattered throughout New Jersey, Reformed churches baptized black men, women, and children during the Early Republic and admitted them to membership. Some blacks were also married by Dutch clergymen or buried in Dutch church cemeteries.[33]

In some Reformed churches, only a few blacks were baptized, but in other churches, dozens of black people were baptized and admitted to membership. Together, the action of these men and women in formally affiliating with these churches suggests patterns of their religious values.

In many of these cases, black adults chose to affiliate with Reformed churches and were allowed, if not encouraged, by whites to do so. At the Reformed Dutch Church of Middleburgh, located in Schoharie County, New York, nineteen black people were baptized between 1798 and 1803. Many of them were enslaved, and masters' names were included in the records before the slaves' names, such as "Lowrense Lawyer's Caesar Cobuskill" and "Stas Vrooman's Scipio." Seven African Americans, five women and two men, joined the Reformed Protestant Dutch Church on Staten Island from 1804 to 1818, including Fortune, "a free coloured man," who was baptized and "Sare, a black woman, servant of John Blake, on confession of their faith." The Reformed Church of Fonda (Caughnawaga), which began regularly baptizing blacks in the 1770s, baptized ninety-five black people between 1791 and 1820.[34] The Madison Avenue Reformed Church in New York City, founded in 1808, baptized three children whose parents were identified as "people of colour" between 1816 and 1819. These black families could have gone to one or more black churches for their children's baptism, but they went to this new Reformed Church. Larger numbers of blacks also participated at the First Reformed (Collegiate) Church of New York City's and the Reformed Church in Greenwich Village. Reflecting the growth in black church membership, the Classis of New-York presented "Mark Jordan, a man of colour, who is desirous of entering the ministry," to the General Synod in 1822, and Jordan became a Reformed minister in New York City.[35]

The increase in black baptisms and members was the result of denomination-wide policies that made Reformed churches more accessible and welcoming to blacks. The Reformed Synod in 1783 voted that the consent of a slave's master or mistress was not required if a slave wished to join a Reformed Church. The Synod also stated that marriages recognized only by enslaved men and women (not officially conducted by clergy) should not be a barrier to church admittance.[36] The 1792 Constitution of the Reformed Dutch Church in the United States of America went even further:

> In the Church there is no difference between bond and free, but all are one in Christ. Whenever therefore, slaves or black people shall be baptized or become members in full communion of the Church, they shall be admitted to equal privileges with all other members of the same standing; and their infant children shall be entitled to baptism, and in every respect be treated with the same attention that the

children of white or free parents are in the Church. Any Minister who, upon any pretense, shall refuse to admit slaves or their children to the privileges to which they are entitled, shall, upon complaint being exhibited and proved, be severely reprimanded by the Classis to which he belongs.[37]

The Reformed Church Constitution repudiated notions that blacks were inferior and stated that black church members were entitled to equal privileges, but it is telling that the language of this passage still equated slavery with blackness and freedom with whiteness. Segregating seating by class and race continued in these churches, and official policy was not necessarily widely accepted among the laity; however, the policy that blacks be admitted and baptized on equal terms was taken seriously by Reformed pastors during the Early Republic. White leaders and pastors put the new policies into practice by reaching out to blacks, asking them about their spiritual state, catechizing them, and encouraging their participation in sacraments and devotional activities.[38]

Not all Reformed Christians, however, were amenable to the inclusion of black people into their churches. The opposition of some and the ambivalence of many Reformed and Presbyterian Christians caused the exclusion of blacks from these churches throughout most of the eighteenth century. In 1788, some African Americans whom Reverend Peter Lowe believed were qualified to become members of a New York Reformed Church were prevented from doing so because of direct opposition from white congregants.[39] Among the long-standing reasons given to prevent black baptisms in the eighteenth century was that blacks were seeking baptism only to escape slavery. But this objection to the inclusion of blacks in Reformed churches diminished as hundreds of blacks gained freedom through individual manumissions and as slavery was put on a path to extinction with New York's 1799 gradual emancipation act. With gradual emancipation enacted, some masters may have felt that introducing black people to Reformed Christianity would reduce the social ills that slaveholders claimed would result from black freedom.[40]

Mid-Atlantic Presbyterian churches also became more welcoming and accessible to black people, and a greater number of Presbyterian churches baptized and admitted black people between 1791 and 1820 than during any previous period. At least twenty-three predominantly white Presbyterian churches baptized or admitted African Americans. Out of this sample, only seven had done so between 1764 and 1790 (five between 1764 and 1776 and five between 1777 and 1790). In churches located in Philadelphia, New Jersey, and New York, black men, women, and children made an increasing number of Presbyterian churches sites of interracial worship.[41]

Presbyterians, beginning in 1786, moved toward making access to baptism and church membership more routine and possible for enslaved black children. As had long been the practice of Congregationalists, Anglicans, and Lutherans, the Mid-Atlantic Presbyterians began baptizing black children on the authority of their owners, even if the black parents were not church members. After the Revolution, Presbyterians increasingly considered how to include blacks within their churches instead of questioning whether they should be included. Some black people responded by joining or being baptized in Presbyterian churches.[42]

The locations of Presbyterian churches in which free and enslaved blacks joined included both urban and rural locations. At the First Presbyterian Church of New York City, thirty-five black people (all but two of them women) were admitted to membership between 1809 and 1820.[43] This church provided a venue for black women to connect with one another and with white members. Thirty-one black people were baptized at the Presbyterian Church of Newtown (now Elmhurst) on Long Island, New York, between 1791 and 1809. At the First Presbyterian Church of Ballston, New York (located north of Albany), a few blacks were admitted as members, including Maria Brown, "a black woman," but she left this church and "joined the Baptists" in 1811. Even in the rural and relatively isolated upstate New York community of Whitestown (Oneida County), the First Presbyterian Church admitted two black women to membership between 1808 and 1815.[44]

The records of the First Presbyterian Church of Elizabeth, New Jersey, provide greater details about black Presbyterians in this era, and a congregation-wide list of households puts black church participation within the context of nineteenth-century slavery in New Jersey. Although the extant records are incomplete, between 1811 and 1820, at least twenty-six blacks were baptized in this church. Most of these people were enslaved, but four free blacks were baptized. Many of the adults were also admitted to communion and membership when baptized. At least twenty-three black people were admitted to communion between 1806 and 1820, including "York property of Gov. Aaron Ogden." In another case, Jude, "a black woman property of Wid. Dayton," and several whites requested baptism and admittance to communion in 1808. The church session, "after conversing with them on their knowledge & experimental acquaintance with religion," admitted Jude and the other candidates.

In 1818, this church's pastor listed 180 blacks and 2,350 whites as parts of "families in the Presbyterian congregation." The vast majority of the blacks listed were identified as part of white households, where they lived as slaves or perhaps as free servants. Nine black households contained a total of thirty-seven individuals, only three of whom were church members. The First Presbyterian of Elizabeth, New Jersey, was an interracial church, but most blacks who worshipped there were enslaved. Only a fraction (probably not more than 13 percent) of all black people in town were church members; the black community most likely lacked the resources necessary to maintain a separate church before 1820.[45]

Dozens of Congregational churches baptized blacks between 1791 and 1820, but the decline in black affiliation with Congregational churches evident between 1776 and 1790 continued into the early nineteenth century. Although some black people still affiliated with Congregational churches, overall, fewer Congregational churches baptized blacks in these decades than during most of the eighteenth century. At least forty-four Congregational churches included multiple black baptisms or members between 1791 and 1820.[46] Conversely, seventy-five Congregational churches had baptized or admitted blacks between 1764 and 1790 (sixty-five between 1764 and 1776 and twenty-nine between 1777 and 1790). While the total number of Congregational churches that baptized black people exceeded the number of Presbyterian, Dutch Reformed, or Lutheran churches that did so, the number of Congregational churches declined while the number of Reformed and Presbyterian churches increased.

Ironically, the Revolutionary principles that led to the relatively quicker end of slavery in New England also seemed to result in a decline in interracial Congregational churches, quickening the downward trend in black affiliation that began in the 1760s. The movement to disestablish churches and the increased competition for religious adherents in New England may have led Congregationalists to shy away from racial inclusion at the same time that Reformed Christians were implementing more equalitarian principles. Because slavery ended after 1780 in Massachusetts and gradually after 1784 in Connecticut and Rhode Island, the black populations in rural New England decreased faster than the rural black populations in New York and New Jersey, as more African Americans moved to urban centers. Although small numbers of black people remained in most New England towns, there were fewer African Americans to participate in the Congregational churches of many rural New England towns. Blacks also affiliated with Episcopal and Baptist churches in New England in significant numbers, which suggests that they may have preferred these churches to Congregational ones. A significant number of New Englanders had moved from Congregational to Anglican churches in the second half of the eighteenth century. Also, by 1820, there was a small number of independent black churches in the largest cities.[47] Nevertheless, the migration of blacks to cities and the increase in black Baptists can only partially explain the decline in black affiliation with Congregational churches.

The black population of Canton, Connecticut, exhibits the decrease in black inhabitants of rural New England towns and the corresponding drop in black Congregationalists. A black man named Charles Prince married Tabatha Qummenor (or Qumino) in 1800. He joined the Congregational Church in Canton Center in 1807, and Tabatha was baptized and admitted to membership in 1816. Their four children were also baptized. Captain Dudley Case employed Charles Prince, and people in this town viewed Prince as "an honest, industrious and meritorious citizen, and . . . worthy members of the church." Unfortunately, Prince died of consumption in 1828 at age fifty-four, but even before his death, he and his family were "wronged out of the small pittance of landed estate which his deceased patron had given him years before, but had not executed the deed." The "family appeared to sink under misfortunes" after Prince died, and some family members died and others left town. Tabatha moved to Hartford and transferred membership from the Canton Church to the African Church in Hartford in 1839. Demographic change and migration within New England affected church affiliation in the nineteenth century.[48]

Some Congregational churches may have become less accepting of black congregants and members as free blacks asserted their rights and demanded equality. It appears that Congregationalists were more comfortable including enslaved blacks than free African Americans within their covenanted communities of faith. As Congregational churches, which had monopolized religion in colonial New England, now had to compete for adherents with the growing number of Baptists, Methodists, and Episcopalians, excluding people of color was one way to attract and maintain white adherents. In the colonial era, most New England towns had only Congregational churches, which ideally included all people in each town. However, in the Early Republic, the tide turned away from inclusiveness. "Whiteness," widely associated with "respectability," may have become an asset for Congregationalists trying to attracting middle-class congregants. They distinguished themselves from Baptist and

Methodist churches, which were associated with African Americans. At the very least, Congregationalists, on the whole, preceded Presbyterian and Reformed churches in separating blacks and whites.[49] Nonetheless, some Congregational churches remained the spiritual homes of black men and women during the Early Republic.

Some black men and women exhibited strong attachments with the First Congregational Church of Newport, Rhode Island, through membership, donations, and pew ownership. At least nine black people were baptized there between 1791 and 1807, including the youngest five children of Newport and Limas Gardner (see chapter 4). Reverend William Patten admitted fourteen African Americans to full membership in the First Congregational Church between 1804 and 1815. In 1805 "black people" contributed money to help paint and repair the church. Several African Americans built and owned pews in the gallery; in 1806, church members voted "that the pews on the South Gallery which were built by the black people six in number shall be their property." In 1819, the church approved that "Abby Stodard coloured woman" and "Henry Clark coloured person" could have "liberty to build" pews in the gallery "joining the blacks."[50]

One of the black church members most invested in the church was Newport Gardner. He was able to purchase his freedom and the freedom of most of his family in 1791 with his share of a winning two-thousand-dollar lottery ticket. In addition to other jobs, he worked as the church sexton from 1807 to 1825.[51] Gardner and Reverend Samuel Hopkins became close associates, if not friends. Hopkins wrote that Newport Gardner was "a discerning, judicious, steady, good man, and feels greatly interested in promoting a Christian settlement in Africa." Gardner was a key person in the black community. He was a leader in the Free African Union Society and the African Benevolent Society, which ran the African Free School for black children, and Gardner served as a teacher. A separate black church was founded in Newport in 1823 with the help of Gardner. Earlier, the black community of Newport either lacked the will or the resources to establish an independent church, especially as many blacks left the city. Newport was the only major northern town whose black population declined from the Revolution into the 1840s.[52]

As had long been the case, Episcopal churches appealed to enslaved and free blacks across the northern states. Black participation in Episcopal churches remained relatively consistent over the second half of the eighteenth century and into the first decades of the nineteenth century. Roughly the same number of Episcopal churches recorded black baptisms between 1791 and 1820 as had done so between 1764 and 1790. At least twenty-four predominantly white Episcopal churches, ranging from Portsmouth, New Hampshire, south to Philadelphia, Pennsylvania, baptized black men, women, and children.[53] Episcopal priests also performed the rites of marriage, burial, and communion for blacks. The number of black people married by Episcopal priests seems to have been even greater between 1791 and 1820 than in earlier periods. As the number of free blacks continued to rise, many of them still chose Episcopal churches as their places of worship. The long-standing black affiliation with Episcopal churches also provided the context for the formation of African American Episcopal churches in New York City and Philadelphia.

In the largest northern cities, Episcopal churches appealed to black people for spiritual and material benefits (that is, access to education) even after separate black churches were available. White Episcopalian layman Jeremiah Taylor, who attended St. George's Episcopal Church in New York City, helped organized Sunday Schools in this period, including "Sunday School No. 34 attached to St. George's church for the instruction of colored men." In 1817, this Sunday School included "twenty-six scholars between the ages of 16 and 50 years," and by 1818, it included "74 coloured men, 9 teachers, 5 assistant teachers."[54] Sixty black people (roughly half male and half female) were baptized at Trinity Church in Boston, which had been a center of black religious life since the 1770s. Among the black baptisms at Trinity Church were the children of Butterfield and Clarissa Scotland, who had moved from Philadelphia to Boston after the Revolution. About 48 percent of the sixty black baptisms at Trinity Church occurred between 1806 and 1820, a time when these men and women could have affiliated with the African Baptist Church.[55] At Trinity Church in Newport, between 1798 and 1820, twenty-six blacks were baptized. Eighteen of them were adults and eight were children.[56] In several locations, Episcopal churches persisted in baptizing more black men and women than any other denomination.

Many blacks affiliated with and attended the predominantly white Episcopal churches in New York City, particularly Trinity Church and its St. Paul's and St. George's chapels. At least 240 black people and perhaps dozens more were baptized at Trinity Church and its chapels from 1791 to 1820. Many of these baptisms occurred even after the independent black Methodist church was founded. Trinity Church provided several services to black New Yorkers, including marriages and burials. Reverend Benjamin Moore married approximately four hundred black couples between 1791 and 1806, and others were married by additional Trinity Church ministers.[57] In 1795, "Isaac Fortune and other Free Black persons" requested financial assistance to "enable them to purchase a piece of ground as a Burial place to bury Black persons of Every denomination and description in this city whether Bond or Free"; Trinity Church's vestry provided five hundred pounds for this purpose. The vestry also affirmed that blacks who were communicants or children of communicants could be buried in any of the church's burial grounds, and at least some black people were buried in these locations between 1813 and 1820. In the same period, the church periodically provided money for teachers who ran schools or classes for black men, women, and children.[58]

Reverend (and later Bishop) Benjamin T. Onderdonk was well acquainted with some of the black communicants and attendees at the predominantly white Episcopal churches of New York, and his ministerial efforts among black New Yorkers perhaps made these churches feel welcoming to African Americans. Onderdonk noted marrying, visiting the sick, administering communion at homes, and attending funerals of many Episcopalians, including black New Yorkers. He married at least seventeen black couples between 1812 and 1820, and most of these ceremonies occurred at his personal residence. On six occasions, Onderdonk visited James Stevens, "a coloured man" and a communing member of St. Paul's Church, at his home on Cedar Street in 1813, and Onderdonk visited Stevens's widow after his death. Onderdonk spent time praying and conversing with Stevens and sought to comfort him. He noted that Stevens "Expresses his grateful sense of the goodness of Providence towards him, . . . Joined heartily in prayer. Being able to read, he is thankful for the blessing & is edified & consoled by the Diligent use he makes of his Bible & prayer Book." Onderdonk also described Stevens as a man of "great piety."[59] Scores of black New Yorkers found satisfaction in the teachings and sacraments of the Episcopal Church, and ministers like Onderdonk were ready to provide the spiritual sustenance that drew some blacks into these parishes.

Even though Philadelphia had two of the oldest black churches in the North, at least thirty-eight blacks were baptized at the Episcopal churches of Christ Church, Saint Peter's, and Saint James's between 1791 and 1820. Among the "coloured" Philadelphians baptized by Reverend Jackson Kemper in 1819 were Mary and Thomas Forten, two children of the wealthy businessman and activist James Forten and his wife, Charlotta. James had served as a leader in the St. Thomas African Episcopal Church since 1796, but he had long-standing connections to predominantly white Episcopal churches. In 1819, he had two children baptized at a predominantly white Episcopal church (probably because Reverend Absalom Jones died in 1818). According to historian Julie Wench, Forten had worshipped for years at St. Paul's Episcopal Church, "where his sister had been married and where Rev. Joseph Pilmore presided. The evangelical Pilmore had proven himself most sympathetic to the needs and concerns of his black parishioners. . . . At least in the early 1790s, James Forten saw no reason to abandon Rev. Pilmore and St. Paul's."[60] Even with the development of separate black churches, some black northerners remained in predominantly white Episcopal churches because they continued to find benefits from such an affiliation, because they did not agree with the theology of the existing black churches, and because of their long-standing ties to these congregations.

Lutheran churches paralleled Episcopal ones in terms of black affiliation. At least thirteen Lutheran churches in the Mid-Atlantic region baptized blacks between 1791 and 1820, which was about the same rate of affiliation as earlier in the eighteenth century.[61] In urban centers, such as New York City and Philadelphia, as well as in small towns and remote locations, these Lutheran churches were accessible to a small number of black people who participated in the sacraments and worshipped there. The First Lutheran Church of Albany, New York, baptized at least nine blacks in this period, including "Dina, Nigro Wench, born in Guinea, belonging to Miss'trs. Lamb." "Elisabeth Huth, *freie schwarze*" (free black), was among the communicants in 1795. At least fifteen black people, most of whom were free, were baptized at Trinity Lutheran Church in Reading, Pennsylvania, including Dinah, a "free negress" about sixty years old.[62] In Somerset, Pennsylvania (135 miles west of Harrisburg), one enslaved black woman named Rachel joined Samuel's Lutheran Church in 1791. The record indicates the steps she undertook to be baptized in this predominantly white, rural church: "On the 17th of April, 1791, a negress who belonged to Peter Angane, and named Rachel having promised to lead her life as much as possible according to God's Commandments, was received through Holy Baptism into the Covenant of Grace with God and His Congregation, and in order that she may have some protection and refuge in Christian faith; so have the Elder and Deacon— Messrs. Peter Angane and Henry Stahl take upon themselves the office of God-parents."[63] Rachel was accepted into this church after she promised to live according to God's commands, and two white men, one of whom was her owner, were the sponsoring godparents. She was likely among the very few black people at this rural church. Similarly, a sketch drawn by Lewis Miller of the Lutheran Church of York, Pennsylvania, shows a crowded Lutheran congregation that included at least one black man, whom Miller depicted as kneeling in prayer on the stairs to the gallery.[64]

Blacks and some Afro-Indians participated in predominantly white Baptist churches between 1791 and 1820, especially as white Baptists reached out to them.[65] For example, the First Baptist Church of Providence, Rhode Island, admitted forty-one black people to membership between 1791 and 1820, and, by 1800, almost 10 percent of the members were people of color. Several of the people who were identified as "black" or "of colour" in the First Baptist Providence records were Afro-Indians. In 1812, "Mrs. Sarah Warmsley [Walmsley] of colour of Olneyville" was received as a member and baptized. She was thirty-nine and had both African and Narragansett ancestors. When black people, such as Abigail Hopkins, joined the church, they followed the same requirements as whites. In 1791, Hopkins "related her religious experiences to the church and was approved as a person fit to follow Christ & to be admitted a member of his visible church." Although it was uncommon for churches to allow African American members to vote, at least five people of color voted in 1791 regarding whether or not "compliance with the imposition of hands shall be a bar to Church membership." Some church members also showed their affiliation with this church through monetary gifts. In 1811, Patience Sterry Bordon, a black woman and member, upon her death, gave $230 to the First Baptist Church "as a fund for the relief of the poor of Colour of that Church." Most black members did not leave this predominantly white congregation until 1840, when a black Baptist church was founded in Providence.[66]

The First Baptist Church of New York City also became more of an interracial church between 1791 and 1808, as thirty-four black people were admitted to membership. Only eight of them were identified as enslaved. Even they likely chose to become members. The strict requirements for membership hedged against forcing anyone to join. In one case, an enslaved woman's owner was a Dutch Reformed minister, but she chose to join this Baptist Church. In 1796, "Flora, a black woman, belonging to the Rev'd Dr. Linn, of this City, was baptized in the N. River, on a profession of her faith; and the next day rec'd into the church, as a member thereof."[67]

A brief account of Susan Wright's family and church affiliation exhibits the slow and uneven process of manumissions in New York and the circumstances that facilitated one black woman's membership in a mostly white Baptist church. Susan, the daughter of York Wright, a free black man, and Mary Wright, an enslaved woman, was born in April 1791. All members of the Wright family lived in the household of Governor George Clinton (future vice president of the United States), and Mary, Susan, and her sister, Celia, were all slaves. In 1800, Mary became free, and Susan became the property of Elisabeth Clinton Tallmadge. Wright described her admission to the Baptist Church of Poughkeepsie, New York, in the following way: "It having pleased God though Grace to call me to repentance & newness of life, I went while our family were at Poughkeepsie before the baptist church at that place, and upon a declaration of faith was unanimously accepted by them, and on the first Sunday in September 1810, baptized by Mr. Wayland their pastor & admitted a member of the church." Her status as a slave limited her mobility, and she was unable to reside in a place with a black church. But, Susan experienced a "newness of life" and affiliated with a church that appealed to her.[68]

In some cases, black men preached to predominantly white Baptist churches. Reverend John Pitman, while pastor of a Baptist church in Pawtuxet, Rhode Island, noted that "Amos Cubit a black man," in 1793, "preached 4 times in this town [and] was thought much of." Reverend Charles Bowles was also among the black men in New England who routinely preached at white Baptist churches. Bowles was born in Boston in 1761. Like Lemuel Haynes, Bowles had an "African" father and a white mother, he was indentured as a child, and he served in the American forces during the Revolution. Sometime after the Revolution, Bowles was baptized and admitted as a member of the predominantly white Calvinistic Baptist Church in Wentworth, New Hampshire. An early biographer, John W. Lewis, wrote that Bowles promoted the Baptist faith among other New Englanders. Years after his baptism, Bowles rejected Calvinist theology and became a Free Will Baptist. By 1808, he preached the Free Will theology to mostly white audiences across New England, including areas of Vermont, Massachusetts, and Rhode Island, and a Baptist church council ordained him in 1816. Subsequently, he preached and administered sacraments across Vermont.[69]

Bowles's preaching was apparently well received by white churchgoers, but Lewis also noted that Bowles's dark skin subjected him to "some frigid looks and discouraging words, and some still sterner opposition" from residents of Huntington and Hinesburg, Vermont. Nonetheless, Bowles did not separate himself from predominantly white churches or colleagues, nor did he establish separate black churches. He approached his opponents with a firm assuredness and forbearance that disarmed scoffers. Whether as an enslaved church member or as an ordained preacher, black men and women continued to participate in predominantly white Baptist churches.

Although divisions between white and black Methodists in the Mid-Atlantic states increased between 1791 and 1820, some northern Methodist churches remained sites of interracial worship. The official membership rolls of the Methodist circuits indicate that some predominantly white Methodist churches included black members between 1791 and 1820, although blacks usually attended segregated class meetings. In 1801, the Boston circuit reported sixty-five white members and ten "colored" members; Boston did not yet have an independent black Methodist church. The First Methodist Church of New Haven also listed a "colored class" whose twelve members in 1812 were more than 20 percent of the church's total membership. Conversely, in the same year, Philadelphia's membership was listed at 707 whites and 448 blacks. However, most of these blacks were members of the separate Methodist church and no longer participated in interracial Methodist meetings.[70]

Table 5.1 presents state-by-state tabulations of white and "colored" members of Methodist churches between 1796 and 1801. The membership figures from the Annual Conferences reveal a couple of trends. First, white leaders still characterized Methodism as a biracial religious movement in their published descriptions, and numerous local churches continued to be sites of interracial worship even as separate black Methodist churches were formed. Second, white Methodists significantly outnumbered black Methodists, and whites joined Methodist churches at a faster rate than blacks. Finally, Methodists designated people only as "white" or "colored," so it is probable that some of the "colored" Methodists, especially in New England, were Indians or Afro-Indians. For example, William Apess, a Pequot, participated in Methodist meetings at Montville, Connecticut, between 1809 and 1813 and was baptized by Methodists in Bozrah, Connecticut, in December 1818. Apess wrote: "I had a desire to attend Methodist meeting. . . . This was altogether new to me; but it was interesting to attend them, and so much so that I desired to be a constant attendant of them." This Pequot man was one of the "colored" members of the Methodist Church.[71]

Before separate black Methodist churches were formed, some blacks participated in and joined predominantly white Methodist churches. Their numbers, however, declined as more and more black Methodist churches were formed after 1810. In 1795, New York City and Elizabeth, New Jersey, Methodist churches each contained a minority of black

TABLE 5.1. Numbers of white and "colored" members in the Methodist churches in northern states, 1796–1801

		Pa.	N.J.	N.Y.	Conn.	R.I.	Mass.	N.H.	Vt.	Maine	Total
1796	White	2,631	2,246	3,826	1,042	220	822	68	0	357	11,212
	Col.	380	105	218	8	0	2	0	0	0	713
1797	White	2,900	2,433	4,612	1,186	175	905	92	0	616	12,919
	Col.	198	127	238	15	2	8	0	0	0	588
1798	White	2,964	2,663	5,081	1,433	161	1,183	122	285	936	14,828
	Col.	224	163	245	22	1	11	0	1	0	667
1799	White	3,000	2,725	5,681	1,480	195	1,398	131	603	1,117	16,330
	Col.	309	167	276	17	1	11	0	1	0	782
1800	White	2,887	2,857	6,140	1,546	224	1,571	171	1,095	1,197	17,688
	Col.	300	173	223	25	3	6	0	1	0	731
1801	White	3,321	2,987	6,750	1,543	234	1,653	521	1,601	1,386	19,996
	Col.	507	172	284	24	3	12	3	6	0	1,011

Source: *Minutes of the Methodist Conferences, Annually Held in America from 1773 to 1813, Inclusive*, vol. 1 (New York: John C. Totten, 1813).

members. The New York City church reported 600 white members and 155 colored members, and Elizabeth listed 270 white and 10 black members. Neither city had a separate black church at that date. Small numbers of black people were also members of the Smithfield Street Methodist Church in Pittsburgh, Pennsylvania. In 1819, there was a "colored class" with twenty-three members that met Monday evenings and a "colored class" with thirty-two members that met Sunday afternoons. Additionally, a "country" class included twenty-seven white and three "colored" members. A few blacks continued to participate in Pittsburgh's predominantly white Methodist church until at least 1823.[72]

Hardly any people identified in church records as Indians participated in predominantly white churches between 1791 and 1820, but Indian communities in New England were places of interracial worship. Of all the churches included in this study, only six predominantly white churches had one or more Indians identified in baptismal or membership records in these years.[73] At least two of the Indians who participated in these churches were servants in white households, and several of these churches were located near Indian communities. The Dutch Reformed pastor of Herkimer, New York, baptized several Oneida adults at one of this tribe's settlements.[74]

Many of the Indian communities that remained in New England and New York had their own churches, most of them Baptist, Congregational, or ecumenical. Missionary societies sometimes supported these Indian churches financially and provided schoolteachers. Predominantly white churches carried the burden of white prejudice and racism, and they had shown little interest in helping Indians retain control over their lands and resources. In Pennsylvania and New Jersey, moreover, the systematic violence that white men inflicted upon Indians during the Revolutionary era either killed or drove away numerous Indians.[75] By 1790, there were few Indians in Pennsylvania and New Jersey, and no churches sampled from these states included Indians.

Northern Indian churches, conversely, were sites of interracial worship as some whites, blacks, and Afro-Indians attended these churches as both congregants and preachers. Gideon Hawley continued to minister to the Mashpee, Massachusetts, community until his death in 1807, and other people occasionally ministered there as well. Hawley, in May 1806, described a remarkable interracial communion service led by himself and "a man of colour":

On the last Lords Day, I met about 70 Indians and persons of Colour; all Clad in a decent manner, and with a serious & devout Countenance; when I celebrated the Lords supper of which a goodly, but Small number, partook. . . . After they were consecrated, by the pastor a man of Colour served in carrying the Bread and wine to the Communicants. The occasion was solemn—The meeting house was crowded . . . besides the black people, we had about an hundred others.[76]

At times, Hawley used the terms Indians, blacks, and people of color interchangeably to describe Mashpee residents, but, at other times, he distinguished between them. On several occasions, Hawley noted that the whites attended his services along with Indians, Afro-Indians, and blacks. The whites, according to Hawley, were relegated to the back seats in the meetinghouse, which was a reversal of the seating arrangements of predominantly white churches. John Freeman also led a short-lived Baptist church in Mashpee between the 1790s and 1806, and at least two of the attendees at this church were of mixed race. Hawley identified an Indian woman named Sarah and "two young Indians of mixed blood" as people who preferred Baptist preaching in 1795. White ministers, along with black and Indian ministers, continued to serve Indians at other Indian communities as well. During this period, the Society for Propagating the Gospel among the Indians and Others in North America employed Reverend Curtis Coe to minister to Indians in Rhode Island, Reverend John Sergeant for the New Stockbridge Indians in New York, and others in Maine and elsewhere.[77]

As the Wampanoags on Martha's Vineyard began to mix with black people after the Revolution, one of their churches also became more racially diverse. An Indian Congregational church had existed on the Vineyard since the seventeenth century. However, their Wampanoag Congregational minister, Reverend Zachariah Howwoswee Jr., betrayed the trust of his community and alienated some church members by refusing to preach in English at a time when the Wampanoag language was falling out of use. The Wampanoag Baptist minister Thomas Jeffers, who arrived in 1801, appealed to the increasingly diverse Wampanoag community of Indians, Afro-Indians, and blacks disaffected with Howwoswee. English-language sermons were part of his appeal. Another part might have been that he resembled his diverse parishioners. Hawley wrote that Jeffers was "half blooded, and came from Middlebury and is half Negroes mixt with Indians." Jeffers was also married to one of the "mixt-blooded females" from Mashpee. Hawley wrote that Sarah Jeffers had "a Sprinkling of white blood in her veins, mixt with both Indian & negroe: her mother was all Indian, and her father half White." Thomas and Sarah Jeffers identified themselves as Wampanoags and were important members of the Aquinnah community, but their diverse ancestry reminds us that the racial categories constructed in North America did not neatly correspond with the complexity of individuals' ancestors or personal identities. By 1811, many people at Gay Head had some African and/or white ancestors, as well as Indian ancestors.[78] Consequently, the churches, like the community overall, reflected a diverse human tapestry. Frequent black and Afro-Indian participation in Indian churches and communities also influenced how whites perceived racial distinctions.

Changing Notions of Race and Christian Equality

The terminology used by whites to describe and categorize people of African and Indian descent shifted significantly between 1790 and 1820, as did the words used by blacks and some Indians to describe themselves. These shifts in language reflected the changes in how blacks and Indians related to whites in the Early Republic, especially as many black people left predominantly white churches and as fewer northern blacks were enslaved. Throughout the colonial period, most English-speaking whites used the word "negro" to describe blacks, and this term was the primary racial identifier in northern church records until around 1790. Sometimes, whites also used terms such as "mulatto" or "mustee" for persons of mixed races and "Indian" to describe people from many different tribal nations. However, in churches across denominational and regional divides, many whites began using "black" and occasionally "African" to denote persons of African descent and sometimes to denote Indians. This shift occurred around 1790 (the term "negro" continued to be used as a pejorative term in other oral and written discourses). Racial terminology shifted again between 1810 and 1820, as whites began to write "coloured" or "people of colour" in the records instead of "black" or "blacks." Although the term "Indian" was still occasionally used in church records, "colored" or an abbreviated form of this word was increasingly used to describe a wide range of people with at least partial African or Indian ancestry, including Afro-Indians, Indians, and blacks. The ways blacks and Indians described themselves influenced how whites conceived of these groups of people. Changes in the words that whites used also resulted from racism and exclusionary practices that followed the gradual end of legal slavery in northern states. Some whites used obstinate forms of racism to control the labor of free blacks and to "imagine" the disappearance of Indians from northern states. Even the most sympathetic whites envisioned the political and increasingly civil society in the United States as exclusively white.[79]

While the timing varied slightly from congregation to congregation, the vast majority of Protestant church records reveal similar trends in the words that whites used to identify people of African and Indian descent. For example, at Christ Episcopal Church in Philadelphia, the term "negro" was uniformly used in the records from 1730 to 1786. The term "blacks" began to appear in 1786, but "negro" was still used occasionally. By 1789, "black" was overwhelming used in the records, but "negro," "mulatto," and "coloured" also appeared. By 1818, "colored" was the only racial identifier.[80] At Old South Congregational Church in Boston, the shift from "negro" to "black" occurred after 1787, and the shift to "colored" happened by the 1820s. Christ Church in Boston switched to "blacks" by 1794 and to "colored" by 1809. The Reformed Protestant Dutch Church on Staten Island used the term "black" from at least 1808 to 1811 and "coloured" by 1818. In the records of the First Presbyterian Church in Ballston, New York, "negro" was used in 1792, "blacks" was used between 1807 and 1809, and "colored" was used after 1817. The First Lutheran Church of Albany, whose records were partly in German and partly in English, included the racial identifier "Negroes" and "*ein sklave*" (a slave) or "*Sklaven*" (slaves) before 1790. In 1789 and other years, "*eine schwarze*" (a black) was used. In 1809 and 1814, "blacks" was written. Finally, after 1817, "colored people" was used in these records. Although local factors affected the words and categories used, most churches shifted from "negro" to "black" and to "colored" between 1790 and 1820. In similar ways, categories on census forms and other public documents also shifted.[81]

In addition to the changes in words used to describe persons of African descent, there was a tendency among whites, especially in New England, to lump Indians and blacks together beginning in the 1790s. In the racially diverse community of Mashpee, white minister Gideon Hawley's journals reflected some of the broader changes in racial categorization. However, Hawley had detailed knowledge of people's lineages, and because people do not always easily fit into narrow categories of race, his use of racial identifiers was more fluid and inconsistent. In 1803, Hawley talked about "the Indians & people of Colour at Mashpee" and "white people" as three distinct groups, and he described himself as "missionary to the Indians." Although he distinguished between people of color and Indians, undoubtedly, some of the "people of colour" had at least partial Indian ancestry. At a different point in 1803, Hawley described himself as the missionary to "the people of Colour." In this case, he described the whole community of Mashpee as "people of colour," suggesting that all Indians, whether of mixed ancestry or not, fit into the "people of color" category.[82] For Hawley, and more so for people less knowledgeable about New England Indians, it became common to categorize blacks, Afro-Indians, and Indians as "people of color." This phrase commonly superseded the use of "mustee" and "mulatto." Moreover, changes in the terminology reflected broader fluctuations in society. One of the reasons for whites' increasing perception of Indians as "blacks" or "colored" was the relatively frequent marriages among blacks and Indians in New England.[83] By identifying Indians in New England as "blacks" or "colored people," whites were remaking racial identities and simplifying racial categories in a way that benefited white employers and landowners. Some whites even argued that no Indians existed in New England because there were only "negroes" on Indian land reserves.[84]

Although white people had a substantial role in changing terminology, blacks, Afro-Indians, and Indians also influenced these changes. Whites wrote the racial designations in church records, but minorities affected and contributed to this rhetorical shift by how they addressed themselves.[85] Phillis Wheatley used "Ethiop" and "African" as descriptors in her 1773 published book of poetry. Free black leaders deliberately included "African" in the name of their early fraternal organizations, benevolent societies, and churches. The Free African Society of Philadelphia, founded in 1787 by Absalom Jones and Richard Allen, and the Boston African Baptist Church, founded in 1805, both used "African" instead of other labels. This name choice reflects a conscientious effort to build a group identity, which was important for the founding and growth of these institutions. Newly freed men and women also sought to distance themselves from the term "negro," which had strong ties to enslavement.[86]

During the years 1815 to 1820, black people began to identify themselves more often as "colored Americans," so the shift in church records from "blacks" to "colored people" at least partially resulted from African Americans using one label over another. The creation of white-led colonization societies, which sought to promote migration of blacks out of the United States, caused free blacks to reevaluate the use of the term "African," even though many black people continued to view Africa as an important part of their identity. Northern blacks began to insist that they were colored Americans who had every right to be treated as equal citizens of the United States and should not be expected to leave the country. Many pastors acquiesced to this preference and used the term "people of color" after the 1810s.

The primary identity for most Indians in this period was their specific tribal nation or community, but Native Americans also identified themselves collectively as Indians. Writing in the late 1820s and early 1830s, William Apess identified himself as a Pequot specifically but also as part of the collective group of "Indians" or "Natives." Afro-Indians sometimes chose to identify as blacks and sometimes as Indians. The Cuffee family in Massachusetts had Indian and African ancestors, and members of this family identified themselves sometimes as black and sometimes as Indian depending on local factors and the purposes of self-identification. Cuffee family members maintained ties to both African American and Indian communities. Several tribal nations and individual Indians spoke against white people classifying Indians as "black" or "colored," and some Indians insisted that mixed ancestry did not necessarily invalidate or exclude an Indian identity or tribal membership.[87]

In 1830, white Philadelphian John Watson indicated that it was black people who had pressed whites to use the term "colored people" instead of other designators. "In the olden times," Watson stated, "dressy blacks and dandy colour'd beaux and belles, as we now see them issuing from their proper churches, were quite unknown. Their aspirings and little vanities have been growing ever since they got those separate churches. Once they submitted to the appellation of servants, blacks, or Negroes, but now they require to be called coloured people, and among themselves, their common call of salutation is—gentlemen and ladies."[88] The image of the African Episcopal Church of St. Thomas in Philadelphia (figure 5.1) was created in the year before Watson recorded these words, so his prejudicial hostility may have even been directed at some of the people in that engraving. Apparently, Watson could not understand why blacks did not want to be called "servants, blacks, or Negroes," and he ascribed this change to "vanity" and their separate institutions. However, most northern clergymen did not object to using "coloured" by 1820.

As much as blacks, Indians, and Afro-Indians sought to influence how they were treated by emphasizing and promoting the use of some words and not others, white Americans and state governments also promoted these changes to the benefit of whites. In the context of the continued exploitation of black labor and Indian lands, whites gained from identifying both groups as "people of color." Describing how Afro-Indians and Indians came to be identified as colored people, historian David Silverman argues that according to dominant American ways of reckoning race, "Blackness trumped Indianness, and racial identity trumped community or tribal identity—a racial construction that conveniently enlarged the servile black labor pool while shrinking the number of Indians on the land." By claiming that no "pure" Indians or even any Indians existed in communities across Massachusetts, Connecticut, and elsewhere, early nineteenth-century whites nearly completed their appropriation of Indian lands in the Northeast. Whites asserted that being a "pure blood" was necessary for a person to be an "Indian." If they categorized remaining Indians as "people of color," then the Indians lacked any legal claim to ancestral lands and could be forced into menial forms of labor like blacks in the "free" North.[89]

It was not coincidental that the terms used to describe blacks and Indians changed in the period when northern slavery was ending and when independent black churches formed. As many blacks and Afro-Indians, especially newly freed African Americans, moved to port cities, this migration and emancipation made issues of identity especially visible and pressing. As all white men were increasingly treated as equals in the political sphere, race became a more significant identifier than class in northern society. Differences between the economic conditions of whites and blacks were increasingly ascribed to a supposed "innate inferiority" of blacks and not to the legacy of hundreds of years of enslavement. By creating separate institutions and by participating in interracial churches, blacks and Indians influenced the changing notions about race. Black people's influence upon interracial churches were evidenced by the ways that churches changed the words used to describe people. However, the ways that whites categorized people of color in churches also contributed to the rise of separate black churches and a broader range of racial segregation in northern society.[90]

Racism and racial segregation increased in northern states after slavery ended. Many black northerners founded and started worshipping in their own churches because of the prejudice they faced and because they believed separate churches would better promote their communities' interests. But, during the Early Republic from 1790 to 1820, black people's affiliation with predominantly white churches also increased, especially in Reformed and Presbyterian churches. After the 1820s, however, all churches became starkly divided by race, and thereby churches influenced segregation and the distancing of blacks and whites throughout northern society. As the era of the Early Republic transitioned into the antebellum era of the 1830s and 1840s, long-standing white prejudices against blacks and Indians developed into an inflexible and obstinate racism that increasingly stereotyped and degraded blacks and Indians and made interracial churches even more problematic and less common.

6 / "Suffering under the Rod of Despotic Pharaohs": The Segregated North and Black and Indian Christian Radicalism, 1821–1850

In 1833 Methodist minister and Pequot Indian William Apess published a tract in Boston that included this challenge to northern ministers and church leaders:

> Now, my brethren in the ministry, let me ask you a few sincere questions. Did you ever hear or read of Christ teaching his disciples that they ought to despise one because his skin was different from theirs? . . . If you can find a spirit like Jesus Christ and his Apostles prevailing now in any of the white congregations, I would like to know it. I ask: Is it not the case that everybody that is not white is treated with contempt and counted as barbarians? And I ask if the word of God justifies the white man in so doing.[1]

As if those questions were not convicting enough, Apess continued: "Why do you, who profess the Gospel and to have his [God's] spirit, act so contrary to it? Let me ask why the men of a different skin are so despised. Why are not they educated and placed in your pulpits?"[2] From Apess's perspective, whites' actions toward people of color in northern states were blatantly unchristian. Apess was not simply pointing out white hypocrisy or inconsistency; he was arguing that their actions proved that white northerners were not, in fact, Christians. He, therefore, called on whites to convert to the religion of Jesus, which would lead them to treat their "colored" brothers and sisters as equals. In this charge, he was joined by African American activists and preachers such as David

Walker. These black and Indian religious critiques were innovative and unprecedentedly radical. Although relatively few of these critiques were published, it seems likely that they were echoed and disseminated in oral forms. Blacks and Indians criticized whites throughout the colonial era, but it was no coincidence that these new types of Christian critiques occurred in a period when the number of interracial churches reached a century low point and when violence and antiblack and anti-Indian racism reached a peak in the nineteenth-century North. More than ever before, African Americans joined separate black churches not only because these churches better met their spiritual and practical needs but also because black people experienced greater resistance to their participation in white churches. Their exodus to separate churches was both willful and forced. Rejection and withdrawal were reciprocated by black and white Christians, but white northerners held a greater preponderance of power in churches and society.

Increasingly in the period of 1821 to 1850, northern whites expressed antiblack and anti-Indian sentiments, instigated race riots, and promoted segregation in churches, schools, public transportation, work, and neighborhoods. Writing in 1835, Englishman Edward Strutt Abdy saw such actions as constituting an "aristocracy of the skin." He was shocked that white Americans "should condemn nearly one-fifth of their fellow citizens, without pity, without remorse, and without a trial, to contempt and obloquy, for no reason but that of the strongest, and no crime but that of color." White northerners had expressed prejudicial views toward black and Indian peoples throughout the colonial era, but nineteenth-century racism was different from earlier forms of prejudice. The North, a group of states that contemporaries increasingly saw as a unified and distinct region, had instituted systematic segregation that was enforced by law and custom.[3]

In the early nineteenth century, northern states began to roll back the political rights they had earlier extended to black people. New Jersey (1807), Connecticut (1818), New York (1821), Rhode Island (1822), and Pennsylvania (1838) either eliminated laws that had allowed some blacks to vote, made it more difficult for blacks to vote, or explicitly restricted voting to whites. As states instituted universal suffrage for white men, they also generally excluded suffrage for all African Americans. The Connecticut Legislature made it illegal in 1833 for anyone to educate black children from other states without their town's permission to prevent schoolteacher Prudence Crandall from opening a school for black children in Canterbury. Even as the number of slaves continued to decline through gradual emancipation laws, private manumissions, and deaths, segregation expanded in the areas of education, employment, transportation, and entertainment.[4]

Urban race riots targeting black churches, upwardly mobile African Americans, and abolitionists became all too common. In October 1824, a white mob attacked a black neighborhood in Providence, Rhode Island, after a group of blacks refused to yield a sidewalk to some whites, and another antiblack riot occurred in 1831. In New York, a white mob targeted black people and white abolitionists in a riot lasting several nights in 1834. They destroyed the St. Phillip's African Episcopal Church building, a black school, two white churches that supported abolitionism, and at least a dozen African American homes. A mob attacked Philadelphia's African American community in 1834 and destroyed one black church, defaced another, and injured many people. Other incidents of mob violence directed at Philadelphia's black residents or their white allies took place in 1835, 1838, 1842, and 1849. White people attacked Hartford's black community in 1835 and destroyed a church and several homes. Mob violence against people of color marginalized them economically, politically, and socially.[5]

Increased discrimination and segregation had critical economic repercussions. Most antebellum whites were unwilling to work with people of color in any job, and they increasingly took steps to restrict black people's employment options. Some skilled black craftsmen in the eighteenth century worked alongside whites, but in the nineteenth century, white people gradually excluded African Americans from most skilled occupations. In describing the economic situation of the 1830s, Edward Strutt Abdy explained how one black man "had experienced great difficulty in obtaining an employment in which he could get his bread decently and respectably: with the exception of one or two employed as printers, one blacksmith, and one shoemaker, there are no colored mechanics in the city." Likewise, Abdy wrote that "there is not, I believe, one trade in New York, in which its colored inhabitants are allowed to work with the whites."[6]

Whites became so committed to racial separation that many advocated for colonization plans that they hoped would eventually eliminate people of color from the United States. The movements promoting Indian removal from the Southeast and Midwest to western reservations and black colonization to Africa or the Caribbean were grounded in the same desire to remove free people of color from the United States. Colonization plans were popular ideas among whites in the North and

FIGURE 6.1. *Colored Schools Broken Up, in the Free States* was created by northern abolitionists to depict the violence that northerners inflicted on free black communities. Illustration in the *American Anti-Slavery Almanac* for 1839 (New York: Published for the American Anti-Slavery Society, 1838), p. 15, Library Company of Philadelphia digital repository, www.librarycompany.org.

the South. Even "friends" of blacks and Indians argued that people of color could never prosper in the United States because of white prejudice. They believed that the best chance for blacks and Indians was their colonization to distant lands. According to historian Graham Hodges: "In the past, white churches had provided some amelioration to blacks for their painful existence. Even this changed for the worse in the antebellum years as white churches spent much of their efforts promoting colonization." The Society for the Colonization of Free People of Color of America was founded in 1816, and it was a white organization that sought to promote the voluntary migration of free African Americans to territories outside the United States. Numerous slave owners joined this society, and not coincidentally, most blacks and Indians opposed colonization and removal plans. Many (perhaps most) whites in both the North and South did not want free blacks or free Indians to remain in the United States.[7]

As evidenced by popular literature and town histories, white New Englanders came to believe that northern Indians were becoming extinct. *The Last of the Mohicans: A Narrative of 1757* by James Fenimore Cooper, first published in February 1826, is the most famous of many accounts that described the last living members of the "dying" or "vanishing" Indian "races." Indians did not disappear, but New Englanders sometimes classified Indians as "blacks" or "colored," which helped perpetuate the belief in vanishing Indians (see chapter 5). Myths that suggested all New England Indians were dead and gone corresponded with growing segregation in public life and colonization plans that sought to create an entirely white North.[8]

The substantial decline in black participation in predominantly white churches, the rise of systematic segregation in northern society, and the articulations of radical Christian critiques of whites are important because they complicate the traditional historical narrative that stresses the North's progressiveness and opposition to slavery in the South. Between the Missouri Compromise of 1820 and the Compromise of 1850, northerners in Congress tended to oppose the extension of slavery to western territories. After 1830, a vocal minority of white northerners joined African Americans to create abolitionist campaigns that included organizations such as the American Anti-Slavery Society and publications such as the *Liberator*. Some northern reformers also opposed the forced removals of Cherokees, Creeks, and others from the Southeast. These antebellum political developments, as well as southern proslavery activism and the Civil War, tend to obscure the fact that the North instituted widespread segregation, morally supported by churches, during the same period. From the perspective of David Walker, William Apess, and many others, the antebellum North did not look particularly progressive.[9]

The North became the first thoroughly segregated society in America as whites further disenfranchised, economically marginalized, and segregated blacks, Afro-Indians, and Indians in all public spaces and encouraged them to leave the United States. Churches played a significant, albeit usually passive, role in these developments. If any institutions could have minimized or critiqued the rising segregation and antiblack and anti-Indian racism, it was churches because of their widely accepted moral authority. Abolitionists in 1834 noted that "vast moral power is thus wielded over our republic" by its churches.[10] However, the growing separation of whites and blacks in churches gave moral sanction to segregation in other aspects of society.

Black participation levels decreased in all types of predominantly white churches in this period, especially after 1830. In locations where they had not done so already, African Americans routinely formed new congregations by withdrawing from predominantly white ones. After protesting against segregation within the church for more than a decade, twenty black members of the Second Congregational Church in Portland, Maine, withdrew and formed the Abyssinian Congregational Church in 1835.[11] Separate black churches were increasingly available across the North, and growing discrimination encouraged blacks to leave white churches. Black men and women worshipped in African American churches because these congregations fostered black leaders, supported the education of black children, and were politically organized to help black communities. Racism or being ejected from a white church may not have always been the strongest reason for why blacks withdrew from white churches, but hostility to black worshippers increased in white churches during this era. Overall, only small numbers of black Christians chose to remain part of predominantly white churches after the 1820s, including a group of Christians who believed that the reintegration of churches was the best hope for combatting racism. The overwhelming majority of people of color favored greater religious separation. The precipitous decline in black affiliation across all Protestant denominations after 1820 gave implicit moral sanction to segregation in other areas of society, which in turn helped to provoke militant Christian critiques of white Americans.

Black Participation in Predominantly White Churches

David Walker, Frederick Douglass, and William Apess criticized the segregated seating arrangements in predominantly white churches and the ways that these congregations tended to push away people of color instead of welcoming them during the antebellum years. Walker lamented how "pretended" white Christians, particularly in his adopted home of Boston, were prejudiced toward blacks. "Even here in Boston, pride and prejudice have got to such a pitch," Walker wrote, "that in the very houses erected to the Lord, they have built little places for the reception of coloured people, where they must sit during meeting, or keep away from the house of God, and the preachers say nothing about it—much less go into the hedges and highways seeking the lost sheep of the house of Israel, and try to bring them in to their Lord and Maker." Walker specifically mentioned the expulsion of a black man from a ground-floor pew, describing it as "an act of cruelty inflicted a few days since on a black man, by the white Christians in the PARK STREET CHURCH, in this (CITY) which is almost enough to make Demons themselves quake and tremble in, their FIERY HABITATIONS" (an ironic phrasing because Park Street Church is nicknamed "Brimstone Corner"). The treatment that black people received in northern predominantly white churches was a significant factor that caused the low rates of black affiliation with these churches.[12]

Between 1821 and 1850, and especially in the latter part of this period, there was a substantial decrease in the number of predominantly white churches baptizing and admitting African Americans, despite the proliferation of new churches and the engagement of some churches in antislavery politics. As absolute numbers and as percentages of the membership, black participation rates in white Protestant churches were lower in the middle of the nineteenth century than they had been in the late eighteenth century. The decline in black baptisms correlated with the increased availability of independent black churches in northern cities and towns. Increased hostility toward blacks in white churches paralleled and reinforced separation across society as a whole. African Americans denounced the ways that predominantly white churches treated people of color, but they also did not want to attend these churches because they asserted that whites were not adhering to true Christianity.[13]

Black men and women affiliated with only a small number of Con-gregational churches. Although black baptismal and membership rates had been declining since the 1760s in many locations, they plummeted after the 1810s. Whereas forty-four Congregational churches had mul-tiple black baptisms or members between 1791 and 1820, only fifteen of the Congregational churches examined for this study had multiple black, Indian, or Afro-Indian baptisms or members between 1821 and 1850. These fifteen churches baptized or admitted only a total of fifty-two people of color. During the same time period, the number of Congre-gational churches in New England rose substantially, but few of these churches included black congregants. Undoubtedly, very few black peo-ple affiliated with either the Trinitarian or the Unitarian Congregational churches after 1820.[14]

At least twenty-four northern Episcopal churches continued to admit and baptized black people, which was the same number of Episcopal churches that did so between 1791 and 1820. At these churches, 237 African Americans were baptized or became a communicant (see table 6.1). However, most of these Episcopal churches contained fewer black

TABLE 6.1. Predominantly white Episcopal churches with multiple black
baptisms or communicants admitted, 1821–1850

Church	Location	Approximate number of black baptisms
St. John's Church Portsmouth	Portsmouth, N.H.	7
Christ Church Boston	Boston, Mass.	5
Trinity Church Boston	Boston, Mass.	24
Trinity Church Newport	Newport, R.I.	8
Christ Church Westerly	Westerly, R.I.	4
Holy Trinity/Christ Church Middletown	Middletown, Conn.	11
St. Paul's Church	Norwalk, Conn.	6
Christ Church	Norwich, Conn.	7
St. John's Church	Stamford, Conn.	3
Christ Church North Guilford	North Guilford, Conn.	3
Christ Church Bethany	Bethany, Conn.	6
St. John's Church Bridgeport	Bridgeport, Conn.	4
Christ Church Stratford	Stratford, Conn.	8
Trinity Church New York & its parishes	New York, N.Y.	19
Saint Andrew's Church Richmond	Staten Island, N.Y.	7
Saint Paul's Church Tompkinsville	Tompkinsville, N.Y.	36
St. John's Church Yonkers	Yonkers, N.Y.	24
St. John's Church Johnstown	Johnstown, N.Y.	2
St. Michael's Church	Trenton, N.J.	9
St. Peter's Church in Perth Amboy	Perth Amboy, N.J.	12
Trinity Church (Old Swedes)	Swedesboro, N.J.	8
St. Mary's Burlington	Burlington, N.J.	9
Trinity Church of Oxford	Philadelphia, Pa.	4
St. James Church Lancaster	Lancaster, Pa.	11
Total		237

persons than in preceding decades, and the baptisms were concentrated in the 1820s and not the 1830s or 1840s. For example, at Trinity Church Boston, about twenty-four blacks were baptized between 1821 and 1850, compared to sixty between 1791 and 1820. Even Episcopal churches, which had often included the highest number of black people of any denomination in northern cities, baptized fewer African Americans.[15]

The number of burials for African Americans exceeded the number of black baptisms at some of these churches, which also suggests a trend away from black participation in Episcopal churches. At least eight black people were baptized at Trinity Church Newport between 1821 and 1840, but twenty-seven deceased African Americans (many who died elderly) were buried under the auspices of this Episcopal church in the same period. A small number of blacks remained active members of this Episcopal parish through the 1840s, even after a separate black church was founded in Newport in 1824, but there was a definite decline in the number of new African Americans affiliating with Trinity and other Episcopal churches compared to previous eras.[16]

Black participation rates declined in predominantly white Presbyterian and Reformed churches, although some of these churches continued to baptize blacks. At least twenty-two Reformed churches (down from thirty-two in the 1791–1820 period) and at least fifteen Presbyterian churches (down from twenty-three in the 1791–1820 period) included multiple black baptisms. These churches baptized or admitted at least 383 African Americans (see table 6.2).

In at least a couple of cases, Dutch Reformed and Presbyterian churches baptized a significant number of black people, but, on the whole, black participation in these churches declined rapidly in the 1830s and 1840s. The First Reformed Church of Coxsackie, New York (located south of Albany on the Hudson River), baptized and admitted to membership a remarkable number of blacks in the 1820s, but fewer were baptized there in the 1830s and 1840s. Sixty-five blacks, including both enslaved and free people, were baptized there between 1821 and 1836. Fifty-three African Americans were admitted to membership and communion at this church in 1821 alone, including twenty-eight free people. During that year, large numbers of both whites and blacks were baptized and admitted to this church. Reverend Gilbert Livingston explained that so many people joined his church during this religious revival that the church's building "became too small to accommodate the Worshippers." Because of this local revival, many blacks joined the First Reformed Church of Coxsackie in 1821, and twenty-eight more blacks joined between 1822

TABLE 6.2. Reformed and Presbyterian churches with multiple black baptisms and/or black members, 1821–1850

Church	Location	Approximate number of black baptisms/members
Reformed Dutch Church at Greenwich	New York, N.Y.	12
First Presbyterian Church New York	New York, N.Y.	14
First Presbyterian Church Albany	Albany, N.Y.	3
Second Reformed Church Albany	Albany, N.Y.	5
Wawarsing Reformed Dutch Church	Wawarsing, N.Y.	3
Presbyterian Church Elmhurst (Newtown)	Elmhurst, N.Y.	18
Staten Island Dutch Reformed Church	Staten Island, N.Y.	4
Reformed Dutch Church in Tompkinsville	Tompkinsville, N.Y.	2
First Presbyterian Church Ballston	Ballston, N.Y.	2
First United Presbyterian Church Cambridge	Cambridge, N.Y.	4
First Reformed Church of Coxsackie	Coxsackie, N.Y.	65
Reformed Dutch Church Wynantskill	Wynantskill, N.Y	3
Pompton Plains Reformed Dutch Church	Pompton Plains, N.Y.	10
Reformed Dutch Church of Catskill	Catskill, N.Y.	4
Presbyterian Church in Charlton	Charlton, N.Y	2
Presbyterian Church of Johnstown	Johnstown, N.Y.	2
German Reformed Church New Rhinebeck	Cobleskill, N.Y.	4
Protestant Dutch Church of Greenbush	Greenbush, N.Y.	11
Reformed Protestant Dutch Church of Florida	Florida, N.Y.	2
Dutch Reformed Church Schenectady	Schenectady, N.Y.	5
Kingsborough Ave Presbyterian Gloversville	Gloversville, N.Y	13
Reformed Protestant Dutch Church of Nassau	Nassau, N.Y.	8

TABLE 6.2 (*continued*). Reformed and Presbyterian churches with multiple black baptisms and/or black members, 1821–1850

Church	Location	Approximate number of black baptisms/members
Reformed Dutch Church of Schodack	Schodack, N.Y.	18
Hurley Reformed Dutch Church,	Ulster County, N.Y	2
Reformed Protestant Dutch Church Bloomingburgh, N.Y.		5
Saddle River Reformed Dutch Church	Saddle River, N.J	34
Old Brick Reformed Dutch Church	Marlboro, N.J.	19
First Reformed Dutch Church	Hackensack, N.J.	3
First Presbyterian Church Cranbury	Cranbury, N.J.	19
First Presbyterian Congregation	Mendham, N.J.	8
Presbyterian Church of Lawrenceville	Lawrenceville, N.J.	17
Rockaway Presbyterian Church	Rockaway, N.J.	3
Bloomfield Presbyterian Church	Bloomfield, N.J.	6
Reformed Church at Readington, N.J.	Readington, N.J.	8
Presbyterian Church in Flemington	Flemington, N.J.	13
Pascack Dutch Reformed Church	Park Ridge, N.J.	15
First Presbyterian Church Elizabeth, N.J	Elizabeth, N.J.	17
	Total	383

and 1843. Some of the black people admitted to membership did not remain members for very long, but a couple dozen of them continued to be "recognized as members" through 1852.[17] Coxsackie was exceptional because almost all the other Reformed and Presbyterians churches included fewer than twenty black participants and many of them had fewer than five black participants during these decades.

In the Presbyterian churches that baptized African Americans, the rate of baptisms declined relative to earlier periods. For example, between 1811 and 1820, twenty-six blacks were baptized, and between 1806 and 1820, twenty-three blacks were admitted to communion in the First Presbyterian Church of Elizabeth, New Jersey. Conversely, only seventeen persons of color were baptized or admitted as members between 1821 and 1850. In 1835, nine black persons were members of this church, which represented only 2 percent of the 445 Presbyterian church members in Elizabeth, New Jersey.[18]

The tendency toward separation was also strong among Methodists, Baptists, and Lutherans. Methodist and Baptist churches were by far the most common types of independent black churches. If a separate black church was available in a given location, in all likelihood, it was a Baptist or Methodist church. Black Methodists worked tirelessly to found new African Methodist Episcopal (AME) and African Methodist Episcopal Zion (AMEZ) churches, and relatively few predominantly white Methodist churches contained black members by the 1830s. The process for ordaining Baptist and Methodist ministers was comparatively easy and did not require extensive theological training, so black Baptists and Methodists were ordained much more frequently than black Episcopalians, Congregationalists, and Presbyterians. Moreover, black men, including Alexander Crummell, were denied admittance to the General Theological Seminary of the Episcopal Church, making the path to ordination for black Episcopalians even more difficult.[19]

The process that began in the 1790s of groups of black Methodists removing themselves from predominantly white Methodist churches continued into the antebellum period in locations where African Americans had yet to form separate churches. Take, for instance, the Methodist church in Gettysburg, Pennsylvania. This predominantly white Methodist church included a class for black Methodists, and the black Methodists sat in a segregated seating area of the church during worship services. Around 1838, black people in Gettysburg began forming a separate Methodist church, "the Coloured People's Church." In February 1841, white leaders reported that "the colored class" had "withdrawn from the Methodist E. Church and joined with the parties called the Bethelites excepting twenty one who still remain." Some blacks remained at the predominantly white church for a time, but the trend toward greater separation among Methodists was unmistakable.[20]

Although some northern Baptist and Lutheran churches contained black members and congregants, most of these churches saw declines in black participation levels. Of all the churches sampled, fourteen predominantly white Baptist churches and only two Lutheran churches baptized or admitted multiple African Americans to their congregations. The First Baptist Church of Providence, Rhode Island, and First Baptist of Newport, Rhode Island, exceeded all others by each admitting nineteen African Americans in this era.[21]

For all northern denominations, policies that marginalized or excluded black people contributed to the decline in African American affiliation rates. More evidence exists from this era regarding the intentional exclusion of blacks from predominantly white churches than from any earlier decade. Public resistance to integration was a major factor in the decline of black participation in predominantly white churches. As David Walker noted, whites forcibly excluded a black man from a seat at the Park Street Congregational Church, although he had the legal claim to a church pew. Frederick Brinsley, a "colored man" who lived on Elm Street, was given the pew at Park Street Church as payment for a debt. Unable to sell the pew for his desired price, Brinsley, his wife, and children occupied the pew one Sunday in February or March 1830. After the service, he received a note from the church informing him that his pew had been rented to another man without his consent. Another note dated March 6, 1830, read as follows:

> Mr. Frederick Brinsley.
>
> Sir, The Prudential committee of Park Street Church, notify you not to occupy any pew on the lower floor of Park Street Meeting-house on any Sabbath, or on any other day, during the time of Divine worship, after this date—and, if you go there, with such intent, you will hazard the consequences. The pews in the upper galleries are at your service. George Odiorne, for the Committee.

When Brinsley returned to the church, he found a constable "at the pew-door," and he made no more attempts at sitting anywhere in this church. A similar affair occurred in a Baptist church in Randolph, Massachusetts. In 1842 James G. Birney noted that "in a large proportion of Congregational churches the arrangement of the negro pew as in the other sects is maintained and colored members are not welcomed to the same seats with their white brethren." Some churches explicitly indicated that black people would not be accepted as equal church members or attendees if they were welcome at all.[22]

Some white Presbyterians in New York City also displayed an aggressive opposition to including blacks on equal terms in their churches. In 1834, the merchant and antislavery activist Arthur Tappan brought Samuel Cornish, "an almost-white Presbyterian clergyman," to sit with him in his ground-floor pew at the Laight Street Presbyterian Church in New York City. This action caused such a controversy that some white church members threatened to leave the church. In 1837 Reverend Cornish wrote: "The Church of Jesus Christ, at the present day, has become corrupt to the very core. Slavery in her southern sections and prejudice in her northern have eaten out her very vitals." Racial distinctions and separation more and more permeated northern society, and since the churches were rarely different from other social institutions in separating blacks from whites, they implicitly supported segregation across all of society.[23]

The predominantly white Baptist Church of Geneva, New York, included black members, but at least some white people took steps to make them feel unwelcome and unequal. The church was founded in the late 1820s, and African Americans had been members since 1827. Around 1830, a conflict about seating developed between whites and blacks. The church members "voted that the back seats in the Gallery be reserved to the use of the Coloured people from this time forward." To make matters worse, the church built a high partition to separate whites and blacks sitting in the gallery. The black members objected to this partition and to separate seating during communion. They reached a compromise in late 1831, and nine more blacks joined the church between April and July 1832, but the unequal treatment of blacks at communion continued. By 1837, most of the black members had determined to withdraw and form a separate Baptist church.[24]

White churches' support for separating people was also made public by their consistent support of colonization plans and the American Colonization Society. On several occasions in the late 1820s and 1830s, the General Association of Congregational Churches in Connecticut adopted resolutions in favor of colonizing blacks overseas. In 1827, the convening white ministers voted that they "highly approve of the object and exertions of the Colonization Society, and do recommend to the ministers in our connection, in this state, to use their influence in that way they shall judge proper, to aid the Society." Reformed and Presbyterian churches also supported African American colonization, which likely caused some black Christians to question their affiliation with white churches. The General Synod of the Reformed Dutch Church endorsed the American Colonization Society's plan to send free blacks to Africa in 1820. Like other northern Christians, Reformed ministers and laity justified colonization and separatism under the guise of benevolence. As slave owners were dominant figures in the American Colonization Society, northern African Americans, including David Walker, denounced colonization plans and those who supported them. It seems hard to imagine that blacks would have felt welcome in predominantly white churches whose ministers used "their influence" to promote the removal of people of color from American society.[25]

The missionary approach of Congregationalists also shifted away from a strategy of including Indians and other nonwhites within their churches, schools, and towns following an attempt to educate and convert "heathens" at a "Foreign Mission School" in Cornwall, Connecticut, between 1817 and 1826. Native Americans, Pacific Islanders, and people from distant parts of the globe were educated there in the hope that they would bring Christianity back to their homelands. The school became mired in controversy when two Cherokee scholars married local white women in 1824 and 1826. In newspapers and private correspondence, some whites pronounced intense opposition to the missionary school and cross-racial interactions. These weddings led to a collapse in donations for the school and its closure, and Congregationalists shifted their evangelization strategy to sending white missionaries overseas instead of seeking to include, convert, and civilize racialized others at home.[26]

Despite the treatment that many of them faced and the fact that most blacks and Indians chose separate churches, small numbers of black people decided to remain active in white churches for theological, social, or practical reasons. In September 1834, when the Second Congregational Church of Woodstock, Connecticut, ordained a new minister, the church included two "colored" women among the 124 church members. For some African Americans, business connections or personal relationships with white people were important factors in keeping them connected to these churches. Other black people stayed at a predominantly white church because of long-standing attachments or for a theological preference. Roughly 5 percent of Philadelphia's black churchgoers (about 150 households) attended one of the twenty-three predominantly white churches, indicating that not everyone moved their affiliation to a black church.[27]

The case of the Kingston Congregational Church in Kingston, Rhode Island, and the Fayerweather family is instructive for why a minority of blacks and Afro-Indians selectively remained in predominantly white churches. For this family, their blacksmith business required connections to the white community. Reverend Oliver Brown, associated with the Massachusetts Society for Promoting Christian Knowledge, began ministry work in Kingston in 1819 and organized a church a year later. Nancy Rodman Fayerweather and Isabella Fayerweather were among the thirteen people received as members of the church in 1836. The church records state, "Nancy wife of George Fayerweather (col'd) rcd 1836." This

George Fayerweather was the son of George Fayerweather Sr., who had been enslaved to Reverend Samuel Fayerweather, minister of St. Paul's Episcopal Church in Narragansett, Rhode Island. George Fayerweather II married Nancy Rodman, an Indian or Afro-Indian, and he opened a blacksmith shop in the village of Kingston in 1820. They attended the predominantly white Congregational church located just down the road from their home and blacksmith shop. Relationships with fellow congregants would have been important to the success of George's business. Although it is not clear whether or not George Fayerweather II joined the church, his wife and at least one daughter became members. In addition, 18 of 169 students in the church's Sunday School in 1833 were African Americans. The Fayerweathers, who can be described as black or Afro-Indian, chose this mostly white Congregational church as their spiritual home, likely for both spiritual and commercial reasons.[28]

The presence of the Fayerweather family at the Kingston Congregational Church and the relationships that they had with other congregants may have had a direct effect on the church's politics. At a congregational meeting in December 1841, the church members adopted a strong anti-slavery position grounded in their theology. The members unanimously acknowledged slavery "as a great sin against God," which was "opposed to the fundamental principles of the gospel of the blessed Savior." They rejected fellowship with anyone "who participate in its guilt or encourage or abet the holding of slaves in any way whatever." Although the Kingston Congregational church retained some black members and installed antislavery into their church polity, these two trends did not necessarily correlate in other churches. Ironically, some northern churches began directing antislavery petitions against southern states even as fewer blacks affiliated with their churches. The moral crusade of abolitionism, of which some churches played important roles, was not built upon the widespread existence of interracial churches. Moreover, numerous churches did not adopt an antislavery position in the antebellum era.[29]

Boston had five predominantly white Congregational churches with which black people affiliated during this period despite the existence of a black Baptist church and a black Methodist church. The records from Hanover Street Congregational Church (name changed to Bowdoin Street Church in 1831), during the pastorate of Reverend Lyman Beecher, suggest why some black people affiliated with white churches in this era. Personal relationships and Beecher's theology and preaching style influenced the black people who sought to join this congregation. Beecher was so popular that between March 1826 and January

1833, 195 men and 330 women became members.[30] At least four African Americans applied for membership at this church, and two were admitted. Ann Maria Clary, Mary Stanley, Dorcas Lew, and Phillip Harris met with church leaders to discuss their religious experiences and beliefs and the reasons for seeking admission to this church, and notes from these meetings survived.[31]

Ann Maria Clary, who had recently moved to Boston from Milford, was the first black person to seek membership at Hanover Church. She was interviewed at the home of Deacon Daniel Noyes in January 1828. Clary stated that her recent interest in religion was the result of a conversation with a Miss Newell (at least two Miss Newells were members by 1828). Afterward, she was engaged in prayer and Bible reading, and she felt that God had redeemed her about three weeks before her confession, evidenced by her beginning to feel happy, loving other Christians as never before, and sensing a nearness to Jesus Christ. If the Miss Newell who encouraged her interest in religion had gone to this church, then a personal relationship perhaps explains Clary's interest in attending this church.[32]

Mary Stanley, who was a single black woman, interviewed for membership in March 1828, and she was admitted to the church. Stanley had been a member since 1825 of the Green Street Congregational Church. She was one of two black members of the Green Street Church, which was founded in 1823. Stanley indicated that a sermon preached by Reverend Benjamin Wisner, pastor of the Old South Church, initiated her attention to religion. Although Stanley lived in the household of a man who attended Reverend Thomas Paul's African Baptist Church, she felt stronger ties to the evangelical Congregational churches. Stanley was influenced by the preaching of Old South's pastor and affiliated with one and then with a second predominantly white Congregational church. Stanley's move to the Hanover Church seems to have been based on a practical concern, "because her situation is such that she cannot hear" at the Green Street Church. Such a statement suggests that the segregated seating arrangement at Green Street Church, either because of poor acoustics, distance from the pulpit, or a quiet preacher, made sermons difficult for her to hear. Stanley was also acquainted with a person who belonged to Hanover Church, which may have influenced her decision. Stanley married a man with the last name of Pierre sometime after she joined Hanover Church. She was still a member in 1843 when she lived on Holden Place, but Mary Stanley-Pierre died sometime between 1844 and 1849.[33]

Phillip Harris was the third African American to seek membership at Hanover Church, and he was admitted in May 1829. He had attended Hanover Church for about a year before seeking membership, and he attended this church because he "Enjoys the preaching." Harris indicated that he had been a member of an Episcopal church for four years. Harris lived on Ann Street (now known as North Street), close to Hanover Church. Since Harris stated that he "prays in his family," he likely brought other family members to the Hanover Church for worship services. Harris's whereabouts were "unknown" to the church in 1843.[34]

For both Harris and Stanley, early published directories, such as the 1837 list, included a racial notation next to their names. However, the list of members published in 1856 did not include racial notations, even though it listed Harris and Stanley as historic (now deceased) members. Since the number of black people associated with this church declined in the 1840s, the absence of such designations in 1856 could mean that the church had no black members by that date. It appears that the African American presence was erased from the public memory after their physical presence in the church had ceased.[35]

Dorcas Lew was interviewed for church membership in August 1832. She was a member of the African Baptist Church, but she sought membership in the Bowdoin Street Church located nearby. In addition to knowing Mary Stanley, she also mentioned that she was acquainted with several white congregants. These relationships, which could have been personal or business in nature, seemed to influence her decision to seek membership in this church. The African Baptist Church was also in a state of flux and transition between the 1829 resignation of Reverend Paul and the 1838 settlement of Reverend G. H. Black, and the state of this church may have affected Lew's desire to change churches. The committee gave her a "favorable" recommendation for membership, but other church records indicate that her request for membership was "Deferred." She may have chosen to remain at the African Baptist Church, or the Bowdoin Street Church's leadership may have developed other reservations about her application for membership.[36]

Some of the African Americans who remained members of predominantly white churches in the 1830s and 1840s were older adults who had spent most of their lives affiliated with a certain church or theological tradition. Ichabod Pease, for example, was a member of St. James Episcopal Church in New London, Connecticut, for more than sixty years. Pease continued to attend this predominantly white church because, in the words of his pastor: "He loved the church and her ways. The words of the liturgy were to him as household words, and were as manna to his mouth." The burial records note his 1842 death with the following statement: "Mar. 5, 1842. Buried Ichabod Pease, aged 86. A man of colour, who for more than sixty years was a communicant in this parish, and, adorned, as few do, his Christian professions." Reverend Robert Hallam preached a sermon at his burial that was subsequently published, and Hallam could not have been more effusive in eulogizing Pease. He stated that Pease's "naked goodness, without the adventitious aids of wealth, rank, learning, distinguished talents, or brilliant deeds, shines in its simple majesty and loveliness, and secures the regard and homage of all hearts." Hallam continued that he "believed in the Lord with all his heart." Hallam described how Pease started attending the church while confined by the "miserable system" of slavery and was taught about Christianity by his Episcopalian owner. During the Revolution, he ran away from his Loyalist owner, Robinson Mumford, but Pease was claimed by John Deshon after the war as payment for Mumford's debt. Pease received religious instruction from Bishop Seabury and became a communicant in 1785. Although it was relatively common for paternalistic whites to praise a particular African American as a moral example for other blacks, it was unheard of for a white person to hold up an African American as a moral example for whites. Hallam did tell the "people of color" to honor the memory of Pease by resolving "to be like him; to do as he did," but he also told all the church's communicants, who were mostly white, that Pease's "life and death solemnly admonish them to be steadfast, unmoving, always abounding in the work of the Lord." This black Episcopalian, a longtime member of a Connecticut parish, was held up as a model Christian for the entire, mostly white community. Pease's standing in this church was rare for black people within predominantly white churches, but long-standing ties kept some blacks affiliated with white churches well into the antebellum era.[37]

Sometimes black men and women joined white churches for reasons particular to their circumstances or their location. Susan James was an African American woman who joined the predominantly white First Baptist Church of Boston in 1830. James had been a member of the African Baptist Church in Boston. She was "a young lady who was awakened under the ministry of Elder Paul, &, when very young, joined the Chh under his care." However, she left the African Baptist Church following the resignation of Reverend Thomas Paul as that church faced internal divisions. Perhaps because of the contentious departure of her mentor, James decided to try a different church. Benjamin Wigden and his wife,

Mary Wigden, both "colored" people, were constituent members of the Friendship Seventh Day Baptist Church in rural Friendship, New York (located in western New York near the border with Pennsylvania), when it was founded in 1824. Another black woman soon joined this church also. Especially in some rural locations such as Friendship, New York, no black churches existed nearby.[38]

African Americans may have remained members of some predominantly white churches because of the racial equality that at least a few churches actually practiced. Cato Pearce, for example, affiliated with a couple of predominantly white churches that, according to his autobiography, treated him with a great deal of respect. Cato Pearce was born to enslaved parents in Kingston, Rhode Island, in 1790. For most of his childhood, he was an unfree laborer, but he ran away in 1808 and again a couple of years later. Pearce attended a variety of Protestant churches, including both predominantly black and predominantly white ones, before settling into an interracial Baptist community. Pearce attended services with mostly African Americans in Providence, Rhode Island, that were led by white Methodist minister V. R. Osborn. However, after he moved from Providence, his spiritual journey took a different direction. Pearce preached to predominantly white audiences on several occasions. In describing one of the religious gatherings, Pearce wrote that "I got up and talked, and we had a first rate meeting."[39]

After another move for work, Pearce was invited to attend a Presbyterian church service, and when he arrived, he was ushered into "the *box* for the colored people." He stated that this service did not do him any good because he could hardly hear the minister who preached, unlike Pearce, from prepared notes: "I was so fur [far] off from him, and he preached by note, that I could n't understand hardly any thing he said— only once in a while, 'Lord Jesus Christ.' I thought to myself I wished I had n't come; for the meetin' did n'nt do me any good." In contrast, when Pearce went to the Chestnut Hill Baptist Church in Killingly, Connecticut, on the next Sunday, "many pew doors was opened for me to come in and set down . . . and I felt as if I was to home—for them was my people." Congregants invited him to share his religious testimony, and at his request, the church soon accepted Pearce as a member. In subsequent gatherings, Pearce preached to predominantly white audiences. While one of his employers, Elisha Potter, cursed Pearce, saying, "I wo' n't have no nigger preachers," Pearce seemed to have maintained good relationships with the white Baptists of his church, particularly deacon Thomas Cole of Cranston, Rhode Island. In some churches, whites and blacks continued to worship and preach together, but such religious communities were uncommon in the antebellum North.[40]

All types of northern Protestant churches became increasingly homogeneous during the antebellum period. A long history of interracial religious worship gave way to increasing segregation. Most blacks, Afro-Indians, and Indians worshipped in separate churches, and they founded many more such institutions during this period. Although small numbers of people of color remained in Congregational, Episcopalian, Presbyterian, Reformed, Baptist, and other churches, the number of black baptisms and members decreased in these churches, especially in the 1830s and 1840s. While people of color resolutely supported their own churches, some white Christians also took actions to expel and discourage black participation in their churches. White churches lent their moral authority to segregation and separation across society when they supported colonization or prevented African Americans from sitting with white attendees. However, small bands of white and black Christians challenged this new status quo by explicitly arguing that segregation was unchristian.

Church Integrationists

Some black and white Christians responded to the rise of segregation in northern churches and society by arguing that churches should reintegrate. These integrationists were a small minority of northerners, but they identified the increased separation of blacks and whites as a cause of the worsening conditions for African Americans in northern society. They advocated integration as the best option available for combatting antiblack sentiments and actions. Many of the integrationists were abolitionists who saw integration as part of their moral crusade to eliminate sin from America, but a few integrationists were not outspoken abolitionists. These white and black Christians supported integration based on their reading of scripture, and they included people such as William C. Nell, William Lloyd Garrison, and Harvey Newcomb.

The most famous of Boston's integrationists of the mid-nineteenth century was African American historian and activist William C. Nell. He spearheaded campaigns to integrate Boston's schools, public transportation, and theaters, but he also stated that churches should be integrated. Nell opposed all forms of segregation, arguing that separate institutions, even those that sought to elevate blacks, should be phased out because of their implicit support of inequality. Nell not only promoted integration through speeches and newspapers, but he also lived out this principle. He attended the integrated worship services of the radical Unitarian Theodore Parker, along with self-emancipated slaves William and Ellen Craft, whom Parker described as "sober and industrious people" and "members of my parish." Nell was also a close friend and associate of William Lloyd Garrison, who was one of the vocal white promoters of integration.[41]

Northern abolitionists fought against racial segregation in churches. Garrison's work as an abolitionist organizer and publisher was complemented by his work as an integrationist, and he promoted church integration with his newspaper, the *Liberator*. Other abolitionists followed Garrison's lead and opposed segregated seating within churches and sometimes racially distinct churches. "God 'is no respecter of persons,'" insisted Gerrit Smith in 1841, "'nor regardeth he the rich more than the poor, for they are all the work of his hands;'—therefore the Abolitionist must refuse to attend worship in those Churches, where a colored skin is made a badge of inferiority, and a justification for contempt and hatred." The Broadway Tabernacle of New York City, organized by abolitionists in 1836, included at least five "colored" members in the 1840s. The antislavery activist Lewis Tappan, who was more conservative than Garrison, tried but was unsuccessful in eliminating the segregation of black worshippers at the Chatham Chapel in New York City. New England's local antislavery organizations in the 1840s defined segregated seating in churches as one of the principal evils in America. One antislavery convention after another condemned "Negro pews" and the ambivalent position of most churches on the issue of slavery. Radical abolitionists believed that they should attend neither churches that did not condemn slavery nor churches that maintained segregated seating. This insistence on racial integration in churches likely made abolitionists even less popular among other northerners. It was easier to condemn slavery in the somewhat distant South than it was to change the practices of segregation in one's own church, among one's own personal and professional relationships. Abolitionists, in these years, were an unpopular minority in the North because they called for radical social changes. However, some of the more moderate people in New England who supported the Liberty Party and the Free Soil Party also opposed segregation in northern society.[42]

One of the most articulate condemnations of segregated church seating came from the writer, journalist, and Congregational minister Harvey Newcomb. In 1837, he published a book titled *The "Negro Pew":*

Being an Inquiry Concerning the Propriety of Distinctions in the House of God, on Account of Color. This work contained a lengthy condemnation of segregated seating in churches and argued that blacks were not intellectually or morally inferior to whites. Newcomb provided a sensitive articulation of how many black people felt in predominantly white churches and argued that "No man would be willing that his constitutional peculiarities, which God gave him, should exclude him from equal privileges in the house of God." Although Newcomb was particularly concerned about eliminating white prejudice in churches, he argued that prejudice against skin color in any sphere of life was shameful and sinful. He stated that "there never was a more narrow-minded, ignoble, and despicable sentiment than the prevailing prejudice against color" and that "the church, as such, wherever these practices prevail, is guilty of countenancing, upholding, and perpetuating . . . A SIN!" This sort of condemnation of racism and segregated churches was heard from white and black abolitionists, but even some Christians who were less connected to abolitionism, such as Newcomb, fought for integration in churches. For Newcomb and others, their Christian faith caused them to oppose racial prejudices.[43]

Two Unitarian ministers of the elite West Church in Boston also sought to eliminate segregated seating in worship services. Reverend Charles Lowell, pastor of this church from 1806 to 1861, and the assistant pastor, Reverend Cyrus Bartol, eventually promoted the integration of church pews. Beginning in about 1837, Bartol and some parishioners sought to eliminate segregated seating at West Church. Years later, Bartol related that "colored men and women were seen every Sunday" in a segregated portion of the gallery, and he found this practice incompatible with the doctrine of the unity in Christ. Although Lowell initially resisted the idea, he soon became a forceful advocate of integration despite the objections of wealthy congregants. Nonetheless, Lowell and Bartol did not initially convince a majority in their church that they should be "no respecter of persons," and the policy of segregated seating did not quickly change. The black Unitarians at West Church also protested the inequitable treatment by the 1850s, but to no avail. In June 1854, Lowell sent a letter to his congregation and again made known his disappointment that the church excluded black people from seating in ground-floor pews. Lowell noted that an elderly black woman, who was a "respectable, modest, humble, sensible, pious woman," sat in the segregated gallery. When this church had communion, this black woman sat in Lowell's pew, but the church's seating policy kept her otherwise confined to the gallery. When the black members were finally "invited and descended actually from the roof to the floor," sometime after 1854, one of the older white congregants "in unappeasable wrath wholly withdrew" from the church. The efforts of Lowell and Bartol reveal the wide extent of racist feelings among white Christians in Boston, and they illustrate the variety of people who promoted integration. The church integrationists were not confined to any one denomination or tradition. Unitarians, Trinitarian Congregationalists, Baptists, and other denominations contained some examples of integrationists.[44]

Tremont Temple Baptist Church of Boston was organized as a church explicitly opposed to racial and class segregation. Established in 1836 as the First Free Baptist Church, it did not sell pews, which caused class segregation, and it did not exclude black people. One of the founders and earliest promoters of the Free Church was Timothy Gilbert. Some histories claim that Gilbert was expelled from the Charles Street Baptist Church because he attempted to integrate seating at that church. After he left this church, Gilbert and his wife, Mary, became members of the Federal Street Baptist Church in 1838, where he tested the attitude of parishioners regarding racial segregation. His friend and early biographer noted: "Soon after he united with the [Federal Street Baptist] church, he filled his pew with colored people. [And] no one objected." This Baptist church, in contrast to the Charles Street Baptist Church, did not oppose racial integration. Gilbert, however, soon formed a new church where there would be no segregation by class or race. He wrote in 1843 that "the rich and poor can meet together; and the black and white are entitled to the same privileges" at Tremont Temple Baptist Church. For Timothy Gilbert, as well as a minority of other white Christians, segregated seating was inconsistent with their faith.[45]

For a small number of blacks and whites in the antebellum era, segregation was inherently sinful and must be opposed. They also felt that the best response to white people's antiblack attitudes and actions was the integration of schools, churches, and public spaces. Many northern whites imagined complete separation, in the form of black and Indian removal to settlement colonies, as the only available option for ending conflicts between whites, blacks, and Indians. Conversely, a small group of Christians, especially in Boston, advocated integration instead. These integrationists, keenly aware of how segregated black and white Christians had become, sought to bring reconciliation through reintegration. Other activists, however, argued that reconciliation could occur only through whites' conversion to true Christianity.

Black and Indian Radical Christian Critiques

Although a small number of black people argued in favor of reintegration, the more common responses to increased racial violence and segregation in northern society were militant or radical Christian critiques of whites. The writings of William Apess, David Walker, Robert Alexander Young, Maria Stewart, Henry Highland Garnet, Frederick Douglass, and others epitomized the critiques that people of color leveled against white Christians from the late 1820s forward. All these Christian activists were part of a generation that was more militant in their civil rights activism than the preceding generations of Indian and African American leaders. In their critiques, these writers argued not that whites needed to live up to their Christian professions but rather that whites had not really been Christians because their actions did not coincide with the teachings of Jesus Christ. These published critiques probably corresponded closely to unrecorded sermons and speeches articulated in black and Indian churches.[46]

Black and Indian leaders, including Reverends Richard Allen, Absalom Jones, and Samson Occom, had critiqued white hypocrisy and unjust actions long before the antebellum era. Indian leaders had been critical of Europeans since the earliest years of colonization. However, black and Indian writers after 1829 reached a level of radicalism and militancy unseen in preceding generations of published writings, especially in terms of religious polemics. Walker, Apess, and other writers suggested that the actions of white Americans proved that they were not Christians at all. In a reversal of the logic of colonialism and white paternalism, these people of color argued that it was whites, not Indians and blacks, who needed to convert to Christianity and be civilized. If whites embraced true Christianity, then God's coming wrath against them would be stayed and colored and white Americans would be able to live in peace.[47]

Indian and African American radical, Christian critiques shared similar traits during this period because there was substantial overlap between northern Indian, Afro-Indian, and black communities, especially in New England. Sometimes Indian, Afro-Indian, and African American communities were, in fact, united communities of diverse people. The inclusion of blacks and Afro-Indians into New England Indian communities, often through marriage, grew substantially from the Revolutionary era into the antebellum years. Places such as the Wampanoag community at Mashpee, Massachusetts, were rural locations in

New England with mixed populations. Afro-Indians and some Indians also incorporated into black communities in cities. William Apess may have been exposed to David Walker's writings or ideas when he visited Boston in 1831. People of mixed ancestry, especially Afro-Indians, were able to maintain ties to both rural Indian communities and urban African American communities. The experiences of white oppression shared by blacks, Indians, and Afro-Indians in their overlapping communities fostered similar Christian radicalism.[48]

Harsh critiques from black and Indian leaders were a response to the growing oppression experienced by people of color, and William Apess and David Walker wrote some of the most damning. Walker was born free in Wilmington, North Carolina, in 1785, and his firsthand knowledge of southern slavery deeply influenced his writings. His father was enslaved, but his mother was a free woman. Until he was thirty years old, he lived and traveled in the South, always observing American slavery. In 1826, he moved to Boston and opened a clothing store near the city's wharves. By the fall of 1829, he had written the *Appeal*, which reflected decades of his personal experiences and his extensive readings of history and contemporary publications. The *Appeal* was a series of articles that Walker also delivered as speeches in Boston and other towns. Most of his speeches were likely given at black churches. Walker made minor revisions to the *Appeal*, and it was published in three editions by his death in 1830.[49]

Reverend William Apess was a Pequot Indian from Connecticut, whose ancestry may have included European, African, and Indian peoples. He became no less forceful a critic of whites' injustices than David Walker. Apess was born in 1798 in Colrain, Massachusetts. During much of his childhood, he was indentured to whites in Connecticut, although he had some contact with his father and other relatives. Apess first began attending Methodist meetings around 1809, and he marked March 13, 1813, as the day he converted to Christianity. He served briefly with American forces in the War of 1812 and was baptized by immersion in 1818. Shortly thereafter, he began to preach at Methodist meetings and to travel as an itinerant preacher among whites, Indians, blacks, and mixed audiences. He was ordained in 1829 as a minister by the Protestant Methodist Church (a group that broke away from the Methodist Episcopal Church), and in 1833, he went to the Wampanoag community of Mashpee, Massachusetts, where he helped lead the "Mashpee Revolt," a peaceful Wampanoag protest against white economic exploitation and interference in the Indian community. Their protest was especially directed against white dominance and, specifically, against what was

FIGURE 6.2. Reverend William Apess, Pequot. Rare Book Division, NYPL, *Mr. William Apes, a Native Missionary of the Pequot Tribe of Indians*, Image ID 5188591, NYPL Digital Collections, http://digitalc-ollections.nypl.org/.

supposed to be a Wampanoag church being run by a white minister whom the tribe had not selected.[50]

As the overall claim in the *Appeal*, Walker argued that "we Colored People of these United States, are, the most wretched, degraded, and abject set of beings that ever lived since the world began, down to the present day, and, that, the white Christians of America, who hold us in slavery, (or, more properly speaking, pretenders to Christianity,) treat us more cruel and barbarous than any Heathen nation did any people whom it had subjected." He could not have been more direct about or damning toward white Americans' exploitation of blacks, and he drew evidence from religious and secular histories to prove his point. Walker maintained that whites not only degraded blacks through slavery but that America's race-based slavery was the worst form of slavery in world history. Whites kept blacks in their wretched condition in the South, the West, and the North, he asserted, by keeping them ignorant of history and literacy. Whites sought to maintain slavery and their dominance by colonizing free blacks abroad. In response to the systematic oppression, he called on blacks to be united, to educate themselves, and to resist slavery, even by violent means. Apess felt similarly about how whites had made Indians among the most degraded and oppressed people in history. On the reservations in New England, "with but a few exceptions," Apess explained, you will find that Indians are "the most mean, abject, miserable race of beings in the world," mostly because of the injustices of contemporary whites and their Puritan ancestors.[51]

Because of their deep and abiding faith in a God of justice who acts in history, Walker and Apess were confident that the oppression of people of color would eventually end. The *Appeal* reflected the preaching tradition of Walker's church, and he petitioned for God's help in reaching the hearts of readers and in bringing an end to injustice. Walker was a member of Reverend Samuel Snowden's African Methodist Episcopal Church in Boston, which contained a high number of black activists. In many respects, Walker's words, especially when presented orally, drew from the Methodist preaching tradition, and he emphasized turning to God and away from sin. He argued that white Americans needed to repent and reform before God's judgment came down hard upon them. Early in the *Appeal*, Walker showed his dependence on God's active work by stating that "these positions I shall endeavor, by the help of the Lord, to demonstrate in the course of this APPEAL, . . . and may God Almighty, who is the Father of our Lord Jesus Christ, open your hearts to understand and believe the truth." Moreover, he had confidence that an end to white oppression was imminent. God "being a just and holy Being will at one day appear fully in behalf of the oppressed." Because of these beliefs, Walker encouraged blacks to do their part in God's work of bringing an end to oppression and called whites to repent. Likewise, Apess admonished: "Oh white man! How can you account to God for this? Are you not afraid that the children of the forest will rise up in judgment and condemn you?" In other words, "have not the great American nation reason to fear the swift judgment of heaven on them for nameless cruelties, extortions, and exterminations inflicted upon the poor natives of the forest?" In his sermon *The Increase in the Kingdom of Christ*, published in 1831, Apess looked forward to "the kingdom of Christ" where justice would finally destroy "every vicious principle and impure motive of the heart is sought out and corrected." In such a time and place, brought about by God's work of redemption, "the white man, who has most cruelly oppressed his red brother, under the influence of that Gospel which he has long professed to believe, and just now begins to feel, pours out unavailing tears over the wasted generations of the mighty forest hunters and, now they are almost dead and buried, begins to pity and lament them." Finally, in the Kingdom of Christ, God would correct the hearts of the wicked, and whites would see their actions toward people of color for what they truly were.[52]

Both Walker and Apess critiqued white Americans as "pretended Christians." Walker forcibly argued that white professors of Christianity were actually not Christians because their actions toward blacks were contrary to the teachings of Jesus Christ, and he bluntly asked: "Can any thing be a greater mockery of religion than the way in which it is conducted by the Americans?" Walker made sharp distinctions between white "pretended" Christianity and the Christianity taught to him and other African Americans by Jesus, the true "master." "Indeed, the way in which religion was and is conducted by the Europeans and their descendants," Walker continued, "one might believe it was a plan fabricated by themselves and the devils to oppress us. But Hark! My master has taught me better than to believe it—he has taught me that his gospel as it was preached by himself and his apostles remains the same, notwithstanding Europeans have tried to mingle blood and oppression with it." By arguing that blacks possessed true Christianity, as established by Jesus and the disciples, Walker and Apess contended that it was white Americans who were in need of conversion to Christianity.[53]

Walker charged that white Christians were worse than "Pagans, Jews, and Mahometans" because these groups, unlike white Christians, protected the people who converted to their faiths. He also pointed out how white Christians did not follow the biblical injunction to treat all people equally as beings created in the likeness of God. "Can the American preachers," he wrote, "appeal unto God, the Maker and Searcher of hearts, and tell him, with the Bible in their hands, that they make no distinction on account of men's colour? . . . Let them answer the Lord; and if they cannot do it in the affirmative, have they not departed from the Lord Jesus Christ, their master?" Walker repeatedly reinforced the point that the behavior of white Americans proved that they had, at the very least, departed from true religious principles, if they had had any in the first place.[54]

Walker and Apess criticized Americans for sponsoring expensive missionary enterprises to foreign lands while neglecting to do justice in the United States. "Let the ministers and people use the colored people they have around them like human beings," Apess pleaded, "before they go to convert any more" people around the world. Antebellum northerners sponsored missionaries to foreign countries, published many religious periodicals, and promoted various reform movements, so Walker was specifically critiquing northerners when he addressed these topics. Walker asked why "the American ministers send out missionaries to convert the heathen, while they keep us and our children sunk at their feet in the most abject ignorance and wretchedness"? Walker was even more direct in his condemnation of white "pretended" Christians in regard to their opposition to many social sins except for slavery, which was "hardly noticed by Americans." "The preachers and people of the United States," Walker argued, "form societies against Free Masonry and Intemperance, and write against Sabbath breaking, Sabbath mails, Infidelity, &c. &c." However, for the most part, the reformers did little against the sin of slavery by 1830.[55] He further contended:

> They have newspapers and monthly periodicals, which they receive in continual succession, but on the pages of which, you will scarcely ever find a paragraph respecting slavery, which is ten thousand times more injurious to this country than all the other evils put together, which will be the final overthrow of its government, unless something is very speedily done; for their cup is nearly full. . . . I tell you Americans! that unless you speedily alter your course, *you* and *your Country are gone*!!!!!! For God Almighty will tear up the very face of the earth!!![56]

Walker was particularly enraged at white reformers because they put so much energy and money into sending missionaries abroad and into opposing mail delivery on Sundays, but they did relatively nothing to oppose the monstrous sin of slavery in the South or racial prejudice in the North.

After completing the third revised edition of his work, Walker was found dead on June 18, 1830, near his clothing shop on Brattle Street. Boston's black community maintains that he was murdered. Walker himself stated in the *Appeal* that he would likely be killed for preaching the truth. His legacy lived on, however, through his only son, Edward G. Walker, who was elected to the Massachusetts legislature in 1866, and through the influence of his writing on future generations of black activists. Reverend Henry Highland Garnet, for example, echoed many of Walker's themes in his 1843 "Address to Slaves in the United States." Garnet was the minister of the African American Liberty Street Presbyterian Church in Troy, New York, and he delivered this address to an

African American convention in Buffalo, New York. Garnet implored American slaves to resist slavery at all costs, and he described whites from the earliest days of colonialism to the present as pretended Christians. Speaking of the first slaves brought to the Americas, Garnet wrote that "the first dealings they had with men calling themselves Christians, exhibited to them the worst features of corrupt and sordid hearts; and convinced them that no cruelty is too great, no villainy and no robbery too abhorrent for even enlightened men to perform, when influenced by avarice and lust." Garnet implied that the behavior of white Christians revealed that they were not Christians and that God would bring judgment against whites and an end to slavery unless white people soon repented.[57]

Echoing Walker's *Appeal*, Frederick Douglass critiqued the ways that white Americans used religion to sustain slavery. In 1845, Douglass wrote, "I love the pure, peaceable, and impartial Christianity of Christ: I therefore hate the corrupt, slaveholding, women-whipping, cradle-plundering, partial and hypocritical Christianity of this land." While he mostly focused on how slavery corrupted religion in the South, Douglass made clear that his condemnations applied to most white Christians in the North as well: "I mean, by the religion of this land, that which is revealed in the words, deeds, and actions, of those bodies, north and south, calling themselves Christian churches, and yet in union with slaveholders. It is against religion, as presented by these bodies, that I have felt it my duty to testify." Douglass believed that any church that did not explicitly oppose slavery and support equality was a corrupted version of Christianity. His 1855 autobiography describes his attendance at the predominantly white Elm Street Methodist Church in New Bedford, Massachusetts, in 1838 or 1839. He went intending to join this church, but he was appalled not only by the segregated seating arrangement but also by the way that white Methodists treated the six or so colored Methodists during the sacrament of communion. Communion was administered after nonmembers were dismissed, so Douglass expected that the true believing Christians would treat black Methodists as equals. To his astonishment and sadness, however, the white Christians' behavior, in keeping blacks apart even at the communion table, showed they were under "the dominion of this wicked prejudice." Douglass argued that the actions of whites showed that they were not genuine Christians.[58]

Apess's texts, *The Experiences of Five Christian Indians of the Pequot Tribe* and *An Indian's Looking-Glass*, published together in 1833, asserted that Indians were true Christians because of their love for all people and that the white people needed to become like the colored Christians. Apess related the religious narrative of Hannah Caleb, Pequot, to show the type of transformation in sensibilities that Christianity would have wrought among whites if they were converted.[59] Hannah Caleb (as recorded by Apess) spoke about her early perceptions of Christianity and white Christians:

> I saw such a great inconsistency in their precepts and examples that I could not believe them. They openly professed to love one another, as Christians, and every people of all nations whom God hath made—and yet they would backbite each other, and quarrel with one another, and would not so much as eat and drink together, nor worship God together. And not only so, the poor Indians, the poor Indians, the people to whom I was wedded by the common ties of nature, were set at naught by those noble professors of grace, merely because we were Indians.[60]

The great hindrance for Caleb when contemplating Christianity was that white people's actions contradicted their professions about their unity and love for all people. As the narrative progressed, however, Caleb implied that she became a Christian through the work of God's spirit, despite white professors of Christianity. Furthermore, after her conversion, her faith was proved genuine, unlike the faith of white people, because, as she stated, "I could say there was no more enmity in my heart, that I loved white people as well as my own." Caleb wondered "if all white Christians love poor Indians. If they did, they would never hurt them anymore. And certainly, if they felt as I did, they would not." Apess likewise related that after his conversion, "My love now embraced the whole human family." Through the consistency of their professions and actions, Caleb and Apess indicated that they were true Christians who loved even their enemies. Their religion forged stronger bonds among a community of Indians and Afro-Indians and critiqued the oppression that their community faced.[61]

Apess believed that American Indians were Jews by ethnicity, as descendants of one of the biblical tribes of Israel, and he confronted white Christians' prejudice by linking their treatment of Indians to how they would treat Jesus Christ if he were to appear in the nineteenth-century United States. Apess: "Now, if the Lord Jesus Christ, who is counted by all to be a Jew—and it is well known that the Jews are a colored people, especially those living in the East, where Christ was born—and if he should appear among us, would he not be shut out of doors by many, very quickly? And by those too who profess religion?" Christ, like other people of color, Apess argued, would be made to feel unwelcome in northern churches, the places where white people invoked his name but did not follow his example.[62]

Apess further attached whites' prejudice toward blacks and Indians in *An Indian's Looking-Glass* by insisting that God created all peoples in his image and that it was preposterous for whites to believe that God favored the minority of people in the world with light skin to the exclusion of most humans:

> If black or red skin or any other skin color is disgraceful to God, it appears that he has disgraced himself a great deal—for he has made fifteen colored people to one white and placed them here upon the earth. Now let me ask you, white man, if it is a disgrace for to eat, drink, and sleep with the image of God, or sit, or walk and talk with them? Or have you the folly to think that the white man, being one in fifteen or sixteen, are the only beloved images of God?[63]

From his point of view, whites disrespected God by their prejudice toward other people, who were made in his image. He asked sarcastically, "Can you charge the Indians with robbing a nation almost of their whole continent, and murdering their women and children, and then depriving the remainder of their lawful rights?" Apess further connected whites' theft of Indian lands with the sin of African slavery: "And to cap the climax, rob another nation to till their grounds and welter out their days under the lash with hunger and fatigue under the scorching rays of a burning sun?" From Apess's point of view, whites, "who profess to have pure principles and who tell us to follow Jesus Christ," had not matched righteous actions with their professions.[64]

Throughout his life, Apess remained convinced of the universal nature of Christianity and God's equal favor to all people, and these beliefs formed a major part of his critique of white Christians who acted contrary to their belief that all people were created in God's image. Apess "felt convinced that Christ died for all mankind—that age, sect, color, country, or situation made no difference. I felt an assurance that I was included in the plan of redemption with all my brethren." Apess regarded Indians, "in some sort, as a tribe of Israelites suffering under the rod of despotic pharaohs." Like African American Christians, Apess and other Indian Christians associated themselves with the ancient Israelites who suffered in bondage in Egypt, and white Americans, instead of being God's chosen people, symbolically became heathens and oppressive Egyptians.[65]

In his autobiographical *A Son of the Forest*, written in 1828–29, Apess argued that whites were neither civilized nor Christian people. A central part of his autobiography is his conversion, but he also implied that whites were still in need of true religion. Apess asked, "How much better would it be if the whites would act like a civilized people and, instead of giving my brethren of the woods 'rum!' in exchange for their furs, give them food and clothing for themselves and children." He related a hypothetical story of Indians reacting to white missionaries, which may have been grounded in his own experiences. "If a good missionary goes among them, and preaches the pure doctrine of the Gospel," Apess explained, "he must necessarily tell them that they must 'love God and their neighbor as themselves—to love all men, deal justly, and walk humbly.'" The Indian hearers of this doctrine "would naturally reply, 'Your doctrine is very good, but the whole course of your conduct is decidedly at variance with your profession—we think the whites need fully as much religious instruction as we do.'" Once again, it was white people who needed civilization and Christianity. Other American Indians in the nineteenth and twentieth centuries made similar arguments, especially that Christians who advocate segregation are not Christians at all and that Indian people are better Christians than many white people.[66]

Apess connected the seventeenth-century oppression of Indians by Pilgrims and Puritans with his own experience of injustices at the hand of whites in the *Eulogy on King Philip*, and he did so in front of predominantly white audiences in Boston in 1836 and through a published version of this sermon. "O thou pretended hypocritical Christians," he charged, you have said, "it was the design of God that we should murder and slay one another because we have the power." In contrast, he argued that King Philip and the Wampanoags acted more like Christians than the Pilgrims did: "for injuries upon injuries, and the most daring robberies and barbarous deeds of death that were ever committed by American Pilgrims, were with patience and resignation borne, in a manner that would do justice to any Christian nation or being in the world," and "Philip treated his prisoners with a great deal more Christian-like spirit than the Pilgrims did." English colonists from Plymouth and Massachusetts did murder and enslave many Indians during King Philip's War.[67]

Many blacks and Indians in the North were able to build strong communities around separate churches where people such as Walker, Douglass, and Apess leveled Christian critiques against white Americans. Their writings reveal the extent of the divide between white and colored Christians. Although the racism, economic marginalization, and segregation were severe, northern African Americans and Indians had the liberty to build and maintain independent institutions and to use them as platforms to freely critique white Americans. Between 1821 and 1850, blacks, Afro-Indians, and Indians built strong bonds within separate churches. These authors (and likely other ministers whose sermons were not published or recorded) defended their communities against the rising wave of white racism that demanded greater and greater separation between whites and people of color. Their radical writings did not simply criticize whites, however. These writers reversed the religious ideology and underpinnings of white exploitation by arguing that blacks and Indians were the true Christians and chosen people of God and that white people were the ones in need of the civilizing and purifying gospel of Christianity.

During the antebellum years, blacks and Indians affiliated with few predominantly white Protestant churches. The number of Congregational and Episcopal churches that baptized blacks and the number of black Congregationalists and Episcopalians in predominantly white churches fell to their lowest levels of the century. Predominantly white Reformed, Presbyterian, Lutheran, Baptist, and Methodist churches also included fewer blacks, especially in the 1830s and 1840s. Only small numbers of blacks and Afro-Indians affiliated with predominantly white churches, and they did so for various spiritual and material reasons. Black Unitarians at Boston's West Church continued to affiliate with that predominantly white congregation perhaps because of their theological preferences, and people such as William C. Nell attended a predominantly white church to promote the cause of integration. The vast majority of blacks, Afro-Indians, and Indians, however, affiliated with independent black or Indian churches because separate churches better met their needs and because white churches made clear that people of color could not participate in white churches on equal terms.

The growth in church segregation gave moral sanction to the segregation in schools, workplaces, transportation, and entertainment. The churches helped create stark segregation in the North but were also clearly influenced by a broader social trend. Just as Frederick Brinsley was forcibly prevented from occupying a ground-floor pew at Park Street Church (part of today's "Freedom Trail" in Boston), so were blacks forced out of higher-paying jobs and formerly interracial urban spaces. Segregation was enforced with the sanction of laws and through mob violence. People of color critiqued the pervasive and sometimes violent segregation in the North in at least two ways. Some blacks and a small group of white allies argued in favor of church reintegration. They argued that racial distinction in houses of worship was a sin that needed to be eradicated and that integration was the best means of changing white racist attitudes. The more common response, conversely, was the radical Christian critiques published by Walker, Apess, Douglass, and others and preached in some black and Indian churches. These activists argued that the United States was not a Christian nation and that the actions of whites in oppressing blacks and Indians proved that white people were not Christians. For those whites who were willing to listen, these messages were a compelling call to turn away from prejudice, but few were listening, and few appeared to make changes in their behavior.

Conclusion

Through much of the eighteenth century and into the early nineteenth century, most northerners experienced formal religious worship in interracial contexts. Although the levels of black and Indian affiliation with northern churches fluctuated nearly every decade and varied by location, the interracial churches that were widespread across the North were mostly a memory by 1850. By that date, northern societies had changed dramatically since colonial times; not only had the broad extent of interracial religious activity collapsed, but northerners also transformed racial categories and the social significance of race.

During the 1730s and 1740s, most Congregational churches in New England and most Anglican parishes across northern colonies included blacks or Indians within their religious communities. Smaller numbers of Lutheran and Moravian churches did so as well. The educational opportunities offered at some of these churches, along with spiritual concerns, made them appealing to many black and Indian peoples. These congregations baptized, admitted to membership, and administered communion to many enslaved and free blacks and Indians. Even more black and Indian people attended worship services than were baptized. While the ministers who promoted revivals sought black and Indian converts more deliberately than some of their colleagues, blacks and Indians affiliated not only with the revivalist "New Light" congregations but also with the more traditional or liturgical churches, especially Church of England parishes.

The interracial practices in northern Anglican, Congregational, Lutheran, and Moravian churches were influenced by developments from other parts of the Atlantic world. Moravians around the Atlantic world frequently stayed in close communication with one another and shared common strategies. Developments in the Caribbean, including planters' opposition to baptizing slaves and missionaries' arguments that Christianity made enslaved people more obedient, heavily influenced the entire Anglican missionary enterprise. For example, Elias Neau, who began catechizing enslaved people in New York City, had connections to the West Indies, and a Barbados sugar plantation funded the Society for the Propagation of the Gospel in Foreign Parts (SPG). As Katharine Gerbner shows, Anglican missionaries played crucial roles in developing the vision of a "Christian slavery" in which black people's baptism and conversion did not undermine slavery, and these ideas influenced Anglicans and other Protestants from Boston and New York City through the Protestant Caribbean.[1] Therefore, Anglican missionaries brought ideas and practices from the Caribbean plantation colonies to the northern colonies, even though they met with less resistance from northern slave owners when evangelizing slaves after 1730. Rebecca Goetz explains how English colonists in seventeenth-century Virginia "conflated religious and racial categories" and generally excluded blacks and Indians from Christian rituals by the mid-seventeenth century, and many churches continued to exclude them during the eighteenth century. Anglican missionaries and enslaved people pushed back against these trends, and in the eighteenth century, small numbers of black people participated in Christian churches in Virginia, Barbados, and elsewhere.[2] Anglican priests baptized enslaved black people across the British Empire in the eighteenth century, but not uniformly from colony to colony.

Race relations in northern churches were also different and distinct from the religious practices in other British colonies. Northern churches, especially Anglican and Congregational ones, on average, were more interracial than most southern churches in the eighteenth century. Goetz describes a "growing gulf between colonial and metropolitan ideas about race and religion" that developed in Virginia and the Caribbean, but the extensive participation of black people in northern Anglican and Congregational churches suggests that the "gulf" between them and the metropole was slighter. Eighteenth-century evangelism toward blacks and Indians and their participation in numerous northern churches came closer than southern churches to meeting the expectations of Christians in England. The relatively smaller enslaved population in most northern colonies likely made Christian enslaved people feel less threatening to slaveholders there. Northern slaveholders were not as opposed to slaves learning to read as their counterparts in Caribbean colonies or as compared to antebellum southerners.[3]

From 1730 until the 1780s, conversely, very few Dutch Reformed, German Reformed, or Presbyterian churches in the northern Mid-Atlantic colonies baptized or admitted to membership blacks or Indians. The standards for baptism and church membership in these denominations made them less accessible to people of color, and some of these Christians believed that conversion or baptism undermined their ownership and control of slaves, a step few were willing to take. Moreover, these churches generally lacked the missionary organizations or evangelical zeal of Moravians, Congregationalists, and Anglicans. Since these denominations were not racially inclusive, the experiences of slavery in areas of New York, New Jersey, and Pennsylvania where Reformed and Presbyterian churches predominated differed from northern slavery in areas where Congregational, Anglican, Lutheran, or Moravian Christianity was most prevalent. Slavery among these latter types of churches regularly entailed shared religious experiences and religious justifications for slavery. Slaves who lived in towns with only Presbyterian and Reformed churches were unlikely to gain an education or other services from churches, especially when compared to the enslaved people who lived near Anglican or Congregational churches. This comparison is crucial for detailing a more accurate and nuanced history of slavery by establishing how slavery differed not only between northern and southern colonies but also among the northern colonies themselves. On the whole, the reluctance of northern Presbyterian and Reformed churches to baptize black or Indian peoples before the 1780s resembled the resistance to baptizing slaves that Protestant planters in Virginia and the Caribbean expressed throughout much of the seventeenth and eighteenth centuries (what Katharine Gerbner terms "Protestant Supremacy").[4]

Northern Protestant churches reflected the hierarchy of colonial society that ranked people by wealth, skin color, and gender, but black and Indian engagement in predominantly white churches did not mean that they acquiesced to their place in society. In the vast majority of cases, whites did not allow blacks and Indians to vote in church matters or to hold leadership positions in predominantly white churches. Because churches were a part of the structures that supported the exploitation of blacks and Indians (like churches around the English Atlantic world), the participation of these groups in churches at times supported their marginalization. However, since blacks and Indians also resisted slavery and white oppression, often creatively, they sometimes sought to change or counter their marginalized position in white churches. Greenwich and Nim used Christianity and the physical space of churches to confront slavery and prejudice. Indians, in a very high proportion, decided to withdraw in the 1750s from the predominantly white churches in which they had earlier affiliated. Instead, Reverend Samson Occom (Mohegan), Reverend Samuel Niles (Narragansett), and other ministers led separate Indian churches. These churches became long-lasting and vital institutions for Narragansett, Mohegan, Montaukett, Wampanoag, and other communities.

After 1790, many African Americans, especially in urban centers, also created their own churches, which led the struggles against northern disenfranchisement and southern slavery from 1790 to 1860 and beyond. In the decades after the Revolution, numerous free African Americans, including Reverends Richard Allen, Thomas Paul, and Peter Williams Jr., withdrew from white churches to worship free from white prejudice and because they believed that separate congregations were better equipped to convert unchurched community members.

The number of northern interracial churches increased in the long Revolutionary era despite the challenges posed to religious worship during the war. The presence of blacks in Anglican churches increased during the 1750s to 1770s. After the 1760s, the development of American Methodism and the expansion of Baptist churches created many more interracial churches, especially in the Mid-Atlantic region. Early Methodists, in particular, were dedicated to the inclusion of all people, and some predominantly white Methodist societies included remarkably high numbers of black members. This expansion of interracial worship even began to affect the denominations that had been most resistant to the inclusion of blacks within their sacramental communities, particularly Dutch Reformed and Presbyterian churches. Independent Indian churches, including ones at Mashpee, Massachusetts, and Narragansett, Rhode Island, also became more diverse over time as they included Afro-Indian, black, and occasionally white worshippers.

The antislavery message of early Methodists, their willingness to license black preachers, and their deliberate outreach to black people made Methodist churches appealing to many black people. Besides the Methodists, however, the connections were tenuous between churches' stance on abolitionism and black affiliation levels in the Revolutionary era. Although some Congregationalists pushed for ending slavery in

New England, black affiliation levels decreased in these churches. The rates of black affiliation in Presbyterian, Anglican, and Baptist churches generally increased before these types of churches adopted direct stances against slavery.

Following the Revolution and continuing through the 1810s, many churches became more racially inclusive. More Dutch Reformed and Presbyterian churches baptized and admitted black people. Remarkably, the expansion in black participation in these churches occurred during the same period as black northerners formed their first separate churches. Black participation declined in most Congregational churches and some other churches in specific locations, but for many northern churches, the period of 1791 to 1820 witnessed widespread interracial public worship. For a time, the expansion of interracial churches and the development of independent black churches proceeded together, and this fact is significant in retrospect because of how extensive segregation became in the coming decades. From the last decades of the eighteenth century and into the nineteenth century, people like Phillis Wheatley, Cuffee Wright, Chloe Spear, and Ichabod Pease indicated the importance of Christianity to their lives, and they retained their affiliation with predominantly white churches.

The expansion of both interracial churches and independent black churches in northern states during the Early Republic resembled similar developments in some southern states. As evangelical Baptist, Methodist, and Presbyterian churches spread across the South after the Revolution, many of them were biracial or interracial. Black Baptist churches and African Methodist churches, which eventually helped to create the AME denomination, spread rapidly through Maryland and Virginia and reached as far south as Charleston, South Carolina, Savannah, Georgia, and Mobile, Alabama. The amount of relative autonomy that southern black churches maintained varied by decade and location, but white southerners had more ability and desire to supervise African Americans' religious practices and churches.[5] In the North and the South, both interracial churches and separate black churches expanded during the Early Republic, but the regional religious trends grew further apart during the antebellum era.

Predominantly white churches played a role in the rise of northern racism during the Early Republic because the inclusion and exclusion of people of color in churches was part of how whites delineated the boundaries and meanings of race. As whites felt anxiety about the growing population of free blacks and saw a need to define citizenship for the first time after the break with Britain, their treatment of blacks in churches was part of their approach to the issue of race. Between the 1770s and 1820s, white conceptions and categorizations of blacks, Afro-Indians, and Indians changed, as did the labels used by black Americans for themselves and their institutions. Gradual emancipation, increased rates of intermarriage among blacks and Indians, and near-universal white male political participation all contributed to the changing notions and meaning of race. However, the distancing of whites and blacks in northern churches also contributed to changes in racial categorizations and the increase in segregation across society. Churches reflected broader social changes, but the withdrawals and ejections of blacks and Indians from churches built upon and further exacerbated preexisting racial divisions and provided a moral justification for segregation (if it is acceptable for churches to be segregated, it must be okay other institutions to segregate).

During the Early Republic, northern missionary organizations also embarked on ambitious plans to evangelize Native Americans in the South and West. Northerners exported to the South and the West their long tradition of missionary organizations that funded concerted efforts to evangelize American Indians. The American Board of Commissioners for Foreign Missions (ABCFM), headquartered in Boston, eventually sponsored missions to the Cherokees, Chickasaws, Choctaws, and other American Indians. The Society for Propagating the Gospel among the Indians and Others in North America still sponsored missionaries to Native Americans in New England and New York, and the ABCFM funded the Foreign Mission School in Cornwall, Connecticut, between 1817 and 1826. However, as white northerners became convinced that Indians were "vanishing" from their midst, northern Christians put more energy and resources into evangelizing Indians elsewhere. African Americans relied heavily on their churches to protect themselves in antebellum America, but the presence of white missionaries and Indian churches did not prevent the forced removals of numerous tribal nations to the West during the 1830s.[6]

Changing attitudes about race in churches after 1820 halted and then reversed the expansion of interracial churches that had coexisted alongside separate black churches and, as a result, churches were on the frontline of creating and supporting segregation in antebellum northern society. Segregation of free blacks and Indians in all parts of northern society was on the rise in the 1820s and 1830s, and sometimes churches argued for colonization under the guise of benevolence. Increasingly, whites barred people of color from forms of employment, public accommodations, schools, and churches through laws, harassment, and occasionally mob violence. Discriminatory practices in the churches were one reason that blacks and Indians created separate churches, and, as a result, northern predominantly white churches gave moral sanction to segregation as they increasingly functioned as another segregated space. Some African Americans had preferred separate churches since the 1790s, but in the antebellum era, most white churches made it very clear that equality was not an option, and sometimes they pushed black congregants out of their churches.

By 1850 interracial Christian churches had all but disappeared. White churches had generally shown themselves inhospitable to African Americans, and separate black churches had proven their religious, social, and educational worth. However, in the year that Congress passed a new compromise over slavery that threatened the freedom of black northerners through a harsh fugitive slave law, African American churches became even more essential to black northerners. The 1850 Fugitive Slave Act made every person of color liable to being seized and taken as a slave to the South. African American churches did their best to protect their members, but some northern black churches lost numerous members who fled to Canada for freedom. Although some white churches protested against the injustice of this 1850 law, most northern churches (apart from ones, such as Theodore Parker's church, that were dedicated to abolitionism) had proven themselves indifferent or hostile to the interests of black and Indian Christians. After 1850, to an extent never seen before, black northerners needed their own churches as organizations to help prevent the return of runaway slaves and the kidnapping of free blacks to the South. Their churches were centers for African American spiritual, social, and political action.[7]

The stark division of northern churches along perceived racial lines, which was an integral part of the creation of a thoroughly segregated society, predated and, in some ways, anticipated what happened in the South only after the Civil War. It was northerners, not southerners, who created the first thoroughly segregated societies in America where racist laws, social norms, and antiblack violence thoroughly marginalized and segregated African Americans. Charles Irons shows that biracial churches and quasi-independent African American congregations (along with the "Invisible Institution" of the South) persisted in Virginia throughout the Early Republic and antebellum eras, despite the fallout from Nat Turner's Rebellion. It was only during and immediately after

the Civil War that black Virginians overwhelming joined fully independent churches under their control. So, the crucial turning point away
from interracial churches and toward widespread segregation in the
North was the 1820s and 1830s; in Virginia and other parts of the South,
the 1860s and 1870s were the decades when churches became most fully
separated and when postslavery racism led to new laws and violence
that marginalized and segregated African Americans.[8] During the era
of Reconstruction, many white northerners convinced themselves that
they were the moral saviors of the nation, but they, too, had perpetu-
ated the types of racism and exclusion in their neighborhoods that they
decried elsewhere. The "whitening" of the North's history and its historical amnesia have had long-standing ramifications for American history
that have stretched into the present.[9]

  While a small number of blacks and whites argued for integration
across northern society as a practical means of combatting racism and as
a necessary step in the moral perfection called for by their religious principles, the vast majority of whites, Indians, and blacks favored separate
institutions by the antebellum era. For whites, their racism precluded
the possibility of inclusion of blacks or Indians on equal terms. Indians
and blacks fostered community cohesion and group identity centered on
churches. Moreover, ministers and activists such as David Walker and
William Apess (Pequot) favored separate churches because they argued
that most white churches did not actually practice real Christianity. They
reasoned that the oppressive actions of whites toward people of color
showed that whites needed to be civilized and converted to the peaceable
religion of Jesus. For Walker, Apess, and scores of other people of color,
from the nineteenth century through the twentieth century, churches
could be reintegrated only if white Americans repented and started
treating all people as equals.

Acknowledgments

Writing this book was an arduous journey for me, and had it not been for the many generous and gifted people who encouraged, supported, and critiqued my work over the past decade, I surely would have faltered and failed. I am genuinely grateful for the personal and institutional backing that my research has received. Along this journey, the recompenses of friendships and intellectual growth that developed were considerable.

Financial support from grants and fellowships made possible research at more than twenty-five archives and libraries in ten states. Thank you to the institutions that provided this crucial support and to the many knowledgeable librarians and archivists who made my research possible and often pleasant. I want to particularly recognize the financial support from the American Congregational Association, American Historical Association, Boston Athenæum, College of Arts and Sciences and Department of History at Oklahoma State University, College of Liberal Arts and Sciences of the City College of New York, Columbian College of Arts and Sciences and History Department at the George Washington University, Cosmos Club Foundation, Gilder Lehrman Institute of American History, Massachusetts Historical Society, New England Regional Fellowship Consortium, and Professional Staff Congress–City University of New York.

When this academic journey brought my family and me first to New York City and then to Stillwater, Oklahoma, I was grateful to find collegial and supportive departments that maintained lively faculty writing groups. Thank you to my former and current colleagues at the City

College of New York and Oklahoma State University for being interested in my scholarship, and especially thank you to those who provided invaluable advice on in-progress chapter drafts: in New York—Lale Can, Craig Daigle, Gregory P. Downs, Emily Greble, Jennifer E. Johnson, Andreas Killen, Anne M. Kornhauser, Adrienne Monteith Petty, Seiji Shirane, and Judith Stein; in Oklahoma—Laura Arata, Laura A. Belmonte, Thomas A. Carlson, Yongtao Du, Emily Graham, James L. Huston, Holly M. Karibo, John M. Kinder, Jason Lavery, Douglas K. Miller, Jennifer M. Murray, Richard C. Rohrs, Matthew Schauer, Louise Siddons, and Anna Zeide.

Other colleagues have graciously offered suggestions, mentoring, and practical assistance that significantly contributed to the development of this project, especially Benjamin L. Carp, Linford D. Fisher, Jared Ross Hardesty, William Keegan, Cynthia L. Lyerly, Joanne Pope Melish, Andrea C. Mosterman, Rebecca Nedostup, Ross Newton, Jonathan D. Sassi, Keith W. Stokes, David Waldstreicher, Jonathan W. White, and Gloria Whiting. Conversations with fellow Interpretive Park Rangers at the Boston African American National Historic Site inspired the initial research questions of this book. Questions and observations from participants and commentators at several conferences and a Boston Area Early American History Seminar were instructive for me. The participants in the Early American Seminar Series at the University of Maryland, College Park, especially Holly Brewer, Matthias Ball, and Richard Bell, provided valuable advice on a draft of chapter 1. Thank you also to the anonymous reviewers of my manuscript, who offered insightful questions and suggestions. I appreciate the skillful and dedicated work of the New York University Press team, especially editor Clara Platter and editorial assistant Veronica Knutson, and consulting editors Tim Roberts and Susan Murray.

No other person has read more drafts and versions of my research than Stephen Jackson. Since our graduate studies in DC and throughout several multistate moves, I have always been able to rely on you for help. Thank you for all the suggestions, and especially for encouraging me to write bolder and clearer prose.

I was incredibly fortunate to study and develop as a historian at the George Washington University with a group of brilliant graduate students and faculty. David J. Silverman and Dewey Wallace, thank you for mentoring and challenging me and for carefully reading and commenting on my early scholarship. David, thank you for continuing to offer me sage advice. Tyler Anbinder, Eric Arnesen, Denver Brunsman, Robert

J. Cottrol, and Christine Leigh Heyrman, thank you for the substantial contributions that you made to my development as a scholar.

Subsections of this book were previously published, and I would like to thank the *Lutheran Quarterly* for allowing me to reproduce material from my article "African Americans and Northern Lutherans during the Eighteenth Century" (Summer 2019) and the *New England Quarterly* for permitting me to reproduce parts of "Documents Relating to African American Experiences of White Congregational Churches in Massachusetts, 1773–1832" (June 2013).

Most of all, I leaned heavily upon family and friends throughout this long journey. To my parents, sister, in-laws, and extended family, I am grateful for your support and unfailing encouragements. Carol, Bruce, and Allison assisted me in countless ways, from patient listening to critiquing parts of my in-progress work. Thank you, Christiane, for supporting and loving for me even during the times when this work was most difficult. I am grateful that our lives together have grown and flourished even during long research trips and moves to new states. This book is for you and our daughters.

Abbreviations

ABHS	American Baptist Historical Society, Atlanta, Ga.
ANTL	Andover Newton Theological School Library, Newton Centre, Mass.
BPL	Boston Public Library, Boston, Mass.
CHS	Connecticut Historical Society, Hartford
CL	Congregational Library and Archives, Boston, Mass.
CSL	Connecticut State Library and Archive, Hartford
HSP	Historical Society of Pennsylvania, Philadelphia
LOC	Library of Congress, Washington, D.C.
MHS	Massachusetts Historical Society Library, Boston
NEC	New England Company
NEHGS	New England Historic Genealogical Society, R. Stanton Avery Special Collections, Boston, Mass.
NEHH	New England's Hidden Histories: Colonial-Era Church Records, CL (available online at www.congregationallibrary. org/nehh/main)
NHS	Newport Historical Society Library, Newport, R.I.
NJHS	New Jersey Historical Society, Newark
NYGBS	New York Genealogical and Biographical Society
N-YHS	New-York Historical Society Library, New York
NYPL	New York Public Library, New York
PHS	Presbyterian Historical Society, Philadelphia, Pa.
RIHS	Rhode Island Historical Society Library, Providence
SPG	Society for the Propagation of the Gospel in Foreign Parts
WMQ	*William and Mary Quarterly*

Records from hundreds of church congregations, located in dozens of archives, are the foundational sources for this book. All sorts of church records—original manuscripts and transcriptions—include racial notations, especially on lists of baptisms, members, communicants, marriages, and deaths. Financial records, meeting minutes, and discipline records sometimes also note racial, gender, and other characteristics of congregants. To understand and contextual church records, I have examined and used diaries, sermons, missionary organization papers, letters, slavery-related documents, and other manuscript and published sources.

Most of the Massachusetts church records (manuscript and typescript) used in this project are located at the Massachusetts Historical Society, Congregational Library and Archives, Boston Public Library Rare Books and Manuscripts Department, and New England Historic Genealogical Society R. Stanton Avery Special Collections Department. These archives also hold collections of missionary organizations. Many of the records that I examined in person are now available electronically through the Congregational Library's New England's Hidden Histories project (www.congregationallibrary.org/nehh/main). Information about black people at St. Michael's Episcopal Church, Marblehead, Massachusetts, and St. Paul's Episcopal Church, Newburyport, Massachusetts, was provided by Frances Stith Nilsson and Bronson de Stadler, respectively. I examined the records of Boston's First and Second Baptist churches at the Andover Newton Theological School Library, Deerfield church records at the Memorial Libraries in Historic Deerfield, and Northampton church records at the Forbes Library in Northampton.

Rhode Island church records are located at the Rhode Island Historical Society, Newport Historical Society Library, University of Rhode Island Archive, and Pettaquamscutt Historical Society Library (Kingston, R.I., Congregational church). James N. Arnold's *Vital Records of Rhode Island* (multiple volumes) is also an important published source of Rhode Island church records.

The Connecticut State Library and Archive and the Connecticut Historical Society preserve the records of most extant eighteenth- and early-nineteenth-century Connecticut church records. At the Connecticut Historical Society, in addition to manuscript church records, I used bound copies of records transcribed under the supervision of Mary Kingsbury Talcott by the National Society of Colonial Dames of America. At the Connecticut State Library and Archive, I examined microfilm copies of Congregational, Episcopal, and Baptist church records, but I also extensively used the State Library Indexes of Connecticut Church Records.

For New Hampshire church records, I examined manuscripts and transcriptions at the New Hampshire Historical Society and Portsmouth Athenaeum. I examined Maine church records at the Maine Historical Society and the New England Historic Genealogical Society R. Stanton Avery Special Collections Department.

For New York State church records, I relied heavily upon the bound typescripts transcribed by the New York Genealogical and Biographical Society, edited by Royden Woodward Vosburgh. These Episcopal, Dutch Reformed, Lutheran, German Reformed, Presbyterian, Methodist, Congregational, and Baptist church records are available at the New York Public Library, Milstein Division, and the Library of Congress, Local History and Genealogy Reading Room. The Milstein Division has many carbon-copy typescripts of church records, often listed without an editor, that are part of the New York Genealogical and Biographical Society Collection. I am grateful to the staff of Trinity Episcopal Church Wall Street and the First Baptist Church of New York City for granting me access to the historical records that they maintain and preserve. I also examined church records and other collections (Benjamin T. Onderdonk Papers and Daniel Rogers Diary) at the New-York Historical Society and the New York Public Library Manuscript and Archive Division (in particular Records Relating to the Lutheran Church in Colonial New York, 1649–1772). At the Schomburg Center for Research in Black

Culture, I examined archival material from St. Philip's Church (Harlem, New York) and Zoar United Methodist Church (Philadelphia, Pa.). Some copies of New York church records are also available at the New England Historic Genealogical Special Collections Department.

At the Monmouth County Historical Association Museum & Library, in Freehold, New Jersey, are the Upper Freehold Baptist Church, Hightstown First Baptist Church, Dutch Reformed Church Marlboro Township, Old Tennent Presbyterian Church, and St. Peter's Church records. At the New Jersey Historical Society Library in Newark, I examined records from the Dutch Reformed Church of Stone House Plains, First Presbyterian Church of Hanover, First Reformed Presbyterian Church in Knowlton Township, Reformed Church of Totowa, and Scotch Plains Baptist Church.

For Pennsylvania church records, I heavily relied on published and transcribed records, including many available at the Library of Congress. At the Historical Society of Pennsylvania, I used the Collections of the Genealogical Society of Pennsylvania, particularly bound transcripts of church records of Philadelphia congregations. For western Pennsylvania, I used transcriptions available at the Carnegie Library of Pittsburgh's Pennsylvania Department and manuscripts at the Senator John Heinz History Center's Thomas & Katherine Detre Library & Archives, especially the Historical Society of Western Pennsylvania collections. At the Adams County Historical Society Library, Gettysburg, Pennsylvania, I examined copies of records from Christ Lutheran Church York, Christ's Episcopal Church York Spring, and First Methodist Episcopal Gettysburg.

Other denomination libraries provided access to the church records in their holdings, including the Presbyterian Historical Society, Philadelphia, Pennsylvania (Evangelical Society of Philadelphia records, First Presbyterian Church Elizabeth, New Jersey, records, and First Presbyterian Church New York, New York, records) and the American Baptist Historical Society, Atlanta, Georgia (Old First Baptist Church of Middletown, New Jersey, First Baptist Church of Philadelphia, Baptist Church of Hightstown, New Jersey, Fifth Baptist Church/Sansom Street Church of Philadelphia, Pennsylvania, Seventh Day Baptist Church in Piscataway, New Jersey, Baptist Church of Stillwater, New York, and the Baptist Church of Upper Freehold, New Jersey).

I examined many published church records at the Library of Congress, Boston Athenaeum, and New England Historic Genealogical Society, including significant numbers of Pennsylvania church records edited by

Phillip A. Rice, Paul Miller Ruff, Glenn P. Schwalm, F. Edward Wright, Frederick S. Weiser, and others. Massachusetts town vital records, mostly published in the early twentieth century by the New-England Historical Genealogical Society, provided information about additional church records. Records published by the Colonial Society of Massachusetts and the Baptist Churches in Early America Series of Mercer University Press were valuable published resources. Finally, I used some transcriptions of records from New England town histories, church anniversary publications, published church covenants and membership lists, church directories, and genealogical magazines. For a bibliography that includes many of the primary and secondary sources that I examined for this project, see Richard J. Boles, "Dividing the Faith: The Rise of Racially Segregated Northern Churches, 1730–1850" (Ph.D. diss., George Washington University, 2013).

NOTES

Introduction

1. Vincent Carretta, *Phillis Wheatley: Biography of a Genius in Bondage* (Athens: University of Georgia Press, 2011); Cedrick May, *Evangelism and Resistance in the Black Atlantic, 1760–1835* (Athens: University of Georgia Press, 2008).

2. Catherine Brekus, "Contested Words: History, America, Religion," *WMQ* 75, no. 1 (January 2018): 3–36.

3. No other scholar has examined the levels of black, Afro-Indian, and Indian participation in so many northern churches, though a few historians have gestured in this direction. Linford D. Fisher and Graham Russell Hodges have made significant use of church records in their histories, which focus on Indians' participation in the Congregational churches of southern New England and African Americans in New York and New Jersey, respectively.

4. I use "interracial" over "integrated" because the latter implies more of an equal status for blacks and Indians in white churches, which these churches did not grant to people of color. "Interracial" should not be read as implying equality. I use "interracial" in the same way that Charles F. Irons and Janet Moore Lindman uses the term "biracial" (Irons, *The Origins of Proslavery Christianity: White and Black Evangelicals in Colonial and Antebellum Virginia* [Chapel Hill: University of North Carolina Press, 2008]; Lindman, *Bodies of Belief: Baptist Community in Early America* [Philadelphia: University of Pennsylvania Press, 2008]).

5. Records kept by Rev. Ebenezer Gay, First Parish (Hingham, Mass.) records, MHS. At the Second Parish of Hingham one Indian and six blacks were baptized between 1730 and 1747 (Rev. Nehemiah Hobart's records, 1721–47 [Second Parish], First Parish [Hingham, Mass.] records, MHS).

6. I examine black and Indian participation rates in most northern Protestant denominations, but I do not address the Society of Friends (Quakers). In this period, Quakers did not generally proselytize, and they did not baptize members. Since much

of this study is dependent on baptismal records, and since the Society of Friends' mixed attitudes toward blacks has been well studied by others, they are excluded from my study. The small number of Roman Catholic parishes in northern colonies were also excluded from this study, although at least some early Catholic congregation included black people (Katharine Gerbner, *Christian Slavery: Conversion and Race in the Protestant Atlantic World* [Philadelphia: University of Pennsylvania Press, 2018]; Ryan P. Jordon, *Slavery and the Meetinghouse: The Quakers and the Abolitionist Dilemma, 1820–1865* [Bloomington: Indiana University Press, 2007]; Jane R. Soderlund, *Quakers and Slavery: A Divided Spirit* [Princeton, N.J.: Princeton University Press, 1985]; Henry J. Cadbury, "Negro Membership in the Society of Friends," *Journal of Negro History* 21 [1936]: 151–213).

7. Daniel R. Mandell, *Behind the Frontier: Indians in Eighteenth-Century Eastern Massachusetts* (Lincoln: University of Nebraska Press, 2000); Jean M. O'Brien, *Dispossession by Degrees: Indian Land and Identity in Natick, Massachusetts, 1650–1790* (Cambridge: Cambridge University Press, 1997); Jared Hardesty, *Unfreedom: Slavery and Dependence in Eighteenth-Century Boston* (New York: New York University Press, 2016); Gloria McCahon Whiting, "Power, Patriarchy, and Provision: African Families Negotiate Gender and Slavery in New England," *Journal of American History* 103, no. 3 (December 2016): 583–605; Margaret Ellen Newell, *Brethren by Nature: New England Indians, Colonists, and the Origins of American Slavery* (Ithaca, N.Y.: Cornell University Press, 2015); Wendy Warren, *New England Bound: Slavery and Colonization in Early America* (New York: Norton, 2016); Heather Miyano Kopelson, *Faithful Bodies: Performing Religion and Race in the Puritan Atlantic* (New York: New York University Press, 2016); Joyce D. Goodfriend, *Who Should Rule at Home? Confronting the Elite in British New York* (Ithaca, N.Y.: Cornell University Press, 2017); John Wood Sweet, *Bodies Politic: Negotiating Race in the American North, 1730–1830* (Philadelphia: University of Pennsylvania Press, 2003); Jenny Hale Pulsipher, *Subjects unto the Same King: Indians, English, and the Contest for Authority in Colonial New England* (Philadelphia: University of Pennsylvania Press, 2005); Graham Russell Hodges, *Slavery and Freedom in the Rural North: African Americans in Monmouth County, New Jersey, 1665–1865* (New York: Rowman and Littlefield, 1997); Graham Russell Hodges, *Root & Branch: African Americans in New York and East Jersey, 1613–1863* (Chapel Hill: University of North Carolina Press, 1999); Robert K. Fitts, *Inventing New England's Slave Paradise: Master/Slave Relations in Eighteenth Century Narragansett, Rhode Island* (New York: Taylor and Francis, 1998); Catherine Adams and Elizabeth Pleck, *Love of Freedom: Black Women in Colonial and Revolutionary New England* (New York: Oxford University Press, 2010); Gary B. Nash, *Forging Freedom: The Formation of Philadelphia's Black Community 1720–1840* (Cambridge, Mass.: Harvard University Press, 2003); Joanne Pope Melish, *Disowning Slavery: Gradual Emancipation and "Race" in New England, 1780–1860* (Ithaca, N.Y.: Cornell University Press, 1998); Richard Bailey, *Race and Redemption in Puritan New England* (New York: Oxford University Press, 2014); Christy Clark-Pujara, *Dark Work: The Business of Slavery in Rhode Island* (New York: New York University Press, 2016); C. S. Manegold, *Ten Hills Farm: The Forgotten History of Slavery in the North* (Princeton, N.J.: Princeton University Press, 2010); Stephanie E. Smallwood, "The Politics of the Archive and History's Accountability to the Enslaved," *History of the Present* 6, no. 2 (Fall 2016): 117–32; Carol V. R. George, *Segregated Sabbaths: Richard Allen and the Rise of Independent Black Churches 1760–1840*

(New York: Oxford University Press, 1973); James Oliver Horton and Lois E. Horton, *In Hope of Liberty: Culture, Community and Protest among Northern Free Blacks, 1700–1860* (New York: Oxford University Press, 1997); Kyle T. Bulthuis, *Four Steeples over the City Streets: Religion and Society in New York's Early Republic Congregations* (New York: New York University Press, 2014); Richard S. Newman, *Freedom's Prophet: Bishop Richard Allen, the A.M.E. Church, and the Black Founding Fathers* (New York: New York University Press, 2008).

8. Newman, *Freedom's Prophet*; George, *Segregated Sabbaths*; Craig D. Townsend, *Faith in Their Own Color: Black Episcopalians in Antebellum New York City* (New York: Columbia University Press, 2005); Genna Rae McNeil, Houston Bryan Roberson, Quinton Hosford Dixie, and Keven McGruder, *Witness: Two Hundred Years of African-American Faith and Practices at the Abyssinian Baptist Church of Harlem, New York* (Grand Rapids, Mich.: Eerdmans, 2014).

9. As Joanne Melish argues, after the 1780s, "New England whites employed an array of strategies to . . . efface people of color and their history in New England," and only recent generations of historians have replaced this erasure with detailed histories of black and Indian New Englanders (Melish, *Disowning Slavery*, 2). Jared Hardesty, Gloria McCahon Whiting, Linford Fisher, Richard Bailey, Graham Russell Hodges, Edward Andrews, Heather Miyano Kopelson, and others have recently written about the racial diversity of New England and are exceptions to the trend of neglecting church records as sources.

10. In recent years, Old South Church and Trinity Episcopal Church, both in Boston, Massachusetts, First Church of Cambridge, Massachusetts (www.firstchurchcambridge.org), and other congregations have studied their congregation's connections to slavery and historic African American and Native American members and attendees. Other examples of recent engagements with these histories include the Episcopal Diocese of Rhode Island's Center for Reconciliation and Deborah B. Knowlton, *The African Americans of Hampton's First Church and Its Descendant Parishes, 1670–1826* (Portsmouth, N.H.: Peter E. Randall, 2015).

11. Anne C. Loveland and Otis B. Wheeler, *From Meetinghouse to Megachurch: A Material and Cultural History* (Columbia: University of Missouri Press, 2003), 96–98.

12. David Silverman, *This Land Is Their Land: The Wampanoag Indians, Plymouth Colony, and the Troubled History of Thanksgiving* (New York: Bloomsbury, 2019); David Silverman, "Racial Walls: Race and the Emergence of American White Nationalism," in *Anglicizing America: Empire, Revolution, Republic*, ed. Ignacio Gallup-Diaz, Andrew Shankman, and Silverman (Philadelphia: University of Pennsylvania Press, 2015).

13. Henry H. Mitchell discusses "the inevitable desire of mixed churches to separate by race." By stating that segregation or separation was "inevitable," however, Mitchell and others somewhat avoid the difficult task of analyzing the specific circumstances that produced segregation in different locations. An "inevitable" history tends to oversimplify and downplay the agency and options available to black people. It also tends to be dismissive toward those black people who chose to stay in predominantly white congregations (Mitchell, *Black Church Beginnings: The Long-Hidden Realities of the First Years* [Grand Rapids, Mich.: Eerdmans, 2004], xvi, 51).

14. Hardesty, *Unfreedom*; Whiting, "Power, Patriarchy, and Provision"; Newell, *Brethren by Nature*; Warren, *New England Bound*; Kopelson, *Faithful Bodies*.

15. Black people in a number of settings tended to favor charismatic churches, but there is also plenty of evidence, especially in northern colonies, that significant numbers of blacks did not. Travis Glasson argues that "the experience of black members of the Church of England have been studied less extensively than those of black Baptists, Methodists, and Moravians." Scholars who have argued that revival preaching of evangelical churches was alluring to blacks include Albert J. Raboteau, William D. Piersen, Catherine Adams, Elizabeth Pleck, Sylvia R. Frey, and Thomas Kidd (Glasson, *Mastering Christianity: Missionary Anglicanism and Slavery in the Atlantic World* [New York: Oxford University Press, 2011], 8; Raboteau, *A Fire in the Bones: Reflections on African-American Religious History* [Boston: Beacon, 1995], 20–23; Piersen, *Black Yankees: The Development of an Afro-American Subculture in Eighteenth-Century New England* [Amherst: University of Massachusetts Press, 1988], 68; Adams and Pleck, *Love of Freedom*, 82–85, 101; Sylvia R. Frey, "Shaking the Dry Bones: The Dialectic of Conversion," in *Black and White Cultural Interactions in the Antebellum South*, ed. Ted Ownby [Jackson: University Press of Mississippi, 1993], 33; Kidd, *The Great Awakening: The Roots of Evangelical Christianity in Colonial America* [New Haven, Conn.: Yale University Press, 2007], 214).

16. In recent decades, several histories have complicated the story of segregation and discrimination in southern churches, and many of these histories inform my study. Conversely, there have been surprisingly few attempts to comprehensively portray race relations within northern churches. Histories by Jon Sensbach, Christine Heyrman, Charles Irons, Cynthia L. Lyerly, Robert Olwell, Randolph F. Scully, Nicholas M. Beasley, Katharine Gerbner, and others chronicle race relations in southern churches. Several of these books reveal that surprising degrees of integration or interracial practices existed within some southern congregations. The foundational work on the origins of African American Christianity in southern colonies is Sylvia Frey and Betty Wood, *Come Shouting to Zion: African American Protestantism in the American South and British Caribbean to 1830* (Chapel Hill: University of North Carolina Press, 1998). See also Christine Heyrman, *Southern Cross: The Beginnings of the Bible Belt* (Chapel Hill: University of North Carolina Press, 1998); Irons, *Origins of Proslavery Christianity*; Jon F. Sensbach, *A Separate Canaan: The Making of an Afro-Moravian World in North Carolina, 1763–1840* (Chapel Hill: University of North Carolina Press, 1998); Cynthia Lynn Lyerly, *Methodism and the Southern Mind, 1770–1810* (New York: Oxford University Press, 1998); Robert Olwell, *Masters, Slaves, and Subjects: The Culture of Power in the South Carolina Low Country, 1740–1790* (Ithaca, N.Y.: Cornell University Press, 1998); Rhys Isaac, *The Transformation of Virginia, 1740–1790* (Chapel Hill: University of North Carolina Press, 1982); Randolph F. Scully, *Religion and the Making of Nat Turner's Virginia: Baptist Community and Conflict, 1740–1840* (Charlottesville: University of Virginia Press, 2008); Nicholas M. Beasley, *Christian Ritual and the Creation of British Slave Societies 1650–1780* (Athens: University of Georgia Press, 2009); Rebecca Anne Goetz, *The Baptism of Early Virginia: How Christianity Created Race* (Baltimore: Johns Hopkins University Press, 2012); and John W. Catron, *Embracing Protestantism: Black Identities in the Atlantic World* (Gainesville: University of Florida Press, 2016).

17. Gerbner, *Christian Slavery*; Beasley, *Christian Ritual*; Glasson, *Mastering Christianity*; Thomas N. Ingersoll, "'Releese Us out of This Cruell Bondegg': An Appeal from Virginia in 1723," *WMQ*, 3d ser., 51, no. 4 (October 1994): 777–82.

18. Daniel R. Mandell, "Shifting Boundaries of Race and Ethnicity: Indian-Black Intermarriage in Southern New England, 1760–1880," *Journal of American History* 85, no. 2 (September 1998): 470, 466; Daniel R. Mandell, *Tribe, Race, History: Native Americans in Southern New England, 1780–1880* (Baltimore: Johns Hopkins University Press, 2011); David J. Silverman, *Red Brethren: The Brothertown and Stockbridge Indians and the Problem of Race in Early America* (Ithaca, N.Y.: Cornell University Press, 2010); Sweet, *Bodies Politic*.

19. I try to explain their actions in ways that are supported by available evidence and that are respectful of the complexities and diversity of early blacks and Indians. Though imperfect, this approach is better than drawing conclusions from a wider range of sources whose origins were outside the time and geographic specificity of this study.

20. Michael D. McNally, "The Practice of Native American Christianity," *Church History* 69, no. 4 (December 2000): 834–59; Neal Salisbury, "Embracing Ambiguity: Native Peoples and Christianity in Seventeenth-Century North America," *Ethnohistory* 50, no. 2 (Spring 2003): 247–59; David A. Snow and Richard Machalek, "The Sociology of Conversion," *Annual Review of Sociology* 10 (1984): 167–90; Jane T. Merritt, "Dreaming of the Savior's Blood: Moravians and the Indian Great Awakening in Pennsylvania," *WMQ*, 3d ser., 54, no. 4 (October 1997): 739–44.

1 / "Not of Whites Alone, but of Blacks Also"

1. Silas Leroy Blake, *The Later History of the First Church of Christ, New London, Conn.* (New London: Day, 1900), 25–34, 72, 502; Peter Benes, *Meetinghouses of Early New England* (Amherst: University of Massachusetts Press, 2012).

2. Blake, *The Later History of the First Church of Christ, New London*, 25–34, 72, 502; Connecticut Church Records, State Library Index, New London First Congregational Church, 1670–1888 (Hartford: CSL, 1949); New London Church Records, vol. 1, microfilm, pp. 23, 128–31; Eliphalet Adams, Bill of sale or indenture made by Eliphalet Adams of New London, Conn., to Joseph and Jonathan Trumble of Lebanon, Conn., Main Vault 326 Ad15, CSL.

3. Manuscript Records of the First Church of Christ in New London, pp. 23, 128, microfilm, CSL; Index, pp. 449–53, New London First Congregational Church, CSL; Linford D. Fisher, *The Indian Great Awakening: Religion and the Shaping of Native Culture in Early America* (New York: Oxford University Press, 2012); Frances Manwaring Caulkins, *History of New London, Connecticut: From the First Survey of the Coast in 1612 to 1852* (Hartford, Conn.: Press of Case, Tiffany and Company, 1852), 194; Blake, *Later History of the First Church of Christ, New London*, 491–519. Adams was not consistent in identifying people as Indian or black, so the number of baptism noted in this chapter might be an underaccounting of the total.

4. Rebecca Anne Goetz, *The Baptism of Early Virginia: How Christianity Created Race* (Baltimore: Johns Hopkins University Press, 2012); Katharine Gerbner, *Christian Slavery: Conversion and Race in the Protestant Atlantic World* (Philadelphia: University of Pennsylvania Press, 2018); Nicholas M. Beasley, *Christian Ritual and the Creation of British Slave Societies 1650–1780* (Athens: University of Georgia Press, 2009).

5. I use "interracial" over "integrated" because the latter implies more of an equal status for blacks and Indians in white churches. See the introduction for more details on this term. Gerbner, *Christian Slavery*, 36–37; Beasley, *Christian Ritual*.

6. Douglas L. Winiarski, *Darkness Falls on the Land of Light: Experiencing Religious Awakenings in Eighteenth-Century New England* (Chapel Hill: University of North Carolina Press, 2017); Thomas Kidd, *The Great Awakening: The Roots of Evangelical Christianity in Colonial America* (New Haven, Conn.: Yale University Press, 2007); Jon Butler, *Awash in a Sea of Faith: Christianizing the American People* (Cambridge, Mass.: Harvard University Press, 1990); Frank Lambert, *Inventing the "Great Awakening"* (Princeton, N.J.: Princeton University Press, 2001).

7. For examples of historians who focus on examples of the emotionalism of revival preaching or the Great Awakening revivals as alluring to black people, see Paul Harvey, *Through the Storm, through the Night: A History of African American Christianity* (New York: Rowman and Littlefield, 2001), 29–32; Albert J. Raboteau, *A Fire in the Bones: Reflections on African-American Religious History* (Boston: Beacon, 1995), 21–22; William D. Piersen, *Black Yankees: The Development of an Afro-American Subculture in Eighteenth-Century New England* (Amherst: University of Massachusetts Press, 1988), 68; Catherine Adams and Elizabeth Pleck, *Love of Freedom: Black Women in Colonial and Revolutionary New England* (New York: Oxford University Press, 2010), 82–85, 101; Richard Bailey, *Race and Redemption in Puritan New England* (New York: Oxford University Press, 2014), 17–18; Sylvia R. Frey, "Shaking the Dry Bones: The Dialectic of Conversion," in *Black and White Cultural Interactions in the Antebellum South*, ed. Ted Ownby (Jackson: University Press of Mississippi, 1993), 33; Winiarski, *Darkness Falls*, 181–86; Sylvia Frey and Betty Wood, *Come Shouting to Zion: African American Protestantism in the American South and British Caribbean to 1830* (Chapel Hill: University of North Carolina Press, 1998).

8. John Sweet and Joseph Conforti also argue that some blacks and Indians found Old Light, antirevivalist churches appealing. Craig Townsend critiques the "essentialism" of the claim that black people necessarily preferred evangelical, Baptist, or Methodist churches, and Katharine Gerbner, focused mostly on the Caribbean, argues that "historians have overstated the significance of emotional worship for the appeal of Christianity" (John Wood Sweet, *Bodies Politic: Negotiating Race in the American North, 1730–1830* [Philadelphia: University of Pennsylvania Press, 2003], 108–10, 122–23; Joseph A. Conforti, *Saints and Strangers: New England in British North America* [Baltimore: Johns Hopkins University Press, 2006], 190–91; Craig D. Townsend, *Faith in Their Own Color: Black Episcopalians in Antebellum New York City* [New York: Columbia University Press, 2005], 35; Gerbner, *Christian Slavery*, 11; Travis Glasson, *Mastering Christianity: Missionary Anglicanism and Slavery in the Atlantic World* [New York: Oxford University Press, 2011], 8).

9. Margaret Ellen Newell, "Indian Slavery in Colonial New England," in *Indian Slavery in Colonial America*, ed. Alan Gallay (Lincoln: University of Nebraska Press, 2009), 31.

10. Daniel R. Mandell, *Behind the Frontier: Indians in Eighteenth-Century Eastern Massachusetts* (Lincoln: University of Nebraska Press, 2000); David Silverman, *Faith and Boundaries: Colonists, Christianity, and Community among the Wampanoag Indians* (Cambridge: Cambridge University Press, 2005); Sweet, *Bodies Politic*; Daniel K. Richter, *Facing East from Indian Country: A Native History of Early America* (Cambridge, Mass.: Harvard University Press, 2001); Richard W. Cogley, *John Eliot's Mission to the Indians before King Philip's War* (Cambridge, Mass.: Harvard University Press, 1999); Jean M. O'Brien, *Dispossession by Degrees: Indian Land and Identity*

in Natick, Massachusetts, 1650–1790 (Cambridge: Cambridge University Press, 1997); Edward E. Andrews, *Native Apostles: Black and Indian Missionaries in the British Atlantic World* (Cambridge, Mass.: Harvard University Press, 2013).

11. Ira Berlin, *Many Thousands Gone: The First Two Centuries of Slavery in North America* (Cambridge, Mass.: Belknap Press of Harvard University Press, 1998), 49, 51, 54, 369; Lawrence W. Towner, *A Good Master Well Served: Masters and Servants in Colonial Massachusetts, 1620–1750* (New York: Garland, 1998), 115.

12. Berlin, *Many Thousands Gone*, 54, 369; Towner, *A Good Master Well Served*; Adams and Pleck, *Love of Freedom*; Sweet, *Bodies Politic*; Graham Russell Hodges, *Slavery and Freedom in the Rural North: African Americans in Monmouth County, New Jersey, 1665–1865* (New York: Rowman and Littlefield, 1997); Robert K. Fitts, *Inventing New England's Slave Paradise: Master/Slave Relations in Eighteenth Century Narragansett, Rhode Island* (New York: Taylor and Francis, 1998); Bailey, *Race and Redemption*, 93–106; Graham Russell Hodges, *Root & Branch: African Americans in New York and East Jersey, 1613–1863* (Chapel Hill: University of North Carolina Press, 1999); Gary B. Nash, *Forging Freedom: The Formation of Philadelphia's Black Community 1720–1840* (Cambridge, Mass.: Harvard University Press, 2003); Lorenzo Johnston Greene, *The Negro in Colonial New England* (New York: Athenaeum, 1969); Jared Hardesty, *Unfreedom: Slavery and Dependence in Eighteenth-Century Boston* (New York: New York University Press, 2016); Glasson, *Mastering Christianity*, 96; Gloria McCahon Whiting, "Power, Patriarchy, and Provision: African Families Negotiate Gender and Slavery in New England," *Journal of American History* 103, no. 3 (December 2016): 583–605; Robert H. Romer, *Slavery in the Connecticut Valley of Massachusetts* (Florence, Mass.: Levellers, 2009).

13. For other examples, see records of First Church Cambridge, Massachusetts, and Old South Church, Boston, Massachusetts; Jeff G. Johnson, *Black Christians: The Untold Lutheran Story* (St. Louis, MO: Concordia, 1991), 29; Hodges, *Root & Branch*, 16, 54–63; Hardesty, *Unfreedom*, 154; *The Manifesto Church: Records of the Church in Brattle Square Boston, 1699–1872* (Boston: Benevolent Fraternity of Churches, 1902), 129–51; and First Church Dorchester, *Records of the First Church at Dorchester, in New England, 1636–1734* (Boston: G. H. Ellis, 1891), 220.

14. Goetz, *Baptism of Early Virginia*, 153–54. When I began this research, my assumption was that the Great Awakening was the primary cause of black people's affiliation with New England churches. So, I anticipated that looking at records starting in 1730 would give me about ten years where I would find very few or no black baptisms before Whitefield's arrival in New England. To my surprise, I found more black baptisms in the 1730s than I anticipated and throughout the 1730s and 1740s many black baptisms in churches opposed to Whitefield's revivalism.

15. Michael D. McNally, "The Practice of Native American Christianity," *Church History* 69, no. 4 (December 2000): 834–59; Neal Salisbury, "Embracing Ambiguity: Native Peoples and Christianity in Seventeenth-Century North America," *Ethnohistory* 50, no. 2 (Spring 2003): 247–59; David A. Snow and Richard Machalek, "The Sociology of Conversion," *Annual Review of Sociology* 10 (1984): 167–90; Jane T. Merritt, "Dreaming of the Savior's Blood: Moravians and the Indian Great Awakening in Pennsylvania," *WMQ*, 3d ser., 54, no. 4 (October 1997): 739–44; Glasson, *Mastering Christianity*, 33–34; Sweet, *Bodies Politic*, 58–130; Gerbner, *Christian Slavery*, 78.

16. For an example of slaves owned by an Anglican pastor who attended church but were not ready for baptism, see Frank J. Klingberg, "The S.P.G. Program for Negroes in Colonial New York," *Historical Magazine of the Protestant Episcopal Church* 8, no. 4 (December 1939): 341; James MacSparran, *A Letter Book and Abstract of Our Services Written during the Years 1743-1751*, ed. Daniel Goodwin (Boston: Merrymount, 1899), 15, 29; Bailey, *Race and Redemption*, 104; Sweet, *Bodies Politic*, 154-55; Glasson, *Mastering Christianity*, 114-18.

17. Bailey, *Race and Redemption*, 61-71; Parish book, 1731-1739, and Parish record book, 1731-1840, in the York, Maine, First Parish Church records, 1731-1927, RG5392, CL, NEHH.

18. Qtd. in Klingberg, "The S.P.G. Program for Negroes in Colonial New York," 339; Charles F. Irons, *Origins of Proslavery Christianity: White and Black Evangelicals in Colonial and Antebellum Virginia* (Chapel Hill: University of North Carolina Press, 2008), 5. In 1724 an Anglican priest named Peter Stouppes wrote that some enslaved people came "out of their free will to church without their master's order" (Robert Bolton, *History of the Protestant Episcopal Church in the County of Westchester from its Foundation A.D. 1693 to A.D. 1853* [New York: Stanford and Swords, 1855], 436).

19. Abington, MA: UCC of Abington, 1724-1749, manuscript records, RG 4969, CL (available on NEHH); Abington, Mass., church records and private records (Mss A 8169), p. 33, NEHGS; Benjamin Hobart, *History of the Town of Abington, Plymouth County, Massachusetts, from Its First Settlement* (Boston: T. H. Carter and Son, 1866), 251-55; Winiarski, *Darkness Falls*.

20. William Stevens Perry, ed., *Papers Related to the History of the Church in Massachusetts, A.D. 1676-1785* (Privately printed, 1873), 297, 307; William Barry, *A History of Framingham Massachusetts: Including the Plantation from 1640 to the Present Time* (Boston: James Munroe and Company, 1847), 63; Towner, *A Good Master Well Served*, 126.

21. Some scholars anglicize his name and call him Andrew. For detailed analysis of Andreas and Moravians of Bethlehem, Pennsylvania, see John W. Catron, *Embracing Protestantism: Black Identities in the Atlantic World* (Gainesville: University of Florida Press, 2016), 101-49; Katherine Faull Eze, "Self-Encounters: Two Eighteenth-Century African Memoirs from Moravian Bethlehem," in *Crosscurrents: African Americans, Africans, and Germany in the Modern World*, ed. David McBride, Leroy Hopkins, and C. Aisha Blackshire-Belay (Columbia, S.C.: Camden House, 1998); Daniel B. Thorp, "Notes and Documents: Chattel with a Soul: The Autobiography of a Moravian Slave," *Pennsylvania Magazine of History and Biography* 112, no. 3 (July 1988): 434-48. In his autobiography, Andreas states that his name was Ofodobendo Wooma and uses Andreas to describe himself at the time of composition.

22. Thorp, "Chattel with a Soul," 442-46, 449-50.

23. Thorp, "Chattel with a Soul," 442, 445-46, 449-50; Catron, *Embracing Protestantism*, 101-49; Joyce D. Goodfriend, *Who Should Rule at Home? Confronting the Elite in British New York* (Ithaca, N.Y.: Cornell University Press, 2017), 82-83, 120, 195.

24. The scholarship about African and Indian conversion to Christianity has become robust and nuanced in recent decades: Catron, *Embracing Protestantism*, 15-49, 105-15; Sweet, *Bodies Politic*, 107-20; Andrews, *Native Apostles*; Jeroen Dewulf, *The Pinkster King and the King of Kongo: The Forgotten History of America's Dutch-Owned Slaves* (Jackson: University Press of Mississippi, 2017); David J. Silverman,

Red Brethren: The Brothertown and Stockbridge Indians and the Problem of Race in Early America (Ithaca, N.Y.: Cornell University Press, 2010); Linford D. Fisher, *The Indian Great Awakening: Religion and the Shaping of Native Culture in Early America* (New York: Oxford University Press, 2012), 5–8, 66–67, 72–73, 86–88, 101–2; Gerbner, *Christian Slavery*, 6–11; Joel W. Martin and Mark A. Nicholas, eds., *Native Americans, Christianity, and the Reshaping of the American Religious Landscape* (Chapel Hill: University of North Carolina, 2010), 2–4, 13–16; David Silverman, "Indians, Missions, and Religious Translation: Creating Wampanoag Christianity in Seventeenth-Century Martha's Vineyard," *WMQ*, 3d ser., 62, no. 2 (April 2005); Rachel Wheeler, *To Live upon Hope: Mohicans and Missionaries in the Eighteenth-Century Northeast* (Ithaca, N.Y.: Cornell University Press, 2008); William Simmons, "Red Yankees: Narragansett Conversion in the Great Awakening," *American Ethnologist* 10, no. 2 (May 1983): 253–71; James Axtell, ed., *After Columbus: Essays in the Ethnohistory of Colonial America* (New York: Oxford University Press, 1988); Craig Wilder, *In the Company of Black Men: The African Influence on African American Culture in New York City* (New York: New York University Press, 2001); Walter Rucker, *The River Flows On: Black Resistance, Culture, and Identity Formation in Early America* (Baton Rouge: Louisiana State University Press, 2008). Douglas Winiarski examines many of the surviving Congregational testimonies in Winiarski, *Darkness Falls*.

25. Qtd. in William D. Johnson, *Slavery in Rhode Island 1755–1776: Papers from the Historical Seminary of Brown University*, vol. 5, ed. J. Franklin Jameson (Providence: Publication of the Rhode Island Historical Society, 1894), 11–12; Bailey, *Race and Redemption*, 83; Sweet, *Bodies Politic*, 125.

26. Erik R. Seeman, "'Justise Must Take Plase': Three African Americans Speak of Religion in Eighteenth-Century New England," *WMQ*, 3d ser., 56, no. 2 (April 1999): 396; Winiarski, *Darkness Falls*, 177, 274, 279, 382, 479.

27. Seeman, "Justise Must Take Plase," 396–99, 407–11; Adams and Pleck, *Love of Freedom*, 87–88.

28. For more about seating arrangements and the connections among gender and race in churches, see Kyle T. Bulthuis, *Four Steeples over the City Streets: Religion and Society in New York's Early Republic Congregations* (New York: New York University Press, 2014), 53–54, 80, 95–119. "CR 1: Records of the Old South Church and Congregation, 1735–1767," Records of Old South (Third) Church, Boston, MA, CL (available on NEHH); Hezekiah Spencer Sheldon, ed., *Documentary History of Suffield in the Colony and Providence of the Massachusetts Bay, in New England 1660–1749* (Springfield, Mass.: Clark W. Bryan Company, 1879), 257–58; J. Rupert Simonds, *A History of the First Church and Society of Branford, Connecticut 1644–1919* (New Haven, Conn.: Tuttle, Morehouse, and Taylor, 1919), 73–74; Diana Ross McCain, "Seating the Meetinghouse," *Early American Life* 22, no. 4 (August 1991): 18–20; Sweet, *Bodies Politic*, 109–11; Susan Juster, *Disorderly Women: Sexual Politics and Evangelicalism in Revolutionary New England* (Ithaca, N.Y.: Cornell University Press, 1996).

29. Sweet, *Bodies Politic*, 102–10; Goetz, *Baptism of Early Virginia*; McCain, "Seating the Meetinghouse," 18–20; Bailey, *Race and Redemption*, 119–22; Richard W. Pointer, "Native Freedom? Indians and Religious Tolerance in Early America," and Jon Sensbach, "Slaves to Intolerance: African Christianity and Religious Freedom in Early America," in *The First Prejudice: Religious Tolerance and Intolerance in Early America*, ed. Chris Beneke and Christopher S. Grenda (Philadelphia: University of

Pennsylvania Press, 2011); Olwell, *Masters, Slaves, & Subjects*, 103–40; Glasson, *Mastering Christianity*, 47–54; Romer, *Slavery in the Connecticut Valley of Massachusetts*, 20–22, 240–44.

30. Sweet, *Bodies Politic*, 121–30; Glasson, *Mastering Christianity*, 105; Jon F. Sensbach, *A Separate Canaan: The Making of an Afro-Moravian World in North Carolina, 1763–1840* (Chapel Hill: University of North Carolina Press, 1998), 3–4, 40, 55, 58–59; Winiarski, *Darkness Falls*, 53–114; Gerbner, *Christian Slavery*, 81.

31. Kidd, *Great Awakening*, 219; Sweet, *Bodies Politic*, 121; Glasson, *Mastering Christianity*, 105–8; Winiarski, *Darkness Falls*, 184; Sensbach, *A Separate Canaan*, 3–4, 40, 55, 58–59. For extended discussions on why some Indians affiliated with Christianity, see Fisher, *Indian Great Awakening*; O'Brien, *Dispossession by Degrees*; and Silverman, *Faith and Boundaries*.

32. "Mr. Cotton's church record 1728," vol. 14, box 1, folder 20, First Congregational Church of Providence Records, 1722–1945, Mss 419, RIHS; Genesis 17:13; Acts 10: 34–35 (King James Version); Winiarski, *Darkness Falls*, 165, 169, 185, 495; Douglas L. Winiarski, "'A Jornal of a Fue Days at York': The Great Awakening on the Northern New England Frontier," *Maine History* 42, no. 1 (2004): 46–85.

33. Congregational churches that admitted to membership or baptized multiple blacks and/or Indians were located in at least the following towns: in Connecticut— Ashford, Bolton, Bozrah, Branford, Brooklyn, Canterbury, Colchester, Cromwell, Durham, East Haddam, East Hartford, Fairfield, Griswold, Groton, Hampton, Hartford, Lebanon, Lisbon, Mansfield, Meriden, Middletown, New Hartford, New Haven, New London, Newtown, North Stonington, North Woodstock, Norwich, Old Lyme, Old Saybrook, Oxford, Plainfield, Portland, Redding, Somers, Southington, Stonington, Suffield, Trumbull, Windham, Windsor, Woodbury, and Woodstock; in Massachusetts—Abington, Amesbury, Barnstable, Beverly, Boston, Boxford, Bradford, Brewster, Bridgewater, Brockton, Brookline, Cambridge, Charlestown, Deerfield, Dorchester, Falmouth, Franklin, Grafton, Hanover, Hingham, Hull, Ipswich, Lancaster, Longmeadow, Mattapoisett, Methuen, Middleborough, Middleton, Milton, Newbury, Northampton, Plymouth, Rehoboth, Revere, Rowley, Salem, Salisbury, Scituate, Stoneham, Tewksbury, Topsfield, Truro, Wakefield, Watertown, Wenham, Weston, West Roxbury, and Weymouth; in Rhode Island—Barrington, Bristol, Little Compton, Newport, Providence, and Westerly; in New Hampshire—Dover, Greenland, Hampton, Hampton Falls, Kingston, Newington, Portsmouth, and West Nottingham; in Maine (still part of Massachusetts)—Berwick, Falmouth (now Portland), Scarborough, and Wells; and in New York—Huntington, Long Island, and East Hampton, Long Island (First Presbyterian East Hampton functioned like a Congregational church in this period).

34. Massachusetts towns whose church record did not clearly include multiple black baptisms or members: Cambridge (Second Church), Harwich, Haverhill (First Church), Lincoln, Lynnfield, Marblehead, Marlborough, Marshfield, Medford, Pembroke, Rochester, Sharon, South Danvers, and Westborough. Some of the records for these congregation do not fully cover 1730 to 1749. I do not have an accurate number of Connecticut Congregational churches that did not baptize black people because I used the Church Record Indexes at the Connecticut State Library to narrow my search to congregations that I knew baptized some black people. In Maine and New Hampshire, probably a higher percentage of Congregational churches did not baptize multiple

black people because the black populations there were smaller. Based on original and transcribed records that at least partially cover 1730–49 at the New Hampshire Historical Society, churches in these New Hampshire towns did not have multiple black baptisms or members during these years: Portsmouth First Church (1747–1835), North Hampton (1739–1850), Kingston East Church (1738–1785), Epping First (1748–1848), Amherst (1741–1826), Exeter First (1744–1763), South Hampton (1743–1790), Stratham (1746–1850), and Salem (1739–1850). Winiarski, *Darkness Falls*.

35. A list of Such Persons as have ben Received Into the Church by the Holy Sacrem't of Baptism Since the 11th Day of October 1719 at Newport Rhod Island, Trinity Church Records, NHS. According to Winiarski, "Even a single new black communicant struck some New Englanders as a significant departure from past affiliation practices, especially in towns with small enslaved populations" (Winiarski, *Darkness Falls*, 184).

36. Winiarski, *Darkness Falls*.

37. Winiarski notes that the terms "half-membership" and "halfway Covenant" originated with Strict Congregationalists, who opposed these practices, and that "in many churches, the practice of owning the covenant declined among whites during the early 1740s but not among enslaved and free black people" (Winiarski, *Darkness Falls*, 14, 38–53, 98, 184, 383). Anne A. Brown and David D. Hall, "Family Strategies and Religious Practice: Baptism and the Lord's Supper in Early New England," in *Lived Religion in America: Toward a History of Practice*, ed. Hall (Princeton, N.J.: Princeton University Press, 1997), 41–68; Robert G. Pope, *The Half-Way Covenant: Church Membership in Puritan New England* (Princeton, N.J.: Princeton University Press, 1969).

38. Windsor, Connecticut, First Congregational Church Records, 1639–1840, p. 185, copied from the original under the supervision of Mary Kingsbury Talcott, Registrar 1894–1914 (National Society of Colonial Dames of America in the State of Connecticut, 1938), handwritten transcription, CHS. "A Mallatto Servt [mulatto servant] made Profession of Faith, owned the Covt and was baptized on his own Right named John. Baptized here on Right of his Master, London, Lueit. Samuel Enos, his negro servant (Windsor, Connecticut, First Congregational Church Records, p. 185). More research is still needed into the religious affiliation histories of slaveholders to see how common it was for slaves to be baptized when their owners were halfway members.

39. Old North Church Records, N-2249, MHS; James N. Arnold, ed., *Vital Records of Rhode Island 1636–1850, First Series, Birth, Marriages and Deaths, A Family Register for the People*, vol. 8: *Episcopal and Congregational* (Providence, R.I.: Narragansett Historical Publishing Company, 1896); Andrew Oliver and James B. Peabody, eds., *Publications of the Colonial Society of Massachusetts*, vol. 56: *Collections: The Records of Trinity Church, Boston, 1728–1830, II* (Boston: Published by the Society, 1982); King's Chapel (Boston, Mass.) Records 1686–1942, MHS; Vital Records from the Parish Register of Queen's Chapel Portsmouth, New Hampshire, copied and indexed by Priscilla Hammond 1943, NEHGS; Trinity Church Newport Records, NHS; William Updike, *A History of the Episcopal Church in Narragansett, Rhode Island, including a History of the Other Episcopal Church in the State*, vol. 3, 2nd ed. (Boston: Merrymount, 1907), 72–88; "Baptisms of coloured people," Queen Anne's Chapel/St. Paul's Church records, Newburyport, Mass., information kindly provided by Bronson de Stadler; "St. Michael's Records of Baptisms, Marriages and Burials of Individuals of

Non-European Origins," St. Michael's Church, Marblehead, Mass. Archive, compiled September 2010; James N. Arnold, ed., *Vital Records of Rhode Island 1636–1850, First Series, Birth, Marriages and Deaths, A Family Register for the People*, vol. 10: *Town and Church* (Providence, R.I.: Narragansett Historical Publishing Company, 1898); Connecticut Church Records, Stratford/Christ Church and Episcopal Society, 1722–1932, vols. 1–4, 8, 12, reel #367, CSL. At least one Indian was baptized at Trinity Church Newport, Rhode Island; St. Paul's Narragansett, Rhode Island; and Christ Church Stratford, Connecticut.

40. Wilkins Updike, *History of the Episcopal Church in Narragansett, Rhode Island, Including a History of Other Episcopal Churches in the State, with an Appendix* (New York: Henry M. Onderdonk, 1847), 462–63; A list of Such Persons as have ben Received . . . Since the 11th Day of October 1719, Trinity Church Records, NHS. Fifteen of seventy-one baptisms (21.1 percent) in 1746; thirteen of fifty-two baptisms (25 percent) in 1747; eight of fifty-one baptisms (15 percent) in 1748; and four of thirty-nine (10 percent) in 1749 were identified as black people (A list of Such Persons as have ben Received . . . Since the 11th Day of October 1719, Trinity Church Records, NHS).

41. Society for the Propagation of the Gospel in Foreign Parts, *A collection of papers, printed by order of the Society for the Propagation of the Gospel in Foreign Parts* (London: Printed by T. Harrison and S. Brooke, 1788), 17–21; Holly Brewer, "Subjects by Allegiance to the King? Debating Status and Power for Subjects—and Slaves—through the Religious Debates of the Early British Atlantic," in *State and Citizen: British America and the Early United States*, ed. Peter Thompson and Peter S. Onuf (Charlottesville: University of Virginia Press, 2013), 29.

42. Qtd. in Klingberg, "The S.P.G. Program for Negroes in Colonial New York," 339; Glasson, *Mastering Christianity*, 150; Jean Fittz Hankins, "Bringing the Good News: Protestant Missionaries to the Indians of New England and New York, 1700–1777" (Ph.D. diss., University of Connecticut, 1993).

43. Greene, *Negro in Colonial New England*, 338; Mary H. Mitchell, "Slavery in Connecticut and Especially New Haven," *Papers of the New Haven Colony Historical Society*, vol. 10 (New Haven: Printed for the Society, Whaples-Bullis Company, 1951), 300; Robert E. Desrochers Jr., "Slave-for-Sale Advertisements and Slavery in Massachusetts, 1704–1781," *WMQ*, 3d ser., 59, no. 3 (July 2002): 630; George W. Harper, *A People So Favored of God: Boston's Congregational Churches and Their Pastors, 1710–1760*, 2nd ed. (Eugene, Ore.: Wipf and Stock, 2007), 47; Hardesty, *Unfreedom*, 5, 22.

44. Since blacks and some Indians participated in Anglican churches and other nonrevivalist churches, sometimes in significant numbers, I argue that blacks did not always come to churches in search of emotional or enthusiastic revivalism. The scholars who claim otherwise usually use evidence from later time periods and other places (such as the South) and/or base conclusions on the assumption that few blacks affiliated with Anglican churches (Raboteau, *A Fire in the Bones*, 21–22; Piersen, *Black Yankees*, 68–69; Adams and Pleck, *Love of Freedom*, 82–85, 101).

45. Harper, *A People So Favored of God*.

46. Harper, *A People So Favored of God*, xv.

47. Old South Church Records, manuscript, CL; *The Manifesto Church*; Manuscript Records of the New North Church in North-Street Boston, BPL; Harper, *A People So Favored of God*, 158–59; Winiarski, *Darkness Falls*, 28, 184; Adams and Pleck, *Love of Freedom*, 31; Whiting, "Power, Patriarchy, and Provision." At least twenty-six male

and twenty female black people were baptized at Brattle Street Church; fourteen male and twenty-one female blacks were baptized at Old South Church; and fifteen male and sixteen female black people were baptized at New North Church. Winiarski notes that in the early eighteenth century, "women, especially, understood church affiliation as an extension of parenting responsibilities" (Winiarski, *Darkness Falls*, 79).

48. Harper, *A People So Favored of God*, xv, 63–99, 146; Benjamin Colman, *Souls flying to Jesus Christ pleasant and admirable to behold: A sermon preach'd at the opening an evening-lecture, in Brattle-Street Boston, Tuesday October 21. 1740* (Boston: G. Rogers and D. Fowle, 1740), 24–25; Winiarski, *Darkness Falls*, 154, 162, 171–77, 185–94, 204, 215, 267–68, 307; Perry, ed., *Papers Related to the History of the Church in Massachusetts*, 345–48. Bailey argues that New Englanders offered redemption or spiritual salvation to slaves in part to redeem themselves from the contradictions and guilt they felt about slavery (Bailey, *Race and Redemption*, 115–133).

49. Qtd. in Harper, *A People So Favored of God*, 67; Benjamin Colman, *An Argument for and Persuasive unto the great and important Duty of Family Worship: With Rules and Directions for the due Performance of it* (Boston: Gamaliel Rogers, 1728), 36.

50. Harper, *A People So Favored of God*, 40–41, 66–67; J. Richard Olivas, "Partial Revival: The Limits of the Great Awakening in Boston, Massachusetts, 1740–1742," in *Inequality in Early America*, ed. Carla Gardina Pestana and Sharon V. Salinger (Hanover, N.H.: University Press of New England, 1999), 75, 81; Kidd, *Great Awakening*, 86, 98, 115, 129; Daniel Rogers Diary, Manuscript, Rogers Family Papers, MS 523, N-YHS; Cato Pearce, *Jailed for Preaching: The Autobiography of Cato Pearce, a Freed Slave from Washington County, Rhode Island*, ed. Christian M. McBurney (Kingston, R.I.: Pettaquamscutt Historical Society, 2006).

51. Robert Dunke and Ann Smith Lainhart, eds., *Hollis Street Church Boston Records of Admissions, Baptisms, Marriages and Deaths 1732–1887* (Boston: New England Historical Genealogical Society, 1998); Manuscript Records of New South Church Boston, BPL; Second Church (Boston, Mass.) Records 1650–1970, MHS; "Records of the West Church, Boston, Mass.," *New England Historic and Genealogical Register* 91 (1937), 92 (1938), 93 (1939), 94 (1940); *Publications of the Colonial Society of Massachusetts*, vol. 39: *The Records of the First Church in Boston, 1630–1868*, ed. Richard D. Peirce (Boston: Published by the Society, 1961); "New Brick Church, Boston," *New England Historical & Genealogical Register and Antiquarian Journal* 19, no. 3 (July 1865): 237; Harper, *A People So Favored of God*, 47–63, 99–123.

52. Perry, ed., *Papers Related to the History of the Church in Massachusetts*, 326; Harper *A People So Favored of God*, 47–63, 99–123; Glasson, *Mastering Christianity*, 89. Churches located nearest to the concentrations of urban blacks did not always have the highest levels of black participation, and churches in the same neighborhood did not always have similar levels of black engagement.

53. Old North Church (Christ Church in the City of Boston) records, MHS; Perry, ed., *Papers Related to the History of the Church in Massachusetts*, 345–50. For examples of opposition to slave baptism on the grounds that the slaves would be freed, see Glasson, *Mastering Christianity*, 75–110. Some seventeenth-century English theorists made direct connections between baptism and inclusion as English subjects. This idea likely influenced some slave owners to oppose slave baptisms (Brewer, "Subjects by Allegiance to the King," 38).

54. Dunke, *Hollis Street Church Boston Records*, 44, 229–30.

55. Winiarski, *Darkness Falls*, 93; Brown and Hall, "Family Strategies and Religious Practice," 53–54; Berlin, *Many Thousands Gone*, 73; John Thornton, "The Development of an African Catholic Church in the Kingdom of Kongo, 1491–1750," *Journal of American History* 25 (1984): 147–67; John Thornton, *Africa and Africans in the Making of the Atlantic World, 1400–1800*, 2nd ed. (Cambridge: Cambridge University Press, 1998).

56. *A Report of the Record Commissioners of the City of Boston, Containing the Boston Marriages from 1700 to 1751* (Boston: Municipal Printing Office, 1898), 129; Ira Berlin, "From Creole to African: Atlantic Creoles and the Origins of African-American Society in Mainland North America," *WMQ*, 3d ser., 53, no. 2 (April 1996): 251–88.

57. Records kept by Rev. Ebenezer Gay, MHS; Samuel Eliot, *Heralds of the Liberal Faith*, vol. 1: *The Prophets* (Boston: American Unitarian Association, 1910), 1–19; Rev. Nehemiah Hobart's records, MHS; Church book, 1734–1837, First Church (Weymouth, Mass.) records, MHS; Winiarski, *Darkness Falls*, 235, 259–61, 316, 373, 437–44. Eight blacks and three Indians were baptized by Reverend Gay (Records kept by Rev. Ebenezer Gay, MHS).

58. Qtd. in Peter Benes, "Slavery in Boston Households, 1647–1770," in *Slavery/Antislavery in New England: The Dublin Seminar for New England Folklife Annual Proceedings 2003*, ed. Benes (Boston: Boston University , 2005), 12–13; Charles Chauncy, *Seasonable thoughts on the state of religion in New England: A treatise in five parts* (Boston: Rogers and Fowle, for Samuel Eliot, 1743); *Records of the First Church in Boston*, 113, 399–402; Winiarski, *Darkness Falls*.

59. Perry, ed., *Papers Related to the History of the Church in Massachusetts*, 341; Glasson, *Mastering Christianity*, 99; Simonds, *History of the First Church and Society of Branford*, 72. Olivas concluded that Benjamin Colman of Brattle Street Church "welcomed blacks and indentured servants, but he welcomed others more," and that "ministers encountered deep resistance when they sought to admit enslaved persons" to membership in the church (Olivas, "Partial Revival," 78–79).

60. Bernard Christian Steiner, *History of Slavery in Connecticut*, Johns Hopkins University Studies in Historical and Political Science, eleventh series, ed. Adams Herbert (Baltimore: Johns Hopkins University Press, 1893), 386; see also A. Leon Higginbotham, *In the Matter of Color: Race and the American Legal Process: The Colonial Period* (New York: Oxford University Press, 1978).

61. Fisher, *Indian Great Awakening*, 43–53, 67–83, 92.

62. Box 2, book of meeting minutes 1731–1747 and 1748–1775, Papers, 1685–1787, Mss B C40, Company for the Propagation of the Gospel in New England and the Parts Adjacent in America, NEHGS.

63. Location/name of Congregational Churches with multiple Indian baptisms or members and the approximate number of Indians at each church in parentheses, 1730–49: Westerly, R.I. (64); Stonington, Conn. First (West) Church (47); East Stonington, Conn. (35); North (Second) Stonington, Conn. (21); First New London, Conn. (16); East Parish Lyme, Conn. (13); First New Hartford, Conn. (12); Evangelical Congregational Grafton, Mass. (9); First Groton, Conn. (9); Middleborough, Mass. (5); First Lebanon, Conn. (4); First Parish Dorchester, Mass. (4); First Old Lyme, Conn. (4); First Parish Hingham, Mass. (3); Barnstable East Parish (3); First Colchester, Conn. (3); Meriden, Conn. (3); Second Church Scituate, Mass. (2); Milton, Mass. (2); First

Providence, R.I. (2); Norwich, Conn. (2); Old Saybrook, Conn. (2). Location/name of Congregational Churches with one Indian Baptism or member, 1730–49: Bristol, R.I.; Bradford, Mass.; Weston, Mass.; Cambridge, Mass.; First Church Scituate, Mass.; Old South Boston, Mass.; Hollis Street Boston, Mass.; Second Church Beverly, Mass.; Pilgrim Church Merrimac, Mass.; First Charlestown, Mass.; Second Parish Hingham, Mass.; Hull, Mass.; First Watertown, Mass.; First Truro, Mass.; First Marlborough, Mass.; First Cromwell, Conn.; Redding, Conn.; Griswold, Conn.; First Kent, Conn.; First Hartford, Conn.; White-Haven/New Haven, Conn.; First Plainfield, Conn.; Canterbury, Conn.; and First Brooklyn, Conn.

64. Index, pp. 449–53, New London First Congregational Church, CSL; Fisher, *Indian Great Awakening*, 102–3; Kidd, *Great Awakening*, 8, 9, 112, 153; Winiarski, *Darkness Falls*, 304, 308.

65. Newell, "Indian Slavery in Colonial New England," 34; Ruth Wallis Herndon and Ella Wilcox Sekatau, "Pauper Apprenticeship in Narragansett County: A Different Name for Slavery in Early New England," in *Slavery/Antislavery in New England: The Dublin Seminar for New England Folklife Annual Proceedings 2003*, ed. Peter Benes (Boston: Boston University, 2005), 56–70; Karen Halttunen, *Murder Most Foul: The Killer and the American Gothic Imagination* (Cambridge, Mass.: Harvard University Press, 1998), 7–32; *Historical Magazine: Notes and Queries Concerning the Antiquities, History, and Biography of America*, 3d ser., 3, no. 1 (January 1874): 83; New London Church Records, 1:23, 128; Eliphalet Adams, *A sermon preached on the occasion of the execution of Katherine Garrett: an Indian-servant [. . .]* (New London: T. Green, 1738), 39–40; Katherine Grandjean, "'Our Fellow-Creatures & Our Fellow-Christians': Race and Religion in Eighteenth-Century Narratives of Indian Crime" *American Quarterly* 62, no. 4 (December 2010): 925–50.

66. Natick, Mass. First Congregational Church, Church records, 1721-1794 , CL (available on NEHH); O'Brien, *Dispossession by Degrees*; Daniel Mandell, "'To Live More Like My Christian English Neighbors': Natick Indians in the Eighteenth Century," *WMQ*, 3d ser., 48, no. 4 (October 1991): 552–79; Harold Field Worthley, *An Inventory of the Records of the Particular (Congregational) Churches of Massachusetts Gathered 1620–1805* (Cambridge, Mass.: Harvard University Press, 1970), 399–400.

67. Kidd, *Great Awakening*, 143; Thomas S. Kidd, "Daniel Rogers' Egalitarian Great Awakening," *Journal of the Historical Society* 7, no. 1 (March 2007): 111–35; Winiarski, *Darkness Falls*, 181–86; Daniel Rogers Diary, March 27, 1740/1 to May 17, 1740/1, N-YHS.

68. Kidd, *Great Awakening*, 47, 48, 85; Glasson, *Mastering Christianity*, 30, 113, 119–20; Goodfriend, *Who Should Rule at Home?*, 99–101.

69. John E. Stillwell, ed., *Historical and Genealogical Miscellany: Data Relating to the Settlement and Settlers of New York and New Jersey*, vol. 2 (Baltimore: Genealogical Publishing Company, 1970); Records of Christ Church Philadelphia Vol. 1: Bap. 1709–1768, red. 10, exp. 6.5. microfilm XCH11.4, HSP; Records of Trinity P.E. Church, Oxford, Philadelphia 1711-1855, Collections of the Genealogical Society of Pennsylvania, vol. 12 (Philadelphia, 1894), HSP; Klingberg, "The S.P.G. Program for Negroes in Colonial New York," 345–46; Hodges, *Root & Branch*, 85–86; Hodges, *Slavery and Freedom in the Rural North*, 28.

70. Vol. 40: Register of burials, 1714–1843, and vol. 41: Register of marriages, 1718–1841, King's Chapel (Boston, Mass.) Records, MHS; Arnold, ed., *Vital Records of*

Rhode Island, 10:333; St. Michael's Church (Pawtucket, R.I.), Records of St. Michael's Church, Bristol, University of Rhode Island Archive; Arnold, ed., *Vital Records of Rhode Island*, 8:187, 191, 196; Thomas Thompson, *An Account of Two Missionary Voyages by the Appointment of the Society for the Propagation of the Gospel in Foreign Parts: The one to New Jersey in North America, the other from America to the coast of Guiney* (London: Benj. Dod, 1758), 11. Some of the people married or buried by Anglican priests in various parishes do not appear elsewhere in the church records. The vestry minutes from Trinity Church New York indicate that blacks took communion there in this period (Copy of Minutes of the Vestry, 1697–1791, Corporation of Trinity Church, vol. 1, Trinity Church Wall Street Archive, New York).

71. John H. Hewitt Jr., *Protest and Progress: New York's First Black Episcopal Church Fights Racism* (New York: Garland, 2000), 1–12; Gerbner, *Christian Slavery*, 111–23; Klingberg, "The S.P.G. Program for Negroes in Colonial New York," 309–24.

72. July the 5th 1726 letter, copy of Minutes of the Vestry, 1697–1791, Corporation of Trinity Church, vol. 1, Trinity Church Wall Street Archive.

73. Hodges, *Root & Branch*, 85–86; William B. Sprague, *Annals of the American Episcopal Pulpit; or Commemorative Notices of Distinguished Clergymen of the Episcopal Church in the United States of America* (New York: Robert Carter and Brothers, 1859), 17.

74. Travis Glasson, "'Baptism Doth Not Bestow Freedom': Missionary Anglicanism, Slavery, and the Yorke-Talbot Opinion, 1701–30," *WMQ*, 3d ser., 67, no. 2 (April 2010): 279, 280, 297, 301, 304, 308; George Berkeley, *The Works of George Berkeley, D.D., Formerly Bishop of Cloyen*, vol. 4, ed. Alexander Campbell Fraser (Oxford: Clarendon, 1871), 638–40; Hugh Hastings, ed., *Ecclesiastical Records State of New York*, vol. 3 (Albany: J. B. Lyon Company, 1902), 1673; Glasson, *Mastering Christianity*, 81–82; Anthony S. Parent Jr., *Foul Means: The Formation of a Slave Society in Virginia, 1660–1740* (Chapel Hill: University of North Carolina Press, 2003), 114; Brewer, "Subjects by Allegiance to the King," 33.

75. Records of Christ Church Philadelphia, vol. 1, HSP; Deborah Mathias Gough, *Christ Church, Philadelphia: The Nation's Church in a Changing City* (Philadelphia: University of Pennsylvania Press, 1995), 68; Nash, *Forging Freedom*, 9–11. Adults were identified as adult, woman, or man. Children/infants were identified as child, infant, boy, or girl (Records of Christ Church Philadelphia, vol. 1, HSP).

76. St. Michael's Church (Pawtucket, R.I.), Records of St. Michael's Church, Bristol University of Rhode Island Archive; Records of Christ Church Philadelphia Vol. 1, HSP; Whiting, "Power, Patriarchy, and Provision."

77. William Bryan Hart, "For the Good of Our Souls: Mohawk Authority, Accommodation, and Resistance to Protestant Evangelism, 1700–1780" (Ph.D. diss., Brown University, 1998), 213–17, 228–38.

78. Arthur C.M. Kelly, ed., *Vital Records of Queen Anne Chapel (Episcopal) Fort Hunter, NY, Town of Florida, Montgomery County, 1735–1746* (Rhinebeck, N.Y.: Kinship, 2000); Daniel K. Richter, "'Some of Them . . . Would Always Have a Minister with Them': Mohawk Protestantism, 1683–1719," *American Indian Quarterly* 16, no. 4 (Autumn 1992): 471–84; Hankins, "Bringing the Good News," 44–48.

79. Richard J. Boles, "African Americans and Northern Lutherans during the Eighteenth Century," *Lutheran Quarterly* 33, no. 2 (Summer 2019): 153–79.

80. Aaron Spencer Fogleman, *Hopeful Journeys: German Immigration, Settlement, and Political Culture in Colonia America, 1717–1775* (Philadelphia: University

of Pennsylvania Press, 1996); A. G. Roeber, *Palatines, Liberty, and Property: German Lutherans in Colonial British America* (Baltimore: Johns Hopkins University Press, 1993); Charles H. Glatfelter, *Pastors and People,* vol. 2: *The History* (Breinigsville: Pennsylvania German Society, 1981), 20, 27–29; Mark Häberlein, *The Practice of Pluralism: Congregational Life and Religious Diversity in Lancaster, Pennsylvania, 1730–1820* (University Park: Pennsylvania State University Press, 2009).

81. Glatfelter, *Pastors and People:* 2:288; Gary B. Nash, "Slaves and Slaveowners in Colonial Philadelphia," *WMQ,* 3d ser., 30, no. 2 [April 1973]: 254–55, 299–32). Häberlein, *The Practice of Pluralism,* 173–79; James Van Horn Melton, "Colonial Germans and Slavery on the Eve of the American Revolution: The Case of Ebenezer," *Bulletin of the German Historical Institute* 61 (Fall 2017): 17–19. According to Glatfelter, "few German farmers had slaves," and Gary Nash argues that Germans in Philadelphia "eschewed slaveholding to a remarkable degree" (Glatfelter, *Pastors and People:* 2:288; Nash, "Slaves and Slaveowners," 254–55, 299–332).

82. St. Michael's & Zion Lutheran Church, Philadelphia, PA, Baptisms 1745–59 Part 1, Collections of the Genealogical Society of Pennsylvania, vol. 30, pp. 19, 27, 31, Philadelphia, 1897, HSP; F. Edward Wright, *Berks County Church Records of the 18th Century,* vol. 1 (Westminster, Md.: Family Line Publications, 1994), 11. St. Gabriel's Church joined the Episcopal denomination after the American Revolution (Kim-Eric Williams, *The Eight Old Swedes' Churches of New Sweden* [New Sweden Centre: Kalmar Nyckel Museum Institute, 1999]).

83. Charles H. Glatfelter, *Pastors and People: German Lutheran and Reformed Churches in the Pennsylvania Field, 1717–1793,* vol. 1: *Pastors and Congregations* (Breinigsville: Pennsylvania German Society, 1980), 215–17; Records relating to the Lutheran Church in Colonial New York, 1649–1772, box 2, November 1/12, 1725, p. 270, Evangelisch Luthersche Kerk (Netherlands), NYPL. See Graham Russell Hodges, "The Pastor and the Prostitute: Sexual Power among African Americans and Germans in Colonial New York," in *Sex, Love, Race: Crossing Boundaries in North American History,* ed. Martha Hodes (New York: New York University Press, 1999), 60–71.

84. Records relating to the Lutheran Church in Colonial New York, p. 331, NYPL; Hodges, "The Pastor and the Prostitute," 64–65.

85. Johnson, *Black Christians,* 32; Karl Kretzmann, "The Constitution of the First Lutheran Synod in America," *Concordia Historical Institute Quarterly* 9, no. 1 (April 1936): 7.

86. Simon Hart and Harry J. Kreider, eds., *Lutheran Church in New York and New Jersey 1722–1760: Lutheran Records in the Ministerial Archives of the Staatsarchiv, Hamburg, Germany* (United Lutheran Synod of New York and New England, 1962), 25.

87. Hodges, *Root & Branch,* 86; Hodges, "The Pastor and the Prostitute," 63.

88. Lutheran church records, 1703–1802, New York, Albany, and other places, manuscript, pp. 98, 101, 102, 141, NYGBS Collection, NYPL; Hodges, "The Pastor and the Prostitute," 61–64.

89. Jon F. Sensbach, *Rebecca's Revival: Creating Black Christianity in the Atlantic World* (Cambridge, Mass: Harvard University Press, 2005); Corinna Dally-Starna and William A. Starna, eds., *Gideon's People: Being a Chronicle of an American Indian Community in Colonial Connecticut and the Moravian Missionaries Who Served There,* vols. 1 and 2 (Lincoln: University of Nebraska Press, 2009); Gerbner, *Christian Slavery,* 138–88.

90. Merritt, "Dreaming of the Savior's Blood," 727, 736; Wheeler, *To Live upon Hope*, 67–171; Gerbner, *Christian Slavery*, 156–57, 163–88.

91. Merritt, "Dreaming of the Savior's Blood," 728–29, 731, 737, 737n48.

92. Amy C. Schutt, "Female Relationships and Intercultural Bonds in Moravian Indian Missions," in *Friends and Enemies in Penn's Woods: Indians, Colonists, and the Racial Construction of Pennsylvania*, ed. William A. Penack and Daniel K. Richter (University Park: Pennsylvania State University Press, 2004), 87, 94, 96, 99; Wheeler, *To Live upon Hope*, 146, 167–71.

93. Jane T. Merritt, *At the Crossroads: Indians and Empires on a Mid-Atlantic Frontier, 1700–1763* (Chapel Hill: University of North Carolina Press, 2003), 8–9; Merritt, "Dreaming of the Savior's Blood," 746.

94. Hodges, *Slavery and Freedom in the Rural North*, 26, 39, 76; *Records of the Reformed Dutch Church of Albany, New York, 1683–1809: Marriages, Baptism, Members, Etc., Excerpted from Year Book of the Holland Society of New York*, introd. Louis Duermyer (Baltimore: Genealogical Publishing Co., 1978), 3:45–110; Old Tennent Church, Freehold, N.J., Records, vol. 1: Records 1730–1820, Monmouth County Historical Association Library; Frank R. Symmes, *History of the Old Tennent Church*, 2nd ed. (Cranbury, N.J.: George W. Burroughs Printer, 1904), 181–223, 465. Here are examples of Dutch Reformed Church records in which I did not find any identified black or Indian baptisms between 1730 and 1749: Royden Woodward Vosburgh, ed., Records of the First Reformed Church of Coxsackie in West Coxsackie, Greene County, N.Y., vol. 1, transcribed by the NYGBS (New York City, 1919); Royden Woodward Vosburgh, ed., Records of the Reformed Protestant Dutch Church of Catskill in the town of Catskill, Greene County, N.Y., transcribed by the NYGBS (New York City, 1919); Collections of the NYGBS, vol. 5, Minister Valley Reformed Dutch Church Records (New York: Printed for the Society, 1917); Charlotta Taylor Luckhurst, ed., Schenectady Dutch Church members, 1694–1839, carbon-copy typescript, NYPL; Maria Noll Cormack, ed., Schenectady, New York First Dutch Reformed Church: Births and Baptisms, 1649–1781, typescript, NYPL; Josephine C. Frost, ed., Baptismal record of the Reformed Dutch Church at Newtown, Long Island, New York, 1736 to 1846, carbon-copy typescript, NYPL; M. M. Bowman and. Lilia Smith Seegmiller, eds., Pompton Plains Reformed Dutch church: marriage records, 1735–1746, 1793–1809, baptismal records, 1735–1871, typescript, NYPL; Ralph H. Weller, ed., Members of the German Reformed Church, Montgomery, Orange County, New York, 1732–1802, photocopy of typescript, NYPL; B. Fernow and Gerritt Hubert van Wagenen, eds., The records of the Dutch Reformed Church at New Paltz, Ulster County, N.Y.: from 1683 to 1816, manuscript, NYPL; Records of the Reformed Church of Linlithgo in the town of Livingston, Columbia County, New York, carbon-copy typescript, NYPL. Examples of Presbyterian churches that did not baptize or admit to membership any blacks or Indians between 1730 and 1770 include the First Presbyterian Church Philadelphia, Pa.; the Presbyterian Church Newtown (now Elmhurst) Long Island, N.Y.; and the First Presbyterian Church Cranbury, N.J. (Collections of the NYGBS, vol. 8, The Presbyterian Church Records, Newtown [now Elmhurst] Queens County, Long Island, N.Y. [New York: Printed for the Society, 1928]; Gertrude A. Barber, ed., Congregational and First Presbyterian Church records at Cranbury, N.J., carbon-copy typescript, NYPL; Records of First Presbyterian Church, Philadelphia, Baptisms 1701–1856, Collections of the Genealogical Society of Pennsylvania, vol. 27, PHS; Viola E. Shaw and Barbara

S. Parker, eds., *Madison, New Jersey Presbyterian Church, Vital Records, 1747–1900* [Madison, N.J.: Presbyterian Church of Madison, ca. 1982]).

95. Bolton, *History of the Protestant Episcopal Church in the County of Westchester*, 243, 250. J. Earl Thompson Jr. writes that, especially regarding Presbyterians, "Some Christians refused or neglected to teach their bond servants the rudiments of Christianity while others were reluctant to allow their instructed slaves to be baptized for fear of being morally obligated to emancipate them" (Thompson, "Slavery and Presbyterianism in the Revolutionary Era," *Journal of Presbyterian History* 54, no. 1 [Spring 1976]: 121).

96. Gerald Francis De Jong, "The Dutch Reformed Church and Negro Slavery in Colonial America," *Church History* 40, no. 4 (December 1971): 432; Noel Leo Erskine, *Black People and the Reformed Church in America* (Lansing, IL: Reformed Church Press, 1978); Dewulf, *The Pinkster King and the King of Kongo*; Patricia Bonomi, "'Swarms of Negroes Comeing about My Door': Black Christianity in Early Dutch and English North America," *Journal of American History* 103, no. 1 (June 2016): 34–58; Henry B. Hoff, "A Colonial Black Family in New York and New Jersey: Pieter Santomee and His Descendants," *Journal of the Afro-American Historical and Genealogical Society* 9, no. 3 (Fall 1988): 101–34; Andrea C. Mosterman, "'I Thought They Were Worthy': A Dutch Reformed Church Minister and His Congregation Debate African American Membership in the Church," *Early American Studies: An Interdisciplinary Journal* 14, no. 3 (Summer 2016): 610–16; Goodfriend, *Who Should Rule at Home?*, 200–203; James W. Van Hoeven, ed., *Piety and Patriotism: Bicentennial Studies of the Reformed Church in America, 1776–1976* (Grand Rapids, Mich.: Eerdmans, 1976); Carla Gardina Pestana and Sharon V. Salinger, *Inequality in Early America* (Hanover, N.H.: University Press of New England, 1999); Shane White, "'It Was a Proud Day': African Americans, Festivals, and Parades in the North, 1741–1834," *Journal of American History* 81, no. 1 (June 1994): 13–50; Charles H. Glatfelter, *Pastors and People*: 1:160–61; Glatfelter, *Pastors and People*, vol. 2; William John Hinke, *A History of the Goshenhoppen Reformed Charge, Montgomery County, Pennsylvania (1727–1819)* (Lancaster: Pennsylvania-German Society, 1920); Gerbner, *Christian Slavery*, 27; Thompson, "Slavery and Presbyterianism in the Revolutionary Era"; Andrews, *Native Apostles*; Peter Kalm, *Travels into North America; containing its natural history, and a circumstantial account of its plantations and agriculture in general, with the civil, ecclesiastical and commercial state of the country, the manners of the inhabitants, and several curious and important remarks on various subjects*, translated into English by John Reinhold Forster, 2nd ed., 2 vols. (London, T. Lowndes, 1772), 1:ix, 172, 178, 196, 311.

2 / "I Claim Jesus Christ to Be My Right Master"

1. "A Remarkable Account of a Reformation among Some Gentlemen, at Boston in New-England; Being an Abstract of a Letter from G. D. of that Place, to His Friend W. N. in Biddiford, Dated Nov. 22, 1740," in *Proceedings of the Massachusetts Historical Society, October 1919–June 1920*, vol. 53 (Boston: Published by the Society, 1920), 200; Douglas L. Winiarski, *Darkness Falls on the Land of Light: Experiencing Religious Awakenings in Eighteenth-Century New England* (Chapel Hill: University of North Carolina Press, 2017), 326.

2. The letter that included this story was printed in a newspaper in Glasgow, Scotland, the *Glasgow-Weekly-History*. The printer sought to further promote revivalism by sharing stories of its successes. From the point of view of the publisher and writer, the central significance of the story lay in the apparent suddenness and completeness of the gentleman's conversion from sinful to godly living at hearing Whitefield's message (even though it was delivered by a slave).

3. "A Remarkable Account of a Reformation among Some Gentlemen," 200; Travis Glasson, *Mastering Christianity: Missionary Anglicanism and Slavery in the Atlantic World* (New York: Oxford University Press, 2011), 103–5. There were no black churches in Boston at this time, and interracial church services were common, so this black man likely heard the message of Christianity at interracial religious services.

4. Winiarski, *Darkness Falls*, 378–402.

5. Qtd. in Frank J. Klingberg, "The S.P.G. Program for Negroes in Colonial New York," *Historical Magazine of the Protestant Episcopal Church* 8, no. 4 (December 1939): 359–60.

6. Names of persons offending & their acknowledgments Received, Records of the Church in Deerfield 1731–1810, bound volume, p. 67 (page missing from microfilm version), Memorial Libraries Deerfield Mass; Linford D. Fisher, *The Indian Great Awakening: Religion and the Shaping of Native Culture in Early America* (New York: Oxford University Press, 2012).

7. Douglas Leach, *Northern Colonial Frontier, 1607–1763* (New York: Holt, Rinehart, and Winston, 1966); Richard Johnson, "The Search for a Usable Indian: An Aspect of the Defense of Colonial New England," *Journal of American History* 64, no. 3 (December 1977): 623–51; Fred Anderson, *Crucible of War: The Seven Years' War and the Fate of Empire in British North America, 1754–1766* (New York: Vintage, 2000); Peter Silver, *Our Savage Neighbors: How Indian War Transformed Early America* (New York: Norton, 2008).

8. Gary B. Nash, "Slaves and Slaveowners in Colonial Philadelphia," *WMQ*, 3d ser., 30, no. 2 (April 1973): 229; Robert E. Desrochers Jr., "Slave-for-Sale Advertisements and Slavery in Massachusetts, 1704–1781," *WMQ*, 3d ser., 59, no. 3 (July 2002): 654–61; Graham Russell Hodges, *Root & Branch: African Americans in New York and East Jersey, 1613–1863* (Chapel Hill: University of North Carolina Press, 1999), 104–5; Connecticut General Assembly, A List of the Number of Inhabitants in Each Town in the Colony of Connecticut Taken in the Year 1762, 2 pp. (Ms Stacks, Connecticut), CHS; Account of the People in the Colony of Rhode Island, Whites and Blacks, 1755, Mss 9003, vol. 12, p. 12, RIHS.

9. Anderson, *Crucible of War*, xxi.

10. Winiarski, *Darkness Falls*, 436–56, 491–95. The only other historians who have paid careful attention to baptismal and membership records in regards to blacks and Indians are Graham Russell Hodges for New York and New Jersey; Linford Fisher for Indians in southern New England; and John Sweet for southern New England (Hodges, *Root & Branch*; Graham Russell Hodges, *Slavery and Freedom in the Rural North: African Americans in Monmouth County, New Jersey, 1665–1865* [New York: Rowman and Littlefield, 1997]; Fisher, *Indian Great Awakening*; John Wood Sweet, *Bodies Politic: Negotiating Race in the American North, 1730–1830* [Philadelphia: University of Pennsylvania Press, 2003]).

11. Fewer black people participated through baptism in Boston's Congregational churches from 1750 to 1763 than from 1730 to 1749. For example, the yearly average

number of black baptisms at Brattle Street Church decreased from 2.3 yearly to 0.93 yearly, and the percentage of all baptisms that were black baptisms decreased from 4.06 percent to 2.95 percent. At three of the Congregational churches, the percentage of all baptisms that were black increased only because the rate of white baptisms decreased substantially (*The Manifesto Church: Records of the Church in Brattle Square Boston, 1699-1872* [Boston: The Benevolent Fraternity of Churches, 1902]).

12. William D. Piersen, *Black Yankees: The Development of an Afro-American Subculture in Eighteenth-Century New England* (Amherst: University of Massachusetts Press, 1988), 164; Lorenzo Johnston Greene, *The Negro in Colonial New England* (New York: Athenaeum, 1969), 338, 347; George W. Harper, *A People So Favored of God: Boston's Congregational Churches and Their Pastors, 1710-1760*, 2nd ed. (Eugene, Ore.: Wipf and Stock, 2007); Desrochers, "Slave-for-Sale Advertisements," 654, 662; Thomas Kidd, *The Great Awakening: The Roots of Evangelical Christianity in Colonial America* (New Haven: Yale University Press, 2007), 213.

13. Baptisms 1669-1875, VS B I, Old South Church Records, CL available on NEHH. I chose Old South for this example because the number of black baptism in both periods was high enough to provide for a comparison.

14. Locations of Congregational churches in which multiple blacks were baptized and/or admitted 1750-1763: in Connecticut—Berlin Kensington, Bloomfield, Bolton, Bozrah, Canterbury (Separate/Strict Congregational Church), Colchester, Cromwell, Durham, East Haddam, East Hartford, East Haven, Fairfield, Griswold, Groton, Hartford, Lebanon, Lisbon Newent, Mansfield, Middletown, New Hartford, New Haven, New London, Newtown, North Woodstock, Northford, Norwich, Old Lyme, Old Saybrook, Oxford, Plainfield, Portland, Preston, Woodstock Hill, Redding, Southington, Stamford, Trumbull (North Stratford), Westchester, Wethersfield, Windsor, and Woodbury; in Massachusetts—Amesbury (North Parish and South Parish churches), Barnstable (West Parish and East Parish churches), Beverly, Billerica, Boston (First Church, Old South, Brattle Square, New North/Fifth, New South/Sixth, New Brick/Seventh, Hollis Street, and West/Ninth), Boxford (First and Second churches), Bradford, Brockton, Cambridge (First and Second churches), Charlestown, Deerfield, Dorchester, Groton, Hingham (First Parish), Lancaster (Second Church/Chocksett Church), Lincoln, Middleton, Medway (Second Church), Merrimac (Pilgrim Congregational), Milton, Northampton, Newbury (Third Church), Pembroke (Second Church) Plymouth, Rehoboth (Newman Congregational), Rochester/Mattapoisett (Second Church), Rowley, Salem, Scituate (First and Second churches), Stoneham, Sturbridge, Topsfield, Truro, Watertown, Wenham, Weymouth, and West Roxbury; in New Hampshire—Hampton, Kingston, North Hampton, Portsmouth (First/North and South churches), and Rye; in Rhode Island—Bristol and Tiverton; in Maine—Congregational Church at Black Point, Scarborough.

15. Church Covenant, baptisms, marriages, other administrations of 4th Church of Christ in Bridgewater, box 1, Brockton, Massachusetts, Christ Congregational Church Records, 1738-1980, CL (available on NEHH); Baptisms in Amesbury, Pilgrim Congregational Church (Merrimac, Mass.) manuscript records, CL (available on NEHH); Greene, *Negro in Colonial New England*, 340 . In Brockton, Massachusetts, six blacks were baptized during each time period (1740-49 and 1750-63). The First Church of Hartford, Connecticut, baptized twelve blacks between 1730 and 1749 (yearly average of 0.60 baptisms) and thirteen blacks between 1750 and 1763 (yearly average of 0.93

baptisms). By 1762, Hartford had a population of 152 blacks (*Historical Catalogue of the First Church in Hartford, 1633–1885* [Published by the Church, 1885], 199–226; A List of the Number of Inhabitants in Each Town in the Colony of Connecticut Taken in the Year 1762, CHS).

16. Connecticut Church Records, State Library Index, Mansfield First Congregational Church, 1710–1892 (Hartford: CSL, 1967); Susan W. Dimock, ed., *Births, Baptisms, Marriages, and Deaths from the Records of the Town and Churches in Mansfield, Connecticut, 1703–1850* (New York: Baker and Taylor Company, 1898), 360–89; Index, New London First Congregational Church, CSL; Blake, *Later History of the First Church of Christ New London*, 491–522; A List of the Number of Inhabitants in Each Town in the Colony of Connecticut Taken in the Year 1762, CHS; Winiarski, *Darkness Falls*, 304–6, 364.

17. A list of Such Persons as have ben Received . . . since the 11th Day of October 1719, Trinity Church Records, NHS; Catherine Brekus, *Sarah Osborn's World: The Rise of Evangelical Christianity in Early America* (New Haven, Conn.: Yale University Press, 2013), 28; Records of Christ Church Philadelphia, vol. 1, HSP; Richard I. Shelling, "William Sturgeon, Catechist to the Negroes of Philadelphia and Assistant Rector of Christ Church, 1747–1766," *Historical Magazine of the Protestant Episcopal Church* 8, no. 4 (December 1939): 388–401.

18. John Egerton, *A Sermon Preached before the Incorporated Society for the Propagation of the Gospel in Foreign Parts: At their Anniversary Meeting in the Parish Church of St. Mary-le-Bow, on Friday, February 18, 1763* (London: E. Owen and T. Harrison, 1763), 33–36, 61–71; Glasson, *Mastering Christianity*; Katharine Gerbner, *Christian Slavery: Conversion and Race in the Protestant Atlantic World* (Philadelphia: University of Pennsylvania Press, 2018); Nicholas M. Beasley, *Christian Ritual and the Creation of British Slave Societies 1650–1780* (Athens: University of Georgia Press, 2009); Rebecca Anne Goetz, *The Baptism of Early Virginia: How Christianity Created Race* (Baltimore: Johns Hopkins University Press, 2012).

19. Marriages Parish 1746–1816 and Baptisms 1759, p. 22, Trinity Church Wall Street Archive, New York; Kyle T. Bulthuis, *Four Steeples over the City Streets: Religion and Society in New York's Early Republic Congregations* (New York: New York University Press, 2014), 18–20, 27.

20. Qtd. in Klingberg, "The S.P.G. Program for Negroes in Colonial New York," 332–33.

21. Klingberg, "The S.P.G. Program for Negroes in Colonial New York," 332–36; Hodges, *Root & Branch*, 119–20; Bulthuis, *Four Steeples over the City Streets*, 27; Glasson, *Mastering Christianity*; Joyce D. Goodfriend, *Who Should Rule at Home? Confronting the Elite in British New York* (Ithaca, N.Y.: Cornell University Press, 2017), 189–97.

22. Qtd. in Klingberg, "The S.P.G. Program for Negroes in Colonial New York," 359–60. Hodges writes, "Between 1740 and 1782 Anglican missionaries baptized at least 350 blacks in New Brunswick, Newark, Elizabethtown, and Perth Amboy," New Jersey (Hodges, *Root & Branch*, 121).

23. St. Michael's & Zion Lutheran Church, Philadelphia, PA Baptisms 1745–59 Part 1, HSP; Christ Evangelical Lutheran Church, York, York County, PA, Part I, Baptisms 1733–1794, Adams County Historical Society; Lutheran church records, 1703–1802 New York, Albany, and other places, NYPL; First Moravian Church

Phila, PA Baptism, Marriages, HSP; New York Moravian Church records: baptisms 1744–1890, with an index compiled by Thelma E. Smith, 1991, NYPL; F. Edward Wright, ed., *Bucks County, Pennsylvania Church Records of the 17th and 18th Centuries*, vol. 1 (Westminster, Md.: Willow Bend, 2001); F. Edward Wright, ed., *18th Century Records of the Germantown Reformed Church of Pennsylvania* (Westminster, Md.: Family Line Publications, 1994); *The Journals of Henry Melchior Muhlenberg*, 3 vols., trans. Theodore G. Tappert and John W. Doberstein (Philadelphia: Evangelical Lutheran Ministerium of Pennsylvania and Adjacent States, 1942–58), 1:342; Goodfriend, *Who Should Rule at Home?*, 195; John W. Catron, *Embracing Protestantism: Black Identities in the Atlantic World* (Gainesville: University of Florida Press, 2016), 101–49.

24. Location/name of churches with Indian baptisms or members and the approximate number of Indians at each church, 1750–1763: Reformed Congregation at Schoharie, N.Y. (41); Congregational Church Tiverton, R.I. (4); First Congregational Hanover, Mass. (3); Second Congregational Scituate, Mass. (1); Second Congregational Medway, Mass. (1); West Parish Congregational Barnstable, Mass. (1); First Congregational Cromwell, Conn. (1); First Congregational Southington, Conn. (1); Second Congregational Guilford, Conn. (1); Congregational Groton, Conn. (1); Congregational Church New London, Conn. (1); East Stonington Congregational Stonington, Conn. (1); North Stonington Congregational Church Stonington, Conn. (2); First Church New Hartford, Conn. (2); First Congregational Mansfield, Conn. (2); First Congregational Plainfield, Conn. (1); Christ Anglican Church Stratford, Conn. (1); King's Anglican Chapel Boston, Mass. (1); Trinity Anglican Church Newport, R.I. (4); and St. Michael's Anglican Bristol, R.I. (1). Sources: Arnold, ed., *Vital Records of Rhode Island*, vol. 8; *Vital Records of Scituate*; Connecticut Church Records, Stratford/Christ Church and Episcopal Society, 1722–1932, vols. 1–4, 8, 12, reel #367, CSL; King's Chapel (Boston, Mass.) Records, MHS; Book of Record Trinity Church Rhode Island 1709, Trinity Church Newport Records, NHP; Connecticut Church Records, State Library Index, Cromwell First Congregational Church 1715–1875, CLS; Connecticut Church Records, State Library Index, Southington First Congregational Church 1728–1876, CLS; Connecticut Church Records, State Library Index, Guilford Second Congregational Church at Northern Guilford 1720–1859, CLS; Connecticut Church Records, State Library Index, New Hartford First Congregational Church (Old Town Hill Church) 1739–1854, CLS; Index, Mansfield First Congregational Church 1710–1892, CLS; Connecticut Church Records, State Library Index, Plainfield First Congregational Church 1747–1832, CLS; Index, New London First Congregational Church, CSL; Royden Woodward Vosburgh, ed., Records of the High and Low Dutch Reformed Congregation at Schoharie, now Reformed Church in the town of Schoharie, Schoharie County, N.Y., vol. 1 pt. 1, pp. 34–58, bound typescript, transcribed by the NYGBS (New York City, June 1917), LOC.

25. Linford Fisher shows that fewer and fewer Indians in Connecticut and Rhode Island affiliated with predominantly white churches after the Great Awakening waned, sometimes dropping sharply after 1742 (Fisher, "'Traditionary Religion': The Great Awakening and the Shaping of Native Cultures in Southern New England, 1736–1776" [Th.D. diss., Harvard University, 2008], 198).

26. Linford Fisher's scholarship deeply influenced my treatment of these Indian churches (Fisher, *Indian Great Awakening*).

27. For a discussion on reasons behind the Indian exodus from white churches, especially separatist theology, see Fisher, "Traditionary Religion," 211–22; Fisher, *Indian Great Awakening*; and Winiarski, *Darkness Falls*.

28. Fisher, "Traditionary Religion," 231, 240, 246.

29. Joanna Brooks, ed., *The Collected Writings of Samson Occom, Mohegan: Leadership and Literature in Eighteenth-Century Native America* (New York: Oxford University Press, 2006), xxi, 52–54, 248–51; Fisher, "Traditionary Religion," 222–25; Company for the Propagation of the Gospel in New England and the Parts Adjacent in America, Papers, 1685–1787 (manuscript), Mss B C40, box 2, book of meeting minutes etc. 1731 to 1747, NEHGS.

30. Fisher, "Traditionary Religion," 225–29; Brooks, ed., *Collected Writings of Samson Occom*, 54–55.

31. Brooks, ed., *Collected Writings of Samson Occom*, 253–64; Fisher, "Traditionary Religion," 231–32.

32. Brooks, ed., *Collected Writings of Samson Occom*, 57–58, 64, 67; Fisher, "Traditionary Religion," 229–31.

33. William S. Simmons and Cheryl L. Simmons, eds., *Old Light on Separate Ways: The Narragansett Diary of Joseph Fish, 1765–1776* (Hanover, N.H.: University Press of New England, 1982), xxviii.

34. Simmons and Simmons, eds., *Old Light on Separate Ways*, xxx; *The Christian History: Containing Accounts of the Propagation and Revival of Religion in England, Scotland and America*, Saturday August 27, 1743, no. 26, pp. 201–8; *The Christian History: Containing Accounts of the Propagation and Revival of Religion in England, Scotland and America*, Saturday September 3, 1745, no. 27, p. 209; *The Christian History: Containing Accounts of the Propagation and Revival of Religion in England, Scotland and America*, Saturday, March 17, 1744, no. 55, pp. 23–24; Fisher, "Traditionary Religion," 244; William Simmons, "Red Yankees: Narragansett Conversion in the Great Awakening," *American Ethnologist* 10, no. 2 (May 1983): 261–62.

35. *The Christian History: Containing Accounts of the Propagation and Revival of Religion in England, Scotland and America*, Saturday, March 24, 1744, no. 56, p. 25; Fisher, "Traditionary Religion," 218–19.

36. Simmons, "Red Yankees," 262–63; Ezra Stiles, *The Literary Diary of Ezra Stiles, D.D., LL.D.*, vol. 1, ed. Franklin B. Dexter (New York: Charles Scribner's Sons, 1901), 232; Company for the Propagation of the Gospel in New England and the Parts Adjacent in America, Papers, Mss B C40, box 2, Book of meeting minutes etc. circa 1748 to 1774, NEHGS. For more on Fish and Niles, see Sweet, *Bodies Politic*, 131–41; and Edward E. Andrews, *Native Apostles: Black and Indian Missionaries in the British Atlantic World* (Cambridge, Mass.: Harvard University Press, 2013), 115–23.

37. Simmons and Simmons, eds., *Old Light on Separate Ways*, 4; Fisher, "Traditionary Religion," 246–47.

38. Simmons and Simmons, eds., *Old Light on Separate Ways*, 3–5, 29.

39. Simmons and Simmons, eds., *Old Light on Separate Ways*, xxxi–xxxvi; Simmons, "Red Yankees," 264; Sweet, *Bodies Politic*, 15–57.

40. Fisher, "Traditionary Religion," 258–361.

41. Michael J. Crawford, "Indians, Yankees, and the Meetinghouse Dispute of Natick, Massachusetts, 1743–1800," *New England Historical and Genealogical Register* 132 (October 1978), 279. Whites also displaced Indians in Stockbridge, Massachusetts

(Patrick Frazier, *The Mohicans of Stockbridge* [Lincoln: University of Nebraska Press, 1992]; Rachel Wheeler, *To Live upon Hope: Mohicans and Missionaries in the Eighteenth-Century Northeast* [Ithaca, N.Y.: Cornell University Press, 2008]; David J. Silverman, *Red Brethren: The Brothertown and Stockbridge Indians and the Problem of Race in Early America* [Ithaca, N.Y.: Cornell University Press, 2010]).

42. O'Brien, *Dispossession by Degrees*; Daniel Mandell, "'To Live More Like My Christian English Neighbors': Natick Indians in the Eighteenth Century," *WMQ*, 3d ser., 48, no. 4 (October 1991); Natick, Mass. First Congregational Church Records, NEHH.

43. Qtd. in O'Brien, *Dispossession by Degrees*, 119–25, 190–92; Mandell, "To Live More Like My Christian English Neighbors"; Crawford, "Indians, Yankees, and the Meetinghouse Dispute of Natick"; Stephen Badger, "Historical and Characteristic Traits of the American Indians in General and Those of Natick in Particular," *Massachusetts Historical Society Collections*, 1st ser., 5 (1798): 32–45; Natick, Mass. First Congregational Church Records, church records, 1802–1833, NEHH.

44. Mandell, "To Live More Like My Christian English Neighbors," 562.

45. Elisha Tupper, Sandwich, Mass., to Andrew Oliver, May 20, 1756; List of Indians attending the meetinghouse in Sandwich, Mass., August 7, 1757; and Elisha Tupper to the commissioners of the NEC, November 18, 1761, all in Miscellaneous Bound Manuscripts, MHS; Harold Field Worthley, *An Inventory of the Records of the Particular (Congregational) Churches of Massachusetts Gathered 1620–1805* (Cambridge, Mass.: Harvard University Press, 1970), 106–9.

46. Proceedings of a meeting held by a group of Indians in Sandwich, Mass., concerning the possibilities of constructing a new meetinghouse, Minutes kept by Joseph Lawrence, in Miscellaneous Bound Manuscripts, MHS.

47. Company for the Propagation of the Gospel in New England and the Parts Adjacent in America, Papers, Mss B C40, box 2, Book of meeting minutes etc. circa 1748 to 1774, September 4, 1753, NEHGS.

48. Certificate listing the members of the Indian meetinghouse in Sandwich, Massachusetts, with an explanation of why a new, larger meetinghouse is needed, compiled by Zaccheus Burge, Joseph Lawrence, and Thomas Swift, in Miscellaneous Bound Manuscripts, MHS; Tupper, to the commissioners of the NEC, November 18, 1761, Miscellaneous Bound Manuscripts, MHS.

49. Certificate listing the members of the Indian meetinghouse in Sandwich, MHS.

50. Mandell, *Behind the Frontier*; David J. Silverman, "The Church in New England Indian Community Life: A View from the Islands and Cape Cod," in *Reinterpreting New England Indians and the Colonial Experience*, ed. Colin G. Galloway and Neal Salisbury (Boston: Colonial Society of Massachusetts, 2003), 265–67, 272, 284–85; David Silverman, *Faith and Boundaries: Colonists, Christianity, and Community among the Wampanoag Indians* (Cambridge: Cambridge University Press, 2005).

51. John H. Lockwood, *Westfield and Its Historic Influences, 1669–1919: The Life of an Early Town*, 2 vols. (Springfield, Mass.: Press of Springfield Printing and Binding Company, 1922), 2:324–25; Winiarski, *Darkness Falls*, 383.

52. Sweet, *Bodies Politic*; Hardesty, *Unfreedom*; Goodfriend, *Who Should Rule at Home?*

53. James F. Cooper Jr. and Kenneth P. Minkema, eds., *The Colonial Church Records of First Church of Reading (Wakefield) and the First Church of Rumney Marsh (Revere)*

(Boston: Colonial Society of Massachusetts, 2006), 16–18 and 34–38; Bailey, *Race and Redemption*, 55, 107–9, 126.

54. Names of persons offending & their acknowledgements Received, Records of the Church in Deerfield 1731–1810, bound volume, pp. 65–68 (pages missing from microfilm version), Memorial Libraries Deerfield; Richard Bailey, *Race and Redemption in Puritan New England* (New York: Oxford University Press, 2014), 55, 107–9, 126; Robert H. Romer, *Slavery in the Connecticut Valley of Massachusetts* (Florence, Mass.: Levellers, 2009), 240–44; David R. Proper, *Lucy Terry Prince: Singer of History: A Biography* (Deerfield, Mass.: Pocumtuck Valley Memorial Association and Historic Deerfield, Inc., 1997), 10–15. In at least one documented case, a black woman testified against white people in a church disciplinary hearing (Bailey, *Race and Redemption*, 126).

55. *Publications of the Colonial Society of Massachusetts,* vol. 22: *Collections, Plymouth Church Records 1620–1859, Part 1* (Boston: Published by the Society, 1920), 295, 297.

56. Church Covenant, baptisms, marriages. . . . 4th Church of Christ in Bridgewater; see also Church records, 1729–1778, box 3, folder 1, First Parish Church in Dorchester Records 1636–1981, Ms. N-258, MHS. For all confession of fornication in the First Church of Brockton (4th Church of Christ in Bridgewater) records, the parents' names were crossed out (for the sake of privacy in later years), but racial notation were not crossed out.

57. Cooper and Minkema, *Colonial Church Records of First Church of Reading (Wakefield) and the First Church of Rumney Marsh (Revere)*, 196–97; Bailey, *Race and Redemption*, 55–56.

58. Index, New London First Congregational Church, CSL, 450; *Records of the Brewster Congregational Church, Brewster, Massachusetts, 1700–1792* (Privately printed, 1911), 95–99. Ann may have been the unidentified "negro woman" baptized and admitted to the church in 1742.

59. Sweet, *Bodies Politic*, 58–130; Bailey, *Race and Redemption*, 103; Lawrence W. Towner, *A Good Master Well Served: Masters and Servants in Colonial Massachusetts, 1620–1750* (New York: Garland, 1998), 163–218; Greene, *Negro in Colonial New England*, 144–67. The struggle between Sarah Osborn and the enslaved woman named Phillis over the fate of Phillis's son, despite their shared evangelical faith, is an instructive example of how religion played into racial disputes (Brekus, *Sarah Osborn's World*, 237–43).

60. Jeroen Dewulf, *The Pinkster King and the King of Kongo: The Forgotten History of America's Dutch-Owned Slaves* (Jackson: University Press of Mississippi, 2017), 137–39; Thomas N. Ingersoll, "'Releese Us out of This Cruell Bondegg': An Appeal from Virginia in 1723," *WMQ*, 3d ser., 51, no. 4 (October 1994); Goetz, *Baptism of Early Virginia*, 99, 138–39; Sweet, *Bodies Politic*, 110, 125–26; Seeman, "Justise Must Take Plase," 399–402, 411–13. By 1762, Canterbury had 29 black and 1,740 white residents. I am relying exclusively upon Erik Seeman's insightful analysis of this text and his research about Greenwich. The original document is missing from the CHS collection (Seeman, "Justise Must Take Plase"; A List of the Number of Inhabitants in Each Town in the Colony of Connecticut Taken in the Year 1762, CHS).

61. Seeman, "Justise Must Take Plase," 399–402, 411–13.

62. Seeman, "Justise Must Take Plase," 399–402, 411–13; Sweet, *Bodies Politic*, 121–24.

63. Stephen Williams Diary, typescript, vol. 5, p. 162, and vol. 6, pp. 26–27, 30–42, Richard B. Storrs Memorial Library, Longmeadow, Mass., www.longmeadowlibrary. org.

64. All quotations from Kenneth Scott, "'Rude and Prophane Behaviour' in Litchfield Meeting House in 1764," *Connecticut Historical Society Bulletin* 19, no. 3 (July 1954): 93–95.

65. Lorenzo J. Green, "The New England Negro as Seen in Advertisements for Runaway Slaves," *Journal of Negro History* 29, no. 2 (April 1944): 126; Desrochers, "Slave-for-Sale Advertisements"; Antonio T. Bly, "A Prince among Pretending Free Men: Runaway Slaves in Colonial New England Revisited," *Massachusetts Historical Review* 14 (2012): 87–118; *Pennsylvania Gazette*, September 11, 1740; Hodges, *Root & Branch*, 127; *Boston Weekly News-Letter*, April 24, 1760, 2; Winiarski, *Darkness Falls*, 315.

66. James MacSparran, *A Letter Book and Abstract of Our Services Written during the Years 1743–1751*, ed. Daniel Goodwin (Boston: Merrymount, 1899), 49, 81, 105; Glasson, *Mastering Christianity*, 113–18; Wilkins Updike, *A History of the Episcopal Church in Narragansett, Rhode Island, Including a History of the Other Episcopal Churches in the State*, vol. 2, pt. 2 (Boston: Merrymount, 1907), 482, 509, 529, 532, 541, 550.

67. C. Bancroft Gillespie, *An Historic Record and Pictorial Description of the Town of Meriden, Connecticut and the Men Who Have Made It, From Earliest Settlement to Close of Its First Century of Incorporation* (Meriden: Journal Publishing, 1906), 249; George William Perkins, *Historical Sketches of Meriden* (West Meriden: Franklin E. Hinman, 1849), 55–56, 86–90. This story about a "surly and unruly" slave was apparently told to the author by descendants of Theophilus Hall (Gillespie, *An Historic Record*, 249).

3 / "Compassion upon These Outcasts"

1. Frederick E. Maser and Howard T. Maag, eds., *The Journal of Joseph Pilmore Methodist Itinerant: For the Years August 1, 1769 to January 2, 1774, With a Biographical Sketch of Joseph Pilmore by Dr. Frank B. Stanger* (Philadelphia: Message Publishing Co., 1969), 96. Dee E. Andrews notes that love feasts did not always remain interracial, and some churches eventually moved to have separate love feasts for blacks and for whites (Andrews, *The Methodists and Revolutionary America, 1760–1800: The Shaping of an Evangelical Culture* [Princeton, N.J.: Princeton University Press, 2000], 133–34).

2. This argument builds on the important insights about evangelism, Enlightenment, and compassion explained by Catherine Brekus, who writes: "By the middle of the eighteenth century, humanitarian ideas became so widely accepted that evangelicals naturally incorporated them into their own fledgling movement. . . . [T]hey gave money to the poor, founded orphanages for needy children, and started schools for Native Americans and slaves." Also, about Christians in the late eighteenth century, Brekus writes: "Many people who prided themselves on their compassion did not oppose slavery, but equated virtue with 'sensibility' (the ability to feel others' pain)" (Brekus, *Sarah Osborn's World: The Rise of Evangelical Christianity in Early America* [New Haven, Conn.: Yale University Press, 2013], 218–19, 225, 284).

3. Brekus, *Sarah Osborn's World*, 262.

4. Fred Anderson, *Crucible of War: The Seven Years' War and the Fate of Empire in British North America, 1754–1766* (New York: Vintage, 2000); Brekus, *Sarah Osborn's*

World, 252; Ira Berlin, *Many Thousands Gone: The First Two Centuries of Slavery in North America* (Cambridge, Mass.: Belknap Press of Harvard University Press, 1998), 369.

5. Richard W. Pointer, *Protestant Pluralism and the New York Experience: A Study of Eighteenth-Century Religious Diversity* (Bloomington: Indiana University Press, 1988), 76–77; Deborah Mathias Gough, *Christ Church, Philadelphia: The Nation's Church in a Changing City* (Philadelphia: University of Pennsylvania Press, 1995), 128, 130–33; Jacqueline Barbara Carr, "A Change 'As Remarkable as the Revolution Itself': Boston's Demographics, 1780–1800," *New England Quarterly* 73, no. 4 (December 2000): 583–84; Benjamin L. Carp, *Rebels Rising: Cities and the American Revolution* (New York: Oxford University Press, 2007), 225; Jacqueline Barbara Carr, *After the Siege: A Social History of Boston 1775–1800* (Chicago: Northwestern University Press, 2005), 13–42.

6. Between 1764 and 1776, at least six Lutheran churches and two Moravian churches baptized blacks: churches in New York City and Athens, New York; a church in Penn's Neck, New Jersey; and churches in Philadelphia, Lancaster, and Stouchsburg, Pennsylvania; Trinity Lutheran Church New York, N.Y.; First Moravian Church New York, N.Y.; Zion Lutheran Church Athens, N.Y.; Swedish Lutheran Church, Raccoon/Penn's Neck, N.J.; St. Michael's & Zion Lutheran Church, Philadelphia, Pa.; First Moravian Church, Philadelphia, Pa.; Trinity Lutheran Church, Lancaster, Pa.; and Christ Lutheran Church, Stouchsburg, Pa. Seven blacks were baptized at St. Michael's & Zion Lutheran Church of Philadelphia from 1767 to 1771 (St. Michael's & Zion Lutheran Church, Philadelphia, PA, Baptisms 1759–71, Collections of the Genealogical Society of Pennsylvania, vol. 31 [Philadelphia, 1898], 426–566). Charles H. Glatfelter, *Pastors and People: German Lutheran and Reformed Churches in the Pennsylvania Field, 1717–1793*, vol. 1: *Pastors and Congregations* (Breinigsville: Pennsylvania German Society, 1980), 289, 411–20.

7. Joyce D. Goodfriend, *Who Should Rule at Home? Confronting the Elite in British New York* (Ithaca, N.Y.: Cornell University Press, 2017), 79–109, 193–95; First Presbyterian Church (New York, N.Y.) Records, 1717–1961, RG 413, box 3, folder 11, Register of Baptism, 1728–1790, pp. 96–191, PHS; Lutheran church records, 1703–1802 New York, Albany, and other places, pp. 215–31, NYPL; New York Moravian Church records: Baptisms 1744–1890, pp. 19–27, NYPL; Frank J. Klingberg, "The S.P.G. Program for Negroes in Colonial New York," *Historical Magazine of the Protestant Episcopal Church* 8, no. 4 (December 1939): 337–38; Tobias Alexander Wright, ed., *Records of the Reformed Dutch Church in New Amsterdam and New York: Baptisms from 1 January 1731 to 29 December 1800, Collections of the New York Genealogical and Biographical Society*, vol. 3 (New York: Printed for the Society, 1902); First Baptist Church Records & Minutes from 1762 to 1812, p. 48, Records of the First Baptist Church of New York City; Pointer, *Protestant Pluralism*, 76–77; Glatfelter, *Pastors and People*, 1:219. From the 1730s to the 1770s, sometimes significant numbers of blacks affiliated with New York's Trinity Lutheran Church and Trinity Anglican Church. Trinity Lutheran baptized seven black people from 1764 to 1776, including two "free negroes." At least three black men and two black women were baptized by the city's Moravian congregation. Although these numbers represent a small portion of the city's black population, they are more than in previous decades. Expansion continued after the Revolution.

8. First Baptist Newport admitted one black person in each period, but other blacks likely attended there too. Second Baptist admitted seven blacks in the 1730s and 1740,

but no new black members between 1750 and 1763. From 1764 to 1776, however, twenty-two black people were admitted to Second Baptist. The small Seventh Day Sabbatarian Baptist Church admitted no blacks in the first period and two in the latter period. Between 1750 and 1763, only one black woman was baptized at First Congregational Church, and no blacks were baptized at Second Congregational Church, but twelve were baptized at First Congregational and eleven were baptized at Second Congregational in the latter period. At Trinity Anglican Church, just over fifty black people were baptized in each period. So, the number of interracial churches grew in Newport as did the rates of black baptism and church membership. Newport had a relatively large black population, accounting for almost 17 percent of the town population in 1748 (Book of Record Trinity Church Rhode Island 1709, Trinity Church Newport Records, NHS; Second Congregation Church Records 838B, Second Congregational Church Records, Newport, Rhode Island, 122–23, NHS; Society Record Second Congregational Church 1733–1834, Records of the Second Congregational Church, Newport, Rhode Island, pp. 58–62, 75–76, 202, 122–23, NHS; Ilou M. and Don A. Sanford, eds., *Newport Seventh Day Baptist Trilogy: Entering into Covenant, Membership Records, Mother Hubbard's Cupboard* [Bowie, Md.: Heritage, 1998], 78–81; Admissions into Full Communion, First Congregational Church Marriages Baptisms 1744–1825, and First Congregational Church. Records 1743–1831, First Congregational Church Newport, NHS; Roll of Members of First Baptist Church 1644–1864 [1169, 67] and Michael Eddy's Marriages & Record Book of the First Baptist Church 1726 [1167, 1660], First Baptist Church Newport, NHS; Second Baptist Church Six Principle 1 and 2 [1656, 1657] and Records of the Six Principals Baptist Society 1786–1886 [804], Second Baptist Church of Newport records, NHS; Benjamin L. Carp, *Rebels Rising: Cities and the American Revolution* [New York: Oxford University Press, 2007], 228; Brekus, *Sarah Osborn's World*, 28; Janet Moore Lindman, *Bodies of Belief: Baptist Community in Early America* [Philadelphia: University of Pennsylvania Press, 2008], 134).

9. If the Quaker Meeting included blacks, then at least 94 percent of Protestants worshipped in an interracial church. Number of families in 1770 according to Stiles: 40 at First Baptist; 150 at the Society of Friends; 200 at Second Baptist; 40 at the Sabbatarian Baptist; 135 at First Congregational; 130 at Second Congregational; 200 at Trinity Anglican; 30 at the synagogue; 35 at the Moravian church; and 20 at a Baptist church led by Dawson and Clark (Second Baptist Church of Newport records, NHS Carp, *Rebels Rising*, 228).

10. Brekus, *Sarah Osborn's World*; Lindman, *Bodies of Belief*; Andrews, *Methodists and Revolutionary America*; Goodfriend, *Who Should Rule at Home?*, 189–97.

11. Cynthia Lynn Lyerly, *Methodism and the Southern Mind, 1770–1810* (New York: Oxford University Press, 1998); Andrews, *Methodists and Revolutionary America*; Kyle T. Bulthuis, *Four Steeples over the City Streets: Religion and Society in New York's Early Republic Congregations* (New York: New York University Press, 2014); John Wesley, *Thoughts upon Slavery*, 3rd. ed. (London: R. Hawes, 1774), 24, 28; Sylvia Frey and Betty Wood, *Come Shouting to Zion: African American Protestantism in the American South and British Caribbean to 1830* (Chapel Hill: University of North Carolina Press, 1998).

12. David Hempton, *Methodism: Empire of the Spirit* (New Haven, Conn.: Yale University Press, 2005).

13. Lyerly, *Methodism and the Southern Mind*, 11–14; Andrews, *Methodists and Revolutionary America*; Graham Russell Hodges, *Root & Branch: African Americans*

in New York and East Jersey, 1613–1863 (Chapel Hill: University of North Carolina Press, 1999), 126; Bulthuis, *Four Steeples over the City Streets*, 22–28.

14. *Minutes of the Methodist Conferences, Annually Held in America from 1773 to 1813, Inclusive*, vol. 1 (New York: John C. Totten, 1813), 2, 6, 25; *Journal of Rev. Francis Asbury, Bishop of the Methodist Episcopal Church*, 3 vols., vol. 1: *From August 7, 1771 to December 31, 1786* (New York: Land and Scott, 1852), 42, 76, 451; Goodfriend, *Who Should Rule at Home?*, 99–101. Since Methodists did not baptize anyone before 1785, firsthand accounts and official membership numbers are the sole means of determining rates of black participation in early Methodist societies.

15. James W. Hood, *One Hundred Years of the African Methodist Episcopal Zion Church; or, The Centennial of African Methodism* (New York: A.M.E. Zion Book Concern, 1895), 1.

16. Maser and Maag, eds., *Journal of Joseph Pilmore Methodist Itinerant*, 74; Lewis R. Streeter, *Past and Present of the John Street Methodist Episcopal Church (First Methodist Society in America) New York* (New York, 1913), 7, 14–19, 22–23; Francis Ashbury, *Journal of Rev. Francis Ashbury, Bishop of the Methodist Episcopal Church*, 1:17; Andrews, *Methodists and Revolutionary America*, 133; Craig D. Townsend, *Faith in Their Own Color: Black Episcopalians in Antebellum New York City* (New York: Columbia University Press, 2005), 11; Hood, *One Hundred Years of the African Methodist Episcopal Zion Church*, 1.

17. *Journal of Rev. Francis Asbury*, 1:17.

18. Maser and Maag, eds., *Journal of Joseph Pilmore Methodist Itinerant*, 26, 58.

19. Maser and Maag, eds. *Journal of Joseph Pilmore Methodist Itinerant*, 107.

20. In 1776, 10.1 percent of all Baptist churches in America were located in Rhode Island, and 57.5 percent of Rhode Island's churches were Baptists. The other northern colonies with substantial numbers of Baptists were Massachusetts, New Jersey, and Pennsylvania (Rodney Stark and Roger Finke, "American Religion in 1776: A Statistical Portrait," *Sociological Analysis* 49, no. 1 [Spring, 1988]: 39–51).

21. Lindman, *Bodies of Belief*, 134–35. Churches with multiple black members 1764–76: First Baptist Church of Boston, Mass.; Second Baptist Church of Newport, R.I.; Seventh Day Baptist Church Newport, R.I.; First Baptist Church Providence, R.I.; Baptist Church of Upper Freehold, N.J.; Baptist Church of Scots Plains, N.J.; and First Baptist Church Philadelphia, Pa. One black person was admitted to the First Baptist Church of New York City and to Second Baptist Church, Richmond, R.I. (which was founded in November 1774) (James N. Arnold, ed., *Vital Records of Rhode Island 1636–1850, First Series, Birth, Marriages and Deaths, A Family Register for the People*, vol. 11: *Church Records* [Providence: Narragansett Historical Publishing Company, 1900], 249; William G. McLoughlin, ed., *The Diary of Isaac Backus*, vol. 1: *1741–1764* [Providence: Brown University Press, 1979], xxx; Stanley Lemons, ed., *Baptists in Early North America, First Baptist, Providence*, Baptists in Early North America Series, vol. 2 [Macon, Ga: Mercer University Press, 2013]; Sanford, *Newport Seventh Day Baptist Trilogy*, 78–81; First Baptist Church Boston, Massachusetts Church Records 1665–1797, microfilm, Pub. No. 461, ANTL; Boston 2nd Baptist Church Records 1743–1787, 1 vol. microfilm, ANTL; Boston Second Baptist Church Records 1789–1793, microfilm, ANTL; Upper Freehold Baptist Church Records, 1766–1805, Monmouth County Historical Society Library, Freehold, N.J.; Scotch Plains Baptist Church, Scotch Plains, N.J., Records, 1747–1809, MG 968, NJHS; First Baptist Church Philadelphia,

Pennsylvania, Membership Records, ABHS; First Baptist Church Records & Minutes from 1762 to 1812, Records of the First Baptist Church in the City of New York). According to Robert G. Gardner, "black Baptists in the New England and Middle provinces/states comprised about 1 percent of all Baptists there from 1750 to 1790" (Gardner, *Baptists in Early America: A Statistical History, 1639–1790* [Atlanta: George Baptist Historical Society], 39–42).

22. Bill J. Leonard, *Baptists in America* (New York: Columbia University Press, 2005), 1–28; Lindman, *Bodies of Belief*; Lemons, ed., *Baptists in Early North America, First Baptist, Providence*, xiii–xviii, xxv; Susan Juster, *Disorderly Women: Sexual Politics and Evangelicalism in Revolutionary New England* (Ithaca, N.Y.: Cornell University Press, 1996), 41. Many Baptist churches did not record meeting minutes or membership lists until after the Revolution (Sydney E. Ahlstrom, *A Religious History of the American People* [New Haven, Conn.: Yale University Press, 1972], 375).

23. Bill J. Leonard, "Baptist Revivals and the Turn toward Baptist Evangelism: 1755/1770," in *Turning Points in Baptist History: A Festschrift in Honor of Harry Leon McBeth*, ed. Michael E. William Sr. and Walter B. Shurden (Macon, Ga: Mercer University Press, 2008), 91; An Account of Persons received into this Church by Baptism or Letter since the constitution of it as a church, Upper Freehold Baptist Church Records, Monmouth County Historical Society Library, Freehold, N.J.

24. McLoughlin, ed., *Diary of Isaac Backus*, 1:xv–xxxvii; C. C. Goen, *Revivalism and Separatism in New England, 1740–1800: Strict Congregationalists and Separate Baptists in the Great Awakening* (Middletown, Conn: Wesleyan University Press, 1987), 208–95.

25. First Baptist Church Boston, Massachusetts Church Records, ANTL; Boston 2nd Baptist Church Records 1743–1787, 1 vol. microfilm, ANTL; Boston Second Baptist Church Records, ANTL; Lemons, ed., *Baptists in Early North America, First Baptist, Providence*, xiii–xxxiii, 2, 12, 40–41, 47–64; Thomas R. McKibbens, ed., *Baptists in Early North America, First Baptist Church, Boston, Massachusetts*, Baptists in Early North America Series, vol. 4 (Macon, Ga: Mercer University Press, 2017).

26. Lemons, ed., *Baptists in Early North America, First Baptist, Providence*, xiii–xxxiii, 2, 12, 40–41, 47–64; Juster, *Disorderly Women*; Richard J. Boles, "'An Unclean Person' or 'A Fit Candidate for a Church Member': Kingston Pease and Northern Baptist Churches," *Rhode Island History* 75, no. 1 (Winter/Spring 2017): 32–45.

27. Lemons, ed., *Baptists in Early North America, First Baptist, Providence*, 52, 56, 57, 60, 87, 91.

28. Locations of churches in which multiple blacks were baptized and/or admitted 1763–76: in Massachusetts—Amesbury (South Parish), Athol, Beverly, Billerica, Boston (First, Second, Old South, Brattle Square, New North, New Brick, and Hollis Street churches), Brockton, Byfield, Cambridge (First), Dorchester (First Parish), Durham, Hanover, Hingham (First Parish), Lancaster (First and Second/Chocksett churches), Lincoln, Marlborough, Merrimac (Pilgrim Congregational Church), Middleton, Peabody (South/Third Church Salem), Pembroke (Second Church), Rehoboth (Newman Congregational), Rochester (Second Church/Mattapoisett), Scituate (First Parish), Tewksbury, and West Roxbury; in Connecticut—Bozrah, Colchester (Colchester First and Westchester churches), East Haddam, East Hampton, East Hartford, East Haven, Fairfield, Guilford (Second Church), Groton, Hartford (First), Hebron Gilead, Lebanon, Middletown, Milford, New Haven (First), Newtown, Northford, Norwich, Old

Lyme, Portland, Redding, Shelton Huntington, Stamford, Trumbull, Wethersfield, Windsor, and Woodstock (Woodstock Hill First); in Rhode Island—Bristol, Newport (First and Second churches), and Tiverton; in New Hampshire—Dover and Rye.

29. Douglas L. Winiarski, *Darkness Falls on the Land of Light: Experiencing Religious Awakenings in Eighteenth-Century New England* (Chapel Hill: University of North Carolina Press, 2017), 372–73, 436.

30. First Congregational Church Marriages Baptisms 1744–1825, Records of the First Congregational Church Newport, NHS; *The Manifesto Church*, 179–98. I have not found any evidence that suggests reasons for why fewer ministers used racial notation in church records during the Revolutionary era. I hypothesize that the pastors, such as Samuel Hopkins, who opposed slavery based on the belief that God was no receptor of persons, may have felt that the use of racial notations implied ideas opposed to this beliefs.

31. A List of ye Male Members of the First Chh in Middleboro Taken Feb. 1775, First Church of Middleboro (Middleboro, Mass.) 1702–1908, RG 4970, CL; The Book of Church Records: 1707–1821, Middleboro, Mass First Church CRII, CL (available on NEHH); James F. Cooper Jr., "Cuffee's 'Relation': A Faithful Slave Speaks through the Project for the Preservation of Congregational Church Records," and Richard J. Boles, "Documents Relating to African American Experiences of White Congregational Churches in Massachusetts, 1773–1832," *New England Quarterly* 86, no. 2 (June 2013): 293–323; Mary Blauss Edwards, "Communications," *New England Quarterly* 86, no. 4 (December 2013): 688–89. Cuffee Wright did not seem to use the last name until years later, perhaps when he became free.

32. A List of the Male Members of the Chh of Christ in Middleborough as appears from the Records under the hand of the Rev. Peter Thacher, First Church of Middleboro (Middleboro, Mass.) 1702–1908, RG 4970, CL; Middleboro, Mass First Church CRII; *Book of the First Church of Christ, in Middleborough, Plymouth County, MA with Notices of Other Church in that Town* (Boston: C. C. P. Moody, 1852), 90–100; Thomas Prince and Peter Thacher, *An Account of the Great Revival: in Middleborough, Mass. A.D. 1741, 1742, during the Ministry of Rev. Peter Thacher; with a Notice of His Character* (Boston: Reprinted by T. R. Marvin, 1842); Winiarski, *Darkness Falls*, 184, 499; Records of Rev. Isaac Backus from 1747/8–1754 being Book I. & Records of the Rev. Solomon Reed from 1756 to 1785 being Book II of the Congregational Church North Middleborough, Mass., Middleboro North Church (Church of Christ) records, 1747–1927, CL; *Collections of the Massachusetts Historical Society, Volume III of the Second Series* (Boston, 1815), 95–97; Richard J. Boles, "Nemasket/Middleborough and Religious Diversity in Colonial New England," in *A Companion to American Religious History*, ed. Benjamin E. Park (New York: Wiley-Blackwell, 2020).

33. Brekus, *Sarah Osborn's World*, 237; Stephen R. Haynes, *Noah's Curse: The Biblical Justification of American Slavery* (New York: Oxford University Press, 2002); Sylvanus Conant, *The Blood of Abel, and the Blood of Jesus Considered and Improved, in a sermon delivered at Taunton, December the first, 1763; upon the day of the execution of Bristol, a Negro boy of about sixteen years old, for the murder of Miss Elizabeth McKinstry* (Boston: Edes and Gill, 1764), 20.

34. Middleboro, MA, First Church of Middleboro, Records, 1707–1908, RG 4970, CL (available on NEHH); Phillis Wheatley, *Poems of Phillis Wheatley: A Native African and a Slave* (Bedford, Mass.: Applewood, 1995), 12; Winiarski, *Darkness Falls*.

35. *The Manifesto Church: Records of the Church in Brattle Square Boston, 1699–1872* (Boston: Benevolent Fraternity of Churches, 1902), 184–89, 408; C VS B I—Baptisms 1669–1875, Old South (Third) Church Boston Records, CL; Adams and Pleck, *Love of Freedom*, 152; J. L. Bell, "Newton Prince and the Struggle for Liberty," *Journal of the American Revolution* (December 2, 2014), https://allthingsliberty.com/.

36. Vincent Carretta, *Phillis Wheatley: Biography of A Genius in Bondage* (Athens: University of Georgia Press, 2011), 22–23; Cedrick May, *Evangelism and Resistance in the Black Atlantic, 1760–1835* (Athens: University of Georgia Press, 2008), 49–63; Wheatley, *Poems of Phillis Wheatley*; Phillis Wheatley to Obour Tanner, March 21, 1774, Misc. Bd. 1774 March 21, MHS.

37. Phillis Wheatley to Obour Tanner, July 19, 1772, Misc. Bd. 1772 July 19, MHS; Carretta, *Phillis Wheatley*, 24; C VS A I—Admission of Old South, Membership 1669–1855, owners of the baptismal covenant 1669–1814, Old South (Third) Church Boston Records, CL; *The Manifesto Church*, 50.

38. Wheatley to Tanner, July 19, 1772, MHS; Phillis Wheatley to Obour Tanner, October 30, 1773, Misc. Bd., MHS; Phillis Wheatley to Obour Tanner, May 10, 1779, Misc. Bd., MHS; May, *Evangelism and Resistance in the Black Atlantic*, 50.

39. Kenneth Silverman, "Four New Letters by Phillis Wheatley," *Early American Literature* 8, no. 3 (Winter 1974): 259, 265; qtd. in Charles W. Akers, "'Our Modern Egyptians': Phillis Wheatley and the Whig Campaign against Slavery in Revolutionary Boston," *Journal of Negro History* 60, no. 3 (July 1975): 406.

40. Brekus, *Sarah Osborn's World*; Mary Beth Norton, "'My Resting Reaping Times': Sarah Osborn's Defense of Her 'Unfeminine' Activities, 1767," *Signs* 2 (Winter 1976): 516–17; Barbara E. Lacey, "The Bonds of Friendship: Sarah Osborn of Newport and the Reverend Joseph Fish of Stonington, 1743–1779," *Rhode Island History* 45, no. 4 (November 1986): 136–37.

41. Brekus, *Sarah Osborn's World*, 174, 202, 218–19, 225, 234–43, 261.

42. Qtd. in Norton, "My Resting Reaping Times," 519–20; Brekus, *Sarah Osborn's World*, 248–88; Lacey, "The Bonds of Friendship," 127–36; Sheryl A. Kujawa, "The Great Awakening of Sarah Osborn and the Female Society of the First Congregational Church in Newport," *Newport History* 65, no. 4 (Spring 1994): 133–53; Carp, *Rebels Rising*, 135–37; William Patten, *Reminiscences of the Late Rev. Samuel Hopkins, D.D. of Newport, R.I., Illustrative of His Character and Doctrines, with Incidental Subjects* (Providence: Isaac H. Cady, 1843), 62–64.

43. Brekus, *Sarah Osborn's World*, 252–53, 281.

44. Obour Tanner, unpublished research notes provided by Bert Lippincott III, NHS; Brekus, *Sarah Osborn's World*, 279, 282; Carp, *Rebels Rising*, 111.

45. Joseph Conforti, "Samuel Hopkins and the Revolutionary Antislavery Movement," *Rhode Island History* 38, no. 2 (May 1979): 39–41; Carp, *Rebels Rising*, 116, 139; Patten, *Reminiscences of the Late Rev. Samuel Hopkins*, 80–83; Brekus, *Sarah Osborn's World*, 284–88.

46. Society Record Second Congregational Church 1733–1834, pp. 58–62, 75–76, 202, 122–23, Records of the Second Congregational Church, Newport, NHS; Carp, *Rebels Rising*, 137; Brekus, *Sarah Osborn's World*, 274. At least three black people were admitted to full communion, six more blacks were baptized and admitted to communion, and two black people owned the covenant and were baptized. Stiles married thirteen black couples during this period.

47. Society Record Second Congregational Church 1733–1834, pp. 58–62, 75–76, 202, 122–23, NHS; Carp, *Rebels Rising*, 137, 138. In 1770, Caleb Gardner paid thirty pounds for a half year's rent on his ground-floor pew and over four pounds for a half year's rent for the gallery pew. Jonathan Otis also rented a ground-floor pew and a gallery pew (Records Second Congregational Church Newport, MS108, folders 1–6 and vol. 1, Pew payment records from 1769–1772, RIHS).

48. Name and locations of Anglican churches in which multiple blacks were baptized 1764–76: Queen's Chapel Portsmouth, N.H.; King's Chapel Boston; Christ Church Boston; Trinity Church Boston; St. Peter's Church Salem, Mass.; St. Paul's Church Newburyport, Mass.; Trinity Church New Haven, Conn.; Holy Trinity Church Middletown, Conn.; Christ Church Norwalk, Conn.; Christ Church Stratford, Conn.; St. John's Church Stamford, Conn.; St. Andrew's Church Simsbury, Conn.; Trinity Church Newport, R.I.; St. Michael's Church Bristol, R.I.; St. Paul's Church Narragansett, R.I.; Trinity Church New York City & its chapels; St. John's Church, Christ Church Shrewsbury, N.J.; St. Mary's Church Burlington, N.J.; and Christ Church Philadelphia, Pa. For Trinity Church New York, see Klingberg, "The S.P.G. Program for Negroes in Colonial New York," 365.

49. John E. Stillwell, ed., *Historical and Genealogical Miscellany: Data Relating to the Settlement and Settlers of New York and New Jersey*, vol. 2 (Baltimore: Genealogical Publishing Company, 1970), 88; Marilyn J. Chiat, *America's Religious Architecture: Sacred Places for Every Community* (New York: Wiley and Sons, 1997), 55.

50. Qtd. in Klingberg, "The S.P.G. Program for Negroes in Colonial New York," 362, 364–65; Andrew Oliver and James B. Peabody, eds., *Publications of the Colonial Society of Massachusetts*, vol. 56: *Collections: The Records of Trinity Church, Boston, 1728–1830, II* (Boston: Published by the Society, 1982); King's Chapel (Boston, Mass.) Records, MHS; Old North Church Records, MHS. In Portsmouth, New Hampshire, the rector recorded four black baptisms in 1767 and 1768 (Vital Records from the Parish Register of Queen's Chapel Portsmouth, New Hampshire, Priscilla Hammond, pp. 26–27, 47, NEHGS).

51. Book of Record Trinity Church Rhode Island 1709, NHS.

52. Qtd. in John B. Hattendorf, *Semper Eadem: A History of Trinity Church in Newport, 1698–2000* (Newport, R.I.: Trinity Church, 2001), 109–10.

53. Hattendorf, *Semper Eadem*, 109–10, 120; George Champlin Mason, *Annals of Trinity Church Newport RI, 1698–1821* (Newport, R.I., 1890), 225; Carp, *Rebels Rising*, 230; Brekus, *Sarah Osborn's World*, 182.

54. Mason, *Annals of Trinity Church Newport*, 132.

55. Hattendorf, *Semper Eadem*, 100–102; Mason, *Annals of Trinity Church Newport*, 155.

56. Gough, *Christ Church, Philadelphia*, 127; Goodfriend, *Who Should Rule at Home?*, 100; Katharine Gerbner, *Christian Slavery: Conversion and Race in the Protestant Atlantic World* (Philadelphia: University of Pennsylvania Press, 2018), 82.

57. Gough, *Christ Church, Philadelphia*, 128, 130–34, 136, 138, 140–41; Benjamin Dorr, *A Historical Account of Christ Church, Philadelphia, from Its Foundation A.D. 1695 to A.D. 1841, and of St. Peter's and St. James, until the Separation of the Churches* (Philadelphia: R.S.H. George, 1841), 142, 176, 181; Carp, *Rebels Rising*, 131.

58. Dorr, *A Historical Account of Christ Church, Philadelphia*, 160. Fort Hunter in Mohawk country had long been the site of Anglican missionary work (see Daniel K.

Richter, "'Some of Them . . . Would Always Have a Minister with Them': Mohawk Protestantism, 1683–1719," *American Indian Quarterly* 16, no. 4 [Autumn 1992]: 471–84).

59. First Moravian Church Phila, PA Baptism, Marriages, HSP; Peter Silver, *Our Savage Neighbors: How Indian War Transformed Early America* (New York: Norton, 2008).

60. Church Record—Rosenthal, New Bethel or Corner Church Albany Township, p. 6, Berks County, Pa., trans. William J. Hinke, 1933, Adams County Historical Society.

61. Daniel R. Mandell, "Shifting Boundaries of Race and Ethnicity: Indian-Black Intermarriage in Southern New England, 1760–1880," *Journal of American History* 85, no. 2 (September 1998): 470, 466.

62. Gideon Hawley, journals, vol. 4, eleventh transcribed binder, p. 150, CL.

63. Gideon Hawley, journals, Mashpee 1 July 1782, vol. 4, twelfth transcribed binder, p. 202, CL.

64. Gideon Hawley, journals, vol. 3, eighth transcribed binder, pp. 3–5, CL.

65. Gideon Hawley, journals, July 8. 1791, vol. 2, sixth transcribed binder, p. 246, CL; Gideon Hawley, journals, vol. 3, eighth transcribed binder, pp. 3–5, CL.

66. Gideon Hawley, journals, vol. 3, eighth transcribed binder, pp. 17–19, CL.

67. Gideon Hawley, journals, vol. 3, eighth transcribed binder, pp. 68–69, CL.

68. Gideon Hawley, December 1805, journals, vol. 3, eighth transcribed binder, p. 121, CL.

69. Gideon Hawley, journals, vol. 4, eleventh transcribed binder, p. 133, CL.

70. William S. Simmons and Cheryl L. Simmons, eds., *Old Light on Separate Ways: The Narragansett Diary of Joseph Fish, 1765–1776* (Hanover, N.H.: University Press of New England, 1982), 55, 59–60, 69, 79.

71. Journal of Samuel Kirkland, Missionary from the Society of Scotland and Corporation of Harvard College, to the Oneida Indians & Other tribes of the Six Nations; from August 1788 to Jan 13, 1789, Society for Propagating the Gospel Among the Indians and Others in North America Records 1752–1948, Ms. N-176, box 1, folder 6–7, pp. 13–14, MHS.

72. Journal of Samuel Kirkland, MHS, box 1, folder 6–7, pp. 8, 15, 16–17, 20.

73. Mandell, "Shifting Boundaries of Race and Ethnicity," 475; David J. Silverman, *Red Brethren: The Brothertown and Stockbridge Indians and the Problem of Race in Early America* (Ithaca, N.Y.: Cornell University Press, 2010), 101–5; Samuel Kirkland, Letter to Ebenezer Pemberton, March 25, 1771, Misc. Bd. 1771 March 25, MHS.

4 / "Slavery Is a Bitter Pill"

1. Journal 1776, Rev. John Pitman Diaries, Mss 622, RIHS.

2. Timothy Mather Cooley, *Sketches of the Life and Character of the Rev. Lemuel Haynes, for Many Years Pastor of a Church in Rutland, VT, and Late in Granville, NY* (New-York: Harper and Brothers, 1837), 75.

3. William B. McClain, *Black People in the Methodist Church: Whither Thou Goest?* (Nashville, Tenn.: Abingdon, 1984), 41–46.

4. *New York Packet*, September 11, 1786, 3, col. 3.

5. Nathan O. Hatch, *The Democratization of American Christianity* (New Haven, Conn.: Yale University Press, 1989), 103.

6. Richard W. Pointer, *Protestant Pluralism and the New York Experience: A Study of Eighteenth-Century Religious Diversity* (Bloomington: Indiana University Press, 1988), 81, 90–107; Randall H. Balmer, *A Perfect Babel of Confusion: Dutch and English Cultures in the Middle Colonies* (New York: Oxford University Press, 1989); George U. Wenner, *The Lutherans of New York: Their Story and Their Problems* (New York: Petersfield, 1918), 12–16; Charles H. Glatfelter, *Pastors and People*, vol. 2: *The History* (Breinigsville: Pennsylvania German Society, 1981), 400–416; Dee E. Andrews, *The Methodists and Revolutionary America, 1760–1800: The Shaping of an Evangelical Culture* (Princeton, N.J.: Princeton University Press, 2000), 61; Jacqueline Barbara Carr, "A Change 'As Remarkable as the Revolution Itself': Boston's Demographics, 1780–1800," *New England Quarterly* 73, no. 4 (December 2000): 583–84; Benjamin L. Carp, *Rebels Rising: Cities and the American Revolution* (New York: Oxford University Press, 2007); Jacqueline Barbara Carr, *After the Siege: A Social History of Boston 1775–1800* (Chicago: Northwestern University Press, 2005), 13–42; Gary B. Nash and Jean B. Soderlund, *Freedom by Degrees: Emancipation in Pennsylvania and Its Aftermath* (New York: Oxford University Press, 1991), 18.

7. Andrews, *Methodists and Revolutionary America*, 63; Deborah Mathias Gough, *Christ Church, Philadelphia: The Nation's Church in a Changing City* (Philadelphia: University of Pennsylvania Press, 1995), 138; Benjamin Dorr, *A Historical Account of Christ Church, Philadelphia, from Its Foundation A.D. 1695 to A.D. 1841, and of St. Peter's and St. James, until the Separation of the Churches* (Philadelphia: R.S.H. George, 1841), 181; Richard W. Pointer, *Protestant Pluralism and the New York Experience: A Study of Eighteenth-Century Religious Diversity* (Bloomington: Indiana University Press, 1988), 79–80, 91–92, 106–10; Frank J. Klingberg, "The S.P.G. Program for Negroes in Colonial New York," *Historical Magazine of the Protestant Episcopal Church* 8, no. 4 (December 1939): 365–68; Kyle T. Bulthuis, *Four Steeples over the City Streets: Religion and Society in New York's Early Republic Congregations* (New York: New York University Press, 2014), 33–36; Nancy L. Rhoden, *Revolutionary Anglicanism: The Colonial Church of England Clergy during the American Revolution* (New York: New York University Press, 1999).

8. The Society of Friends/Quakers are beyond the scope of this study (see the introduction). Ryan P. Jordon, *Slavery and the Meetinghouse: The Quakers and the Abolitionist Dilemma, 1820–1865* (Bloomington: Indiana University Press, 2007); Jane R. Soderlund, *Quakers and Slavery: A Divided Spirit* (Princeton, N.J.: Princeton University Press, 1985); Gary B. Nash, *The Unknown American Revolution: The Unruly Birth of Democracy and the Struggle to Create America* (New York: Penguin, 2005), 124; Nash and Soderlund, *Freedom by Degrees*; Manisha Sinha, *The Slave's Cause: A History of Abolition* (New Haven, Conn.: Yale University Press, 2016).

9. Qtd. in Nash, *The Unknown American Revolution*, 125, 126–27; "Petition by negro servants of Hartford for their freedom, October 1780," vol. XIII, document 286a-d, Trumbull Papers, CSA; Jared Hardesty, *Unfreedom: Slavery and Dependence in Eighteenth-Century Boston* (New York: New York University Press, 2016); Jared Hardesty, "'Taught My Benighted Soul to Understand': African Slaves, Protestant Christianity, and Resistance in Eighteenth-Century Boston," paper presented at the Boston College Biennial Conference on the History of Religion, March 30–31, 2012; Christopher Cameron, *To Plead Our Own Cause: African Americans in Massachusetts and the Making of the Antislavery Movement* (Kent, Ohio: Kent State University Press, 2014).

10. Nash, *Unknown American Revolution*, 62–62, 223, 321; Ira Berlin, *Many Thousands Gone: The First Two Centuries of Slavery in North America* (Cambridge, Mass.: Belknap Press of Harvard University Press, 1998), 228, 230; Douglas R. Egerton, *Death or Liberty: African Americans and Revolutionary America* (New York: Oxford University Press, 2009); Graham Russell Hodges, *Root & Branch: African Americans in New York and East Jersey, 1613–1863* (Chapel Hill: University of North Carolina Press, 1999); Graham Russell Hodges, *Slavery and Freedom in the Rural North: African Americans in Monmouth County, New Jersey, 1665–1865* (New York: Rowman and Littlefield, 1997); Eric G. Grundset, ed., *Forgotten Patriots: African American and American Indian Patriots in the Revolutionary War, A Guide to Service, Sources, and Studies* (Washington, D.C.: National Society of Daughters of the American Revolution, 2008).

11. Joanne Pope Melish, "The 'Condition' Debate and Racial Discourse in the Antebellum North," *Journal of the Early Republic* 19, no. 4 (Winter 1999): 654; Patrick Wolfe, "Land, Labor, and Difference: Elementary Structures of Race," *American Historical Review* 106, no. 3 (June 2001): 879–81; Margot Minardi, *Making Slavery History: Abolitionism and the Politics of Memory in Massachusetts* (New York: Oxford University Press, 2010), 18–19; Berlin, *Many Thousands Gone*, 369, 372.

12. Joanne Pope Melish, *Disowning Slavery: Gradual Emancipation and "Race" in New England, 1780–1860* (Ithaca, N.Y.: Cornell University Press, 1998); Berlin, *Many Thousands Gone*, 228–30; Nash, *Unknown American Revolution*, 125–27; Douglas R. Egerton, *Death or Liberty: African Americans and Revolutionary America* (New York: Oxford University Press, 2009), 97; Gloria Whiting, "Emancipation with Neither Courts nor Constitution: The Remarkable Case of Revolutionary Massachusetts," paper presented at American Historical Association annual meeting, Chicago, Illinois, January 5, 2019.

13. Nash, *Unknown American Revolution*, 125–27.

14. Locations of Congregational churches in which multiple blacks were baptized and/or admitted to membership 1777–90: in Massachusetts—Beverly, Boston (Brattle Square, New North, and West churches), Brockton, Charlestown, Dorchester, Hingham, Groton, and Mattapoisett (Second Church in Rochester); in Connecticut—Branford, Colchester, East Hartford, Fairfield, Glastonbury (Glastonbury Buckingham-Eastbury Church), Guilford (Second Church), Lebanon, Middletown, New Haven, Old Saybrook, Oxford, Shelton/Huntington, Trumbull, and Wethersfield; in Rhode Island—Newport (First Church) and Providence (First Church); in New Hampshire—Epping, North Hampton, and Portsmouth (First).

15. Lorenzo Johnston Greene, *The Negro in Colonial New England* (New York: Athenaeum, 1969), 74–77; Grundset, ed., *Forgotten Patriots*, 79; Ira Berlin, "The Revolution in Black Life," in *The American Revolution: Explorations in the History of American Radicalism*, ed. Alfred F. Young (DeKalb: Northern Illinois University Press, 1976), 349–82.

16. John Louis Ewell, *The Story of Byfield: A New England Parish* (Boston: George E. Littlefield, 1904), 133–35; Theophilus Parsons, *Memoir of Theophilus Parsons with Notices of Some of His Contemporaries* (Boston: Ticknor and Fields, 1859), 16–19; John James Currier, *History of Newburyport, Mass: 1764–1905*, vol. 1 (Newburyport: Published by the author, 1906), 69.

17. Parsons, *Memoir of Theophilus Parsons*, 17.

18. Record book of admission to church covenant, church members, transactions, confessions, etc. 1744–1826, vol. 8, box 2, in the Byfield, Mass., Byfield Parish Church records, 1709–1845, RG5065, CL (available on NEHH); Ewell, *The Story of Byfield*, 134.

19. Kenneth P. Minkema and Harry S. Stout, "The Edwardsean Tradition and the Antislavery Debate, 1740–1865," *Journal of American History* 92, no. 1 (June 2005): 47–74; Peter Hinks, "Timothy Dwight, Congregationalism, and Early Antislavery," in *The Problem of Evil: Slavery, Freedom, and the Ambiguities of American Reform* (Amherst: University of Massachusetts Press, 2007); James D. Essig, *The Bonds of Wickedness: American Evangelicals against Slavery, 1770–1808* (Philadelphia: Temple University Press, 1982); Rupert Charles Loucks, *"Let the Oppressed Go Free": Reformation and Revolution in English Connecticut, 1764–1775* (Madison: University of Wisconsin Press, 1998).

20. Records Congregational Church (Epping, N.H.), 1748–1922, pp. 51–52, 94, 101, 107–9, NHHS.

21. C VS B I—Baptisms 1669–1875, Admission of Old South 1669–1855, Membership 1669–1815, owners of the baptismal covenant, Old South (Third) Church Records, CL; Carr, "A Change 'As Remarkable as the Revolution Itself,'" 583–85; Nash, *Unknown American Revolution*, 62–66, 119–20, 228; Record book, 1741–1816, vol. 6, Second Church Boston Records, MHS; Record book, 1775–1833, vol. 9, Second Church Boston Records, MHS; Carr, *After the Siege*; May, *Evangelism and Resistance in the Black Atlantic*, 61; Akers, "Our Modern Egyptians," 403, 409–10. Following the British evacuation from Boston in 1776, it remained difficult for many churches to resume normal activities, so the baptismal rates for whites and blacks alike remained low for years. There were no baptisms recorded at Old South Church from 1776 to 1782. Other churches were likewise unavailable. The meetinghouse of the Second Church of Boston was destroyed during the British occupation, and Second Church merged with the New Brick (Seventh) Church in 1779. This newly united church apparently baptized no blacks between 1777 and 1790 (C VS B I—Baptisms 1669–1875, Old South [Third] Church Records, CL; Second Church [Boston, Mass.] Records 1650–1970, MHS).

22. William Patten, *Reminiscences of the Late Rev. Samuel Hopkins, D.D. of Newport, R.I., Illustrative of His Character and Doctrines, with Incidental Subjects* (Providence: Isaac H. Cady, 1843), 91; Joseph Conforti, "Samuel Hopkins and the Revolutionary Antislavery Movement," *Rhode Island History* 38, no. 2 (May 1979): 41; Catherine Brekus, *Sarah Osborn's World: The Rise of Evangelical Christianity in Early America* (New Haven, Conn.: Yale University Press, 2013). The records of First Congregational Church Newport contain no church votes between 1777 and 1781 and few baptisms. Second Church did not reopen until 1785. By 1782, Newport's population had rebounded to only about 5,530 people, which included 18 Indians, 51 "mulattos," and 549 blacks (Jay Mack Hollbrook, ed., *Rhode Island 1782 Census* [Oxford, Mass.: Holbrook Research Institute, 1979]; First Congregational Church, Records 1743–1831, First Congregational Church Newport, NHS).

23. Admissions into Full Communion, First Congregational Church Marriages Baptisms 1744–1825, and First Congregational Church Records 1743–1831, First Congregational Church Newport, NHS.

24. William D. Piersen, *Black Yankees: The Development of an Afro-American Subculture in Eighteenth-Century New England* (Amherst: University of Massachusetts Press, 1988), 42, 46, 59–60, 104; Lorenzo Johnston Greene, *The Negro in Colonial New*

England (New York: Athenaeum, 1969), 278, 294, 306; George C. Mason, *Reminiscences of Newport* (Newport: Charles Hammett Jr., 1884), 154–59; William H. Robinson, ed., *The Proceedings of the Free African Union Society and the African Benevolent Society, Newport, Rhode Island, 1780–1824* (Providence: Urban League of Rhode Island, 1976), viii, ix, 58; I use "Newport Gardner" instead of "Occramer Marycoo" because in his role as secretary of two African American organizations, he always used the name Newport Gardner (Robinson, ed., *The Proceedings*).

25. Qtd. in Conforti, "Samuel Hopkins and the Revolutionary Antislavery Movement," 39–47; Patten, *Reminiscences of the Late Rev. Samuel Hopkins*, 80–83; Nash, *Unknown American Revolution*, 137.

26. Cooley, *Sketches of the Life and Character of the Rev. Lemuel Haynes*, 28, 37; John Saillant, *Black Puritan, Black Republican: The Life and Thoughts of Lemuel Haynes, 1753–1833* (New York: Oxford University Press, 2003), xi, 3–12. The First Church Granville, also known as East Church, was gathered in 1747. Jedidiah Smith was pastor from 1756 to 1776. Timothy Mather Cooley was pastor from 1796 to 1859. Cooley knew Haynes personally and wrote the 1837 biography, which includes lengthy quotations from Haynes's writings. There are no surviving records from First Church Granville antedating 1791 (Cooley, *Sketches of the Life and Character of the Rev. Lemuel Hayne*; Harold Field Worthley, *An Inventory of the Records of the Particular [Congregational] Churches of Massachusetts Gathered 1620–1805* [Cambridge, Mass.: Harvard University Press, 1970]; Granville, Mass. First Congregational Church records, NEHH).

27. Cooley, *Sketches of the Life and Character of the Rev. Lemuel Haynes*, 28–59; Saillant, *Black Puritan, Black Republican*, xi, 3–5, 9, 15–46; Eric G. Grundset, ed., *Forgotten Patriots: African American and American Indian Patriots in the Revolutionary War, A Guide to Service, Sources, and Studies* (Washington, D.C.: National Society of Daughters of the American Revolution, 2008), 115.

28. Cooley, *Sketches of the Life and Character of the Rev. Lemuel Haynes*, 60–81.

29. For the whole North, eighteen Anglican parishes baptized blacks between 1777 and 1790 compared to nineteen parishes that had done so between 1764 and 1776. New England Episcopal churches in which multiple blacks were baptized from 1777 to 1790: Christ Church Boston, Mass.; Trinity Church Boston, Mass.; St. Peter's Church Salem, Mass.; St. Paul's Church Newburyport, Mass.; Trinity Church New Haven, Conn.; Holy Trinity Middletown, Conn.; Christ Church Norwalk, Conn.; Christ Church Stratford, Conn.; Christ Church Norwich, Conn.; St. John's Church Stamford, Conn.; St. Andrew's Church Simsbury, Conn.; Trinity Church Newport, R.I.; St. Paul's Church Narragansett, R.I.

30. Travis Glasson, *Mastering Christianity: Missionary Anglicanism and Slavery in the Atlantic World* (New York: Oxford University Press, 2011), 11; C. Bancroft Gillespie, *An Historic Record and Pictorial Description of the Town of Meriden, Connecticut and the Men Who Have Made It, From Earliest Settlement to Close of Its First Century of Incorporation* (Meriden, Conn.: Journal Publishing, 1906), 251; Bulthuis, *Four Steeples over the City Streets*, 42–43, 55–56.

31. Barbara Carr, *After the Siege: A Social History of Boston 1775–1800* (Chicago: Northwestern University Press, 2005), 3–6, 171, 173, 233; Jeffrey Richardson Brackett, "The Beginnings," in *Trinity Church in the City of Boston Massachusetts 1733–1933* (Boston: Merrymount, 1933), 11–12; Andrew Oliver and James B. Peabody, eds., *Publications of the Colonial Society of Massachusetts*, vol. 56: *Collections: The Records of*

Trinity Church, Boston, 1728–1830, II (Boston: Published by the Society, 1982); William B. Sprague, *Annals of the American Pulpit*, vol. 5 (New York: Robert Carter and Brothers, 1861), 296–98; George Frances Marlowe, *Churches of Old New England: Their Architecture and Their Architects, Their Pastors and Their People* (New York: Macmillan, 1947), 32.

32. Grundset, ed., *Forgotten Patriots*, 114, 153; James O. Horton and Lois E. Horton, *Black Bostonians: Family Life and Community Struggle in the Antebellum North* (New York: Holmes and Meier, 1999), 30–31, 76; William C. Nell, *The Colored Patriots of the American Revolution with Sketches of Several Distinguished Persons: To Which Is Added a Brief Survey of the Conditions and Prospects of Colored Americans* (Boston: Robert F. Wallcut, 1855), 25, 29, 48; Daniel Mandell, "'A Natural & Unalienable Right': The 1777 Prince Hall Petition and African American Emancipation in New England," paper presented to the Consortium on the Revolutionary Era, February 26, 2009.

33. Oliver and Peabody, eds., *The Records of Trinity Church, Boston*, 597, 598, 600, 603, 607, 617, 624, 626, 740. Gary Nash states that Prince Hall worshipped at the Eleventh Congregational Church (School Street or Reverend Andrew Croswell's Church) since 1762, but the church disbanded soon after Croswell's death in 1785, and no church records are extant from this congregation. King's Chapel baptized one black person and Christ Episcopal Church baptized five between 1777 and 1790 (Nash, *Race and Revolution* [Madison: Madison House, 1990], 65; King's Chapel [Boston, Mass.] Records 1686–1942, MHS; Old North Church Records, MHS).

34. Book of Record Trinity Church Rhode Island 1709, Trinity Church Newport Records, NHS; Carp, *Rebels Rising*, 104, 123; Mason, *Annals of Trinity Church Newport RI*, 161.

35. New England Baptist churches in my sample that admitted multiple black people to membership from 1777 to 1790: First Baptist Boston, Mass.; Second Baptist Boston, Mass.; Second Baptist Church Newport, R.I.; Seventh Day Baptist Newport, R.I.; First Baptist Providence, R.I.; Baptist Church Tiverton, R.I.; First Sabbatarian Baptist Hopkinton, R.I.; First Baptist North Kingstown, R.I.; and Baptist Church Exeter, R.I.

36. Janet Thorngate, ed., *Baptists in Early North America, Newport, Rhode Island. Seventh Day Baptists*, Baptist in Early American Series, vol. 3 (Macon, Ga.: Mercer University Press, 2017), 168, 162, 177, 182; John Barrington, ed., *Baptists in Early North America, Welsh Neck, South Carolina*, Baptist in Early American Series, vol. 5 (Macon, Ga: Mercer University Press, 2018), i, liii; Sanford, *Newport Seventh Day Baptist Trilogy*, 35, 81–82; Carp, *Rebels Rising*, 138–39.

37. William G. McLoughlin, ed., *The Diary of Isaac Backus*, vol. 1: *1741–1764* (Providence, R.I.: Brown University Press, 1979), 118; William G. McLoughlin, ed., *The Diary of Isaac Backus*, vol. 2: *1765–1785* (Providence, R.I.: Brown University Press, 1979), 720; Minkema and Stout, "The Edwardsean Tradition and the Antislavery Debate," 55.

38. Qtd. in William G. McLoughlin, ed., *The Diary of Isaac Backus*, vol. 3: *1786–1806* (Providence, R.I.: Brown University Press, 1979), 1205.

39. Arnold, ed., *Vital Records of Rhode Island*, 11:249.

40. James N. Arnold, ed., *Vital Records of Rhode Island 1636–1850, First Series, Birth, Marriages and Deaths, A Family Register for the People*, vol. 8: *Episcopal and Congregational* (Providence: Narragansett Historical Publishing Company, 1896), 598–611. In 1740, there were only 25 Baptist churches in New England. By 1790, there were 38 in Rhode Island, 92 in Massachusetts, 55 in Connecticut, 15 in Maine, 32

in New Hampshire, and 34 in Vermont, for a total of 266. Only a fraction of their eighteenth-century church records are extant and available (Sydney E. Ahlstrom, *A Religious History of the American People* [New Haven, Conn.: Yale University Press, 1972], 375).

41. Stanley Lemons, ed., *Baptists in Early North America, First Baptist, Providence*, Baptists in Early North America Series, vol. 2 (Macon, Ga: Mercer University Press, 2013), 77–121.

42. Lemons, ed., *Baptists in Early North America, First Baptist, Providence*, xxxvii–xxxviii.

43. First Baptist Church Boston, Massachusetts Church Records, ANTL; Thomas R. McKibbens, ed., *Baptists in Early North America, First Baptist Church, Boston, Massachusetts*, Baptists in Early North America Series, vol. 4 (Macon, Ga: Mercer University Press, 2017); Boston 2nd Baptist Church Records 1743–1787, 1 vol. microfilm, ANTL; Boston Second Baptist Church Records 1789–1793, ANTL.

44. *Memoir of Mrs. Chloe Spear, a Native of Africa, Who Was Enslaved in Childhood, and Died in Boston, January 3, 1815 . . . Aged 65 Years by A Lady of Boston* [*Rebecca Warren Brown*] (Boston: James Loring, 1832), 21, 27–28, 34, 35–37, 41, 48–50, 86–89; New North Church Records, 1714–1797, MS f. Bos. 22 v.1, BPL; Boston Second Baptist Church Records 1789–1793, ANTL.

45. Melish, *Disowning Slavery*; Nash and Soderlund, *Freedom by Degrees*; Nash, *Unknown American Revolution*, 323–25; Shane White, *Somewhat More Independent: The End of Slavery in New York City, 1770–1810* (Athens: University of Georgia Press, 1991).

46. Nash and Soderlund, *Freedom by Degrees*, 106–7. Other legislators' religious affiliation is uncertain.

47. Nash and Soderlund, *Freedom by Degrees*, 154–64. According to Nash and Soderlund: "While Episcopalians were only about 14 percent of Philadelphia's population in 1790, they comprised 43 percent of slaveholders. . . . For Episcopalians, to free slaves or hold on to them remained an individual decision. The church made no effort to encourage manumission." The fact that German pastors and members of the legislature lagged behind other Philadelphians might account for the lower numbers of black baptism in Lutheran and German Reformed churches, but not enough sources are available to definitively confirm this hypothesis (Nash and Soderlund, *Freedom by Degrees*, 154–64; Glatfelter, *Pastors and People*, 1:290).

48. Presbyterian churches in which multiple blacks were baptized and/or admitted to membership 1777–90: First Presbyterian Church New York City; Old Tennent Presbyterian, Manalapan (Freeport), N.J.; Presbyterian Church in Westfield, N.J.; Second Presbyterian Church Philadelphia; and Big Spring Presbyterian Church Newville, Pa.

49. Dutch Reformed churches within which multiple blacks were baptized and/or admitted to membership 1777–1790: Dutch Reformed Church New York City; Dutch Reformed Church of Fonda, N.Y.; Dutch Church Schenectady, N.Y.; Dutch Church of Greenbush, N.Y.; First Dutch Church Poughkeepsie, N.Y.; Dutch Reformed Church at Schoharie, N.Y.; Reformed Dutch Church of Schodack, N.Y.; and Reformed Church at Readington, N.J. From 1764 to 1776, only the Dutch Church of Schenectady, New York, and the Dutch Reformed Church of Fonda, New York, included multiple black baptisms (Maria Noll Cormack, ed., Schenectady, New York First Dutch Reformed Church: "Births and Baptisms, 1649–1781," typescript, NYPL; Royden Woodward Vosburgh, ed.,

Records of the Reformed Protestant Dutch Church of Caughnawaga, now the Reformed Church of Fonda, in the village of Fonda, Montgomery County, N.Y., vol. 1, pp. 5–35, transcribed by the NYGBS [New York, 1917], bound transcript, NYPL; General Church Book of the Reformed Congregation in Reyn Beck, organized by G. M. Weiss, preacher to the two Low Dutch Congregations in Kats Kill and Kocka Hocky: records of the Reformed Church of Rhinebeck, Dutchess County, New York, p. 11, copied by the Montgomery County Department of History and Archives from a handwritten transcript of the original records, on file in the NYGBS, carbon-copy typescript, NYPL).

50. Gerald Francis De Jong, "The Dutch Reformed Church and Negro Slavery in Colonial America," *Church History* 40, no. 4 (December 1971): 426–27; John De Jong, "Social Concerns," in *Piety and Patriotism: Bicentennial Studies of the Reformed Church in America, 1776–1976*, ed. James W. Van Hoeven (Grand Rapids, Mich.: Eerdmans, 1976), 116–17; John W. Beardslee III, "The American Revolution," *Piety and Patriotism: Bicentennial Studies of the Reformed Church in America, 1776–1976*, ed. James W. Van Hoeven (Grand Rapids, Mich.: Eerdmans, 1976), 17–33.

51. Classis ordinaria den 12 april 1779, 379: Archief van de Nederlandse Hervormde Kerk, pp. 231–35, Classis Amsterdam, Stadsarchief Amsterdam, https://archief.amsterdam/. Thanks to Andrea Mosterman for bringing this document to my attention.

52. Edward Tanjore Corwin, ed., *A Digest of Constitutional and Synodical Legislation of the Reformed Church in American* (New York: The Board of Publication of the Reformed Church in America, 1906), 4, 679–80. Historian Noel Leo Erskine argues that "toward the end of the eighteenth century, however, there was an indication of a new mood in the Dutch Reformed Church's attitude toward black people" (Erskine, *Black People and the Reformed Church*, 39–42).

53. Tobias Alexander Wright, ed., *Records of the Reformed Dutch Church in New Amsterdam and New York: Baptisms from 1 January 1731 to 29 December 1800, Collections of the New York Genealogical and Biographical Society*, vol. 3 (New York: Printed for the Society, 1902), 358, 373, 374, 384, 394, 409.

54. *Records of the Presbyterian Church in the United States of America: Embracing the Minutes of the Presbytery of Philadelphia, from A.D. 1706 to 1716, Minutes of the Synod of Philadelphia, from A.D. 1717 to 1758, Minutes of the Synod of New York, from A.D. 1745 to 1758, Minutes of the Synod of New York and Philadelphia, from A.D. 1758 to 1788* (Philadelphia: Presbyterian Board of Publication, 1841), 527.

55. Minkema and Stout, "The Edwardsean Tradition and the Antislavery Debate," 58; Mark A. Noll, "Observations on the Reconciliation of Politics and Religion in Revolutionary New Jersey: The Case of Jacob Green," *Journal of Presbyterian History* (1962–1985) 54, no. 2 (Summer 1976): 217–37; Thompson, "Slavery and Presbyterianism in the Revolutionary Era," 125–28; Douglas R. Egerton, *Death or Liberty: African Americans and Revolutionary America* (New York: Oxford University Press, 2009), 99; Nash and Soderlund, *Freedom by Degrees*, 157–64.

56. *Records of the Presbyterian Church in the United States of America*, 540; Nash and Soderlund, *Freedom by Degrees*, 157–64.

57. Records of Second Presbyterian Church Philadelphia Baptism, Marriages, Burials, 1745–1833, Collections of the Genealogical Society of Pennsylvania, vol. 32 (Philadelphia, 1898), HSP; Records of First Presbyterian Church, Philadelphia, Baptisms 1701–1856, pp. 258, 368, HSP.

58. Register of Baptism, 1728–1790, First Presbyterian Church (New York, N.Y.) Records, pp. 193–261, PHS.

59. Lutheran churches in which multiple blacks were baptized and/or admitted to membership 1777–1790: Trinity Lutheran Church New York City; First Lutheran Church Albany, N.Y.; Gilead Evangelical Lutheran Church, Brunswick, N.Y.; Zion Lutheran Church Athens, N.Y.; St. Thomas's Lutheran Church Claverack, N.Y.; Trinity Lutheran Church Lancaster, Pa.; and Christ Lutheran Church Stouchsburg, Pa. Baptism at the Swedish Lutheran Churches in Gloucester County occurred during the period when this church was transitioning to the Episcopal denomination (Pointer, *Protestant Pluralism*, 80, 81, 106; Lutheran church records, 1703–1802 New York, Albany, and other places, NYPL; Royden Woodward Vosburgh, ed., Records of the First Lutheran Church in the city of Albany, NY, vol. 1, pp. 4–80, transcribed by the NYGBS [New York City, June 1917]; Royden Woodward Vosburgh, ed., Records of the Gilead Evangelical Lutheran Church at Center Brunswick, in the town of Brunswick, Rensselaer County, NY, vol. 1, pp. 19–122, transcribed by the NYGBS [New York City, June 1913]; Royden Woodward Vosburgh and L. P. de Boer, eds., Records of St. Thomas's Evangelical Lutheran Church at Churchtown, town of Claverack, Columbia County, N.Y., transcribed by the NYGBS [New York, 1912], typescript, NYPL; Records of the Zion Lutheran Church of Athens, Greene County, N.Y., 1704–1865, positive photostatic reproduction, NYPL; *Records of Pastoral Acts at Christ Lutheran Church, Stouchsburg, Berks County, Pennsylvania, Part 1 and 2*, trans. and ed. Frederick S. Weiser (Birdsong: Pennsylvania German Society, 1989, 1990); Paul Minotty, ed., *The Records of Trinity Episcopal Church [Old Swedes], Swedesboro, Gloucester County, New Jersey, 1785–1975* [Woodbury, N.J.: Gloucester County Historical Society, 1979]).

60. John H. Heffner, ed., *The Records of the Swedish Lutheran Churches at Raccoon and Penns Neck, 1713–1786* (Topton, Pa.: J. H. Heffner, 1997); *Trinity Lutheran Church of Reading Berks County Pennsylvania, Translated from the Original by Rev. J. W. Early (ca. 1906)*, pt. 1: *Baptisms 1751–1790* (Apollo, Penn. : Closson, 1990), 103; Christ Evangelical Lutheran Church, York, pt. I, p. 225, Adams County Historical Society.

61. Lutheran church records, 1703–1802, New York, Albany, and other places, pp. 236–63 NYPL; Charles H. Glatfelter, *Pastors and People: German Lutheran and Reformed Churches in the Pennsylvania Field, 1717–1793*, vol. 1: *Pastors and Congregations* (Breinigsville: Pennsylvania German Society, 1980), 219; Hodges, *Root & Branch*, 156; George U. Wenner, *The Lutherans of New York: Their Story and Their Problems* (New York: Petersfield, 1918), 14–15; Pointer, *Protestant Pluralism*, 104–5; Nash, *Unknown American Revolution*, 163.

62. Pointer, *Protestant Pluralism*, 79–80, 91–92, 107; Graham Russell Hodges, ed., *Black Itinerants of the Gospel: The Narratives of John Jea and George White* (Madison, Wisc.: Madison House, 1993), 3; Bulthuis, *Four Steeples over the City Streets*, 30–47; Deborah Mathias Gough, *Christ Church, Philadelphia: The Nation's Church in a Changing City* (Philadelphia: University of Pennsylvania Press, 1995), 138; Benjamin Dorr, *A Historical Account of Christ Church, Philadelphia, from Its Foundation A.D. 1695 to A.D. 1841, and of St. Peter's and St. James, until the Separation of the Churches* (Philadelphia: R.S.H. George, 1841), 181. At Hempstead, Long Island, when it was under British control, Reverend Leonard Cutting baptized twenty-five whites and two blacks. Mid-Atlantic Episcopal churches in which multiple blacks were baptized, 1777–90: Trinity Church & its chapels, New York, N.Y.; Trinity Church Swedesboro,

N.J.; St. Michael's Church Trenton, N.J.; Christ Church Philadelphia, Pa.; St. James Church Lancaster, Pa.; and Robert Ayres's Episcopal ministry, Brownsville, Pa. For Trinity Church New York, see Frank J. Klingberg, "The S.P.G. Program for Negroes in Colonial New York," *Historical Magazine of the Protestant Episcopal Church* 8, no. 4 (December 1939): 338–68.

63. Records of Christ Church Philadelphia Baptisms 1769–1794, Collections of the Genealogical Society of Pennsylvania (Philadelphia 1906), HSP; Gough, *Christ Church, Philadelphia*, 114, 144–61.

64. Trinity Church Baptisms, Trinity Church Wall Street Archive, New York; Hodges, *Root & Branch*, 147; Pointer, *Protestant Pluralism*, 107; Klingberg, "The S.P.G. Program for Negroes in Colonial New York," 338; Hodges, ed., *Black Itinerants of the Gospel*, 3; Bulthuis, *Four Steeples over the City Streets*, 30–47, 55–56.

65. "Ayres baptismal registry," Papers of Robert Ayres, 1785–1837, box 1, folder 1, Heinz History Center.

66. Mid-Atlantic Baptist churches in which multiple blacks were admitted to membership, 1777–90: First Baptist New York City, N.Y.; Baptist Church of Upper Freehold, N.J.; Old First Baptist Church Middletown, N.J. (ABHS); and Mount Moriah Baptist Church Smithfield, Pa. Mount Moriah Baptist Church was constituted in 1784, and at least three blacks were members in its early years (see business meeting minutes between 1785 and 1790) ("Combined Church Record Books, 1784–1871," Moriah Baptist Church, Smithfield [Fayette County] Pa., micofilm, reel 1 [LCCN: 89–798516], LOC).

67. A. D. Gillette, ed., "Minutes of the Philadelphia Baptist Association, Held in Philadelphia, October 6th, 7th, 8th, and 9th, 1789," in *Minutes of the Philadelphia Baptist Association, from 1707 to 1807* (Philadelphia: American Baptist Publication Society, 1851), 247.

68. Janet Moore Lindman, *Bodies of Belief: Baptist Community in Early America* (Philadelphia: University of Pennsylvania Press, 2008), 142–45. German Baptists denounced the slave trade and slavery at their annual meeting of 1782, and they ordered "Brother John Van L." to free his five slaves. In 1797, they prohibited slaveholding (Willis A. Hess, Ray B. Hess, and David G. Benedict, eds., *Minutes of the Annual Meetings of the Old German Baptist Brethren from 1778 to 1955* [Winona Lake, Ind.: BMH Printing, 1981], 8, 24–25). The Baptist Church of Scots Plains, New Jersey, records include an interesting case of a black man who repeatedly sought to join the church but was denied membership for apparently religious reasons (Scotch Plains Baptist Church, Scotch Plains, N.J., Records, 1747–1809, pp. 54–55, MG 968, NJHS).

69. First Baptist Church Records & Minutes from 1762 to 1812, pp. 48–85, 107, 135–249, Records of the First Baptist Church of New York City.

70. *Minutes of the Methodist Conferences*, vol. 1 (1813), 25–26, 46–47; Andrews, *Methodists and Revolutionary America*, 125–32.

71. *Minutes of the Methodist Conferences*, vol. 1 (1813), 12, 14, 22, 31, 49–51, 60–61; Cynthia Lynn Lyerly, *Methodism and the Southern Mind, 1770–1810* (New York: Oxford University Press, 1998), 20–21; Andrews, *Methodists and Revolutionary America*, 47–62.

72. *Minutes of the Methodist Conferences*, vol. 1 (1813), 68.

73. For analysis of the reliability of the membership numbers reported in the Minutes, see Andrews, *Methodists and Revolutionary America*, 133, 259–61.

74. Streeter, *Past and Present of the John Street Methodist*, 21–23; Bulthuis, *Four Steeples over the City Streets*, 38–39, 44–46; Andrews, *Methodists and Revolutionary America*, 136.

75. *Minutes of the Methodist Conferences*, vol. 1 (1813), 61, 67, 95; Andrews, *Methodists and Revolutionary America*, 135, 248–50; Sylvia Frey and Betty Wood, *Come Shouting to Zion: African American Protestantism in the American South and British Caribbean to 1830* (Chapel Hill: University of North Carolina Press, 1998), 105.

76. *Journal of Rev. Francis Asbury, Bishop of the Methodist Episcopal Church*, 3 vols., vol. 1: *From August 7, 1771 to December 31, 1786* (New York: Land and Scott, 1852), 424, 433–34; Andrews, *Methodists and Revolutionary America*, 139; Henry H. Mitchell, *Black Church Beginnings: The Long-Hidden Realities of the First Years* (Grand Rapids, Mich.: Eerdmans, 2004), 50; *Minutes of the Methodist Conferences, Annually Held in America from 1773 to 1813, Inclusive*, vol. 1 (New York: John C. Totten, 1813), 26.

77. Richard S. Newman, *Freedom's Prophet: Bishop Richard Allen, the A.M.E. Church, and the Black Founding Fathers* (New York: New York University Press, 2008), 27–45; Richard Allen, *The Life Experience and Gospel Labors of the Rt. Rev. Richard Allen: To Which Is Annexed the Rise and Progress of the African Methodist Episcopal Church in the United States of America, Containing a Narrative of the Yellow Fever in the Year of Our Lord 1793 . . . with an Introduction of George A. Singleton* (Nashville, Tenn.: Abingdon, 1983), 15–19.

78. Newman, *Freedom's Prophet*, 27–45; Allen, *Life Experience and Gospel Labors*, 15–19; Gary B. Nash, "New Light on Richard Allen: The Early Years of Freedom," *WMQ*, 3d ser., 46, no. 2 (April 1989): 332–38.

79. Allen, *Life Experience and Gospel Labors*, 19–22; Newman, *Freedom's Prophet*, 45–53; Nash, "New Light on Richard Allen," 332–39; character references for blacks, Pennsylvania Abolition Society Collection, microfilm, HSP.

80. Newman, *Freedom's Prophet*, 50–70; Nash, "New Light on Richard Allen," 337; Allen, *Life Experience and Gospel Labors*, 23–25.

5 / "To Restore Our Long Lost Race"

1. William Douglass, *Annals of the First African Church, in the United States of America, Now Styled the African Episcopal Church of St. Thomas, Philadelphia* (Philadelphia: King and Baird Printers, 1862), 58, 66, 79, 85–92.

2. Journal 1793, Rev. John Pitman Diaries, Mss 622, RIHS.

3. Nathan O. Hatch, *The Democratization of American Christianity* (New Haven, Conn.: Yale University Press, 1989), 4, 58.

4. Katherine Wolff, *Culture Club: The Curious History of the Boston Athenaeum* (Boston: University of Massachusetts Press, 2009); James O. Horton and Lois E. Horton, *Black Bostonians: Family Life and Community Struggle in the Antebellum North* (New York: Holmes and Meier, 1999).

5. Charles F. Irons, *Origins of Proslavery Christianity: White and Black Evangelicals in Colonial and Antebellum Virginia* (Chapel Hill: University of North Carolina Press, 2008); Henry H. Mitchell, *Black Church Beginnings: The Long-Hidden Realities of the First Years* (Grand Rapids, Mich.: Eerdmans, 2004), 46–70, 82–97, 190–92; Janet Moore Lindman, *Bodies of Belief: Baptist Community in Early America* (Philadelphia: University of Pennsylvania Press, 2008); Jon F. Sensbach, *A Separate Canaan: The*

Making of an Afro-Moravian World in North Carolina, 1763–1840 (Chapel Hill: University of North Carolina Press, 1998); Mechal Sobel, *Trabelin' On: The Slave Journey to an Afro-Baptist Faith* (Princeton, N.J.: Princeton University Press, 1988); Christine Heyrman, *Southern Cross: The Beginnings of the Bible Belt* (Chapel Hill: University of North Carolina Press, 1998); Lyerly, *Methodism and the Southern Mind.*

6. Richard S. Newman, *Freedom's Prophet: Bishop Richard Allen, the A.M.E. Church, and the Black Founding Fathers* (New York: New York University Press, 2008); Craig D. Townsend, *Faith in Their Own Color: Black Episcopalians in Antebellum New York City* (New York: Columbia University Press, 2005); Mitchell, *Black Church Beginnings*; Horton and Horton, *Black Bostonians*; Genna Rae McNeil, Houston Bryan Roberson, Quinton Hosford Dixie, and Keven McGruder, *Witness: Two Hundred Years of African-American Faith and Practices at the Abyssinian Baptist Church of Harlem, New York* (Grand Rapids, Mich.: Eerdmans, 2014). Janet Lindman notes that "the development of distinct meetings did not end interactions among black and white Baptists" (Lindman, *Bodies of Belief*, 152).

7. Graham Russell Hodges, ed., *Black Itinerants of the Gospel: The Narratives of John Jea and George White* (Madison, Wisc.: Madison House, 1993), 8.

8. James Oliver and Lois E. Horton, *In Hope of Liberty: Culture, Community and Protest among Northern Free Blacks, 1700–1860* (New York: Oxford University Press, 1997), 83–84; Kyle T. Bulthuis, *Four Steeples over the City Streets: Religion and Society in New York's Early Republic Congregations* (New York: New York University Press, 2014), 55.

9. Robert C. Hayden, *Faith, Culture, and Leadership: A History of the Black Church in Boston* (Boston: Boston Branch NAACP, 1983), 3–17; Robert L. Carter Jr., *A History of the Black Churches of Massachusetts, Rhode Island, and New Hampshire*, vol. 1 (Worcester: United Baptist Convention of Massachusetts, Rhode Island, and New Hampshire, 2003), 43, 65, 82–83; Mitchell, *Black Church Beginnings*, 66–70, 82–88, 182–84.

10. Richard Allen, *The Life Experience and Gospel Labors of the Rt. Rev. Richard Allen: To Which Is Annexed the Rise and Progress of the African Methodist Episcopal Church in the United States of America, Containing a Narrative of the Yellow Fever in the Year of Our Lord 1793 . . . with an Introduction of George A. Singleton* (Nashville, Tenn.: Abingdon, 1983), 24, 26, 27; Newman, *Freedom's Prophet*; William Douglass, *Annals of the First African Church, in the United States of America, Now Styled the African Episcopal Church of St. Thomas, Philadelphia* (Philadelphia: King and Baird Printers, 1862); Dee Andrews and Kathryn Zabelle Derounian, "Notes and Documents: The African Methodists of Philadelphia, 1794–1802," *Pennsylvania Magazine of History and Biography* 108, no. 4 (October 1984); Carol V. R. George, *Segregated Sabbaths: Richard Allen and the Rise of Independent Black Churches 1760–1840* (New York: Oxford University Press, 1973); Townsend, *Faith in Their Own Color*; John Jamison Moore, *History of the A.M.E. Zion Church in America, Founded in 1796, in the City of New York* (York, Pa.: Teachers' Journal Office, 1884); Mitchell, *Black Church Beginnings*; Horton and Horton, *Black Bostonians*, 42; George A. Levesque, *Black Boston: African American Life and Culture in Urban America, 1750–1860* (New York: Garland, 1994), 82, 88, 133, 266–71; Hayden, *Faith, Culture, and Leadership*; John H. Hewitt Jr., *Protest and Progress: New York's First Black Episcopal Church Fights Racism* (New York: Garland, 2000); McNeil, *Witness*.

11. Albert Raboteau cautions against viewing "white racism as the reason for the development of the black church" because "black religious independence arose from black initiative and not simply in reaction to white discrimination" (Albert J. Raboteau, *A Fire in the Bones: Reflections on African-American Religious History* [Boston: Beacon, 1995], 80–81).

12. Andrews and Derounian, "Notes and Documents: The African Methodists of Philadelphia, 1794–1802," 474–75; Newman, *Freedom's Prophet*, 62–73; Douglass, *Annals of the First African Church*, 18, 42, 43, 46–51; Raboteau, *A Fire in the Bones*, 84–85; Horton and Horton, *Black Bostonians*, 42–43; George A. Levesque, *Black Boston: African American Life and Culture in Urban America, 1750–1860* (New York: Garland, 1994), 82, 88, 133, 266–71; James O. Horton, "Generations of Protest: Black Families and Social Reform in Ante-Bellum Boston," *New England Quarterly* 49, no. 2 (June 1976): 245–46; Hayden, *Faith, Culture, and Leadership*, 3–4.

13. Townsend, *Faith in Their Own Color*, 27.

14. Allen, *Life Experience and Gospel Labors*, 25; Newman, *Freedom's Prophet*, 59–60.

15. Allen, *Life Experience and Gospel Labors*, 26.

16. Moore, *History of the A.M.E. Zion Church in America*, 15–16; *Journal of Rev. Francis Asbury, Bishop of the Methodist Episcopal Church*, 3 vols., vol. 2: *From January 1, 1787 to December 31, 1800* (New York: Land and Scott, 1852), 270.

17. William T. Catto, *A Semi-Centenary Discourse, Delivered in the First African Presbyterian Church, Philadelphia, on the Fourth Sabbath of May, 1857: With a History of the Church from Its First Organization: Including a Brief Notice of Rev. John Gloucester, Its First Pastor* (Philadelphia: J. M. Wilson, 1857), 18, 19. There are no extant church records from the early decades of this congregation. Catto, when writing the 1857 history, relied on information from a few surviving black members, some white Presbyterians, and some scattered written sources (Catto, *A Semi-Centenary Discourse*).

18. "To the Pious and Benevolent," July 31, 1809, box 1, folder 2, Evangelical Society of Philadelphia, Records, 1809–1815, RG 313, PHS; Catto, *A Semi-Centenary Discourse, 50–53*.

19. Act of Incorporation, Causes and Motives, of the African Episcopal Church of Philadelphia, White-Hall, 1810, Edward Carey Gardiner Collection, 1673–1949, Collection 227A, Section 6: Miscellaneous Section, box 32, file 1, HSP; Douglass, *Annals of the First African Church*, 93–95, 99; Andrews and Derounian, "The African Methodists of Philadelphia," 474, 475–76, 481–84; Allen, *Life Experience and Gospel Labors*, 29, 30; Newman, *Freedom's Prophet*, 70–72.

20. The Petition of Peter Williams, Jnr, Lewis Francis, Andrew Rankins, John Kent, Thomas Zabriskie, John Beas, John Marander, and William Pate, managers of the African Episcopal Catechetical Institution, in the City of New York, November 17th, 1817, Trinity Church Archive, Box 288, VP 3, 1816–1820, folder 288–9, Vestry Papers; To the Rector, Wardens and Vestrymen of Trinity Church, in the City of New York, May 6th, 1819, Trinity Church Archive, Box 288, VP 3, 1816–1820, folder 288–9, Vestry Papers; Townsend, *Faith in Their Own Color*.

21. John Jamison Moore, *History of the A.M.E. Zion Church in America, Founded in 1796, In the City of New York* (York, Pa.: Teachers' Journal Office, 1884), 16–17, 19–20, 28, 29; *Journal of Rev. Francis Asbury, Bishop of the Methodist Episcopal Church*, 3

vols., vol. 3: *From January 1, 1801 to December 7, 1815* (New York: Land and Scott, 1852), 67, 78, 224, 279, 337, 363, 385, 453.

22. Douglass, *Annals of the First African Church*, 101–6, 107–10, 123; Townsend, *Faith in Their Own Color*, 30–31; Absalom Jones, *A Thanksgiving Sermon, Preached January 1, 1808, In St. Thomas's or the African Episcopal, Church, Philadelphia: on Account of the Abolition of the African Slave Trade, on That Day, By the Congress of the United States* (Philadelphia: 1808); *Journal of Rev. Francis Asbury*, 3:67, 78, 224, 279, 337, 363, 385, 453.

23. Sarah Barringer Gordon, "The African Supplement: Religion, Race, and Corporate Law in Early National America," *WMQ* 72, no. 3 (July 2015): 399–400; Andrews and Derounian, "Notes and Documents: The African Methodists of Philadelphia, 1794–1802," 476, 483–84; Allen, *Life Experience and Gospel Labors*, 31; Newman, *Freedom's Prophet*, 70–72; Horton and Horton, *Black Bostonians*, 42; Levesque, *Black Boston*, 82, 88, 133, 266–71; Hayden, *Faith, Culture, and Leadership*, 3–4.

24. Townsend, *Faith in Their Own Color*, 42; copy of Minutes of the Vestry, 1791–1826, Corporation of Trinity Church, vol. 2, June 8, 1818, p. 328, March 15, 1819, p. 335, and May 10, 1819, p. 338; The Petition of Peter Williams, et al., November 17, 1817, and To the Rector, Wardens and Vestrymen of Trinity Church, in the City of New York, May 6, 1819, Trinity Church Archive, box 288, VP 3, 1816–1820, folder 288–89, Vestry Papers.

25. Copy of a Resolution (to purchase a Lot) given to Rev'd John Gloucester, dated Oct 6, 1809, MS EV14, box 1, folder 2, Evangelical Society of Philadelphia, Records, 1809–1815, RG 313, PHS; Catto, *A Semi-Centenary Discourse*, 43–44, 50–53.

26. Andrews and Derounian, "The African Methodists of Philadelphia," 477; Allen, *Life Experience and Gospel Labors*, 32–35; Newman, *Freedom's Prophet*, 72–73, 131–35, 159–81; Raboteau, *A Fire in the Bones*, 90–92.

27. John Jamison Moore, *History of the A.M.E. Zion Church in America, Founded in 1796, in the City of New York* (York, Pa.: Teachers' Journal Office, 1884), 37–54, 61–64; Mitchell, *Black Church Beginnings*, 69; *Journal of Rev. Francis Asbury*, 2:270; *Journal of Rev. Francis Asbury*, 3:67, 78, 224, 385, 474; Townsend, *Faith in Their Own Color*, 11–14. Black Episcopal churches were denied the right to attend the Episcopal Conventions well into the 1850s (Townsend, *Faith in Their Own Color*, 1–8).

28. Horton and Horton, *Black Bostonians*, 42–43; Levesque, *Black Boston*, 82, 88, 133, 266–71; Horton, "Generations of Protest," 245–46; Hayden, *Faith, Culture, and Leadership*, 3–4; Journal 1805, Rev. John Pitman Diaries, Mss 622, RIHS; Carr, *After the Siege*, 257n114; Horton and Horton, *In Hope of Liberty*, 83.

29. Gary B. Nash, *Forging Freedom: The Formation of Philadelphia's Black Community 1720–1840* (Cambridge, Mass.: Harvard University Press, 2003), 260; Catto, *A Semi-Centenary Discourse*, 40–41; Douglass, *Annals of the First African Church*, 101––10, 123; Townsend, *Faith in Their Own Color*, 30–31. Between 1796 and 1818, Reverend Jones baptized 268 adults and 927 infants at St. Thomas Episcopal Church (Douglass, *Annals of the First African Church*, 123).

30. Peter Williams wrote in 1816 that New York City had "three African churches: 2 Methodist, 1 Baptist. Two of which will contain more than 1000 persons. . . . [T]he Episcopal Church have established a lecture room for the coloured people belonging to that denomination, that is usually attended by a decent & orderly congregation of about 300 persons" (Peter Williams to NY Manumission Society, letter giving

statistics on land ownership and religious and literary societies among New York's black people, January 10, 1816, Library Company of Philadelphia, Grellet Mss. vol. I, 1701–1818, p. 219, HSP).

31. Nathan O. Hatch, *The Democratization of American Christianity* (New Haven, Conn.: Yale University Press, 1989), 3.

32. Dutch Church records did not use racial notations as uniformly as other denominations. I have assumed that people identified as servants or as belonging to a person and without last names were black people. I used the same search methods for earlier periods as well. Reformed churches in the following towns had multiple blacks baptized and/or admitted to membership between 1791 and 1820: in New York—Albany, Catskill, Cobleskill, Coxsackie, East Greenbush, Fleming, Fonda (Caughnawaga), German Flatts, Kingston, Machackemeck (Deerpark), Marbletown, Mayfield, Middleburgh, Minden, Nassau, New Paltz, New York City (First Reformed, Madison Avenue Reformed, Reformed Church at Greenwich Village, and Reformed Church on Staten Island), Palatine, Poughkeepsie, Schenectady, Schodack, Schoharie, Shokan, Shawangunk, and Tappan; in New Jersey—Hackensack, Pompton Plains, Readington, and Totowa. For religious and demographic information about New Jersey, see Jedidiah Morse, Aaron Arrowsmith, and Samuel Lewis, *The American Universal Geography: Or, A View of the Present State of All the Kingdoms, States, and Colonies in the Known World*, 7th ed., 2 vols., vol. 1 (Charlestown: Lincoln and Edmands, 1819), 408-411.

33. For black baptism in Dutch Reformed churches 1730–76, see chapter 1. For founding dates of colonial Reformed churches, see Balmer, *A Perfect Babel of Confusion*, 157–59. Graham Hodges states, "officially segregated since the 1660s, the church began accepting black communicants soon after the Revolution," but black membership in Dutch Reformed churches still "remained small compared with the number of African Americans owned by the Dutch" (Hodges, *Root & Branch*, 181).

34. Royden Woodward Vosburgh, ed., Records of the Reformed Dutch Church in the town of Middleburgh, Schoharie County, N.Y., pp. 7–25, 113–17, transcribed by the NYGBS, NYPL; Royden Woodward Vosburg, ed., Records of the Reformed Protestant Dutch Church on Staten Island, in Richmond County, NY., vol. 2, pp. 153–61, transcribed (New York City, 1923), LOC; Vosburgh, Records of the Reformed Protestant Dutch Church of Caughnawaga, vol. 1, pp. 5–152, and vol. 2, pp. 1–213, NYPL. The Reformed Church at Machackemeck (Deerpark) baptized eleven or so blacks in these years (Collections of the NYGBS, vol. 5, Minister Valley Reformed Dutch Church Records, pp. 207, 215, 219, 254, 256, LOC).

35. Royden Woodward Vosburg, ed., Records of the Madison Avenue Reformed Church in the City of New York, vol. 1, New York City, 1921, pp. 39, 42, 57, transcribed by the NYGBS, LOC; Royden Woodward Vosburg, ed., Records of the Reformed Dutch Church at Greenwich in the City of New York, vol. 1, New York City, 1920, pp. 4–21, 115–16, 182–89, transcribed by the NYGBS, LOC; *The Acts and Proceedings of the General Synod of the Reformed Dutch Church in North America at New-York, June 1822* (New-York: George Forman, 1822), 19, 62; *The Acts and Proceedings of the General Synod of the Reformed Dutch Church in North America at Albany, June 1823* (New-York: Abraham Paul, 1823), 58.

36. Corwin, *Digest of Constitutional and Synodical Legislation of the Reformed Church*, 4, 679–80; Erskine, *Black People and the Reformed Church*, 39–40, 42.

37. Corwin, *Digest of Constitutional and Synodical Legislation of the Reformed Church*, lxvi; Hodges, *Root & Branch*, 181.

38. "Report of the State of Religion within the boundaries of the Reformed Dutch Church in North America Made June 1816," *Utica Christian Magazine: Designed to Prompt the Spirit of Research, and Diffuse Religious Information*, vol. 2 (Utica, N.Y.: Printed for Cornelius Davis, 1816), ii–iii.

39. Hugh Hastings, ed., *Ecclesiastical Records, State of New York*, vol. 1 (Albany: J. B. Lyon, 1901), 548; Andrea C. Mosterman, "'I Thought They Were Worthy': A Dutch Reformed Church Minister and His Congregation Debate African American Membership in the Church," *Early American Studies: An Interdisciplinary Journal* 14, no. 3 (Summer 2016): 610–16. I would like to thank Andrea Mosterman for her advice and for sharing an early version of her article with me.

40. Hodges, *Root & Branch*, 168–69; Horton, *In Hope of Liberty*, 101;. In 1787, Presbyterians worried that freeing slaves too quickly might be "dangerous to the community" (*Records of the Presbyterian Church in the United States of America: Embracing the Minutes of the Presbytery of Philadelphia, from A.D. 1706 to 1716, Minutes of the Synod of Philadelphia, from A.D. 1717 to 1758, Minutes of the Synod of New York, from A.D. 1745 to 1758, Minutes of the Synod of New York and Philadelphia, from A.D. 1758 to 1788* [Philadelphia: Presbyterian Board of Publication, 1841], 540).

41. Locations of predominantly white Presbyterian churches in which multiple blacks were baptized and/or admitted to membership, 1791–1820: in New York—Albany, Ballston, Cambridge, Catskill, Durham, Johnstown, New York City (First Presbyterian), Newtown (Elmhurst), Perth (Galloway), Pleasant Valley, Whitesboro, and Yorktown; in New Jersey— Cranbury, Elizabeth, Flemington, Hanover, Lawrenceville, Madison, Manalapan (Old Tennent Presbyterian), Mendham, and Rockaway; in Philadelphia, Pennsylvania—Second Presbyterian Church and Third Presbyterian Church..

42. *Records of the Presbyterian Church in the United States of America* (1841), 527.

43. RG 413, box 3: folder 4, List of Members, 1809–1812; folder 6, List of Members, 1811–1824; folder 12, Register of Baptism, 1791–1802, First Presbyterian Church (New York, N.Y.) Records, 1717–1961, PHS.

44. Presbyterian Church Records, Newtown (now Elmhurst) Queens County, Long Island, NY, LOC, 16–20; Royden Woodward Vosburg, ed., Records of the First Presbyterian Church at Ballston in Ballston Center, Saratoga County, New York, pp. 49–94, 70–81, 108–13, transcribed by the NYGBS, vol. 1 (New York City, 1916), LOC; Royden Woodward Vosburgh, ed., Records of the First Presbyterian Church of Whitesboro in the town of Whitestown, Oneida County, N.Y., pp. 48–53, transcribed by the NYGBS (New York City, June 1920), LOC.

45. List of the families in the Presbyterian congregation of Elizabeth Town taken by the Rev. John McDowell in his pastoral visits begun Nov. 26th, 1818, List of Families, 1810–12, 1834–35, Session Minutes 1817–1824, Session Minutes 1806–1816, Infant Baptism and Adult Baptisms 1811–1824, First Presbyterian Church (Elizabeth, N.J.) Records, 1716–1913, boxes 1 and 2, RG 68, PHS.

46. Locations of predominantly white Congregational churches in which multiple blacks were baptized and/or admitted to membership, 1791–1820. The churches are the first parish/congregation unless otherwise noted: in Massachusetts—Amesbury (North Parish), Beverly, Boston (Second Church, Old South–Third Church, Brattle

Square-Fourth Church, New North–Fifth Church, Hollis Street–Eighth Church, and West–Ninth Church), Charlestown, Dorchester, Groton, Marblehead (Second Church), Newton, and Northampton; in Rhode Island—Bristol, Little Compton, and Newport; in Connecticut—Branford, Bridgeport (United), Canton (Canton Center), East Hampton (Haddam Neck), Essex (Essex Centerbrook Church), Fairfield, Glastonbury (Glastonbury Buckingham–Eastbury Church), Lebanon, Lisbon (Lisbon Newent), Madison, Middletown, New Canaan, New London, Norwalk, Old Lyme, Old Saybrook, Sharon, Trumbull, Westchester, Windham, and Woodbury; in New York—Congregational Church of New Canaan; in Vermont—Bennington, Manchester, and West Rutland; in New Hampshire—Amherst and Portsmouth.

47. Margot Minardi, *Making Slavery History: Abolitionism and the Politics of Memory in Massachusetts* (New York: Oxford University Press, 2010), 61; Douglas L. Winiarski, *Darkness Falls on the Land of Light: Experiencing Religious Awakenings in Eighteenth-Century New England* (Chapel Hill: University of North Carolina Press, 2017), 367–506. The number of Episcopal/Anglican churches in which black affiliated stayed relatively constant between the periods of 1763 to 1790 and 1791 to 1820. The number of Baptist churches with black members increased.

48. Abiel Brown, *Genealogical History, with Short Sketches and Family Records of the Early Settlers of West Simsbury, Now Canton, Conn.* (Hartford: Case, Tiffany, 1856), 139–42; *Connecticut Church Records, Canton Center Church 1785–1890*, 1929, typescript index to church records, pp. 12, 219–20, CSL.

49. This argument about why the number of interracial churches declined among Congregationalists is speculative, but my thinking has been influenced by Joseph A. Conforti, *Imagining New England: Explorations of Regional Identity from the Pilgrims to the Mid-Twentieth Century* (Chapel Hill: University of North Carolina Press, 2001), 130–35; Joanne Pope Melish, *Disowning Slavery: Gradual Emancipation and "Race" in New England, 1780–1860* (Ithaca, N.Y.: Cornell University Press, 1998); Winiarski, *Darkness Falls*, 449, 372–73.

50. Racial notations were not uniformly written in these records; First Congregational Church Marriages Baptisms 1744–1825, Admissions into Full Communion, and Meeting House Booke of the Rev. Mr. Clap commencing September 1743, NHS; Loose paper in the Union Congregational Church 1790–1796 and 1772–1824 record ledgers, Union Congregational Church Newport R.I., NHS; Financial records and receipts, First Congregational Church of Newport records 1805–1825, Mss. 418, RIHS.

51. Meeting House Booke of the Rev. Mr. Clap commencing September 1743, NHS; Financial records and receipts, First Congregational Church of Newport records 1805–1825, Mss. 418, RIHS; Lorenzo Johnston Greene, *The Negro in Colonial New England* (New York: Athenaeum, 1969), 278, 294; George C. Mason, *Reminiscences of Newport* (Newport, R.I.: Charles Hammett Jr., 1884), 154–59; William H. Robinson, ed., *The Proceedings of the Free African Union Society and the African Benevolent Society, Newport, Rhode Island, 1780–1824* (Providence: Urban League of Rhode Island, 1976), viii, ix, 58.

52. Qtd. in Mason, *Reminiscences of Newport*, 157; Richard C. Youngken, *African Americans in Newport: An Introduction to the Heritage of African Americans in Newport, Rhode Island, 1700–1945* (Providence: Rhode Island Historical Preservation and Heritage Commission), 23–24.

53. Locations of predominantly white Episcopal churches in which multiple blacks were baptized, 1791–1820: in New Hampshire—Portsmouth; in Massachusetts—Boston

(Christ Church and Trinity Church) and Salem; in Rhode Island—Bristol, Newport; in Connecticut—Bridgeport, Middletown, New Haven, New London, Stratford, Norwich, and Stamford; in New York—New York City (Trinity Church, St. Paul's Chapel, and Christ Church), Richmond, Staten Island, Hobart, Jamaica, Long Island, and Johnstown; in New Jersey—Burlington, Trenton; in Pennsylvania—Lancaster, Philadelphia, and Pittsburgh.

54. Jeremiah Taylor, A Sketch of Religious Experiences in and around New York City, 1811–1858, Misc. Mss. 1858, pp. 7, 35, 37, 41–43, manuscript department, LOC.

55. The Scotlands' lives are explored in Carr, *After the Siege*, 3–6, 171, 233. Andrew Oliver and James B. Peabody, eds., *Publications of the Colonial Society of Massachusetts*, vol. 56: *Collections: The Records of Trinity Church, Boston, 1728–1830, II* (Boston: Published by the Society, 1982), 634–99. The pastor of Trinity Church did not uniformly write racial notations. For example, "Augustus Caesar son of Caesar Elio by Rosanna Freeborn his wife" may have been blacks, but they were not included in the totals listed above.

56. Trinity Records 1786–1861, NHS. Approximately forty-one blacks were baptized by the ministers of Christ Church (now Holy Trinity Church) in Middletown, Connecticut, between 1809 and 1820 (Baptisms of Persons of Colour, Middletown Holy Trinity, microfilm records, CSL).

57. The exact number of black baptisms is difficult to discern because not all priests included racial notations within the records and because overlapping copies of records exist (Register of Christenings and Births Parish of Trinity Church New-York, 1778–1813, Baptism Trinity 1809–1832, Baptism Trinity Church 1800–06, Baptism St. George's Chapel 1782–1798, Marriages Parish 1746–1816, Trinity Church Archive). Craig Townsend states that at some point between 1803 and 1816, when Peter Williams Jr. began attending Trinity Church, "there were perhaps two hundred African American, both slave and free, attending services in a small chapel on Sunday afternoons and being taught the fundamentals of the Episcopal faith by an assistant minister of the parish. It was a separate congregation, and it was outgrowing what Trinity was willing to make available to it." Townsend provided no citation for this information (Townsend, *Faith in their Own Color*, 14).

58. Minutes of the Vestry, 1791–1826, Corporation of Trinity Church, vol. 2, pp. 40–41, 109, 174, Trinity Church Wall Street Archive; Records of Funerals attended by the Rev'd Benjamin Tredwell Onderdonk, Benjamin T. Onderdonk Papers, 1812–1832, N-YHS.

59. Record of Pastoral Visitations to the Sick, Afflicted, Prisoners, &c. by the Rev'd Benjamin Tredwell Onderdonk, 1813–1814, List of Persons to whom the Holy Communion has been privately administered by the Rev. Benj. T. Onderdonk, Record of Marriages performed by the Rev'd Benjamin Tredwell Onderdonk, Benjamin T. Onderdonk Papers, 1812–1832, N-YHS

60. Julie Winch, *A Gentleman of Color: The Life of James Forten* (New York: Oxford University Press, 2002), 140–43.

61. Locations of Lutheran churches in which multiple blacks were baptized, 1791–1820: in New York—Albany, Athens, Brunswick, Claverack, Livingston (Manorton), New York City, Sharon (New Rhinebeck), West Sandlake; in New Jersey—Perth Amboy; in Pennsylvania— Berrysburg/Mifflin, Lancaster, Reading, and Stouchsburg.

62. Vosburgh, Records of the First Lutheran Church in the city of Albany, N.Y., vol. 1, pp. 77, 80, 90, 96, 101, 115, 129, 136, 209–20, 261, LOC; *Trinity Lutheran Church of Reading Berks County Pennsylvania Translated from the Original by Rev. J. W. Early (ca. 1906) Part Two, Baptisms 1790–1812* (Apollo, Pa.: Closson, 1991), 30, 41–77, 85, 108.

63. Charles R. Shultz, ed., Baptismal and other records of the Samuel's Church, Lutheran and Reformed, 1784–1793 (Swissvale, Pa.: Charles R. Shultz, [1945?]), 1 vol. (unpaged), Carnegie Free Library, Pittsburgh; Glatfelter, *Pastors and People*, 1:433. At Christ Lutheran Church of Stouchsburg, Pennsylvania (between Reading and Harrisburg), at least five blacks were baptized between 1791 and 1806, including "Elisabeth, illegitimate daughter of Bethy, mulatto" (*Records of Pastoral Acts at Christ Lutheran Church, Stouchsburg, Berks County, Pennsylvania, Part 1 and 2*, trans. and ed. Frederick S. Weiser [Birdsong: Pennsylvania German Society, 1989, 1990], 82, 91, 97, 98, 114).

64. Donald A. Shelley, ed., *Lewis Miller: Sketches and Chronicles, The Reflections of a Nineteenth Century Pennsylvania German Folk Artist* (York, Pa.: Historical Society of York County, 1966), 13, 105. See also Patricia U. Bonomi, *Under the Cope of Heaven: Religion, Society, and Politics in Colonial America*, updated ed. (New York: Oxford University Press, 2003), 83.

65. At least nineteen predominantly white Baptist churches admitted African Americans to membership between 1791 and 1820, but the number was likely higher as Baptist record keepers were often inconsistent in how they listed members and in their use of racial notations. Locations of predominantly white Baptist churches in which multiple blacks were baptized or listed as members, 1791–1820: Boston, Mass. (First Baptist and Second Baptist); Swansea, Mass.; Newport, R.I. (First Baptist, Second Baptist, and Seventh Day Baptist); Providence, R.I.; Pawtucket, R.I.; Richmond, R.I.; Tiverton, R.I.; Exeter, R.I.; Westerly, R.I.; New York City, N.Y. (First Baptist); Bedford, N.Y.; Cape May, N.J.; Hightstown, N.J. (ABHS); Scots Plains, N.J.; and Philadelphia, Pa. (First and Sansom Street/Fifth Baptist ABHS). Lindman, *Bodies of Belief*, 134–55.

66. Lemons, ed., *Baptists in Early North America, First Baptist, Providence*, xiii, 124–370; Richard J. Boles, "'An Unclean Person' or 'A Fit Candidate for a Church Member': Kingston Pease and Northern Baptist Churches," *Rhode Island History* 75, no. 1 [Winter/Spring 2017]: 32–45. As another example, the Hill Church, or First Baptist Church of Westerly, had at least a few black members from 1790 to 1810, including a "famous exhorter," Cuffy Stanton (Church book for 1796 of Elkanah Babcock, Westerly, Rhode Island. Church of Christ [Hill Church] Records, 1793, 1893–1963, CL; Frederick Denion, *Westerly [Rhode Island] and Its Witnesses, For Two Hundred and Fifty Years, 1626–1876* [Providence: J. A. and R. A. Reid, 1878], 106).

67. First Baptist Church Records & Minutes from 1762 to 1812, pp. 135–245, Records of the First Baptist Church of New York City.

68. Susan Wright biography, Mathias Tallmadge Papers, N-YHS.

69. 1793 Journal, Rev. John Pitman Diaries, Mss 622, folder 7, RIHS; John W. Lewis, *The Life, Labors, and Travels of Elder Charles Bowles, of the Free Will Baptist Denomination, Together with an Essay on the Character and Condition of the African Race by the Same* (Watertown: Ingalls and Stowell's Steam Press, 1852), 5, 8, 10, 14, 15, 19; Nell, *Colored Patriots of the American Revolution*, 28–29; Eric G. Grundset, ed., *Forgotten Patriots: African American and American Indian Patriots in the Revolutionary War, A Guide to Service, Sources, and Studies* (Washington, D.C.: National Society of Daughters of the American Revolution, 2008), 103, 115–16.

70. Church records, New Haven, First Methodist Church 1806–1897, MS. Stacks, CHS; *Minutes of the Methodist Conferences*, vol. 1 (1813), 257.

71. Barry O'Connell, ed., *On Our Own Ground: The Complete Writings of William Apess, a Pequot* (Amherst: University of Massachusetts Press, 1992), xxxi, xxxiii, lxxix, lxxx, 125.

72. *Minutes of the Methodist Conferences*, vol. 1 (1813), 94–95, 146, 175, 241, 257, 273, 291, 314, 392, 449, 482, 517, 552, 596; *Journal of Rev. Francis Asbury*, 3:337. The earliest extant records are from 1818: General Register of Official Members 1818–1832 Smithfield Street Station Church, Methodist Episcopal Church in the City of Pittsburgh 1818–1832, Smithfield Street Church, Book # 1, 1818–1832, pp. 13–15, 30, Heinz History Center. The 1803 members list from the Asbury Methodist Episcopal Church at New Springville, Staten Island, includes fifty white members and five black members (Royden Woodward Vosburg, ed., Records of the Asbury Methodist Episcopal Church at New Springville, Staten Island, in Richmond County, N.Y., p. 37, transcribed [New York City, June 1922], LOC; Royden Woodward Vosburg, ed., Records of the Woodrow Methodist Episcopal Church at Woodrow, Staten Island, in Richmond County, N.Y., pp. 5–6, transcribed [New York City, 1922], LOC).

73. First Congregational Church West Roxbury, Mass.; First Congregational Church Orleans, Mass.; Tiverton Baptist Church, Tiverton, R.I.; St. James Episcopal Church, New London, Conn.; Canaan Congregational Church, Stillwater, N.Y.; and Reformed Dutch Church of Herkimer, Oneida Castle, N.Y.

74. Royden Woodward Vosburgh, ed., Records of the Reformed Protestant Dutch Church of Herkimer, town of Herkimer, Herkimer County, NY, vol. 1, p. 309, transcribed by the NYGBS (New York City, June 1918).

75. Nash, *Unknown American Revolution*, 378.

76. Gideon Hawley, journals, vol. 3, p. 144, ninth transcribed binder, pp. 81–161, CL.

77. Gideon Hawley, journals, vol. 3, pp. 121, 141, ninth transcribed binder, pp. 81–161, CL; Gideon Hawley, journals, vol. 3, pp. 34, 84, eighth transcribed binder, pp. 1–80, CL; Society for Propagating the Gospel Among the Indians and Others in North America Records, 1752–1948, Ms. N-176, box 2, February 6, 1810–July, 21, 1810, folder and May 6, 1811–June 6, 1811, folder, MHS.

78. David Silverman, *Faith and Boundaries: Colonists, Christianity, and Community among the Wampanoag Indians* (Cambridge: Cambridge University Press, 2005), 181–83, 223–25, 231, 238–40; Silverman, "The Church in New England Indian Community Life," 280; Gideon Hawley, journals, vol. 4, pp. 40–41, tenth transcribed binder, pp. 1–80, CL.

79. For Indians identified as "black," see Richard Bailey, *Race and Redemption in Puritan New England* (New York: Oxford University Press, 2014), 42; John Wood Sweet, *Bodies Politic: Negotiating Race in the American North, 1730–1830* (Philadelphia: University of Pennsylvania Press, 2003), 175–79; Joanne Pope Melish, "The Racial Vernacular: Contesting the Black/White Binary in Nineteenth Century Rhode Island," in *Race, Nation, and Empire in America*, ed. James T. Campbell, Matthew Pratt Guterl, and Robert G. Lee (Chapel Hill: University of North Carolina Press, 2007), 17–34; and Nicholas Guyatt, "'The Outskirts of Our Happiness': Race and the Lure of Colonization in the Early Republic," *Journal of American History* 95, no. 4 (2009): 986–1011.

80. Records of Christ Church Philadelphia Baptisms 1794–1819, Collections of the Genealogical Society of Pennsylvania, vol. 167, Philadelphia, 1906, HSP; Records of Christ Church Philadelphia Baptisms 1769–1794, HSP.

81. C VS B I—Baptisms 1669–1875, and Admission of Old South, Membership, Records of the Old South Church and Congregation 1669–1766, CL; Clark's register, 1723–1851, Old North Church Records, MHS; Vosburgh, ed., Records of the Reformed Protestant Dutch Church on Staten Island, vol. 2, LOC; Vosburgh, ed., Records of the First Presbyterian Church at Ballston in Ballston Center, Saratoga County, New York, vol. 1, LOC; Vosburgh, ed., Records of the First Lutheran Church in the city of Albany, N.Y., vol. 1, LOC; Melish, "The Racial Vernacular."

82. Gideon Hawley, journals, vol. 3, pp. 95–97, ninth transcribed binder, pp. 81–161. See also Theodore G. Mayhew to William Jennison, May 18, 1824, in Miscellaneous Manuscripts, MHS "Many nineteenth-century New Englanders designated as 'colored' or 'mulatto' (or even 'black' or 'negro') were descendants of Nipmucs, Wampanoags, Narragansetts, Pequots, and other Native residents of the region that would come to be called New England. . . . Obscuring the heritage and identity of Native people, nineteenth-century record-keepers' tendencies to lump people of color together under labels such as 'black' and 'colored' facilitated the apparent disappearance of Indians from the New England landscape" (Minardi, *Making Slavery History*, 62–63).

83. Daniel R. Mandell, "'The Indian's Pedigree' (1794): Indians, Folklore, and Race in Southern New England," *WMQ*, 3d ser., 61, no. 3 (July 2004): 534; Daniel R. Mandell, "Shifting Boundaries of Race and Ethnicity: Indian-Black Intermarriage in Southern New England, 1760–1880," *Journal of American History* 85, no. 2 (September 1998): 466–501.

84. Whites outside of New England did not usually identify Indians as blacks or colored people. Whites and Indians had tended to apply the term "red" to Indians in the South since the early eighteenth century (Nancy Shoemaker, "How Indians Got to be Red," *American Historical Review* 102, no. 3 [June 1997] 625–44; Melish, "The Racial Vernacular: Contesting the Black/White Binary in Nineteenth Century Rhode Island," 17; Daniel K. Richter, "'Believing That Many of the Red People Suffer Much for the Want of Food': Hunting, Agriculture, and a Quaker Construction of Indianness in the Early Republic," *Journal of the Early Republic* 19, no. 4 [Winter 1999]: 601–28).

85. Melish, "The 'Condition' Debate and Racial Discourse in the Antebellum North," 659.

86. See Melish, "The 'Condition' Debate and Racial Discourse in the Antebellum North," 667; Newman, *Freedom's Prophet*, 61; James Sidbury, *Becoming African in America: Race and Nation in the Early Black Atlantic* (New York: Oxford University Press, 2007); Phillis Wheatley, *Poems on Various Subjects, Religious and Moral* (1773).

87. Barry O'Connell, ed., *On Our Own Ground: The Complete Writings of William Apess, a Pequot* (Amherst: University of Massachusetts Press, 1992), li–liii, 5, 31, 119, 124; Mandell, "Shifting Boundaries of Race and Ethnicity," 486; Melish, "The Racial Vernacular." As Joanna Brooks writes, Samson Occom "thought of himself first as a Mohegan with profound responsibilities to his own tribal community and to American Indian people in general" (Joanna Brooks, ed., *The Collected Writings of Samson Occom, Mohegan: Leadership and Literature in Eighteenth-Century Native America* [New York: Oxford University Press, 2006], 4).

88. John Fanning Watson, *Annals of Philadelphia: Being a Collection of Memoirs, Anecdotes, and Incidents of the City and Its Inhabitants* (Philadelphia: E. L. Carey and A. Hart, 1830), 479; Emma Jones Lapsansky, "'Since They Got Those Separate Churches': Afro-American and Racism in Jacksonian Philadelphia," in *African Americans in Pennsylvania: Shifting Historical Perspectives*, ed. Joe William Trotter Jr. and Eric Ledell Smith (University Park: Pennsylvania Historical and Museum Commission and the Pennsylvania State University Press, 1997), 100, 107.

89. Silverman, *Faith and Boundaries*, 225; Melish, "The Racial Vernacular," 18–23.

90. Daniel R. Mandell, "'The Indian's Pedigree' (1794): Indians, Folklore, and Race in Southern New England," *WMQ*, 3d ser., 61, no. 3 (July 2004): 535; Lois E. Horton, "From Class to Race in Early America: Northern Post-Emancipation Racial Reconstruction," *Journal of the Early Republic* 19, no. 4 (Winter 1999): 643, 648–49.

6 / "Suffering under the Rod of Despotic Pharaohs"

1. Barry O'Connell, ed., *On Our Own Ground: The Complete Writings of William Apess, a Pequot* (Amherst: University of Massachusetts Press, 1992), 158.

2. O'Connell, ed., *On Our Own Ground*, 159.

3. Edward Strutt Abdy, *Journal of a Residence and Tour in the United States of North America from April 1833 to October 1834*, vol. 1 (London: John Murray, 1835), 44–45; David N. Gellman and David Quigley, eds., *Jim Crow New York: A Documentary History of Race and Citizenship 1777–1877* (New York: New York University Press, 2003); Richard Archer, *Jim Crow North: The Struggle for Equal Rights in Antebellum New England* (New York: Oxford University Press, 2017).

4. James Oliver and Lois E. Horton, *In Hope of Liberty: Culture, Community and Protest among Northern Free Blacks, 1700–1860* (New York: Oxford University Press, 1997). Rhode Island was an exception to this trend in later years. Blacks with some wealth in Rhode Island were extended the right to vote in 1842 by politicians who sought to prevent universal white male suffrage in that state (Robert J. Cottrol, *The Afro-Yankee: Providence's Black Community in the Antebellum Era* [Westport, Conn.: Greenwood, 1982], 6–9, 68–77).

5. Cottrol, *Afro-Yankee*, 53–57; Graham Russell Hodges, *Root & Branch: African Americans in New York and East Jersey, 1613–1863* (Chapel Hill: University of North Carolina Press, 1999), 227–28; NY Riots, 1834, Misc. Microfilm Reel 34, N-YHS; Emma Jones Lapsansky, "'Since They Got Those Separate Churches': Afro-American and Racism in Jacksonian Philadelphia" in *African Americans in Pennsylvania: Shifting Historical Perspectives*, ed. Joe William Trotter Jr. and Eric Ledell Smith (University Park: Pennsylvania Historical and Museum Commission and the Pennsylvania State University Press, 1997), 93, 101, 114–15; Archer, *Jim Crow North*, 83–87.

6. Theodore Hershberg, "Free Blacks in Antebellum Philadelphia: A Study of Ex-Slaves, Freeborn, and Socioeconomic Decline" in *African Americans in Pennsylvania: Shifting Historical Perspectives*, ed. Joe William Trotter Jr. and Eric Ledell Smith (University Park: Pennsylvania State University Press, 1997), 126, 129, 131; Abdy, *Journal of a Residence and Tour in the United States*, 121, 358; Julie Winch, *A Gentleman of Color: The Life of James Forten* (New York: Oxford University Press, 2002).

7. Nicholas Guyatt, "'The Outskirts of Our Happiness': Race and the Lure of Colonization in the Early Republic," *Journal of American History* 95, no. 4 (2009): 986–1011;

Hodges, *Root & Branch*, 238; Charles Carroll Harper, "Address of C.C. Harper," in *The African Repository and Colonial Journal*, vol. 2 (Washington: Way and Gideon, Published by order of the manager of the American Colonization Society, 1827), 188–89; J. B. Harrison, "The Colonization Society Vindicated to Virginia," in *The African Repository and Colonial Journal*, vol. 3 (Washington: James C. Dunn, Published by order of the manager of the American Colonization Society, 1828), 202; Abdy, *Journal of a Residence and Tour in the United States*, 121.

8. Daniel R. Mandell, *Tribe, Race, History: Native Americans in Southern New England, 1780–1880* (Baltimore: Johns Hopkins University Press, 2011), 193; Bernd C. Peyer, *The Tutor'd Mind: Indian-Missionary-Writers in Antebellum America* (Amherst: University of Massachusetts Press, 1997), 121–22, 153, 158, 161, 238, 255; Jean O'Brien, *Firsting and Lasting: Writing Indians out of Existence in New England* (Minneapolis: University of Minnesota Press, 2010).

9. For the history of abolitionist movements, see Manisha Sinha, *The Slave's Cause: A History of Abolition* (New Haven, Conn.: Yale University Press, 2016).

10. George Bourne, *Man-stealing and Slavery Denounced by the Presbyterian and Methodist Churches, Together with an Address to All the Churches* (Boston: Garrison and Knapp, 1834), 3.

11. Church records, 1835–1876, Abyssinian Church Portland, Maine, NEHH, www.congregationallibrary.org/nehh/series1/PortlandMEAbyssinian.

12. David Walker, *David Walker's Appeal, In Four Articles; Together with a Preamble, to the Coloured Citizens of the World, but in Particular, and Very Expressly, to Those of the United States of America, Third and Last Edition, Revised and Published by David Walker, 1830*, introd. James Turner (Baltimore: Black Classic Press, 1993), 60, 73.

13. Boston had two black churches by 1820 and five by 1841. For estimates of the number of each type of church in the United States in 1818, see Jedidiah Morse, Aaron Arrowsmith, and Samuel Lewis, *The American Universal Geography: Or, A View of the Present State of All the Kingdoms, States, and Colonies in the Known World*, 7th ed., 2 vols., vol. 1 (Charlestown: Lincoln and Edmands, 1819).

14. Congregational churches with multiple black, Indian, or Afro-Indian baptisms or members, 1821–1850, and approximate number of people of color at each church: First Congregational Church, Portsmouth, N.H. (4); First Church in Bennington, Vermont (2); Old South Church Boston, Mass. (8); Brattle Square Church (Unitarian), Boston, Mass. (2); West Church (Unitarian) Boston, Mass. (3); Church of Christ in Green Street, Boston, Mass. (2); Bowdoin Street Church Boston, Mass. (2); First Congregational Church Bristol, R.I. (9); Congregational Church Kingston, R.I. (2); Congregational Church of West Woodstock, Conn. (2); First Congregational Church Stonington, Conn. (2); First Congregational Church Madison, Conn. (3); Congregational Church Woodbury, Conn (3); Gilead Congregational Church, Hebron, Conn. (3); and Broadway Tabernacle Church, New York, N.Y. (5).

15. Andrew Oliver and James B. Peabody, eds., *Publications of the Colonial Society of Massachusetts*, vol. 56: *Collections: The Records of Trinity Church, Boston, 1728–1830, II* (Boston: Published by the Society, 1982), 700–710; Trinity Church Register, 1820–1869, H2 N2, Trinity Church Records, MHS. Seven of the twenty-four were adult baptisms.

16. Book of Record Trinity Church Rhode Island 1709, Trinity Church Newport Records, NHS. At Easter 1840, the church's communicant list included fifteen black

members, and the 1848–51 communicant lists included sixteen black members (Book of Record Trinity Church Rhode Island 1709, NHS).

17. Royden Woodward Vosburgh, ed., Records of the First Reformed Church of Coxsackie in West Coxsackie, Greene County, N.Y., vol. 2, pp. 19–62, transcribed by the NYGBS (June 1919); Royden Woodward Vosburgh, ed., Records of the First Reformed Church of Coxsackie in West Coxsackie, Greene County, NY, vol. 3, pp. 9–36, 40, 49, 114, transcribed by the NYGBS (June 1919).

18. Infant Baptism and Adult Baptisms 1811–1824, Session Minutes 1817–1824; Session Minutes 1825–32, List of Families, 1810–12, 1834–35, List Suspended Members, 1824–1851, boxes 1 and 2, First Presbyterian Church (Elizabeth, N.J.) Records, 1716–1913, RG 68, PHS.

19. James G. Birney, *The American Churches, the Bulwarks of American Slavery: By an American, Enlarged with an Appendix* (Newburyport, Mass.: Charles Whipple, 1842), 42.

20. The United Methodist Church of Gettysburg, Adams County, Pa., typescript transcription of records, pp. 15–16, Adams County Historical Society, Gettysburg, Pa.; Margaret S. Creighton, *The Colors of Courage: Gettysburg's Forgotten History: Immigrants, Women, and African Americans in the Civil War's Defining Battle* (Cambridge, Mass.: Basic, 2006), 62, 253. For other examples, see Royden Woodward Vosburg, ed., Records of the Bethel Methodist Episcopal Church at Tottenville, Staten Island, in Richmond County, N.Y., pp. 67–73, transcribed (New York City, 1922), LOC; and Methodist Episcopal Church attendance and collection records, 1841–1851, New Haven, Conn., MS 69819, CHS.

21. At least thirteen Lutheran churches and fifteen Baptist churches included multiple blacks between 1791 and 1820. Name of Baptist and Lutheran churches with multiple black baptisms and/or members, 1821–50, and approximate number of African Americans who affiliated: First Baptist Church Boston, Mass. (2); Baldwin Place (Second) Baptist Church, Boston, Mass. (2); First Baptist Church Providence, R.I. (19); Third Baptist Church of Providence, R.I. (3); First Baptist (United) Church Newport, R.I. (19); First Baptist Church South Kingstown, R.I. (6); Baptist Church in Exeter, R.I. (4); Six Principle Baptist Church East Greenwich, R.I. (2); First Baptist Church Stonington, Conn. (8); Friendship Seventh Day Baptist Church, Nile, N.Y. (3); Baptist Church Upper Freehold, N.J. (3); Baptist Church of Scots Plains, N.J. (3+?); First Baptist Church Middletown, N.J. (7); Fifth/Samson Street Philadelphia, Pa (17); St. Paul's Lutheran Church Berne, N.Y. (3); St. Thomas's Lutheran Church Claverack, N.Y. (3); First Baptist Providence, for years 1820–1825, see Stanley Lemons, ed., *Baptists in Early North America, First Baptist, Providence*, Baptists in Early North America Series, vol. 2 (Macon, Ga: Mercer University Press, 2013).

22. Letter qtd. in Abdy, *Journal of a Residence and Tour in the United States*, 133–36; Archibald Henry Grimké, *William Lloyd Garrison: The Abolitionist* (New York: Funk and Wagnalls, 1891), 160–61; Birney, *The American Churches, the Bulwarks of American Slavery*, 46; Archer, *Jim Crow North*, 9–10.

23. Bertram Wyatt-Brown, *Lewis Tappan and the Evangelical War against Slavery* (Baton Rouge: Louisiana State University Press, 1997), 176; qtd. in Moses N. Moore Jr., "Revisiting the Legacy of Black Presbyterians," *Journal of Presbyterian History* 84, no. 1 (Spring/Summer 2006): 39; *Colored American*, May 13, 1837.

24. Kathryn Grover, *Make a Way Somehow: African-American Life in a Northern Community, 1790–1965* (Syracuse, N.Y.: Syracuse University Press, 1994), 171–74.

25. General Association of Connecticut, *Proceedings of the General Association of Connecticut, June, 1827* (Hartford, Conn.: Peter B. Gleason and Co., 1827), 9; General Association of Connecticut, *Minutes of the General Association of Connecticut, June, 1834* (Hartford, Conn.: Peter B. Gleason and Co., 1834), 10; Firth Haring Fabend, *Zion on the Hudson: Dutch New York and New Jersey in the Age of Revivals* (New Brunswick, N.J.: Rutgers University Press, 2000), 181–82; Guyatt, "The Outskirts of Our Happiness."

26. John Demos, *The Heathen School: A Story of Hope and Betrayal in the Age of the Early Republic* (New York: Knopf, 2014), 142–273.

27. W. Woodstock Connecticut manuscript church records in the Richard Boles' Collection of New England church history, MS 5060, CL; Hershberg, "Free Blacks in Antebellum Philadelphia," 134–35.

28. William D. Metz, *The History of the Kingston Congregational Church, 1695–1995* (Kingston, R.I.: Kingston Congregational Church, 1996), 96; Kingston Congregational Church original copies Torrey, Subject Files, Pettaquamscutt Historical Society, Kingston, R.I.; Cato Pearce, *Jailed for Preaching: The Autobiography of Cato Pearce, a Freed Slave from Washington County, Rhode Island*, ed. Christian M. McBurney (Kingston, R.I.: Pettaquamscutt Historical Society, 2006), 19.

29. Qtd. in Metz, *History of the Kingston Congregational Church*, 73. James Birney argued that "The discussion of slavery has been and still is to a great extent shut out of Congregational churches" (Birney, *The American Churches, the Bulwarks of American Slavery*, 46). Sydney E. Ahlstrom, *A Religious History of the American People* (New Haven, Conn.: Yale University Press, 1972), 675.

30. Richard J. Boles, "Documents Relating to African American Experiences of White Congregational Churches in Massachusetts, 1773–1832," *New England Quarterly* 86, no. 2 (June 2013): 293–323; *The Articles and Covenant of the Bowdoin Street Church, Boston with a List of the Members* (Boston: T. R. Marvin, 1856), 5, 23–36; Debby Applegate, *The Most Famous Man in America: The Biography of Henry Ward Beecher* (New York: Three Leaves, 2006), 57, 58. A third black church, the First African Methodists Episcopal Bethel Society, was organized in November 1833.

31. Bowdoin Street Church Documents, Bowdoin Street Church, Records, 1825–1865, RG 0806, box 2, folder 36, CL; *Articles and Covenant of the Bowdoin Street Church*, 3–5, 22–23; Applegate, *Most Famous Man in America*, 52–58. The church leaders interviewed candidates for membership and made recommendations regarding whether or not they should be admitted. The church required that candidate for membership "give credible evidence of a change of heart, by the renovating influence of the Holy Spirit, implying repentance for sin, and faith in Jesus Christ the Redeemer" (Bowdoin Street Church Documents, Bowdoin Street Church, Records, 1825–1865, RG 0806, box 2, folder 36, CL).

32. Examining Committee Membership Records, 1827, Bowdoin Street Church, Records, 1825–1865, RG 0806, box 1, folder 12, CL.

33. Records of the Congregational Church of Christ in Green Street Boston III, Green Street Church, Records, 1822–1844, CL; Examining Committee Membership Records, 1827, Bowdoin Street Church, CL.

34. Examining Committee Membership Records, 1829 and Membership Records, ca. 1825–1859, Bowdoin Street Church, Records, 1825–1865, RG 0806, box 1, folders 8 and 14, CL; *Articles and Covenant of the Bowdoin Street Church* (1856), 30–31; Robert C. Hayden, *Faith, Culture, and Leadership: A History of the Black Church in Boston* (Boston: Boston Branch NAACP, 1983). The 1828 and 1829 Boston city directories listed him as a "labourer" (*Boston Directory 1828* [Boston: Hunt and Stimpson, 1828], 304; *Boston Directory 1829* [Boston: Charles Stimpson Jr., 1829], 297).

35. *Articles of Faith and Covenant of the Bowdoin Street Church, Boston: with a list of the members* (Boston: T. R. Marvin, 1837), 30–32; *Articles and Covenant of the Bowdoin Street Church* (1856), 30–31. Other published church records and directories from the nineteenth century likewise omitted the racial labels found in the original church records. Old South (Third) Church in Boston did not racially identify its historic black church members on lists printed in 1833, 1841, or 1883 (*The Form of Covenant, of the Old South Church, in Boston, Massachusetts, with Lists of the Founders, The Pastors, The Ruling Elders and Deacons, and the Members* [Boston: Crocker and Brewster, 1833]; *The Confession of Faith and Form of Covenant, of the Old South Church, in Boston, Massachusetts, with Lists of the Founders, The Pastors, The Ruling Elders and Deacons, and the Members* [Boston: Crocker and Brewster, 1841]; *An Historical Catalogue of the Old South Church [Third Church] Boston, 1669–1882* [Boston: Printed for private distribution, 1883]).

36. Hayden, *Faith, Culture, and Leadership*, 5; Membership Records, ca.1825–1859 and Examining Committee Membership Records, [1831?], Bowdoin Street Church, Records, 1825–1865, RG 0806, box 1, folder 17, CL.

37. List of Communicants 1816, 1832–1834, 1835–1871, Baptisms, Confirmations, Marriages and Burials 1792–1874, New London Episcopal Church Records, vol. 2, 1792 to 1874, New London/St. James Church, reel #305, p. 108; Robert A. Hallam, *The Dignity of Goodness: A Discourse, Delivered at the Funeral of Mr. Ichabod Pease, (A Man of Color,) in St. James' Church, New London, March 5, 1842* (New London: Bolles and Williams, 1842), 3–4, 8–12, 15–16; Barbara W. Brown and James M. Rose, *Black Roots in Southeastern Connecticut 1650–1900* (New London County Historical, 2001), 291–92; Hagar Merriman, *The Autobiography of Aunt Hagar Merriman of New Haven, Conn.* (New Haven: Published for the author, 1861).

38. Records of the First Baptist Church of Boston, Beginning January 24, 1800 . . . , First Baptist Church Boston, ANTL; *Minutes of the Eighteenth Anniversary of the Boston Baptist Association, Held at the Federal-Street Baptist Meeting-House, in Boston* (Boston: Lincoln and Edmands, 1829), 4, 17; *Minutes of the Nineteenth Anniversary of the Boston Baptist Association, Held at the Second Baptist Meeting-House, Boston* (Boston: Lincoln and Edmands, 1830), 4, 16; *Minutes of the Twentieth Anniversary of the Boston Baptist Association, Held at the Baptist Meeting-House, Roxbury* (Boston: Lincoln and Edmands, 1831), 4, 7–8; Ilou M. Sanford, ed., *Membership Records of Seventh Day Baptist Churches in Western New York and Northwestern Pennsylvania 1800–1900* (Bowie, Md.: Heritage, 1996), 35–36.

39. Pearce, *Jailed for Preaching*, 5–6, 8, 14–15, 17, 19–20.

40. Pearce, *Jailed for Preaching*, introduction, 17; narrative, 27–28, 31, 34.

41. Dorothy Porter Wesley, "Integration versus Separatism: William Cooper Nell's Role in the Struggle for Equality," in *Courage and Conscience: Black & White Abolitionists in Boston*, ed. Donald M. Jacobs (Bloomington: Indiana University Press,

1993), 214–15; James O. Horton and Lois E. Horton, *Black Bostonians: Family Life and Community Struggle in the Antebellum North* (New York: Holmes and Meier, 1999), 75; James O. Horton, "Generations of Protest: Black Families and Social Reform in Ante-Bellum Boston," *New England Quarterly* 49, no. 2 (June 1976): 249–52; Archer, *Jim Crow North*; Robert P. Smith, "William Cooper Nell: Crusading Black Abolitionist," *Journal of Negro History* 55, no. 3 (July 1970): 182–99; Dean Grodzins, *American Heretic: Theodore Parker and Transcendentalism* (Chapel Hill: University of North Carolina Press, 2002), 472; Theodore Parker (Boston) to Reverend J. Martineau, November 11, 1850, Theodore Parker Papers, vol. 3, p. 324, MHS.

42. *Liberator*, August 27, 1841; Gerrit Smith, "Some of the Duties of an Abolitionist: (and Every Whole Man Is an Abolitionist.) Peterboro, August 27, 1841," Misc. 1841 Sept. 6, MHS; Wyatt-Brown, *Lewis Tappan and the Evangelical War against Slavery*, 177; "Bristol County Antislavery Society Minutes," *Liberator*, December 24, 1841; "Middlesex County Antislavery Society minutes," *Liberator*, August 6, 1841; "Salem Female Antislavery Society Minutes," *Liberator*, 1844; "Strafford County Antislavery Society Minutes," *Liberator*, October 1, 1841; *The Condition of the Free People of Colour in the United States of America, Reprinted from no. XII of the Anti-Slavery Examiner, Published in New York, 1839, To Which Are Added Resolutions Passed at the Late Meeting of the Anti-Slavery Convention, Held in London, June, 1840* (London: Thomas Ward and Co., 1841), 16; Broadway Tabernacle Church Journal Book, Broadway Tabernacle Church and Society Papers, N-YHS; Bruce Laurie, *Beyond Garrison: Antislavery and Social Reform* (Cambridge: Cambridge University Press, 2005); Sinha, *The Slave's Cause*.

43. Harvey Newcomb, *The "Negro Pew": Being an Inquiry Concerning the Propriety of Distinctions in the House of God, on Account of Color* (Boston: Published by Isaac Knapp, 1837), iv, 101, 94. Dewey D. Wallace Jr. notes that Newcomb "expressed indignation about the way in which native Americans had been oppressed and deprived of their rights" (Wallace, "Newcomb, Harvey," American National Biography Online, February 2000, www.anb.org).

44. *The Five Ministers: A Sermon in West Church, by Cyrus Augustine Bartol, on the Fortieth Anniversary of His Ordination* (Boston: A. Williams and Co., 1877), 10–11; Gary Collison, "Anti-Slavery, Blacks, and the Boston Elite: Notes on the Reverend Charles Lowell and the West Church," *New England Quarterly* 61, no. 3 (September 1988): 426–27; Charles Lowell (Cambridge, Mass.) to Theodore Parker, June 23, 1854, Theodore Parker Papers, vol. 11, p. 253, MHS; *Liberator*, October 18, 1850.

45. Justin D. Fulton, *Memoir of Timothy Gilbert* (Boston: Lee and Shepard, 1866), 50, 134; *The Declaration of Faith with the Church Covenant, and List of Members, of the Federal Street Baptist Church, Boston, Constituted July 1, 1827*, 5th ed. (Boston: William D. Ticknor, 1841), 19–20; Collison, "Anti-Slavery, Blacks, and the Boston Elite."

46. Hodges, *Root & Branch*, 244–45; Albert J. Raboteau, *A Fire in the Bones: Reflections on African-American Religious History* (Boston: Beacon, 1995), 37–56; Horton, "Generations of Protest," 254.

47. Richard S. Newman, *Freedom's Prophet: Bishop Richard Allen, the A.M.E. Church, and the Black Founding Fathers* (New York: New York University Press, 2008); Joanna Brooks, *American Lazarus: Religion and the Rise of African-American and Native American Literatures* (New York: Oxford University Press, 2003). Bernd Peyer argues that Apess's "books thus seem to follow the chronological trend in

abolitionist and African American literature from a milder moralistic appeal to the American conscience up until the 1820s to a militant protest rhetoric exposing the moral deficit of the American political ethos at the close of the decade, as represented by the hard-line antislavery statements in *Walker's Appeal*" (Peyer, *The Tutor'd Mind*, 152).

48. Daniel R. Mandell, "Shifting Boundaries of Race and Ethnicity: Indian-Black Intermarriage in Southern New England, 1760–1880," *Journal of American History* 85, no. 2 (September 1998), 467, 470, 485, 500; Mandell, *Tribe, Race, History*, 42–69; Philip F. Gura, *The Life of William Apess, Pequot* (Chapel Hill: University of North Carolina Press, 2015), 54, 58, 61, 150. Russel Lawrence Barsh argues that "African American and Indian communities were so extensively intertwined by kinship and employment that they should be considered together as a single antebellum socioeconomic class, defined by their occupation as well as color" (Barsh, "Colored Seamen in the New England Whaling Industry: An Afro-Indian Consortium," in *Confounding the Color Line: The Indian-Black Experience in North America*, ed. James F. Brooks [Lincoln: University of Nebraska Press, 2002], 81–86, 99).

49. David Walker, *David Walker's Appeal*, 10–13; Horton and Horton, *Black Bostonians*, 88–89; Peter P. Hinks, *To Awaken My Afflicted Brethren: David Walker and the Problem of Antebellum Slave Resistance* (University Park: Pennsylvania State University Press, 1997); Donald Jacobs, "David Walker and William Lloyd Garrison: Racial Cooperation and the Shaping of Boston Abolition," in *Courage and Conscience: Black & White Abolitionists in Boston*, ed. Jacobs (Bloomington: Indiana University Press, 1993).

50. O'Connell, ed., *On Our Own Ground*, lxxviii–lxxxi, 3–97; Gura, *Life of William Apess*; Peyer, *The Tutor'd Mind*, 129–48.

51. Walker, *David Walker's Appeal*, 20, 27; O'Connell, ed., *On Our Own Ground*, 155.

52. Horton and Horton, *Black Bostonians*, 52–53; Walker, *David Walker's Appeal*, 21, 23; O'Connell, ed., *On Our Own Ground*, 102, 106, 114, 121.

53. Walker, *David Walker's Appeal*, 55, 63; O'Connell, ed., *On Our Own Ground*, 287, 301, 304.

54. Walker, *David Walker's Appeal*, 62, 56–57.

55. O'Connell, ed., *On Our Own Ground*, 287, 301, 304; Walker, *David Walker's Appeal*, 57, 60–61.

56. Walker, *David Walker's Appeal*, 59.

57. Walker, *David Walker's Appeal*, 17–19; Horton and Horton, *Black Bostonians*, 89; Henry Highland Garnet, "The Slave Must Throw off the Slaveholder," in *Afro-American History: Primary Sources, Shorter Edition*, ed. Thomas R. Frazier (New York: Harcourt Brace Jovanovich, 1971), 65; Martin B. Pasternak, *Rise Now and Fly to Arms: The Life of Henry Highland Garnet* (New York: Garland, 1995).

58. Frederick Douglass, *Narrative of the Life of Frederick Douglass, an American Slave*, ed. and introd. Houston A. Baker Jr. (New York: Penguin, 1986), 153, 157; Frederick Douglass, *My Bondage and My Freedom*, ed., introd., and with notes by John David Smith (New York: Penguin, 1986), 258–60.

59. For similar and supporting analysis, Brooks, *American Lazarus*, 117.

60. O'Connell, ed., *On Our Own Ground*, 145.

61. O'Connell, ed., *On Our Own Ground*, 129, 147.

62. For analysis of these ideas, see O'Connell, ed., *On Our Own Ground*, 118, 160. Mohican Hendrick Aupaumut explored similar ideas and themes (Rachel Wheeler, "Hendrick Aupaumut: Christian-Mahican Prophet," *Journal of the Early Republic* 25, no. 2 [Summer 2005: 187–220). The Church of Latter Days Saints, which was founded in this era, also believed that Indians were descendants of ancient Israelites.

63. O'Connell, ed., *On Our Own Ground*, 157. Elsewhere Apess also states that "It is my opinion that our nation retains the original complexion of our common father, Adam" (O'Connell, ed., *On Our Own Ground*, 34).

64. O'Connell, ed., *On Our Own Ground*, 157.

65. O'Connell, ed., *On Our Own Ground*, lxviii, 19, 127, 179.

66. O'Connell, ed., *On Our Own Ground*, 33; Charles A. Eastman, *From the Deep Woods to Civilization: Chapters in the Autobiography of an Indian,* introd. Raymond Wilson (repr., Lincoln: University of Nebraska Press, 1977), 142–50; Philip J. Deloria and Neal Salisbury, eds., *A Companion to American Indian History* (Malden, Mass.: Blackwell, 2004).

67. O'Connell, ed., *On Our Own Ground*, 278, 279, 300; Margaret Ellen Newell, *Brethren by Nature: New England Indians, Colonists, and the Origins of American Slavery*; David Silverman, *This Land Is Their Land: The Wampanoag Indians, Plymouth Colony, and the Troubled History of Thanksgiving* (New York: Bloomsbury, 2019).

Conclusion

1. Katharine Gerbner, *Christian Slavery: Conversion and Race in the Protestant Atlantic World* (Philadelphia: University of Pennsylvania Press, 2018), 3, 91–188; Travis Glasson, *Mastering Christianity: Missionary Anglicanism and Slavery in the Atlantic World* (New York: Oxford University Press, 2011).

2. Rebecca Anne Goetz, *The Baptism of Early Virginia: How Christianity Created Race* (Baltimore: Johns Hopkins University Press, 2012), 2, 6, 85–88, 99–105, 138–40, 154–58; Sylvia Frey and Betty Wood, *Come Shouting to Zion: African American Protestantism in the American South and British Caribbean to 1830* (Chapel Hill: University of North Carolina Press, 1998). Gerbner argues that "Planters continued to bar all but their most favored slaves from Christian rituals and they resisted the work of missionaries throughout the eighteenth century" (Gerbner, *Christian Slavery*, 194).

3. Goetz, *Baptism of Early Virginia*, 106, 110–11, 150. Gerbner notes that "the ideology of Protestant Supremacy was strongest in the plantation colonies, and it became more pronounced as the slave populations grew to a majority" (Gerbner, *Christian Slavery*, 47, 74, 133–36). Sylvia Frey and Betty Wood's argument that "the vast majority of bondpeople found little in Anglicanism with which they could or wished to identify" does not hold true for black northerners (Frey and Wood, *Come Shouting to Zion*, 75).

4. Gerbner, *Christian Slavery*, 2–3, 47.

5. Christine Heyrman, *Southern Cross: The Beginnings of the Bible Belt* (Chapel Hill: University of North Carolina Press, 1998); Charles F. Irons, *The Origins of Proslavery Christianity: White and Black Evangelicals in Colonial and Antebellum Virginia* (Chapel Hill: University of North Carolina Press, 2008); Henry H. Mitchell, *Black Church Beginnings: The Long-Hidden Realities of the First Years* (Grand Rapids, Mich.: Eerdmans, 2004); Janet Moore Lindman, *Bodies of Belief: Baptist Community in Early*

America (Philadelphia: University of Pennsylvania Press, 2008); Cynthia Lynn Lyerly, *Methodism and the Southern Mind, 1770–1810* (New York: Oxford University Press, 1998).

6. Emily Conroy-Krutz, *Christian Imperialism: Converting the World in the Early American Republic* (Ithaca, N.Y.: Cornell University Press, 2015); William G. McLoughlin, *The Cherokee and Christianity, 1794–1870: Essays on Acculturation and Cultural Persistence* (Athens: University of Georgia Press, 1994); Jean O'Brien, *Firsting and Lasting: Writing Indians out of Existence in New England* (Minneapolis: University of Minnesota Press, 2010).

7. James O. Horton and Lois E. Horton, eds., *Black Bostonians: Family Life and Community Struggle in the Antebellum North* (New York: Holmes and Meier, 1999), 111–12; Albert J. Von Frank, *The Trials of Anthony Burns: Freedom and Slavery in Emerson's Boston* (Cambridge, Mass.: Harvard University Press, 1998), 23–30, 37, 52, 81, 90, 107–13, 259–66.

8. Irons, *Origins of Proslavery Christianity*.

9. Joanne Pope Melish, *Disowning Slavery: Gradual Emancipation and "Race" in New England, 1780–1860* (Ithaca, N.Y.: Cornell University Press, 1998), 2.

Index

ABOUT THE AUTHOR

Richard J. Boles is Assistant Professor of History at the Oklahoma State University.